Incremental Realism

Post45 Loren Glass and Kate Marshall, Editors
Post•45 Group, Editorial Committee

Incremental Realism

Postwar American Fiction, Happiness,
and Welfare-State Liberalism

Mary Esteve

Stanford University Press
Stanford, California

STANFORD UNIVERSITY PRESS
Stanford, California

© 2021 by the Board of Trustees of the Leland Stanford Junior University. All rights reserved.

No part of this book may be reproduced or transmitted in any form or by any means, electronic or mechanical, including photocopying and recording, or in any information storage or retrieval system without the prior written permission of Stanford University Press.

Printed in the United States of America on acid-free, archival-quality paper

Library of Congress Cataloging-in-Publication Data
Names: Esteve, Mary, author.
Title: Incremental realism : postwar American fiction, happiness, and welfare-state liberalism / Mary Esteve.
Other titles: Post 45.
Description: Stanford, California : Stanford University Press, 2021. | Series: Post*45 | Includes bibliographical references and index.
Identifiers: LCCN 2020021119 (print) | LCCN 2020021118 (ebook) | ISBN 9781503613942 (cloth) | ISBN 9781503614376 (paperback) | ISBN 9781503614383 (ebook) |
Subjects: LCSH: American fiction—20th century—History and criticism. | Authors, American—Political and social views. | Happiness in literature. | Welfare state in literature. | Liberalism in literature. | Realism in literature.
Classification: LCC PS379 .E88 2021 (ebook) | LCC PS379 (print) | DDC 813/.5409—dc23
LC record available at https://lccn.loc.gov/2020021119

Cover photo: Aurélie Le Moigne | Alamy Stock Photo
Cover design: Rob Ehle
Typeset by Motto Publishing Services in 10/15 Minion Pro

Contents

Acknowledgments vii

Introduction: **The Symbolic Economy of Postwar American Happiness** 1

1 **The Art, Sociology, and Library Politics of Happiness in Early Philip Roth** 30

2 **Gwendolyn Brooks and the Welfare State** 56

3 **Queer Consumerism, Straight Happiness:** Patricia Highsmith's "Right Economy" 100

4 **Countries of Health** 123

5 **Writing Mute Liberalism:** Peter Taylor, the South, and Journeyman Happiness 179

Coda: **The Politics of Contemporary Happiness** 221

Notes 231
Index 271

Acknowledgments

The formal opportunity to thank persons and institutions is most welcome. For more than ten years I have benefitted from the formidable intelligence, incisive criticism, and magnificent geniality of the Post•45 research collective. In particular, the board members, both past and present, deserve thanks for tending to the fires of this little institution and for encouraging members and affiliates to polish their gems of literary and cultural knowledge: Danielle Christmas, J. D. Connor, Florence Dore, Merve Emre, Loren Glass, Amy Hungerford, Andy Hoberek, Kate Marshall, Sean McCann, Annie McClanahan, Deak Nabers, Debbie Nelson, Anthony Reed, Dan Sinykin, Richard So, and Michael Szalay.

This book has been a work in progress for so many years that some of the folks thanked here may no longer recall their exchanges with me—their astute comments, their savvy recommendations of literary and critical texts, and their clarifying objections. Others, meanwhile, at Post•45 and elsewhere, may recall all too vividly being buttonholed into extended one-sided conversations about the chapter I happened to be fixated on at the time. To them, too, my debts of gratitude have racked up. Warm thanks to Jennifer Ashton, Phillip Barrish, Robin Blyn, Adrienne Brown, Abigail Cheever, Michael Clune, Dana Dragunoiu, Richard Godden, Cathy Jurca, Michael LeMahieu, Franny Nudelman, Tom Perrin, Stephen Schryer, Evie Shockley, Lisa Siraganian, Andrew Wallace, and Cindy Weinstein. I'm also grateful for the invitations to present substantial chunks of the project at Caltech and at Southern Methodist University. At home in Montreal, the spirited conversation and critical acumen of colleagues and friends have provided intellectual sustenance on a more regular basis; my gratitude goes out to Bob Croskey, Bina Freiwald, Omri Moses, Nicola Nixon, Eyvind Ronquist, and Jon Sachs. When it comes to finishing a book, it's difficult to thank adequately the crew of darlings who put aside their own work and busy lives to give urgently needed feedback on drafts of chapters and book proposals. To Cathy Jurca, Sean McCann, Omri Moses, Jon Sachs, and Stephen Schryer, all I can say is, such ready and tenacious support for this project warrants naming you twice in this paragraph.

I am grateful for the financial support of Concordia University, whose internal grants funded two Post•45 conferences. I also want to thank Canada's Social Science and Humanities Research Council. The residuals of its grant for an earlier project on late-nineteenth-century American literature and political economy paid for the excellent research assistance of Adam Carlson when this mid-twentieth-century project was in its infancy.

Versions of chapters or chapter portions have been published previously. Parts of the coda appeared in "The Idea of Happiness: Back to the Postwar Future," in *Postmodern/Postwar—and After*, ed. Jason Gladstone, Andrew Hoberek, and Daniel Worden (University of Iowa Press, 2016). The third chapter, "Queer Consumerism, Straight Happiness: Patricia Highsmith's 'Right Economy,'" appeared in *Post45 Peer Reviewed* (December 18, 2012); a very early version of the first chapter appeared under the title, "Postwar Pastoral: The Art of Happiness in Early Philip Roth," in *American Literature's Aesthetic Dimensions*, ed. Chris Looby and Cindy Weinstein (©Columbia University Press, 2012).

At Stanford University Press, I am deeply grateful for the two anonymous reviewers' various enthusiasms, suggestions, and quibbles. It has been more than a pleasure to work with the friendly, engaged, and competent editorial staff—Kate Wahl, Erica Wetter, Faith Wilson Stein, and Emily Smith—as well as with the wonderfully adroit editors of the Post•45 book series, Loren Glass and Kate Marshall. Many thanks also to Rob Ehle, who designed the cover, and to Gretchen Otto's copyediting team, who fixed a lot of sentences.

This book is dedicated to my dear mama, Jeanie Gleason Esteve, who, from her perch on the Oregon coast, has been eager to see its completion.

Incremental Realism

INTRODUCTION
The Symbolic Economy of Postwar American Happiness

In 1969, a decade after the appearance of his breakout novella *Goodbye, Columbus*, Philip Roth revisited one of this text's central themes: the status and value of the public library. He published an editorial in the *New York Times* extolling the virtues of that institution—specifically, Newark's—and excoriated the Newark City Council's vote to shut it down for budgetary reasons. He heaped scorn on the council for depriving the city's "mostly black" residents of the profound satisfaction he had experienced as a boy of modest means in the 1940s of accessing "any book [he] wanted" from the stacks "held in common for the common good." The public library, Roth explained, was more than a repository of desirable objects for bookish kids. It was an "exacting haven" that built "trust . . . in both oneself and in systems," thereby offering its patrons multiple "satisfactions." It did not "count for nothing to carry a library card in one's pocket; to pay a fine; to sit in a strange place, beyond the reach of parent and school, and read whatever one chose, in anonymity and peace; finally, to carry home across the city and even into bed at night a book with a local lineage of its own, a family tree of Newark readers to which one's name had now been added." A performative exercise in "municipal citizenship," this boyhood engagement with the library—with its store of common goods and its institutional procedures—illustrates what midcentury liberal activists understood to be the operative purpose of the welfare state.[1] In a socioeconomic system marked by increasing interdependence, the welfare state was supposed to contribute to the flourishing individuality and autonomy of persons, particularly those disadvantaged by poverty or meager opportunity.

Roth's tribute to the public library and its modes of "satisfaction" goes far to confirm what the midcentury liberal economist John Kenneth Galbraith suggested postwar Americans sorely needed, namely, "symbols of happiness" that could draw attention to the moral as well as the material value of public investment.² In *The Affluent Society* (1958) he advanced a "theory of social balance" in which he pressed for the expansion of all manner of public services—the improvement of brick-and-mortar institutions such as schools and hospitals, the construction of housing for low-income Americans, the clearance of rural and urban slums, the establishment of routine municipal services like trash collection, and so forth. Direct public action, he argued, would do much to improve Americans' quality of life. It would counterbalance the American economy's overemphasis on the private sector's production of consumer goods and its obsession with efficiency at the expense of individual and social well-being. It was the absence of trash collection, for instance, that "forced the use of home incinerators" in Los Angeles, leading to atrocious levels of air pollution (*AS* 256). Moreover, in an era of relative indifference to wealth and income inequality, the wide distribution of public goods and services would especially benefit those stricken by poverty—that "small and also inarticulate minority" largely "forgotten" even by most liberals, let alone by conservatives (328).³ In comparison to monetary income transfers, Galbraith's propositions amounted to "less direct but, conceivably, almost equally effective means" of redistribution (330); indeed, to his mind, they offered better chances of breaking the cycle of "self-perpetuating" poverty of dysfunctional individuals, families, and geographical regions (329).

The moral imperative framing these practical schemes of incremental progress reflected the activist strain of postwar liberalism, in which the aim was to "protect and advance basic social justice" (*AS* 266) and to contribute to everyone's "chance for dignity, individuality, and full development of personality" (288). Galbraith thus exemplified the sort of midcentury liberal who saw a need to move beyond what he called the "conventional wisdom" of viewing the welfare state as comprising a matrix of government agencies that merely "softened and civilized capitalism" (15). The welfare state needed to become more active in improving American lives, especially those of the polity's least advantaged members. He brushed off claims such as Friedrich A. Hayek's that government expansion would put the country on the road to totalitarianism, that the "paternalistic welfare state" would become hardly distinguishable from "full-fledged socialism."⁴ Galbraith countered, "That [cities'] residents should have a nontoxic supply of air suggests no revolutionary dalliance with socialism" (252). Similarly, promoting institutions that advanced equal opportunity and plans that reduced poverty need not subscribe to the socialist ideal of a "community," to borrow political scientist J. Donald Moon's description, "in which there would be a strong coincidence of individual destiny and communal norms."[5] The whole point of privileging equal opportunity over equal outcomes was to protect and enlarge persons' individual capacities, or, as Roth put it, to enable trust in oneself as well as in the ordinary experience of systems.

But no less important than the pushback against libertarian ideologues who raised the specter of totalitarianism, Galbraith's call for new forms of happiness struck at the heart of utilitarian ideology, whether conservative or liberal, in which the focus on the greatest happiness for the greatest number often ignored—indeed, could justify ignoring—the least advantaged members of society. He faulted both contemporary and historical versions of this ideology. On the one hand, a lingering Keynesian imperative to stimulate consumer demand distorted productivity demands at midcentury (*AS* 188–90); on the other hand, ever since the "Benthamite test of public policy was 'what serves the greatest happiness of the greatest number,' and happiness was more or less implicitly identified with productivity," modern society had misdirected its economic and ethical energies (288–89). The dismal irony of "private opulence and public squalor," he implied, was practically destined to become the plight of postwar American affluence (257).

Although the mixed economy at midcentury presented occasions for sporadic outrage for Roth and slow-burning disappointment for Galbraith, both writers registered the potential for postwar liberal activists to envision viable alternatives to status quo liberalism and entrenched conservatism. This book offers a revisionist literary and cultural history of progressive liberals' sense of the welfare state's chronic vulnerability and the efforts undertaken by literary realists, public intellectuals, and policy activists to advance the value of public institutions and the claims of socioeconomic justice. Midcentury literary realism contributed significantly to this project. Numerous writers—Philip Roth, Gwendolyn Brooks, Patricia Highsmith, Mary McCarthy, Paula Fox, and Peter Taylor—carved out spaces of representation in which welfare-state "symbols of happiness" circulated, usually in unobtrusive but nevertheless visible and appreciable ways. These writers thus mobilized a trope that was already quite familiar to Americans—the pursuit of happiness—for the promotion both of welfare-state liberalism and, as we'll see, of a small-canvas aesthetics of moderation—what Lionel Trilling, with reference to William

Dean Howells, called "dealings with the ordinary" rather than with the "rare and strange."⁶ If they risked writing what Herbert Marcuse sneeringly dubbed "good-will" literature, they also possessed the temerity to affirm crucial locations and objects of welfare-state value: not only the public library, which was easy to love, but also more troublesome things such as the United Nations (UN) Universal Declaration of Human Rights (UDHR), Chicago's mixed economy, the Home Owners' Loan Corporation, Blue Cross health insurance, Medicaid, and the university.⁷

But that's only half the story. In addition to embracing specific objects and locations of welfare-state happiness, these writers developed narrative modes that made *justifiable* the claims of disadvantaged Americans on the nation-state. To stay with the example of Roth (whose early fiction is the focus of chapter 1), in *Goodbye, Columbus*, he guides the reader not only toward endorsing the protagonist's ultimate satisfaction in returning to his humdrum job at the Newark Public Library after an ugly breakup with his affluent girlfriend but also toward an endorsement of the narrative's cumulative moral logic. Its final scene of emotional satisfaction turns out to be bound up with earlier episodes in which the protagonist's workplace conduct reveals the importance of the public library to the well-being and personal dignity of a disadvantaged black boy. This narrative logic of justification is a central feature of a genre of postwar fiction that I call *incremental realism*. Drawing on the idea of incrementalism that informed midcentury decision-making theory (discussed in chapter 2), I suggest that this literary genre creates a symbolic economy in which referential figures of liberal activism and welfare-state happiness circulate, albeit inconspicuously and in a minor key. Practitioners of incremental realism, as we'll see in each chapter, tend to employ narrative forms of measured analogy as well as steady, linear plot progression (as opposed to extravagant metaphor and sequential confusion); they gravitate toward characters and narrators exemplifying liberal subjectivity and mobilize tropes of happiness (as opposed to vehement emotions such as ecstasy and bliss) to stage the justification of a redistributive institution or program. With happiness as its emblem of committed but temperate activism, the incrementalist style gestures toward the near, possible future in which equitable wealth redistribution, expansion of public infrastructure, and individual flourishing function as operative ideals. Situating tropes of happiness in dialectical relation to liberalism's formal yet pragmatic horizon of redistributive justice, incremental realism tilts the postwar idea of the nation-state toward practical ambitions related to its citizens' flourishing and away from a Cold War national imaginary in which the pursuit of happiness, alongside life and liberty, looked like something worth going to war for.

1948/1971

The literary and cultural history of postwar welfare-state happiness is surprisingly entangled, its many knots resulting from the deeply ambiguous status of happiness, the vexed politics of liberalism, and the dominant preference for a literary aesthetics not of moderation and sociopolitical affirmation but of heightened intensity and alienation. These manifold issues receive attention throughout the ensuing chapters, but here I want to bring into focus some of their salient implications by examining in detail four publishing events—two in 1948 and two in 1971—related to happiness and the welfare state (these dates also serve loosely as this study's temporal bookends). With regard to mainstream happiness discourse, 1948 is the year *Life* magazine published "A *Life* Round Table on The Pursuit of Happiness," and 1971 is the year E. L. Doctorow published what may count as the most damning repudiation of the ideology informing the *Life* article: his novel, *The Book of Daniel*. In welfare-state discourse, 1948 is the year the UN issued the UDHR, and 1971 is the year John Rawls published arguably the most rigorous and expansive justification of the UDHR's principles and values in his liberal manifesto, *A Theory of Justice*. At first glance, these textual artifacts seem to reveal the extent to which the two discourses of happiness and welfare-state liberalism were at cross purposes and practically unintelligible to each other, even where their political and affective vocabularies overlapped. Yet the juxtaposition of the *Life* article and Doctorow, on the one hand, and the UDHR and Rawls, on the other hand, should illuminate the moral, conceptual, and representational claims that liberal activism drew into its orbit. Instead of the rearguard "conventional wisdom" that Galbraith lampooned throughout *The Affluent Society*, such activism may be broadly understood, in keeping with the literary genre identified earlier, to issue from an *incrementalist intelligence*, that is, from a forward-looking sensibility keyed to the ethical and pragmatic tenets of welfare-state justice and to the affirmative mode of happiness exemplified by Roth's tableau of library satisfaction.

I begin with *Life* magazine's roundtable. As a genre of knowledge production, the roundtable was not as uncomplicated as its name suggests. It comprised preliminary discussion groups and three days of dialogue among nearly twenty invited participants, all of which was subsequently compressed into a published report with a byline. These formal elements turned out to be as central to the magazine article's ideology of happiness as the content of the discussions. The author of the piece was the roundtable's moderator, Russell W. Davenport, a liberal conservative who had been managing editor of *Fortune* in the 1930s, political advisor to the 1940 Republican presidential candidate, Wendell Willkie, and on staff at *Life* and *Time* after World War II. He had developed the roundtable "technique" for *Fortune*, touting it as a "democratic device" that created "balance" by drawing together men and women with "different views" for a weekend of discussion and debate.[8] Participating in the forum were numerous academics (including left liberals Sidney Hook, Stuart Chase, and Erich Fromm), a few corporate and advertising executives, one union leader, one museum director, one Hollywood executive, a few religious leaders and magazine editors, one paralytic, one government official, and one Mother of the Year (*Life* 96). As a model of democratic pluralism, the group had predictable deficiencies—the absence of racial minorities, for instance, and a tilt toward corporate interests.[9] But for the present analysis what is more notable is the way the group also served as a model of consensus. Davenport explains that his "task" as moderator is "to unify the conflicting views" and to find "agreement wherever possible" (96). Remarking again and again on the consensus achieved, he creates a narrative of the weekend's production, after "exhausting intellectual struggle," of "a set of agreements, for the most part unanimous," regarding midcentury American pursuits of happiness (97).

"Consensus" was, as Richard Godden has put it, "the bedrock and horizon of liberal optimism"; as such it "blanket[ed] the fifties" and the ensuing decades.[10] And yet, even among liberal optimists, there were distinct ways of construing consensus. *Life*'s construal, as we'll see, differed significantly from the social-contract version that informed Rawls's political philosophy. As reconstructed by Davenport, *Life*'s roundtable was of a piece with concerted postwar efforts of organizations such as the Advertising Council and the American Heritage Foundation to promote "the American way." The historian Wendy Wall offers a concise summary of this project:

> [It was] a wide-ranging and multifaceted effort by an array of influential elites in the immediate postwar years to recapture the sense of national unity and teamwork that had pervaded public discourse in the U.S. during World War II. Those

engaged in this endeavor included social scientists who worried about threats to social cohesion posed by the "group mind"; intergroup activists who hoped to extend their wartime antiprejudice campaigns; business, advertising, and public relations executives determined to derail the rising power of labor and to halt or roll back the policies of the New Deal; and officials of the Truman administration who sought to unify Americans behind their emerging cold war policies.[11]

In 1945, the Advertising Council—the result of a postwar makeover of the War Advertising Council into a nonprofit, "public-service" foundation—solicited support from the editors of *Time*, *Life*, and *Fortune*.[12] Davenport's roundtable on the pursuit of happiness was clearly an instance of this support. Among its participants was Thomas D'Arcy Brophy, advertising executive and president of the American Heritage Foundation, whose concurrent pet project was the Freedom Train. This traveling exhibit of select American documents (such as Jefferson's draft of the Declaration of Independence, Washington's copy of the Constitution, the Emancipation Proclamation, and the American flag that was raised on Iwo Jima) toured the forty-eight states from late 1947 to early 1949. Wall describes the lengths to which Brophy and fellow promoters went to empty the exhibit of political controversy—playing up "freedom," for instance, and back-benching "democracy"—so as to advance "a consensual vision of [the] 'American Way.'"[13] The broad ambition of the American way was to instill cultural unity, religious and racial tolerance, demographic inclusion, and economic prosperity as the nation's hallmarks.

In *Life*'s roundtable the narrative of consensus converges on the group's arrival at a thick description of the meaning of Jefferson's "Third Right"—a description so thick, in fact, that it becomes indistinguishable from a moral and cultural prescription of happiness. The main question at hand, Davenport submits, is not "the nature of happiness itself" but rather "the meaning and use of a *political right*" (*Life* 97, emphasis in original). And yet the participants frequently lapse into stipulating the conditions of happiness. Claims are made, for instance, that peace is "essential" to happiness (98), that happiness and painful self-sacrifice are compatible (98), that happiness can't be intelligently pursued with the threat of atomic warfare looming (98), and that happiness "results from the full use of one's faculties" (100), whereas unhappiness results from monotonous labor (98). When this sort of philosophical opining gives way to the putatively different question of the pursuit of happiness as a political right, the participants seem unable to switch analytical gears.

Their elision of the distinction between existential and political propositions is most apparent in the way they accept as self-evident the truth of what they call "genuine happiness" (97), which they differentiate from the kind of happiness people report themselves in surveys as having experienced—for instance, in the survey that Beatrice Gould, editor of the *Ladies' Home Journal*, brought to the roundtable in which 46 percent of Americans deemed themselves "very happy," as opposed to 9 percent of French people (97). Dismissing such first-person evaluation, the roundtable participants agree with Erich Fromm that "a wide gulf [exists] between what people think they are and what they really are"; the participants thus construct an account of subjective happiness that privileges objective "facts," determined from a third-person perspective, over personal "opinions" (97).

Much follows from these determinations. Understanding themselves as "thoroughly Jeffersonian," everybody at the roundtable is in "fundamental agreement" that "the whole moral question—not only sacrifice, but duty, honor, generosity, courage, fairness, justice, and so forth—is inseparable from the question of happiness. The very idea of pursuing happiness with no reference to moral standards is self-defeating, not to say destructive. The good is implicit in the search for happiness; moral goals must be realized if happiness is to be achieved" (*Life* 98). The group downplays the political tenuousness of this logic of inseparability (which would reduce the *political right* that the Declaration of Independence determines inalienable to exclusively edifying pursuits and thus render the state protecting this right grossly paternalistic). To be sure, Davenport indicates that the group has embraced the results of a preliminary discussion group of Jefferson scholars who concluded that Jefferson substituted "the pursuit of happiness" for "property" because he wanted to broaden the scope of inalienable rights and that he understood "*that the chief end of government is the happiness of the people*" (97, emphasis in original). But despite Davenport's initial assertion to the contrary, the roundtable turns out not to be terribly interested in the pursuit of happiness as a political right. Rather, more like the philosopher Aristotle than the revolutionary Jefferson, the roundtable participants are invested in erecting a moral epistemology to frame the conditions of happiness and thus to secure an alibi for issuing diagnoses of midcentury America. The predicative "facts" about happiness authorize the group's overarching conclusion: "There is a failure in America to achieve genuine happiness" (97). The consensus leaders have spoken. Pointing to the nation's high divorce rate and family disintegration, increasing rates of juvenile delinquency and crime, excessive drinking, and so forth (97), they have positioned themselves to dispense advice on how to improve America and achieve genuine happiness.

With everyone in agreement about the intrinsically moral nature of genuine happiness, the *Life* article concludes with a summary of the roundtable's more specific "agreements [having] to do with the application of this right by those who cannot escape responsibility for its proper exercise" (*Life* 110). These agreements include, redundantly, not construing happiness as mere pleasure or self-indulgence as well as issuing social and economic directives: give workers more opportunity to participate "in [their] job[s] and in profits" (*Life* 110), encourage the patronage of art museums (110), revise Hollywood's censorship policies so as to foster the production of morally serious movies (110, 113), curb the advertising industry's "interfere[nce] with an intelligent pursuit of happiness," and find in the "American democratic heritage . . . the best common ground on which to base the moral principles required for the intelligent pursuit of happiness" (113). In baking so much moral "intelligence" into the cake of acceptable pursuits of happiness, this roundtable's dramatic conversion of democratic pluralism into monolithic consensus renders the pursuit of happiness not merely consonant with "the American way" but effectively inseparable from it.

. . .

By 1959, John Higham's withering critique of the "cult" of "American consensus" made visible the dubiousness of the presumption that America was conflict-free in its ideological commitments and cultural values. His classic essay, "The Cult of 'American Consensus': Homogenizing Our History," took specific aim at academic historians who had abandoned the progressive historiography of "clashing ideologies" and "jagged" processes of protest and reform for a historiography of epochal continuity, cultural placidity, and national unity.[14] Singled out for bracing admonishment is Daniel Boorstin, whom Higham skewers for blithely contending that "American values had emerged from happy experience; here the 'ought' derived from the 'is.'"[15] Giving the lie to consensus liberalism's wish fulfillment, Higham's dissent from mainstream consensus ideology challenged the Cold War fixation on national unity. His critique, however, took place in the relatively cordial sphere of academic exchange.

That is, Higham's objections paled in comparison to the emergent counterculture's radical dissent, its all-out repudiation of the liberal system that made the proposition of intellectual disagreement irrelevant. Doctorow's *Book of Daniel* portrays this oppositional logic, detailing the conditions of the counterculture's hardening over the next decade into the New Left's reactionary disenchantment. A fictionalization of the Rosenberg family, the novel takes the perspective of the executed couple's son Daniel Isaacson, who is a graduate student of history in the late 1960s at Columbia University. It opens and closes with scenes of Daniel in the library, where he works on an unconventional dissertation—the manuscript that becomes *The Book of Daniel*. A kind of grotesque parody of Roth's boyhood expeditions to the library for conditioning in citizenship, Daniel's time in the library indexes the making of a sadistic, aggrieved, alienated anticitizen. Researching and writing there, pondering the personal and political implications of the execution of his parents, he develops a historiography of national accursedness and an indictment of the nation-state's biopolitics. His deeply personal connection to the execution of spies provides the alibi for this historiography. Rather than understanding the episode in the disappointed manner of, say, the historian John Patrick Diggins—that is, as an egregious juridical mistake in a series of Cold War events that an anti–New Deal, right-wing conspiracy theorist like Joseph McCarthy could take advantage of—Daniel internalizes the execution, in effect, as a symptom of the American way.[16] At the outset of his book, Daniel envisions a parallel between himself and his biblical namesake, who, he notes, may have "survive[d] three reigns" of imperious kings "but at considerable personal cost. Toward the end his insights become more diffuse, apocalyptic, hysterical."[17] Speaking apocalyptic hysteria to consensus power is a more analytical affair for the studious Daniel than it is for his countercultural bedfellow, the beat poet Allen Ginsberg, but his book is no less suspicious of liberalism's foundational values and principles and, correspondingly, no less indebted to visionary tropes of abnegation than *Howl* (1956) is.

Central to the narrative's exultant fatalism is a looming figure of absent happiness. Sandwiched between childhood memories of visiting his parents in prison before their execution and thoughts about his recent participation in the 1968 march on the Pentagon, a thirteenth zodiac sign, Starfish, becomes the object of Daniel's ponderous attention. Ostensibly erased long ago by "the famous Egyptian adjustment of the Chaldean calendar, in 4000 B. C.," it was once "considered one of the most beneficial of signs" because it "suggested serenity and harmony with the universe, and therefore great happiness" (*BD* 305). Daniel goes on to surmise that modern astrologers avoid reference to the sign "because modern man can conceive of nothing more frightening than the self-sufficiency of being of the beautiful Starfish: he mistakes it for death" (306). Once conjoining "[b]elief . . . with intellect, language with truth, and life with justice," this sign of beatific virtue has no place in the modern firmament (305). The implications of Daniel's celestial ideal are twofold: it signals the debased condition of consensus liberalism's idea of genuine happiness, while the zodiac sign's total erasure signals the condition of abjection that the modern nation-state induces in its citizens. This is the New Left story: true happiness has been rendered otherworldly and unavailable by modern political regimes. As we'll see shortly, its only chance of revival is through the psychic limit-experience that nowadays travels under the name of jouissance.

Already gesturing toward the sacred in his summons of the zodiac sign, Daniel connects this figure of exiled happiness more closely with what his real-world counterpart Giorgio Agamben designates *homo sacer* when Daniel aligns the Starfish with his suicidal sister. Beholding the unresponsive Susan in a sanitarium, Daniel explores her "starfish" abjection: "Today she practices the silence of the starfish. There are few silences deeper than the silence of the starfish. There are not many degrees of life lower before there is no life" (*BD* 253).[18] Witness to this scene of fatal desperation, Daniel notably also likens her to a Holocaust refugee: "She writhes gently on her back, swaying like something underwater, staring intently with her DP eyes at the ceiling" (252). Reduced to what Agamben calls "bare life" by the childhood trauma of losing her parents, Susan embodies the nation-state's biopolitical capture of and sanctioned violence against humanity. *Bare life* indicates the condition of human beings that the modern nation-state has managed, in its totalitarian mission creep, to command and suppress at once. Modern or "Western politics first constitutes itself through an exclusion (which is simultaneously an inclusion) of bare life."[19] The bare life is lived, according to Agamben, by the "*homo sacer* (the sacred man), who *may be killed and yet not sacrificed*," and this torturous truth becomes "the hidden foundation on which the entire [modern democratic] political system rest[s]."[20]

Moreover, constituting as it does the "specific aporia" of modern democracies, this biopolitical imperative "wants to put the freedom and happiness of men into play in the very place—'bare life'—that marked their subjection."[21] The liberal state's ordinary protections and pursuits ("freedom and happiness") are thus condemned as sites of duplicity. If such intricate masking is baked into modern political logic, the polity is also bound to expose its duplicity during moments of crisis. For instance, the abandoned refugee—exiled from one nation-state and refused protection by another—becomes the stateless exception that not only gives the lie to the universal verities of inalienable human rights (of treating all human life as sacrosanct) but also reveals the nation-state's self-crippling destiny. Agamben describes a long history of the contradictions inhering in the idea of the sacred—its religious, anthropological, and, finally, political ways of identifying the life that, though imbued with paramount worth, can be killed with impunity. He concludes that the sacred refugee is "nothing less than a limit-concept that radically calls into question the fundamental categories of the nation-state." As Daniel's Susan morphs into a Holocaust refugee, Agamben's refugee morphs into Susan's hospitalized counterpart, Karen Quinlan, whose body has been handed over to medical procedures and legal decisions that seek to shape "a life that coincides with death."[22] As befits such biopolitical destitution, in Doctorow's novel Susan becomes a martyr without an intelligible cause: the progressive radicalism of her parents is obsolete by the 1960s and the countercultural radicals she petitions want nothing more from her attachment to her parents' cause than a spectatorial poster that, for them, marks the parents' quaint celebrity in days of red-baiting yore.

We are a long way from Higham's scene of disagreement; the point of New Left historiography is not to disagree (and persuade) but to redescribe. According to this redescription, liberal democracies have led us hopelessly into what Agamben calls "unprecedented biopolitical catastrophe."[23] Just as *homo sacer* is cursed, so too, Agamben and Daniel both imply, is the modern polity.[24] Fleshing out his history of accursed ruination, Daniel finds confirmation in Edgar Allan Poe. Daniel sees him as a figure who exceeded the run-of-the-mill traitors of the incipient nation-state (that is, Benedict Arnold, General Charles Lee, Aaron Burr, Robert E. Lee, and Mormons, among others). Poe embodies "the archetype traitor, the master subversive... who wore a hole into the parchment [of the US Constitution] and let the darkness pour through" (*BD* 218). Poe's "hellish" darkness, in Daniel's projection of him, overturns antebellum America's version of *Life*'s consensus happiness. He works "like the poisonous effulgence of combustion engines over Thrift and Virtue and Reason and Natural Law and the Rights of Man. . . . It's Poe who ruined us, that scream from the smiling face of America" (218). From smile to scream: here, then, is a radical dissident's discovery of a distant forbear who can corroborate his late 1960s project of creating a narrative that turns in on itself.

This involution reaches maximum expression when Daniel deems "monstrous" the proposition of putting down words in "sequence"; he can hardly fathom that a "monstrous reader . . . goes on from one word to the next" just as the "monstrous writer . . . places one word after another" (*BD* 300). A conflation both of the "monstrous magician" whom the biblical Daniel displaces and of the biblical Daniel himself who can read the writing on the wall, here is a historian who is condemned both when he writes or interprets and when he does not (300). It may be impossible to be further away from the literary practices of incremental realism than this.[25] Indeed, Doctorow intimates that his novel—or at least Daniel's book—operates under the totalizing sign of the curse. A letter from Susan strikes Daniel as explicitly taking this "literary form" (101). As Daniel sees it, "[t]his curse" has "two stages." One is the prophecy of ultimate self-destruction whereby Daniel will disappear "into his own asshole" (101). The other is an attempted purgation through writing: in Susan's repudiating declaration, "*You no longer exist*," Daniel "is 'written' out of mind" (101). Daniel observes, however, that he might be less easy to disappear than Susan expects and that she might be subject to her own verbal violence. Doctorow writes, "There is some evidence that she was driven finally to eradicate him from her consciousness by the radical means of eradicating her consciousness" (101). In these losing propositions—either Daniel is destroyed or Susan is, either he writes monstrosity or he is silenced—the prospect of happiness, whether celestial or political, has long disappeared. The sign of the beneficent Starfish rises over the book only so that its figuration of happiness can be unwritten, blotted "out of mind."[26] It is condemned to the status of absent reminder of America's accursed share.

There is one crucial exception, however. There is Artie Sternlicht, who embodies the revolutionary extremist wing of the New Left. Starfish returns from bare life to violent life in the form of "starlight" joy. As though filling the vacuum created by the disappearance of the zodiac sign, the archprovocateur Sternlicht joins Poe in looming over Daniel's book. Daniel describes his biblical namesake as the "Beacon of Faith in a Time of Persecution" (*BD* 14), but in his own time it is Artie's light as much as anything that guides Daniel, fueled by family history, down the mountain of antipathy and onto the plains of radical dissent from all things liberal. The entire system of the nation-state, Sternlicht declares, is "guilty" (186). And it is a kind of guilt for which there is no possibility of exculpation. By this logic, the efforts on the part of Robert Lewin, Daniel's adoptive father and left-liberal lawyer, to have the Isaacson parents' verdict reversed is worthless; it amounts to an act of "good will" that merely exhibits "complicity" with the Cold War system. Daniel can't help but conclude that "[i]t is complicity in the system to be appalled with the moral structure of the system" (276). There's "no substantial difference" between being appalled by a government action—or viewing it with "shame"—and being a government stooge (277). In the face of the country's monstrous guilt, of which the Rosenberg/Isaacson execution is merely a symptom, such fine distinctions melt into air. The historian Doug Rossinow has noted that New Left antipathy toward midcentury liberalism engendered a New Left historiography that was blind to the compatibilities of Old Left radicalism and liberal reformism.[27] In *The Book of Daniel*, the New Left exemplars, Daniel and Sternlicht, insist on the opposite but to the same effect: Popular Front radicals were too much like liberals. As "revolutionary heirs of Jefferson and Lincoln and Andrew Jackson and Tom Paine" (237) who "wore ties[,] . . . held down jobs[,] . . . put people up for President," and so forth, the Popular Front folks were deep "into the system" (185). Committed as they were "to the world of American fair play and justice" (26), they too must be delegitimized.

A key aspect of this delegitimization entails expressing a radical form of happiness, one that bears striking resemblance to what poststructuralist theory often construes as jouissance. The occasion for this limit-experience in *The Book of Daniel* is a magazine writer's visit to Sternlicht's pad in the East Village, where Sternlicht, his girlfriend, and friends are hanging out. During the interview, for a meteoric instant, "[e]veryone gets happy" from blurting out "in unison" the title of the wall collage that Sternlicht's girlfriend has created: "EVERYTHING THAT CAME BEFORE IS ALL THE SAME!" (*BD* 168). Critics have noted that the collage itself, a massive palimpsestic jumble of images mostly from American popular and political culture, performs a postmodern "erasure of history" and a "vocal deracination."[28] The collage's title and the collective enunciation of it also betoken the urge toward ecstatic dissolution that jouissance signifies. As gestures of detachment—from history's referents and from personal identity—the title and collective utterance reach toward a conceptual extremism and radical consensus in which the boundaries marking representational and subjective coherence give way to ontological alterity. This version of otherness, insofar as it can be tapped, offers itself as the revolutionary alternative to liberal autonomy. Even the interviewer gets in on the game. She thinks, "This piece is writing itself," thereby echoing Roland Barthes's version of jouissance, wherein pleasures of the text issue from the undoing of writerly coherence. As she and the New Left claimants get radically happy, they distinguish themselves from the one remaining member of the Isaacsons' Old Left circle, Selig Mindish, the sellout or devious strategist, whose first name means "happy" or "blessed" in German and who for his pains winds up senile and condemned to the mindless (or mindish) pleasures of Disneyland. He becomes yet another example of the moribund Starfish.

If Doctorow is the novelist who, as Fredric Jameson's oft-cited acclamation has it, stands as "the epic poet of the disappearance of the American radical past, of the suppression of older traditions and moments of the American radical tradition," what his *Book of Daniel* reveals in retrospect is that 1960s radicalism doesn't so much disappear as find new platforms from which to operate.[29] Broadly speaking, to be sure, the revolutionary left "will lose its momentum as the war winds down and the draft ceases."[30] But the rise of poststructuralism and critical theory will provide radical thought ample opportunity to articulate antiliberal critiques on paper and in the seminar room—critiques that often envisage the constitutive undoing, the self-ruination, of systems. Daniel is poised to become a New Left academic historian even before the war winds down. He will invest in a historiography that recognizes no forebears in the Old Left, that revels in the undoing of liberal predicates, and that more or less abandons the realm of welfare-state justice and its attendant idea of happiness.

. . .

With the pervasiveness of consensus liberalism, the ongoing pressures of entrenched conservatism, and the increasing hostility of countercultural backlash, the activist wing of the liberal apparatus in the early postwar decades faced difficult odds in its efforts to promulgate a welfare-state vision. It nevertheless did seek suitable venues to clarify and formalize its moral and anthropological conditions of possibility.[31] Genres such as a proclamation from a newly formed international body, like the UN, and a treatise of political philosophy, like Rawls's *Theory of Justice*, may initially have had purchase only for like-minded liberals who were already prepared to build templates for a more equitable future. But the act of elaborating in minimalist form the grounding moral claims and basic social values of the signatory member states, as in the case of the UN's UDHR, and the act of elaborating most of those principles into a systematic justification of redistributive justice, as in the case of Rawls's work, may be understood as aiming over the long term to persuade bureaucratic, governmental, civic, and academic agencies of the merits of welfare-state liberalism. In the American scene, progressive liberals could offer alternatives not only to Cold War illusions of national consensus but also to countercultural visions of radical dissent.[32]

Both the UN and Rawls depended heavily on the legitimacy of Enlightenment ideas of a social contract to anchor their aspirational projects. I turn first to the UN's UDHR. As already indicated in the earlier discussion of Agamben's thought, there is a tendency among poststructuralist critics to dwell on the contradictions they descry at the core of human rights discourse. They often draw on Hannah Arendt's renowned account in *The Origins of Totalitarianism* of the refugee's condition of statelessness, which, contrary to the very idea of the universality of human rights, renders the person bereft of basic legal protections. The editors Ian Balfour and Eduardo Cadava, in their 2004 introduction to a special issue of the *South Atlantic Quarterly* on the status of human rights discourses, go so far as to stage this contradiction as a "crisis" with portentous implications: "The crisis within human rights is that, with the appearance of the refugee, the presumably sacred and inalienable rights of man are shown to be entirely alienable, to lack any protection or reality at the very moment in which they can no longer be understood as rights belonging to citizens of a state, or to members of a particular community."[33] More than exhibiting concern about the latest wave of specific refugees who might be suffering the pains and indignities of having little palpable security, Balfour and Cadava seem to find it logically unacceptable that, despite the universalist presumptions built into human rights claims, historically only nation-states have provided the political structure and enforcement power to bolster them. They write, "This reversal of the priority of human rights over political rights belies the contradictions at the heart of the rights of man: if they are supposed to be inalienable and universal, free from the determinations of any particular nation or state, they are also dependent on the sovereignty of that nation or state for their definition, protection, and realization."[34] Since they deem contradictory the situation in which moral (or metamoral) claims and political (or legal) claims derive from different institutional and historical sources, they set the diagnostic stage as one might imagine Daniel Isaacson Lewin setting it: as rife with complicity and guilt. Hence, their concluding remarks take up modernity's cursed destiny, self-consciously echoing Walter Benjamin: "There is no document of humanitarianism that is not at the same time a document of inhumanity, inequality, and violence, and . . . the human rights activist should therefore dissociate himself or herself from it as much as possible."[35] To which a liberal might respond that the only human rights activists in need of such dissociation are those who deem flawed actualizations of ideal aspirations to delegitimize the aspirational project altogether or who apply a deconstructive logic to the metaphysical abstractions on which human rights are putatively predicated, such that these abstractions are constitutively undone by an underlying materiality.

By contrast, those working with the UN to draft the UDHR understood that conceptual abstractions need not be metaphysical; that what must drive the agenda was the consensus of member states on moral values, not truths; and that barbarous acts wrought by humans were not likely to come to a halt simply by declarative will. The UDHR clearly registers a sense of interdependency (rather than contradiction) between the UN's universalist moral "aspiration" and sovereign nations' political responsibility and legal authority to implement "progressive measures."[36] Although the UN would become a central component of the international apparatus authorizing sanctions and military actions between and among nation-states, what is remarkable about the UDHR is its focus on what each nation-state owes its "peoples" as individual humans. Many of the rights delineated in the thirty articles speak, of course, to protection from the state itself, articulating what are commonly understood as negative liberties—the right to life, liberty, and security (Article 3); the right not to be enslaved (Article 4); the right to privacy (Article 12); the right to marry, to practice religion, to free speech (Articles 16, 18, 19), and so forth. But in addition to negative liberties, the UDHR identifies numerous rights that speak to people's substantive welfare and that, in an international regime of sovereign nation-states, only a modern welfare state can address:

the right to work (Article 23), the right to leisure (Article 24), the right to education, the right to participate in cultural activity (Articles 26, 27), and so forth. Arguably most crucial in this vein are two broader considerations of people's general well-being and, in effect, their existential dignity. Regarding well-being, Article 25 stipulates a substantial package of social-security provision: "Everyone has the right to a standard of living adequate for the health and well-being of himself and of his family, including food, clothing, housing and medical care and necessary social services, and the right to security in the event of unemployment, sickness, disability, widowhood, old age or other lack of livelihood in circumstances beyond his control." This article reiterates and elaborates on the stipulations of Article 22, in which the language of existential dignity is foregrounded: "Everyone, as a member of society, has the right to social security and is entitled to the realization, through national effort and international co-operation and in accordance with the organization and resources of each State, of the economic, social and cultural rights *indispensable for his dignity and the free development of his personality*" (emphasis added). This italicized phrase, repeated in slightly different form in Article 29, may be said to articulate and legitimate, for the UN's consenting member nation-states, the general idea of the very purpose of these nation-states' existence, namely, not only to protect their peoples from various harms and indignities but also to contribute actively to their flourishing over time.

At the dawn of the postwar era, then, the most expansive international institution ever formed staged a kind of enormous roundtable convention in which moral consensus was achieved around the aspirational fundamentals of a welfare-state system, while paternalist moralizing about the specific contents of a good life was largely averted. (Nobody complained about divorce rates or excessive drinking, for instance.) Indeed, Samuel Moyn has argued that the UDHR was much more important for its articulation of a "national welfarist consensus" than for its advancement of international human rights. To corroborate his claim, he refers to the UDHR's denunciation in the United States as a "pink paper." [37] Less direct but more affirmative corroboration would appear in the liberal activist and academic Harry K. Girvetz's book *The Evolution of Liberalism* (1950/1963). In a chapter titled "The Welfare of Nations," he insisted that the "[s]tandard of living" in the United States be understood not as a bare minimum of subsistence but as gauged by what people think "they *can* have and *ought* to have as a matter of right and justice."[38] With its second edition blurbed on the front cover by Hubert H. Humphrey and introduced by Arthur Schlesinger Jr., the book testifies to the existence of postwar relays between the left-liberal American political apparatus and UDHR language and ideals.[39]

. . .

The specific language of happiness is absent from the UDHR, but this absence dovetails with an important aspect of the argument presented in this study: the more the language of personality development—or what political philosophers often call flourishing—could become an adequate synonym for happiness, the more happiness itself could claim legitimacy as a political value. (An early UN offshoot, the World Health Organization, embraced all too gladly the language of happiness in its 1948 constitution, which, as we'll see in chapter 4, rendered it susceptible to science fiction parody.) In *A Theory of Justice*, Rawls explicitly makes the semantic link between happiness and flourishing when he presents arguments for building his theory's principles of justice as fairness into institutional schemes and thus into the life schemes of persons and their varying conceptions of the good. It is important to note, however, that by the late 1950s Rawls was already engaged in conceptualizing a dialectical relation between the pursuit of happiness, broadly construed, and liberalism's formal yet practical sense of redistributive justice.

In this early stage of his thought, his arguments were directed not at what critics of human rights discourse often worry about, namely, that the advocacy of liberal individualism threatens to eclipse collective values.[40] Rawls's concern was instead with dominant strains of social-welfare theory, which did not worry enough about the individual as a person deserving dignity and socioeconomic justice. As Amartya Sen has recently observed, the 1950s were marked by dramatic turns in social-welfare analysis, largely brought about by Kenneth Arrow's "birth of the modern discipline of social choice theory" and by John Rawls's "pioneering" work on the related question of redistributive justice.[41] At issue, among other things, was social-welfare theory's reliance on the utilitarian principle of aggregating individual preference satisfaction for identifying and choosing optimal states of collective well-being. This theory not only ignored the effect of social choice on the least advantaged members of society but also excluded the relevance of objective assessments of well-being. It was both hyperindividualist (in that everybody's personal happiness, pleasure, or preference satisfaction counted toward the aggregate) and conceptually indifferent to the plight of underprivileged individuals (in that the aim was for maximum aggregate happiness).

Rawls, for his part, drew instead on social-contract theory to introduce postulates of fairness, equity, and liberty that could override determinations of aggregate happiness. Such postulates constituted minimum conditions of socioeconomic justice. Without a ubiquitous sense of justice as fairness, Rawls argued, "the liability to pleasure and pain ... might be taken as alone relevant, and the greatest happiness principle would be entirely natural."[42] But *with* a sense of justice as fairness in play, utilitarianism could be defeated. Indeed, the very assumption "that individual preferences have value as such" was questionable with regard to questions of justice. For Rawls, individual preferences were subordinate to a kind of omnilateral reciprocity, that is, to "the mutual recognition of principles [of justice] by participants in a common practice [whose] rules ... define their several relations and give form to their claims on one another."[43] Whereas justice in classical or hedonic utilitarianism amounted to efficient executive decisions that maximized society's happiness, justice in Rawls's view was built into distributive axioms.[44] Most important was the "maximin" (or "difference") principle, whereby any Pareto optimum (that is, preference-driven distribution of efficiency) must also improve the conditions of the least advantaged; this precept excluded the utilitarian "justification of inequalities on the grounds that the disadvantages of those in one position are outweighed by the greater advantages of those in another position."[45]

In Rawls's theory, then, subjective preferences were subordinate but by no means excluded; they were equivalent to aspirations and desires or, more broadly, to personal conceptions of the good. They were distinct from and lower in priority than Rawls's index of objectively measurable (and interpersonally comparable) primary goods: "liberty and opportunity, income and wealth, health and educated intelligence," and, not least, "self-respect," which denotes "a confident conviction of the sense of one's own value, a firm assurance that what one does or plans to do is worth doing."[46] This commitment to the moral idea of an increasingly equalized distribution of primary goods dovetailed with a meatier proposition of happiness than utilitarianism's psychological calculus of pleasure and pain. And yet it was quite minimalist compared to *Life*'s roundtable version of "genuine happiness." Although pleasure and enjoyment were by no means irrelevant in this proposition, what mattered much more was a person's pursuit of a good life extended over time. Happiness signified the "successful execution," more or less, of a life plan, a "human flourishing" reflective of a "life fully worthy of choice."[47] "Someone is happy when his plans are going well, his more important aspirations being fulfilled, and he feels sure that his good fortune will endure," Rawls wrote (*TJ* 409). This description, of course, was an imaginative ideal commensurate with welfare-state ideology, not a guarantee of the actually existing welfare state. If we allow for contingencies of luck and misfortune in areas such as personal aptitude, family circumstance, and current events, a fair share of primary goods should enable one to view one's life as more or less in sync with welfare-state liberalism's modality of happiness.

Informed, to be sure, by Aristotelian ideas of the good life, Rawls nevertheless understood this life plan loosely; it came with minimal expectations of personal virtue or specific conduct. Indeed, even general expectations (such as the desire to pursue challenging rather than monotonous activities) could be "overridden" by individual idiosyncrasy (*TJ* 429). The point of envisioning a happy life plan was not social engineering or paternalist surveillance but rather the state's acknowledgement of actually existing human tendencies. The "design of social institutions" must make "a large place" for patterns of human conduct that do not violate rules of justice (429). Rawls's idea of happiness accommodated, for instance, the eccentric (fictive) individual who makes a living solving math problems but "whose only pleasure is to count blades of grass in various geometrically shaped areas" (432). Although unconventional and possibly "neurotic," this person's pursuit is freely chosen and, in the final analysis, "ties in with the primary good of self-respect" (432, 433).[48] At the same time, the life plan does entail a person to respect a sense of temporal endurance or existential "continuity," which "reminds us that since a plan is a scheduled sequence of activities, earlier and later activities are bound to affect one another" (420). Such self-knowledge generates considerations of a future structured by increments—with provisions for its becoming "relatively less specific for later periods" (410). Rawls's incrementalist protocol, in other words, insists that noncontingent principles of justice inhering in institutions are commensurate with an equally noncontingent principle of self-respect inhering in persons. In this manner, the postwar era's most important liberal theorist envisioned an ongoing dialectic between individual flourishing and the structures of *inter*dependence—both intimate and impersonal—entailed by a socioeconomic system of distributive justice.

. . .

A 1973 dystopian fantasy written by Arrow's and Rawls's slightly younger contemporary Ursula K. Le Guin, "The Ones Who Walk Away from Omelas," may be understood to illustrate the implications for happiness and justice of adhering to Arrow's social choice theory rather than to Rawls's system of justice as fairness. In brief, it is a kind of parable, presenting an idyllic, prosperous, happy, consummately civil, and well-knit society on the occasion of its annual Festival of Summer. The self-reflexive narrator summons the reader to participate in choosing some of the elements comprising the city, thus coyly satisfying utilitarianism's criterion of individual preference. "Perhaps it would be best," the narrator suggests, "if you imagined it as your own fancy bids, . . . for certainly I cannot suit you all." Between all the things that are ruled in as "necessary" and ruled out as "destructive" are innumerable options: "central heating, subway trains, washing machines, and all kinds of marvelous devices not yet invented here, floating light-sources, fuelless power, a cure for the common cold. Or they could have none of that: it doesn't matter. As you like it."[49] The narrator's mounting insistence on the relevance of the reader's nearly unrestricted preferences conforms to Arrow's utilitarian world in which the aggregate of individual sets of preferences constitutes its happiness and its justice.

And yet, there's a gruesome hitch. In the final pages the narrator explains that all this happy prosperity and social cooperation—as all the citizens "understand"—depends on the incarceration and "abominable misery" of a young child. And as though in express violation of Rawls's difference principle of justice, this child's life has suffered a turn for the worse. The child "can remember sunlight and its mother's voice"; it "used to scream for help," but now all it manages to express is "a kind of whining" as it withers away in squalor and infirmity.[50] This is what provokes a few to walk away in the end. Le Guin, in other words, exposes the problem of relying on aggregated preferences instead of on a social contract committed to justice as fairness.

The Argument for Incremental Realist Fiction

One of the strengths of science fiction is its ability to expose through situational schema and diagnostic parable the nightmarish implications of our ostensibly virtuous social and political commitments—such as, in Le Guin's story, the freedom to choose this or that in the name of collective happiness. The genre is arguably less good at affirming a liberal activist's sense of the positive potential inhering in an actually existing system. Even the utopian variety of science fiction has difficulty narrating how a society on planet

Earth got from present-day *x* to future situation *y* in distant year *z*. But as we'll see throughout this study, modernist realism and naturalist realism, as practiced at midcentury, aren't much good at affirming liberal activism either. Problems arise of extravagant metaphor and satire, of rendering psychosocial pathology equivalent to the American norm, of insisting on a privacy of will, and of exalting regional history. These and other elements interfere with the goodwill narration of welfare-state justice that incrementalist realism exhibits, even in works of fiction such as Paula Fox's early novels, which portray considerable conflict, distress, and injury.

To be clear, however, when incremental realists portray conflict, distress, and injury, they are not performing the same kind of cultural work that Heather Love attends to in her account of "the incrementalist turn" in literary criticism as well as in literary styles of description. Exemplified by her practice of "close but not deep" reading and by Claudia Rankine's lyric documentation, Love is concerned to identify a critical practice proportionate to small-scale literary practice, akin to microsociology, and to account for its politics. Deriving the terms of incrementalism from architecture (and drawing on Mark Seltzer's account), she argues that a realism "committed to immanence rather than to transcendence at every point along the scale" can be redeemed from charges of status quo conservatism when understood as "a point of articulation of a larger circuit." In the case of Rankine's work, the larger circuit is defined by "violence."[51] The very smallness of the "small-scale incidents of racism" that Rankine observes again and again points to the banality and thence to the ubiquity of racial injury. This is how Rankine delivers "object lessons," that is, a political pedagogy of resistance. Scaled-back description steers clear of transcendent "wish fulfillment," which Love critiques in Fredric Jameson's account of realism's antinomies.[52] He envisages mainstream realism's detailed attention, for instance, to webs of individual relationships as somehow intimating a utopian totality—what he calls "new macrocosms of collectivity."[53] Like so many poststructuralists who harbor political, ethical, or merely emotional commitments to utopia, Jameson counts on a glimpse or a glimmer or a glow of that which exceeds the regime of representation, thereby transcending the extant world and its history.

Although Love importantly disavows this mode of transcendence, the reduction of incrementalism to a cognition of scale obviates two important aspects of both literary realism and political discourse: temporality and morality.

A microsociology of observational description inhabits a very narrow present; it also abjures moral argument. To be sure, a certain moral awareness of racism's offensiveness obtains; indeed, this awareness must be shared by the reader and Rankine for her observations of microaggression to gain any political (and pedagogical) purchase. But these object lessons have little to no persuasive power, because there isn't anything in them to disagree with. By contrast, the mode of incrementalism derived from midcentury decision theory (discussed in chapter 2), which can be seen to supplement Rawls's incrementalist protocol with thicker notions of practical applicability, is explicitly predicated on liberal democratic values to which everybody in principle consents but around which conflict endlessly coalesces. Not to put too fine a point on it: in an operative social contract of liberal democracy (we must presume in good faith), everybody wants as much liberty as possible, as little state paternalism as possible, and as equitable a socioeconomic order as possible. But everybody does not prioritize these values—in neither their macro- nor their micromanifestations—in the same way. This is why, as Schlesinger put it in his introduction to Girvetz's book, "debate is the essence of liberalism."[54] There is no such thing as debate without disagreement; and settling disagreements usually requires not only observational documentation but also a commitment to persuade. Moreover, the incrementalism of midcentury decision theory was organized around a political grammar of both the present and the future tense: to envision making a decision is to envision acting in and on the future. This mode of incrementalism thus provided midcentury welfare-state activists—whether of the academic, grassroots-organizing, policy-making, or literary variety—with a critical framework for affirming a form of political and social consensus, for disagreeing with those who harbored different priorities, and for attempting to persuade them to change their minds.

To put this problem another way, (Love's account of) Rankine's documentary construction of a social totality of microaggressive violence looks like a milder version of Jameson's diagnostic construction of a postmodern totality (sans transcendent escape hatch). As Deak Nabers notes, Jameson has a way of conflating "blood, torture, death, and terror," of indiscriminately designating these refractions of violence the "underside" of "American military and economic domination throughout the world."[55] The problem, as Nabers, sees it, is that Jameson does not distinguish between the sheer materiality of blood and death and the signifying mechanisms embedded in torture and terror.

Nabers makes the compelling case for understanding the postwar "martial imagination" as one in which torture and terror were message-bearing technologies designed to convey to adversaries a willingness to bring about more bloodshed and death; they were, in other words, attempts to persuade these adversaries to comply with directives. For Jameson and Rankine, though, persuasion and the attendant exercises of interpretation, judgment, and dis/agreement that constitute an interdynamic signifying system have been effectively eliminated from the macrocultural picture. For Jameson and Rankine, injuries of all sorts are nothing if not self-evident markers of the sociopolitical bloodbath in which we're all immersed.

However grisly this martial imagination and its ways of working through the troublesome dialectic of materiality and message, the distinctions Nabers identifies in the broad patterns of postwar thought prove central to liberal activism's reclamation of a symbology of happiness as well. Activists encountered not only the opposition of utilitarian economists for whom the psychological experience of happiness was the prime indicator of preference satisfaction (and thus the driver of their policy decisions). They also, and conversely, had to reckon with a plethora of midcentury social critics for whom the experience of happiness was the self-evident marker of an American culture gone wrong. Discussed more fully in chapter 1, feeling (or exhibiting) happiness indicated middle-class conformity, obsessive consumerism, self-absorption, and/or passive complacency. The critic Robert Warshow, for instance, opened his seminal 1948 essay, "The Gangster as Tragic Hero," with an indictment of American optimism and cheerfulness:

> America, as a social and political organization, is committed to a cheerful view of life. It could not be otherwise. The sense of tragedy is a luxury of aristocratic societies, where the fate of the individual is not conceived of as having a direct and legitimate political importance, being determined by a fixed and supra-political—that is, non-controversial—moral order or fate. *Modern equalitarian societies*, however, whether democratic or authoritarian in their political forms, always base themselves on the claim that they are *making life happier*.... *Happiness thus becomes the chief political issue—in a sense, the only political issue—and for that reason it can never be treated as an issue at all*.... It [thus] becomes an obligation of citizenship to be cheerful.... The citizen may even be compelled to make a public display of his cheerfulness on important occasions.[56]

Naming happiness the American political issue that can't be treated as an issue, Warshow converts the experience of happiness into a symptom of the national form. The nation's constitutional insistence on political equality amounts in this scenario to making everybody happy, hence to a kind of diseased obligation to mirror this form by being happy.[57]

Postwar literary satirists proved eager to participate in this symptomology. For instance, Richard Yates concludes *Revolutionary Road* (1961) with a picture of the white-collar protagonist Frank Wheeler—in the wake of his wife's disastrous death by a DIY abortion—happily spouting psychobabble as a "walking, talking, smiling, lifeless man."[58] He thereby discloses the psychosocial deformities of the self-deceived white suburban male narcissist. Yates resembled the writer of "serious literature" C. Wright Mills envisioned, who made white-collar figures "subjects for lamentation" on account of their diseased fate while leaving "popular writing" to do the false work of promoting happy people as "targets of aspiration."[59] With similar knowingness Flannery O'Connor depicts the self-deceived Emory Enoch in *Wise Blood* (1952) as deservedly punished for his pursuit of secular happiness. He is duped by the confluence of Hollywood commercialism and institutions of secular knowledge. Whereas Hollywood promotes a movie by exhibiting a fake gorilla, a museum of natural history displays a prehistoric "shrunken man."[60] Enoch experiences "the intensest kind of happiness" and believes no one could feel "happier" than he does when he dons the stolen gorilla suit and sets out to greet people near the highway, only to see them run away from him in fright.[61] O'Connor's and Yates's scenarios function as fictive documentation or, to borrow Love's phrase, as points of articulation of a larger circuit. In these cases, the larger circuit is not of racial violence but of false consciousness, which renders the experience of happiness suspect.

When Mills refers to the postwar middle class as "*symptom and symbol* of modern society as a whole," for which Yates's Frank Wheeler could serve as a particular example, he binds the linguistic technology for abstraction and generalization (symbol) to the diagnostic technology for identifying material disease (symptom).[62] With this binding logic in place, abstraction and generalization essentially amount to different scales of evidence, to larger circuits that demonstrate the same thing embodied by the particular example. The symbol doesn't persuade; it merely registers evidence in concentrated form. In the early postwar decades, then, Yates, O'Connor, and Mills all perform the role of third-person diagnostician, as do Jameson, Rankine, and Love in the present, examining sociopolitical evidence and providing reports in the form of example, whether real or fictive, whether extravagant or minimalist. This mode of diagnostic knowledge production participates in what Walter Benn Michaels describes "as the disarticulation of difference from [ideological] disagreement," in that any conflict that might arise from a difference in interpretation or judgment operates only on the level of empirical description.[63] (If, say, two doctors disagree about whether a lump is a cyst indicating an infection or a tumor indicating cancer, the dispute will be resolved by conducting more diagnostic tests. At stake would be empirical accuracy, not ideological faith.) In the realm of cultural knowledge production in which symbol becomes the appendage of symptom, those who deem the world afflicted by the disease of false consciousness and then create symbols to reflect that condition merely differ from—without disagreeing with—those who deem it afflicted instead (or also) by diseases of racism and American imperialism.

By contrast, when Galbraith yearns for new symbols to take the place of dominant aspirations to achieve privatized consumer happiness, he seeks to situate these abstractions or generalizations in a symbolic economy in which differences are bound up with disagreement. To be sure, he proffers diagnoses of American socioeconomic ills, but in his hands, symbols are not symptoms of these ills; rather, they're instruments of persuasion. Just as utilitarians deem preference satisfaction a positive empirical metric, he inflects his envisioned symbols of happiness with a positive valence (pace the era's diagnosticians of false consciousness with whom he doesn't engage). But these affirming symbols, constituting an arsenal of persuasion, invite the long temporal horizon. For in addition to issuing grim diagnoses of the American present, Galbraith makes an argument for a better future. No transcendence here—his symbology of happiness dovetails with Girvetz's sense of "pleading the cause of justice."[64] We'll see that this symbology, as deployed by postwar fiction writers of incrementalist realism, bore the burden of persuading liberals of various stripes to join welfare-state activists in deeming personality development and socioeconomic justice to be more important—that is, of more social, political, and personal value—than utilitarian aggregations of preference satisfaction, more important than free-market ideology, and more important than regional attachment.

The chapters that follow focus on writers who did the cultural work of embedding dimensions of what Nabers calls "the argumentative infrastructures of . . . postwar liberal discourse" in realist fiction.[65] These narratives are paradigmatic examples of a kind of midcentury realism that neither aspired to be, say, the next Great American Novel nor conformed to the social realism of the populist or Marxist variety. They exemplified instead a constrained yet spirited narrative aesthetics that addressed experiential intricacies—including conflict, distress, and injury—while conveying justifications for redress by means of the welfare state. Often inflected by considerations of race, sexuality, and socioeconomic status, incremental realism was atypical in its insistence on the virtues of welfare-state liberalism. For incremental realists, then, symbols of happiness don't express larger circuits of symptomatic evidence but instead contribute to larger arguments for welfare-state justice. They seem to have intuited that the narrative challenge of justifying happiness from the standpoint of the liberal activist had to do both with midcentury politics and midcentury affection. If the welfare state served to mitigate the predatory conditions of capitalism, incremental realists attempted in effect to mitigate the hard truth that Irving Howe discerned in the early 1980s, that "the welfare state does not seem able to arouse strong loyalties" even among its supporters and even though its emergence earlier required the political activity of "large numbers of people."[66] Although the Newark Public Library clearly did arouse Roth's strong loyalty, as we've seen, his librarian protagonist Neil Klugman in *Goodbye, Columbus* finds the path to making his workplace an object of attachment far tougher going; it requires affirmation of his municipal agency, which emerges almost begrudgingly and only through the solicitude he offers an underprivileged black boy. And yet compared to the other writers featured in this study Roth's conversion of the public library into a symbol of happiness is a picnic. Consider *Maud Martha* (1953). Gwendolyn Brooks may be understood in this narrative to take on the assignment of making symbols of happiness out of three things: (1) the entire South Side's depressed mixed economy, (2) a New Deal home-loan agency whose eligibility criteria were notoriously difficult to satisfy, and (3) a set of uninspiring marital preferences. Or consider *Desperate Characters* (1970). Written soon after the passage of Medicare and Medicaid legislation, Paula Fox wrestles with the country's inhospitable health-care system, managing against the odds to pin to the happiness mat a dingy, overcrowded emergency room in Brooklyn. Or consider *The Price of Salt* (1952), often celebrated as the first lesbian novel with a happy ending. Patricia Highsmith here pays tribute to the aspect of the mixed economy that midcentury social critics, including Galbraith, loved to hate—consumerism—by rendering sexual minorities normative partly through their participation in the consumer economy, which facilitated their UDHR-sponsored personality development. Not for nothing does Highsmith dress her protagonist, in the novel's final episode, in a little black dress—the stylish woman's equivalent to the middle-class man's gray flannel suit. Or consider Peter Taylor's answer, in a cluster of short stories, to the incorrigibly regressive South. A university administrator, in "Dean of Men" (1968), crawls out from under the family patriarchy to lead a happy life devoted to modern institutional decision-making; similarly, an academic historian in "*Je Suis Perdu*" (1958) and a creative writing professor in "1939" (1955) attribute much of their happiness to careers within the postwar university system.

Altogether, by showing how postwar writers of fiction linked the era's familiar trope of happiness to less familiar political arguments about the value of individual flourishing within a system committed to advancing socioeconomic fairness, this study seeks to enlarge our sense of the postwar liberal imagination and its attentiveness to better, possible worlds.

1 The Art, Sociology, and Library Politics of Happiness in Early Philip Roth

Esquire's January 1962 issue contained an excerpt from Philip Roth's novel *Letting Go* titled "Very Happy Poems." Taken from the middle of the novel, these are the words that the high-strung Libby Herz is reduced to uttering when encouraged by the representative of an adoption agency to describe the "kind" of poems she writes. None the wiser after his initial line of inquiry ("Do you write nature poems, do you write, oh I don't know, rhymes, do you write little jingles?") the agent tries again, following Libby's breathy declarations of enthusiasm for Keats, Donne, and Yeats:

> "And how about your own poems? I mean—would you say they're, oh I don't know, happy poems or unhappy poems? You know, people write all kinds of poems, happy poems, unhappy poems—what do you consider yours to be?"
>
> "Happy poems," said Libby. "Very happy poems."[1]

The situation is uncomfortable, not least because the flustered Libby desperately wants to demonstrate her motherly fitness to the adoption agent, an "easygoing" young man who nevertheless "intimidate[s]" her (*LG* 332). In turn, she perplexes the agent by disavowing being a writer of poems despite having already told him she was writing a poem just before he arrived, which isn't the truth but isn't exactly a lie either.[2] Roth's intimate focus on Libby's perspective (for the first time in the novel) intensifies the sense of her agonizing difficulty countenancing the specific contingencies of her life—her husband Paul's sexual remoteness, her kidney ailment, their quasi-bohemian poverty and childlessness—and presenting a coherent version of herself to the external world. Although such contingencies are presented as credible sources of frustration, Roth implies that Libby's emotional and psychic predicament is aggravated by an unrealistic expectation of ease and happiness, of ease *as* happiness. She would in fact like to wake up on any given morning and, without prior effort or practice, compose some very happy poems.

Vividly portraying the near crack-up of this intelligent but misguided and overly sensitive character, the *Esquire* excerpt showcased Roth's talent for writing in the key of excruciation. But it also signaled that among the many concerns of the forthcoming novel (released later that year) was the relation between aesthetic value and that paradigmatic postwar American feeling, happiness. What's particularly notable about the exchange between Libby and the adoption agent is neither that it revolves around literary production, a self-reflexive theme that pervades Roth's fiction, nor that it engages the vocabulary of happiness in postwar America, which also recurs often enough in his work. Rather, it is the way this exchange imagines the two distinct pursuits of art and happiness as forming a compound precipitate, the happy poem. Forming, yet also deforming—for even as the two characters summon the happy poem into being, Roth suggests that it remains mere wish fulfillment. With Libby's happy poems claimed but disclaimed, not yet written but yearned for, genuinely esteemed by her but articulated as such only by echoing an affable social worker's prying terms, Roth places this imagined artifact under the pressure of multiple and conflicting valences.

This chapter takes the *Esquire* excerpt's staged problematic as the point of departure for an examination of Roth's aesthetic, affective, and political commitments at midcentury. It is important first to consider how Roth seems at times to join the era's intelligentsia and literati in dismissing happy art as a middle-class monstrosity, a kitschy blob threatening to suffocate postwar America. What might qualify as Exhibit A in the category of happy-art monstrosity, as the historian of happiness Darrin McMahon suggests, is the "smiley face." It was in 1963 that an advertising executive invented this "modern icon," earning him a forty-five-dollar commission, only to see it virally proliferate, selling annually in the form of fifty million buttons alone by 1971 and coming to rival "in certain quarters . . . the Cross and the Star of David."[3] But Exhibit B could well be drawn from one of Roth's early works, *Portnoy's Complaint*, in which Portnoy extols his Jewish family's Thanksgiving tradition over and against that of his WASP girlfriend, Pumpkin, whose family in Davenport, Iowa, all look and act too much like folks in "a painting by Norman Rockwell."[4] At other times, however, happy art becomes for Roth an occasion to explore more deeply the existential, ethical, and political significance of both aesthetic and affective experience. In these instances, he puts into narrative play a range of liberal conditions—conceptual, dispositional, and institutional—that coalesce around the happy-art object and test its precarious viability. He thus reveals the potential for art and happiness to function as mutually animating values and qualities within the welfare state. More specifically, he draws attention to happiness's labile function within mundane circuits of middle-class life, such as working at a white-collar job in a welfare-state institution such as a public library. He thereby registers a commitment to certain middle-class norms—a commitment, however, that is less concerned with reinforcing and perpetuating postwar norms than with imagining them, from the perspective of a liberal activist, as they might be. [5]

If happy art is subject to a rather withering trial by fire in *Letting Go*, its baptism in Roth's better-known earlier work, *Goodbye, Columbus* (1959), proves more promising. In that text, historically actual artifacts such as Gauguin prints and Mantovani records vie for value priority, even if the contest is heavily weighted by authorial favoritism. Despite Roth's relish, as Jonathan Freedman convincingly shows in *Klezmer America*, for "popular and mass culture of the last century, particularly . . . [that of] the 1940s and 1950s," he clearly deems all too easy the mode of listening that Mantovani music elicits.[6] And despite Roth's equally pronounced appreciation, as Ross Posnock richly elaborates in *Philip Roth's Rude Truth*, for high modernism and literary experimentalism,[7] Gauguin's paintings gain significance less for their modernist challenge or formal innovation than for the intense pleasure they bring to the uninitiated beholder and the genial dialogue they prompt. The happy-art object's potential value, Roth implies, involves but is not reducible to its creator's expressive achievement; this value depends in no small measure on the beholder's capacities and ambitions as well as on the art object's relational function within a liberal social system.

Happiness and Midcentury Social Criticism

What might be called Roth's normative (as opposed to modernist or populist) challenge to happy art's smiley-faced normality takes shape within a broader discourse of happiness at midcentury.[8] From 1776 onward, the Declaration of Independence may have etched the right to pursue happiness into Americans' consciousness, but not until the nation's claim to World War II triumph and the ensuing economic boom did happiness come to be equated with an American sense of entitlement, emerging as a kind of affective correlative of the nation-state. It thus became a social critic's veritable obligation to disparage happiness, stigmatizing it as the foremost index of middle-class conformity, complacency, and shallow materialism. In his 1953 book on the subject, *The Pursuit of Happiness*, the eminent historian Howard Mumford Jones summed up the conditions of happiness that rendered it a pox on the nation:

> [T]he United States remains a happy land, the land of good cheer, God's country. It produces the Optimists' Club, the glad books, the Boosters' society, manuals on how to attain peace of mind, songs to the effect that though I want to be happy, I can't be happy unless you are happy too.... Advertisements reveal our folkways. They prove that the effect of purchasing American cigarets [sic], oil furnaces, laxatives, shirts, automobiles, house paint, television sets, coffee, nylon stockings, vacuum cleaners, chewing gum, coated paper, electric trains, and dog food is the instant creation of felicity.[9]

Not just advertisements, of course, but also advice columns, children's books, stories in slick magazines, and excessive leisure—indeed, the ubiquitous insistence on "having a good time"—contribute to "guaranteeing the American citizen the ghastly privilege of pursuing a phantom and embracing a delusion" (*PH* 17, 138). With this ominous witticism Jones manages to turn Kant's well-known statement about happiness's elusiveness on its head. Kant viewed happiness as a natural inclination but one rendered elusively indeterminate by our cognitive limitations on what would make us happy and by the gap between our empirical "wishes and wills" and "the idea of happiness." This idea "require[s] an absolute whole, a maximum of well-being" both in the present and future, which is unknowable: "In short [the human being] is not capable of any principle by which to determine with complete certainty what would make him truly happy, because for this omniscience would be required." Kant thus considered happiness "not an ideal of reason but of imagination."[10] Jones, however, converts postwar happiness's elusiveness into gothic obsessiveness and imagination into a generator of patently false phantasms.

Jones's oddly good-natured book chronicles happiness's demise. It tells how a series of judicial decisions (involving such concerns as the right of inheritance and employment contract) conspired to render happiness a function of libertarian proprietary ideology; it also tracks pernicious shifts in cultural value, exemplified most dismayingly by Emerson's and William James's respective alignments of happiness with self-fulfillment and personal adjustment. By the postwar era, these propensities had devolved into navel-gazing self-expression and personal therapy. This "inheritance," Jones complains, has "translated the problem of the right to happiness out of ethics, out of law, and out of religion into a problem of both national and individual psychology, normal or otherwise" (PH 129–30).[11] Yet Jones is confident that the founders had more in mind than Locke's sense of privacy, that their declaration protecting the pursuit of happiness was predicated on Blackstone's natural-law assumption "that the law of nature being itself the product of divine benevolence, must be the only model for human law, so that in proportion as human law mirrors universal reason, citizens obedient to its ancient sanctions must secure felicity" (105). By Jones's quasi-Aristotelian lights, then, genuine happiness must be keyed to public reason and virtuous action, inscribed within an empirically determinate teleology.

Other critics, even those with less-pointed political concerns, developed a sharper social psychology than Jones's, as exemplified by the Princeton sociologist Melvin Tumin in a 1957 essay (he would befriend Roth some five years later). "A society is in real trouble with itself," he intones, "when its people get unthinking and unfeeling enough to consider 'happiness' as the prime goal in life. . . . The fact is simple: happiness is no guide to anything." Here happiness barely qualifies *as* a feeling; only "unfeeling" people pursue it, threatening open society by eroding "critical, reflective judgment based on sound experience."[12] According to the more radical left, middle-class happiness was essentially a symptom of false consciousness—and thus a historical and ontological problem more than a psychological one—fictively exemplified by the pathetic figure Willy Loman, who names his son Happy. The sociologist C. Wright Mills may harbor more empathy than Tumin for such "trapped" cogs of the military-industrial complex who generally "cannot overcome their troubles," but his verdict is similar: they are the ones whose "authority is confined strictly within a prescribed orbit of occupational actions" and thus whose "power" is at best "a borrowed thing."[13] This quasi-Marxist sense of the white-collar worker's inability to be genuinely happy also dovetailed with the era's Freudian theorists, for whom happiness is always already undone by the psyche's overdetermined, pleasure-thwarting ways. Indeed, as

Catherine Jurca has expansively shown in *White Diaspora*, the unhappier you found yourself at midcentury, the more distinctive and glamorous you might appear. Shored up by narcissistic self-pity, white suburbanites in gray flannel suits could join this special crew of *misérables* when their "houses and furnishings reflexively become evidence of and opportunities for alienation," thereby allowing them to count themselves among the "malcontents" rather than among the "mindless conformists."[14] In such accounts of alienation, Jurca suggests, there may be more bad faith than false consciousness at work.

For all the skepticism of midcentury happiness that Roth appears at times to share with the era's critics, he is less inclined to fix its position on the cultural landscape with witticism, ironic historiography, psychopolitical complaint, or blanket stigmatization. "Everything will turn," Jones contended in his book's penultimate paragraph, "on the question [of] whether happiness is construed in modern America as primarily an individual or primarily a social state" (*PH* 164). Roth doesn't disagree with this claim, but he doesn't share Jones's vision of rectifying the balance by reattaching happiness to its roots in Aristotelian virtue. He harbors some of Jones's suspicion of the postwar era's hyperpersonalization of happiness, but he doesn't abandon an essentially subjective orientation toward its meaning and value.

The alternative route to reinvigorating the idea of happiness that Roth's fiction fleshes out does resonate, however, with the work of other social analysts of the postwar era, such as Lionel Trilling, David Riesman, and William Whyte, who are often identified with Cold War consensus ideology but whose ideas and arguments distinctly contest this ideology's blithe assumptions about American society's achievement of harmonious stability, its "indifferen[ce] to questions about the ultimate worth of capitalism and the underlying values of American life."[15] Roth can be seen in effect to answer Trilling's chastening call, in his 1951 essay on William Dean Howells, to examine more critically the seductions of modernist aesthetics of extremity and to take more interest in Howells's depiction of "civil personalities" and their "moderate sentiments." Trilling's effort to rehabilitate the Howellsian aesthetic of "the 'more smiling aspects' of life" signals, as one sympathetic critic puts it, a "serious" but inadequate "attempt to recover the lost imagination of happiness."[16]

If Trilling's aesthetic revaluation remains overshadowed by his own modernist commitments and polemics, Riesman proves a more illuminating beacon. Better known for his critique of "other-directed" group identification (and conformity more generally) advanced in *The Lonely Crowd* (1950), Riesman took "vitality and happiness, even in a time of troubles" to be a sign of a person's autonomous potentiality.[17] He developed this point as early as 1947 in the essay "The Ethics of We Happy Few," evidently prompted by the appearance the year before of the novel *We Happy Few* by Helen Howe (and by Diana Trilling's review of it in *The Nation*), which satirized the smug and snobbish left-leaning elitism of Harvard humanities professors. In brief, Dorothea, the faculty-wife protagonist who is the smuggest of them all, eventually comes to exalt the "truth" of self-sacrificing wartime service, namely, that it requires "simply the power to forget yourself—completely." After a series of personally humiliating and humbling experiences, Dorothea of the Few is able genuinely to care about, succor, and even join the Many on their knees in prayer because "the albatross of her self had gone."[18] In this manner the novel imagines the discovery of true happiness as assuming the force of a nationalist theology and personal obligation, articulating a social logic that Riesman critiques and against which he advances an alternative set of political and existential propositions. He strenuously objects to Howe's implicit endorsement of Dorothea's self-belittling, self-accusing, and self-sacrificing means of self-correction, which he deems masochistic and ultimately unethical. They reflect her surrender to the "phoniness of 'sharing' common experiences," her abdication of an intellectual's "critical uniqueness" and "individuality of interpretation." With, to quote Howe, the "burden of being one's own arbiter of taste and feeling" removed, Riesman contends that the "ethical convictions that they [Dorothea and others] lack are the belief in their own values."[19] By "belief" Riesman means a commitment to the frame of mind and conceptual conditions that enable the validation of one's values—in other words, being capable of not just having values but also self-consciously valuing one's values.

This valuation logic thus entails an ethical component that subordinates the anthropological or naturalist fact of valuing (which amounts to mere behavior) to the humanist fact of valuing (which is predicated on self-awareness and endorsement). Echoing his mentor Erich Fromm, Riesman sees the acceptance of being one's own arbiter of taste and feeling as a nonnegotiable element of a "rational individualist ethics." It is what enables both the many and the few not just to feel but to assess their happiness. The belief in the value and human capacity of "self-love" is Riesman's ethical, existential, and political-economic starting point. Not to be confused with selfishness or narcissism, Frommian self-love is more akin to the concept of autonomy that Riesman develops elsewhere: "The self-loving person is confident of his own self-evaluation" and is thus "capable of loving [others] as he loves himself."[20] As a dimension of self-love, the pursuit of happiness doesn't threaten the critical faculty, as Tumin and others suppose, but rather enables its cultivation, thus playing a crucial role in the formation of an open society.

The Very Happy Poem

When Libby pronounces those three words, "very happy poems," she allows the adoption agent in effect to put words in her mouth; she thus commits Dorothea's crime of surrendering the arbitration of her own taste and feeling. To be sure, Libby is grasping here for anything on offer that might favorably impress the adoption agent; that is, her authorial claim to very happy poems looks something like the single remaining arrow in her quiver of positive self-projections. But this instrumentalization of her taste and feeling doesn't entirely exonerate her, for she has also committed the misdemeanor of biographical fallacy: she presumes—and wants the adoption agent to presume—that a happy poem reflects its author's happy disposition. Indeed, it is as though the falsity with which she releases the arrow (the falsity arising both from the fact that she hasn't written any poems and from this fallacy's illogic) causes it masochistically to reverse course, rendering Libby herself, along with her esteem for happy poems, its wounded target. Further deepening the wound is that inwardly, too, she seems to think that writing happy poems will make her happy. Although that is theoretically possible—some writers of happy poems doubtlessly derive happiness from their creative production—her affective economy to date evinces its utter unlikelihood. She who is manifestly frustrated and miserable and who has a scheduled appointment with a psychoanalyst that afternoon thus entraps herself in a double bind: she can't write happy poems unless she's happy, but she can't be happy unless she writes happy poems.

At the same time that Roth reveals the crippling aesthetic-authorial psychology underlying Libby's phantasm of the happy poem, he references a work of visual art that reveals Libby's concomitant inability to engage in any meaningful way with actually existing happy art. A painting by the picturesque impressionist Utrillo may not be as immediately recognizable a happy-art object as the Norman Rockwell illustrations that Alexander Portnoy loves to loathe, but in *Letting Go* a print by this painter that Libby has tacked to her and Paul's various apartment walls since college assumes this status, eliciting its beholders' undemanding, mildly positive engagement. It too proves problematic, however, but less because of this engagement's mildness than because of its merely personal orientation. This comes into focus when Libby finds the adoption agent "standing before the Utrillo print," casually regarding it (*LG* 333). Libby now apologetically assesses it as "corny," deploying a term that manages to elide the distinction between her judgment of the painting and her judgment of her personal history of owning the print. As they proceed to discuss its provenance and artistic value, with him suggesting that her fondness for the print is based on "sentimental reasons," she doesn't entirely succumb to the agent's attempt to put words in her mouth, but neither can she quite resist it:

> "Well . . . *I just like it*. Yes, sentiment—but aesthetics, of course, too."
> She did not know what more to say. They both were smiling. (334, emphasis added)

This halting response doesn't so much refute his notion of sentimentality as redirect it away from causal explanation and toward a sentimental aesthetic theory: just liking. As Roth implies with Libby's ensuing speechlessness and both characters' smiles, there's nothing exactly wrong with pleasing art objects, but an aesthetic engagement that involves no critical sense has severely limited social and even existential value. Such stunted engagement as just smiling risks reversion to the "phony" mode of sharing common experience that Riesman critiques. Reduced to just being liked by Libby, the Utrillo print begins to look at best like a prosthetic substitute for writing happy poems, or like compensation for not writing them.

In broader aesthetic-theoretical terms, Roth's portrayal of Libby's predicament renders palpable the hazard of excluding the element of disinterest (in the Kantian sense of purposelessness) from aesthetic production and indeed from the affective experience of art; Libby is all too interested in determining her happy poems' cause and effect and all too personal in her response to happy paintings, and so her aesthetic investments are destined to yield low returns. To put it another way, and to borrow Charles Altieri's provocative terms for theorizing "an aesthetics of the affects," Libby treats happiness too much like an "adjective," an empirical abstraction, rather than an "adverb," a quality of reflexive action. She converts it into a "fixed objective state," one that is describable in "standard adjectival terms" and that conforms too readily to an established belief system.[21] Although "just dying to be happy," Libby proves incapable of experiencing happiness reflexively, because for her, happiness isn't simply an inclination or an elusive pursuit; it *is* a belief system, as indicated in one of the nearly random thoughts that enters her mind right before she opens the door to the adoption agent: "She did not really believe in unhappiness and privation and never would" (*LG* 332, 615). But failing to key her affective and aesthetic belief in happiness to productive imagining, she reverts to the reductive paradigm of aesthetic fantasy and affective abstraction. More than an antidote to her husband's own melancholic "belie[f] in doom" and "mourning" (615), Libby's obsession with happiness is a dispositional affliction that at once totalizes and diminishes her existence. As she replies to Paul's observation that she "think[s] too much about being happy," "that's all there is" (616).

Hello, Suburban Vacation

However negatively inflected, the aesthetic orientation exemplified in *Letting Go* helps to clarify the stakes of Roth's configuration, in *Goodbye, Columbus*, of art and happiness as mutually constructive, as values worth valuing. In this novella, moreover, Roth engages directly with the terms and arguments of the midcentury sociological imagination by situating the happiness problematic in the context of suburban domesticity and white-collar work—that is, where both happiness and art are putatively most compromised by compulsory normality.[22] The novella is contrapuntally structured around the main plot of Newark-dwelling Neil Klugman's summertime romance with suburbanite Brenda Patimkin and the subplot of his workaday tactics in the Newark Public Library to help a black boy maintain access to the art books he more than "just" likes. These narrative vectors pivot on Neil's sense of his employment as public librarian—in effect, as a white-collar bureaucrat. In Brenda's world, Neil is, as Louis Althusser might say, occupationally hailed—and not without chagrin. His lowly job becomes a source of defensiveness, defining him as bereft of ambition and a career plan.[23] But the work he takes upon himself to protect the black boy from his fellow librarians' narrow-minded rigidity and racism not only enables the boy's enjoyment of Gauguin reproductions of Tahitian paradise but also turns out to contribute to Neil's recovery of his own imaginative capacities and self-respect.[24] Directly following the scene in which Neil finds the boy with the "expensive" art book and discusses the "pictures" with him (GC 37), Roth places Neil back "at the Information Desk thinking about Brenda and . . . Short Hills, which [he] could see now, in [his] mind's eye, at dusk, rose-colored, like a Gauguin stream" (38). He stages, in effect, two different versions of the pursuit of happiness, imaged and twinned through the trope of paradise, with each version's stakes and contours rendered more visible by the contrast.

This trope of paradise further serves to intertwine the questions of happiness and art with that other middle-class conundrum—leisure. Midcentury critics of all stripes fretted that Americans, rather than educating or cultivating themselves in their leisure time, "sought distractions . . . [and] the excitement, the spontaneity, and the 'immediate satisfactions' they missed on the job." Others "insisted that only when work and leisure were reintegrated could culture become an important part of, rather than a flight from, daily life."[25] In Roth's novella the fact that Brenda is home on summer vacation and that the romance with Neil fully blossoms when he spends his two-week vacation with her at her parents' suburban home reflects the abundance of their leisure time; it signals as well the degrading effect that the syndrome of work-leisure segregation will have on their work and leisure. Conforming to sociological type, Brenda and Neil do become each other's source of excitement and immediate satisfaction. Indeed, Roth appears to share Riesman's more specific criticism of contemporary youth for its "lack of imagination," for turning "sexual intimacy" into a "chief leisure resort" bereft of "joyful[ness]."[26] Neil and Brenda's sexual intimacy succumbs to this state as it gets bound up with the Patimkin family's entangled hierarchy of affection. The couple may well exploit the suburban home's ample opportunity for privacy, having sex for the first time in the spatially segregated TV room. But Neil can't disentangle the charm of this occasion from the mounting resentment he feels at having been peremptorily assigned to babysit Brenda's coddled little sister Julie, who feeds on the illusion of being the family's crack basketball and Ping-Pong player and is always allowed to win. "How can I describe loving Brenda?" Neil later mulls. "It was so sweet, as though I'd finally scored that twenty-first point" (GC 46).

Moreover, Neil's need to prove that he possesses a winning critical intelligence registers as a kind of metasociological conformity. Throughout the affair with Brenda, he marvels at and indulges in the Patimkin family's overabundance of everything, but he is also apt to sneer at their country-club attitudes, identifying their mind-set with the herd mentality. Indeed, Neil creates opportunities to adopt the stance of a sociologist who witnesses—more precisely, pictures—affluent suburbanites at their most herd-like. Hence his afternoon drive to a nearby deer park where he sees in close proximity the "tawny-skinned mothers" of young deer and the "white-skinned mothers" of young children feeding them popcorn (*GC* 95). For Norman Rockwell this scene would be pastoral perfection. But for Neil, these are mothers who "compared suntans, supermarkets, and vacations," whose "hair would always stay the color they desired," whose "clothes [were] the right texture and shade," whose "homes . . . would have simple Swedish modern when that was fashionable"—in sum, whose "money and comfort" had rendered their individual differences "microscopic" and thus whose "fates had collapsed them into one" (96). With this conspicuously severe but boilerplate analysis, Neil betrays a willingness to parrot the critical condescension of such midcentury analysts as Jones, Mills, and Tumin, an attitude that prepares them to read all evidence of abundance as symptomatic expressions of mindless complacency and/or illusory happiness. This condescension later informs the "psychoanalytical crap," as Brenda calls it (132), that Neil wields to explain her actions. It provokes their recrimination-filled dispute over the outrage her mother expresses after discovering the diaphragm he persuaded her to obtain. After the breakup he finds himself staring at his reflection in the darkened window of Lamont Library, asking himself circular questions: "What was it inside me that had turned pursuit and clutching into love, and then turned it inside out again? What was it that had turned winning into losing, and losing—who knows—into winning?" (135). Such questions reflect the couple's failure to reach beyond predictable, indeed almost compulsory, norms of flirtation and passion, to access what Riesman would deem a more joyful and imaginative level of intimacy.

Roth, however, doesn't let his protagonist languish in a logic of self-loathing, in which winning and losing determine the measure of self-worth. The longer Neil stares at his reflection, the more he sees something else: "I looked hard at the image of me, at that darkening of the glass, and then my gaze pushed through it, over the cool floor, to a broken wall of books, imperfectly shelved" (*GC* 136). Literally, of course, the darkness of the glass makes it difficult for Neil to see what's behind it, an optical reality that figuratively corresponds to his fixation on the surface psychology of injured vanity. But the glass's heightened state of qualitative transformation, its darkening, also prompts Neil to "push through," which figuratively maps onto his more searching inner examination. Only a seasoned librarian would notice shelving imperfections, but only a self-loving white-collar aesthete would be drawn to the impersonal furniture of his work-time consciousness—to books in a library—in search of an objective correlative of his affective plight. As Neil transfers this observational sensitivity to his inner world, taking inventory of what might be called the library of his soul, he discovers it in disarray but not beyond repair. For as though in aesthetic overdrive, Neil turns this crisis-induced introspection into an occasion for the subtle but dramatic revaluation of his own sense of postwar bounty, of plenitude: "I did not look very much longer, but took a train that got me to Newark just as the sun was rising on the first day of the Jewish New Year. I was back in plenty of time for work" (136). Here, at narrative's end, in addition to converting selective details of reality into shopworn tropes of renewal (the rising sun, the New Year), Neil more inventively uncouples the phenomenon of abundance from suburban affluence and draws it into his own sphere of life. Leisure time may be no less a commodity than Swedish furniture, but having "plenty" of it is a function of a prospering mixed economy, of having a public-service job that turns the empty anxious time of the unemployed into positive time off.

For Neil, then, the relation between leisure and work undergoes crucial recalibration. Whereas the romance with Brenda at first serves as an escape from the job that Neil has "beg[u]n to fear" is "pump[ing]" him with "numbness" (*GC* 33), his almost eager thought of returning to work suggests that he now views work not so much as a segregated alternative to a botched love life but as a place for self-validation based on renewed appreciation for the library and his own function in it. Such is the retrospectively implied effect of his earlier solicitude toward the black boy, who continues over the weeks to linger in his mind. During his vacation in Short Hills, for instance, Neil has a somewhat troubling dream of being on a boat with the boy in the harbor of a Pacific island; later, when he's back at work and Brenda is back at school, he observes that he "never did see the colored kid again," wondering if he "discovered" another painter's work or went "back to playing Willie Mays in the streets" (120). These imagined scenes form a temporal continuum extending to (and reinforcing the significance of) Neil's later sense of work-time plenitude, with his reflexive "gaze" into the "darkening" window of another library supplying the realist-symbolic relay between the boy's "playing" and Neil's work.

Library Politics

In other words, Neil's job doesn't so much hail him into occupational identity as open up a world in which he functions as a productive and imaginative municipal agent—indeed, as a liberal activist. In his 1950 book, *The Public Library of the United States*, political scientist Robert D. Leigh noted the "traditionally low temperature of library politics," owing to the relatively low cost of public library services.[27] Still, Roth's attack on the Newark City Council plan to defund the city's library in his 1969 *New York Times* editorial (quoted in the opening paragraph of this book's introduction) suggests that the political heat could rise from time to time. In 1959, when *Goodbye, Columbus* first appeared, Newark's library politics were evidently more in sync with Leigh's description. Yet notwithstanding this relative tranquility, Roth participates in the postwar examination and renewed justification of the role the institution played in American life. The novella, like his later extolment of the Newark Public Library, confirms the liberal-democratic ethos that, according to Leigh, animates "the structure and interpretations of our analysis of public library objectives and practice."[28] Director of a massive two-year-long investigation—the Public Library Inquiry (PLI), of which *The Public Library* was the summary report—Leigh oversaw a raft of social scientists and assistants who modeled their project on Gunnar Myrdal's investigative study of US race relations (and were funded by the same source, the Carnegie Corporation).

According to historian Douglas Raber, the PLI originated with concerns the American Library Association (ALA) had about the low pay and social status of the profession, its weak "power . . . to command respect and resources."[29] The ALA asked the Social Science Research Council to conduct an investigation by expert outsiders—not librarians themselves—whose results the ALA hoped would "provide an empirical basis on which librarianship could justify its claim that it provided a legitimate public good."[30] Growing much broader in scope, the PLI exemplified what public affairs specialist

Redmond Kathleen Molz calls "classic incrementalism in public policy planning," in that it constituted only one component of a set of postwar initiatives—loosely coordinated and not fully consistent—to promote and modernize a civic institution. Other projects included the ALA's sponsorship and publication of the *Post-War Standards for Public Librarians* (1943) and *A National Plan for Public Library Service* (1948) as well as the introduction in the US Congress of the 1946 Public Library Service Demonstration Bill, which evolved into the Library Services Act (LSA) of 1956 and the Library Services and Construction Act of 1964.[31]

Congress's slow motion and Eisenhower's reluctance to sign the LSA—involving as it did grants-in-aid to underserved rural areas—indicate the kinds of difficulty liberal activists faced in their push to reframe even relatively uncontroversial public services like libraries as "political goods," to borrow political philosopher J. Roland Pennock's 1960s phrase. There is "unlimited value" in political goods, he contended, identifying "security, justice, liberty, and welfare" as the categories of primary concern: "These political goods are what the polity is *for*, in the sense that they give it whatever value and justification it has."[32] Besides displacing Cold War visions of the nation-state as quasi-sacred unity, liberal conceptions such as Pennock's challenged those who stigmatized welfare programs as charity or discretionary frill and underscored the legitimacy of public policy designed to meet "human needs."[33] The endeavor to render this standpoint normative is registered in Leigh's elaboration of specific liberal values informing the PLI's study of the US public library. He enumerates six value "assumptions" that frame the PLI's "ideological" orientation and pertain to the library's "social goals."[34] They include the "opportunity to learn"; the "freedom of communication"; the mediation and integration of diverse, insular groups; and the maintenance of bilateral relays between "popular control and expert direction," between "centralization and local participation" in government, and between "technological change and institutional tradition."[35] These macrostructural concerns are supplemented by Leigh's description of public librarians' sense of their particular objectives, including specific "fields of knowledge and interest" that the library should stimulate and guide its clientele toward: public affairs and citizenship, vocational and practical information, aesthetic and cultural appreciation, personal and social recreation, science and technology, and archival research.[36]

For the social scientist, he clarifies, these assumed values are not "considered to be natural laws, self-evident, hallowed by sacrifice, perhaps revealed through sacred writing or dogma" but rather "plausible hypotheses... subject to continued testing and verification."[37] He seems to say (alongside Riesman) that to the extent Americans are willing to revisit the value of their values and endorse the application of this metavaluation procedure to the public library, they will arrive at a verification of this specific institution's plausible worth and a reconfirmation of its underlying value system. In addition to the piecemeal process that Molz describes, in other words, the incrementalist method (discussed more fully in the next chapter) builds itself on ethical reflexivity.

At first glance liberal activism's embrace of the public library as a political good may appear symptomatic of what historian Howard Brick calls the "the postcapitalist vision" of midcentury intellectuals and academics who, in the age of prosperity, shifted their attention from the political economy and its attendant inequities to social and cultural problems.[38] Corroboration of this view would be the controversy generated by the PLI's finding that the public library best served patrons who were self-selecting and "culturally alert."[39] These "natural library users," as Leigh referred to them, could go on to become "opinion leaders"—forming a "widespread network of opinion leadership" that "is quite unofficial, informal, and flexible"—and thus indirectly benefit the broader community.[40] Trickle-down cultural enhancement, by this logic, could offset the unequal access and usage of the library. The Arnoldian tinge of this account suggests that the PLI approached the library as an institution of culture, more or less detached from the political economy. Leigh's acquiescence to unequal access and usage, however, was not received warmly by library professionals at the time who liked to think that they served everybody,[41] or by later social scientists who saw the library as deeply embedded in the political-economic matrix. During the 1960s and early 1970s these social scientists argued that essentially all public-service decisions should be viewed as connected to the political economy. They were, as Robert L. Lineberry italicized in *Equality and Urban Policy* (1977), "*fundamentally redistributive mechanisms*":

> They constitute... "hidden multipliers of income." To those advantaged, services represent an increment of real, as opposed to pecuniary, income; to those in receipt of less than their share, service inadequacies not only diminish real income, but symbolically emblazon their subordinate status.[42]

Others, such as the several authors of *Urban Outcomes: Schools, Streets, and Libraries* (1974), noted that, in contrast to their own approach, some public-policy experts tended to look only to pecuniary income solutions because redistributive justice by other means (such as public services) risked favoritism and the sacrifice of due-process protections in the interest of material outcomes.[43] In rebuttal, these authors elaborated a conception of outcomes that countermanded simplistic consequentialism in which ends justify means. They developed models of research analysis and action recommendation that were specifically designed to allow moral questions of distribution and redistribution to enter into the public-policy calculus. *Outcomes*, they insisted, were different from *outputs* in that they incorporated "the judgments by which citizens evaluate their government." Outcomes thus reflected social science's responsiveness to the evolving needs and tastes of a community, such that it became possible to address a question like, "Ought people who are worse off be made better off?"[44]

The authors of *Urban Outcomes* were part of the 1966 Oakland Project in which UC Berkeley faculty and graduate students designed a "program of policy research and action" that took such questions seriously but also placed them in the broader context of institutional and political realities.[45] They explained, for instance, that aggressive actions of compensatory redistribution were better conducted by the federal government than by municipalities, not only because of the precedent of New Deal grants-in-aid programs but also because of the populace's ease of mobility in and out of localities. This mobility meant that any given municipality implementing redistributive policies risked losing negatively affected taxpayers to other municipalities, "unless [those] other cities in its area [did] the same."[46] This is why, they explained, municipal distributive justice tended to conform to patterns either of market equity (in which benefits received are proportionate to taxes paid) or of equal opportunity (in which the dollar value of services is distributed evenly).

With reference specifically to a public library system, the *Urban Outcomes* authors urged that, at minimum, it should be required to a pursue a policy of equal opportunity. They made clear, however, that this minimum was palpably insufficient due to the financial logic to which a library was ordinarily subject. They dubbed this logic (borrowing from David Riesman), "the more, the more": the more resources a library has, the higher the patronage and book circulation and thus the more funding the library receives.[47] Furthermore, they determined, the Oakland library system was afflicted by an unwillingness to stock popular materials, doing a disservice to low-income persons who wanted them and thereby also driving down patronage and circulation. Similarly, the unwillingness on the part of library professionals to engage in promotional or outreach activity was preventing the library from attracting the uninitiated local populace. Hobbled by a tradition of professional "aloofness," the ordinary librarian worried too much that the library "may be visited by unsavory characters who request the wrong sort of books."[48] In other words, proactive corrections to its everyday internal practices—spend more on books, less on staff; invest more in popular than archival materials; train staff differently—could reshape the library into a hive of low-temperature liberal activism, with redistributive justice supplanting mere equal opportunity.

Roth animates *Goodbye, Columbus* with many of these aspects of library politics. He figures Neil as leaning toward the heightened activism of the later social scientists, while other textual details reveal traces of the PLI's acceptance of "natural library users" as a norm. Embodying the less than 60 percent of librarians with college degrees and the 60 percent without professional library training,[49] Neil inhabits a position at his workplace that recapitulates the inside/outside dynamic that, Andrew Hoberek argues, marks his identity as a "postwar Jewish intellectual who is at once inside and outside the new suburban middle-class Jewish world: inside enough to understand it, outside enough to critique it."[50] It is when Neil is inside Brenda's affluent world that his library job looks like a dead end; it doesn't offer the upwardly mobile opportunities that Brenda seems to expect a serious boyfriend to pursue. But when Neil is inside the library world, not only do such opportunities arise—albeit very modest ones—but his critique from outside operates differently. Rather than positioning him outside the institution per se, his critique positions him outside its current modality.

Neil does not plan to make the library his "lifework" in the manner that his colleague John McKee does, that is, by obtaining professional training at the Newark State Teachers College and "studying at the Dewey Decimal System" (*GC* 32). But Neil turns out to be a model librarian-activist, the type the authors of *Urban Outcomes* hankered after. He abandons the aloof stance of traditional librarians and performs the "social work" that they disavowed.[51] Whereas John McKee targets the black boy—one of those "unsavory characters" suspected by traditional librarians—for likely doing dirty things while "hiding in the art books" section (35), Neil goes to a lot of trouble to encourage the boy's active curiosity. Indeed, he engages in what the Howells-reading

Trilling might call a civil person's act of righteous disobedience to prevent the boy's favorite book of Gauguin reproductions from being checked out by another, far less needy patron. Falsely asserting that someone has put a hold on the book, Neil keeps it available for the boy. This action is retroactively made good by the boy's explanation that he can't take the book home because "somebody [would] dee-*stroy* it" there (60). Although it is possible to criticize Neil for subterfuge and arguably even more for fueling an impoverished kid's desire for unattainable tropical fantasies—as Neil himself momentarily and halfheartedly does when he thinks back on his dream (120)—such fallibility stands in tension with his participation in acts of redistributive justice, going beyond mere equal opportunity.

This little drama of liberal activism, however, is arguably compromised by the manner in which Roth sidesteps the problem of a library's service priorities. In creating the unlikely figure of a black boy who is sufficiently "culturally alert" and self-motivated to seek out reproductions of a high modernist painter, Roth appears to cede to the PLI's status quo ideology of the "natural library user." And yet, this boy's interest in Gauguin's work is an essential component of the narrative's entanglement; it gives rise to a conflict of scarce resources, which is resolved by Neil's activist commitment to redistribute these resources in the direction of those who are worse off. Moreover, Roth's depiction of the everyday scene inside the Newark Public Library indicates that it has little trouble attracting a wide array of users. Neil takes note of the working-class "teen-age girls" of various ethnicities (*GC* 32), the "bums" who "slept over *Popular Mechanics*," the law school students poring over "tort texts," and the elderly suburban "ladies" who "huddle" over "society pages in old old copies of the Newark *News*" (36). Neil's approving observation of these groups' diverse activities redounds to his credit as a self-respecting professional—as does the slight increase in pay that accompanies his promotion (58).[52] On low simmer, the temperature of the novella's library politics keeps things bubbling gently along.

Arts and Recreation

The black boy's Gauguin fixation also allows Roth to intertwine two stated objectives of midcentury libraries into one plot thread: to facilitate patrons' recreation and aesthetic appreciation. Neil's initial encounter with the boy takes place on the library steps outside, where he spies him playfully tormenting one of the "pale cement lions" (*GC* 31): "He would growl, low and long, drop back, wait, then growl again." This behavior has earned him an epithet, "the lion tamer," from Neil (32, 33). In his taunting and taming play, the black boy registers a capacity for what Riesman calls "good play," which involves the "excited concentration" of "tasks" that are neither "too demanding" nor "not demanding enough"—a kind of "new-found mastery."[53] Neil later directs the boy to what Neil, also playful, hears him call the "heart section" (Neil could have opted for the more prosaic phonetic spelling, "hart") and then finds him there with an open book on his lap and in deep enchantment, observing that "his lips were parted, the eyes wide, and even the ears seemed to have a heightened receptivity. He looked ecstatic" (34, 36). Creating opportunities for this activity's repetition and expansion seems the least a conscientious librarian can do; indeed, it is the sort of engagement that enables (in an existential if not remunerative sense) "the boundaries between work and play [to] become shadowy."[54] Neil himself suggests as much in another evocative pun. Hoping not to appear suspicious of the boy and interrupt his contemplative ecstasy, he pretends to search for a book: "I fished around the lowest shelves a moment, playing at work" (36).

It is worth noting that the boy's ecstatic state falls more easily into the category of vehement passion than into that of such moderate feelings as happiness. In his recent book, *The Vehement Passions*, Philip Fisher distinguishes vehement states (such as anger, shame, fear, and wonder) from emotional ones (particularly happiness, discussed at length in his concluding chapter) on the basis of their multiple demands on subjectivity: undivided involvement, suspension of temporal consciousness, and abolition of privacy by inducing bodily (that is, publicly evident) expression, to name the most extreme. These demands work to "reinstall an absolute priority of the self, with its claim to be different from and prior to others both in the claims of its will and in its account of the world."[55] Roth appears, in his portrayal of the black boy's ecstatic state, to endorse Fisher's valorization of vehemence over such "middle-class categories" as emotions and feelings, which instead give priority to "the everyday world"—a world that threatens, in its legislation of reciprocity and goodwill, the self's singularity, that is, its experience of "nonreciprocal intimacy."[56] But as the scene with the black boy unfolds, Roth reveals not only that the library, this paradigmatic middle-class institution, serves as a kind of curatorial site of vehement wonder but also that reciprocity and goodwill themselves enable an enlarged or intensified experience of singularity within the affective realm of happiness. Reciprocity and singularity need not be mutually exclusive, as Neil's orientation toward the black boy makes visible.

To begin with, Neil's interest in the black boy goes beyond institutional solicitude; it could indeed be called aesthetic. Attending to the curious particulars of the boy's painterly appeal, Neil converts him into a work of happy art: "By the light of the window behind him I could see the hundreds of spaces between the hundreds of tiny black corkscrews that were his hair. He was very black and shiny, and the flesh of his lips did not so much appear to be a different color as it looked to be unfinished and awaiting another coat" (*GC* 36). Here Neil exhibits, in distinct contrast to Libby, a capacity for careful but disinterested aesthetic appreciation, enhancing his own self-loving singularity. Roth's emphasis on Neil's reflexive perspective—"I could see," "appear to be," "looked to be"—suggests that the boy's incarnation of the happy-art object doesn't *cause* Neil's appreciative pleasure so much as occasion or inspire Neil's attentive regard, which Neil then relishes for its own productively imaginative, self-prioritizing sake. In other words, this mode of appreciation may be intimately keyed to Neil's goodwill to promote the boy's happiness, but it cannot be reduced to this goodwill.

In similarly pronounced contrast to Libby's doomed aesthetic logic—in which, to recall, her speechlessness signifies an overpersonalization of aesthetic sentiment—the ensuing dialogue between Neil and the black boy indicates their reciprocal engagement as well as their preservation of singularity, of intractable particularity and self-directed intimacy. As ecstasy modulates into more moderate good feelings and communicative agency, much of what transpires assumes a pedagogical cast. Neil supplies the geographical facts of Gauguin's work and attempts to correct the boy's terminology and sharpen his grasp of the distinction between taking a picture and painting one, while the boy absorbs the facts and remains largely indifferent to the corrections. An irony lost on both, though perhaps not on Roth, is that the ecstasy-inducing images are in fact photographs of paintings—that is, reproductions—shrunk to 8 1/2 × 11 book proportions, another indication that for Roth the art object itself matters not nearly as much as the conceptual and subjective conditions underlying the beholder's orientation.

Here the pedagogy contributes to the interlocutors' affective enhancement as well as to their critical sensibility. Learning that Tahiti is in fact a "place you can go" to, the boy's inclination to vehemence resurfaces as "euphoria," prompting an unguarded expression of delight: "That's the fuckin life" (*GC* 37). Less communicative than exclamatory and self-concentrating, this comment tellingly elicits no response from Neil: the more forceful the vehemence, Roth suggests, the closer Gauguin's work will indeed have to come to suiting the claims of the boy's will and his account of the world (which might be called "just enthusing"). Although the boy doesn't exactly relinquish this claim—implied by his continued idiosyncratic reference to Gauguin as a "picture taker" rather than a painter (37)—one could say he tempers it with faint expressions of reflective judgment. However underdeveloped, this capacity emerges when he descriptively expounds on one Gauguin image of "three native women standing knee-high in a rose-colored stream": "These people, man, they sure does look cool. They ain't no yelling or shouting here, you could just see it" (37). As in Neil's description, cited earlier, of the boy himself, the perspectivalist vocabulary—"look" and "see"—suggests the introduction of an interpretive or judgmental orientation, but one relaxed by communicative happiness.

Trading nonreciprocal intimacy for intimate reciprocity, the black boy thus enters the sphere in which critical or interpretive disagreement becomes possible—in which, for instance, an interlocutor might opine that the women look benumbed or sedated rather than cool. Neil turns out not to disagree, but he arrives at a slightly more sophisticated version of the black boy's account, as though completing a circuit of pedagogical reciprocity: "It *was* a silent picture, he was right" (*GC* 37). Here Neil shifts attention away from the appealing absence of noisy actions by particular "people" in the painting toward its overall mood or atmosphere, but he also preserves the boy's initial intuition. Similarly, when the boy asks, rather than exclaims, "Ain't that the fuckin *life*?," Neil finds himself able at least laconically to respond, "I agreed it was and left" (37). No wonder he appears happy, weeks later, to be "back in plenty of time for work" (136).

At the same time, the fact that Neil will soon never see the boy again suggests the functional limitations of Neil's municipal agency: his work as a librarian may be valuable, even crucial, but it remains, like Kantian happiness, elusively indeterminate. For better or worse, training will never be everything. Rather, the important thing in this novella is to illustrate—whether in the form of a public institution's statuary decoration that in part signifies "pale" culture's self-lionizing ways or in the form of expensive reproductions of a "white man['s]" modernist paintings of "young brown-skinned maid[s]" (*GC* 37)—how much the aesthetic object's capacity to elicit its beholder's affective and imaginative engagement depends on the beholder, along with the social value of (and institutional support for) that engagement. The contrast could hardly be greater between the black boy's aesthetic play or Neil's aesthetic work and Brenda's brother Ron's mode of aesthetic engagement: Ron is only too complacently happy to hear again and again the easy-listening records of Mantovani or the "soft patriotic music" of "his Columbus record" before "rumbling down into that exhilarating, restorative, vitamin-packed sleep" of an athlete (74). Like the speechless smiles of Libby and the adoption agent before the Utrillo print, Ron's sleepiness exemplifies ingrained habits of overpersonalized normality that appear beyond the reach of Roth's normative challenge.

Rewriting Bellow

Neil Klugman may figure midcentury liberal activism more fully than other characters populating Roth's first collection, but there's considerable family resemblance between him and such men as Eli Peck, Nathan Marx, and Robert Russo. In "Eli, the Fanatic," the lawyer protagonist mediates between his neighbors—secular affluent Jews—and the ultra-Orthodox Holocaust refugees who move into the suburban town, ultimately assisting these disadvantaged newcomers (despite their violation of a municipal ordinance against boarding schools). In "Defender of the Faith," Sergeant Marx pushes back against a Jewish conscript's string-pulling, thereby preserving military fairness. In "You Can't Tell a Man by the Song He Sings," the high-school teacher, a Popular Front type of patriotic communist, goes out of his way to help a disadvantaged student (a delinquent from the reformatory) find occupational direction. Taken together, these low-level mediators may be read as advancing Roth's liberal-incrementalist agenda. I want to conclude this chapter by suggesting that these characters take their professional cues from the protagonist of Saul Bellow's widely admired and anthologized story of municipal agency, "Looking for Mr. Green" (1951). But they far surpass this hard-boiled relic in their activist wherewithal.[57] A brief discussion of Bellow's story should help to clarify this point and, more broadly, to throw into relief, by way of contrast to Roth, key attributes of Roth's mode of *incremental realism*. To be more specific, I suggest that the two authors' modes of characterization have significant implications for their literary styles. The activist intelligence with which Roth imbues the characters just named enables him to explore narrative situations that address ordinary problems of socioeconomic disparity and the institutions designed to solve them. In Bellow's hands, by contrast, ordinariness is overtaken by the protagonist's ponderous imagination and analogical exaggeration, consequently buttressing Bellow's epiphanic plot trajectory and overall grandiose style.

In "Looking for Mr. Green," Bellow parlays a day in the life of a delivery man of welfare checks on Chicago's South Side into an occasion for pondering world-historical cycles of ruination as well as for conducting an existential search for "the last reality" in a world distorted by shadowy, bleak, grotesque appearances.[58] The protagonist George Grebe's lofty effort to confirm the truths of ancient Greek philosophy and perhaps Spenglerian historiography thus eclipses his work for a public institution that aims to improve the lives of the city's most disadvantaged residents. Grebe's elevated pursuits are not satirized; indeed, they are supposed to index his stoic integrity. They loom over prosaic details imparted during the course of the story, such as the fact that Grebe has gotten the job in the Relief office through connections—"the pull of an old schoolmate" (LFMG 254)—and despite the fact that his boss thinks he "ought to have a Negro doing" the job (252), given South Side blacks' suspicion of white strangers going around asking questions. We also learn that Grebe wants to do the job well, not explicitly out of "consideration" of "the clients [who] would be waiting for their money" but "simply for doing-well's sake" (251).

With a mind-set of near indifference to redistributive justice, then, the "native Chicagoan" and former college Latin teacher proceeds to wander through an unfamiliar city district, "interpreting looks and signs" in the spirit of a philosopher of history (LFMG 251, 252). On this hermeneutic journey, the discrepancy he finds between reality and appearance mirrors the socioeconomic and epistemological chasm separating him from South Side residents. Rather than somehow forming bridges, though, Grebe widens this chasm further by developing a figurative technology of overdrawn analogy to process his experience. He likens wall graffiti to the drawings of primitive men in "caves" and "pyramids" (253); he likens one welfare recipient to "one of the underground kings of mythology" (258); and he calls the search for Mr. Green a "hunting game" whose "prey" lives in "camouflage" (251, 261). Altogether the "terrific, blight-bitten" district of black people (254) becomes an emblem of tragic human history repeating itself—"a second layer of ruins [second only to the Great Chicago Fire of 1871]; centuries of history accomplished through human massing. Numbers had given the place forced growth; enormous numbers had also broken it down" (259). Grotesque enormity defines this world.

Grebe's increasing estrangement from South Side residents ultimately provokes him to interpret a "blundering . . . , heavy . . . , naked and drunk" black woman claiming to be Mrs. Green as the final (although indirect) connection to reality, to the person who now embodies reality instead of appearance: the "real Mr. Green" (LFMG 261). This encounter, for Grebe, is a major existential breakthrough, an epiphany: "'For after all,' he said, 'I *did* get to him'" (261). With his essence-existence mission accomplished, we now see the point of Bellow's figuration of a municipal journey. It isn't about the difficulty of completing a welfare-state objective, metonymized by the delivery of checks to needy recipients; rather, it's about how Mr. Green indeed gets to Grebe. The welfare-state agent, the story's witness to "the real," becomes the story's truly needy recipient. Forget redistributive justice, Bellow implies, when there's spiritual rejuvenation on the horizon.

Tellingly, Grebe deems this boon of epiphany "a reason for elation" (LFMG 261). The story's concluding affect of elation supplants the happiness that Grebe observes earlier, almost in passing, in the "underground king" of the South Side, Winston Field. Grebe considers mere ceremony the way this man insists on showing him his box of official documents "with a certain happy pride" (258). Despite the fact that these papers verify Field's status as welfare recipient, Grebe tries to beg off, telling the man not "to go to all that trouble" (258). It is as though he's capable of honoring welfare-state happiness only in the breach. Grebe thus embodies exactly the sort of misguided liberal agency that goodwill activists such as Neil, Eli, Nathan, and Robert effectively labor to supplant.

For contemporary historians of midcentury American literature, it is perhaps more likely that Roth's story of a solicitous librarian and a vulnerable black youth looks like a naively wishful rewriting of Richard Wright's autobiography, *Black Boy* (1945), rather than a critical rewriting of Bellow. Wright describes how he, a chronically abused black youth, had to muster all kinds of ingenuity to triumph over the racist librarian and gain access to books.[59] Of course, more emblematic yet of American pathologies of race is his portrayal of Bigger Thomas in *Native Son* (1940). This character wouldn't even know what to do with a library book. In this context, Roth's library story may look hopelessly out of touch. But from the standpoint of Gwendolyn Brooks, the author whose midcentury work and career the following chapter takes up, Roth looks like a comrade in liberal activism. Wright's Bigger Thomas becomes emblematic of midcentury black experience only if Brooks's literary figures and lives like hers are ignored. Not unlike the relation between Bellow's and Roth's fictional worlds, Wright's attunement to pathological crisis finds a tempered counterpart in Brooks's incrementalist intelligence, alert as she is both to African American potentiality and to the potentiality of welfare-state institutionalism. She, too, extolled public libraries—as did, for that matter, Saul Bellow.[60] Indeed, in her 1996 autobiography Brooks observed that the Chicago Public Library now contained busts of her and Bellow. She muses, "Just the two of us. What do we say to each other when the library is closed?"[61] The next chapter examines what Brooks's side of the conversation might have sounded like.

2 Gwendolyn Brooks and the Welfare State

Gwendolyn Brooks's novel *Maud Martha* (1953) contains a singularly unhappy black man, David McKempster. He is one of the young fellows Maud Martha Brown dates before she marries Paul Phillips. The source of his unhappiness is his racial and socioeconomic disadvantage. No matter how hard he studies he will never catch up to his white counterparts at the University of Chicago. Their families do things like discuss V. L. Parrington's *Main Currents of American Thought* at the dinner table, so these peers have been hearing about that work since "they were four," whereas David is only now getting wind of it.[1] Excluded in so many ways from the main currents of American middle-class life, he is "agitated" and "depressed": "The unhappiness he felt over there [where he was raised, west of the Midway] was physical. He wanted to throw up" (*MM* 44, 45). There are other things he yearns for to "make up a good background," among them a pet that reveals the depth of his racial abjection: "He wanted a dog. A good dog. No mongrel" (46). A few years later, when we next encounter David, he seems on his way to owning the good dog. All wrapped up in the "University world" to which he now belongs, he snubs Maud Martha when they run into each other at a lecture on campus (128). He's capable of being jovial now but only with the white university chums he comes across. While escorting Maud Martha to the streetcar he's "cold" and claims to be "tired," but then he banters affably with these chums (128–29).

One of *Maud Martha*'s objectives is to present a legitimate alternative to David McKempster as an emblem of South Side culture and personality—an alternative, however, whose legitimacy does not nullify the credence of David's self-abnegation but does question its pervasiveness and inevitability. The novel achieves this objective by centering on Maud Martha, who suffers David's snub but does not succumb to the psychosocial logic that produces it. Structured as a series of vignettes and narrated from an intimate third-person perspective, the novel charts her development from a near-poor yet sensitive girl into a still-poor young married mother who, despite setbacks and frustrations, manages to sustain a margin of autonomy that rests on alternately accepting and rejecting her life circumstances as determinative. Maud Martha is an underprivileged black person who rarely gets what she wants and who experiences a predictable succession of race-based indignities, and yet she remains happy in mood and sense of prospect. Thus she functions as a kind of midcentury model minority. Whereas nowadays a psychologist of happiness might analyze Maud Martha's temperament in entirely apolitical terms of "set points" and declare her genetically fortunate, a midcentury ego psychologist would have understood her as possessing an "integrated" personality, one that "maintain[s] self-identity across a multiplicity of roles, institutional settings, and social positions."[2] Meanwhile, David resembles one of the case histories the neo-Freudian social scientists Abram Kardiner and Lionel Ovesey discussed in *The Mark of Oppression*, their 1951 study of quasi-neurotic Negro personalities. "The social realities, which relegate the Negro to a position of inferiority," they argued, "serve to confirm [his] feelings of worthlessness. His reaction is to reject his own race." David's pursuit of refined things and his snobbish attitude amount to what they called "compensatory devices."[3]

One way to understand *Maud Martha*, then, is as a novel that entered the pre–*Brown v. Board of Education* (1954) debates about the psychosocial effects of racial segregation and systemic discrimination. When numerous American social scientists turned in the 1940s and 1950s to the national and regional problems of racial prejudice, they generally did so as advocates of racial equality, social justice, and progressive reform. As professionalized "social engineers," their ambition was "to cure various social ills."[4] *The Mark of Oppression*, for instance, considered at length the emotionally debilitating conditions of poverty and unemployment in black families. Their conclusion enjoined the "white man" to "stop the oppression" by "removing the forces that create and perpetuate" black "self-hatred."[5] However well intended their assessments, not all liberals welcomed them. Alain Locke hailed the work "a significant ground-breaker in the field of racial psycho-dynamics," but others objected to the methodology of this kind of study.[6] The psychologist Robert M. Hughes, for example, considered its approach "poorly conceived and poorly executed"; it relied on only a couple dozen case studies of Harlem residents who exhibited symptoms of "psychoneurotic maladaptation" and was "therefore unrepresentative of American Negro life."[7] His criticism echoed Ralph Ellison's earlier account of Gunnar Myrdal's book, *An American Dilemma*, which, for all its merits, also problematically construed "Negro culture and personality simply as the product of a 'social pathology'" and as chronically "reacting" to white America rather than exhibiting creative agency.[8] Ironically, Ellison faced the same criticism in 1953 when the sociologist and journalist Marguerite Cartwright attacked *Invisible Man* along with Kardiner and Ovesey's book and Kenneth Clark's testimony in South Carolina on the psychological harm of segregated schools on black children. Considering them all "descendants of Bigger Thomas," she criticized the emergence of "the neurotic Negro" as a new stereotype that "strongly re-enforced existing prejudice and discrimination."[9] It was perhaps the ponderous ubiquity of this neurotic figure in midcentury literature and social science that stirred one early reviewer to describe *Maud Martha* as possessing "a freshness, a warm cheerfulness" along with a main character who "still can feel, in an affirmation of vitality, that life is good."[10]

Critics, in any case, have long recognized Maud Martha as Bigger Thomas's opposite number on the South Side.[11] Her unwillingness to kill a mouse she has trapped in her kitchenette apartment stages her vast distance from Bigger's pathological unraveling—he who in the opening pages of *Native Son* crushes a huge rat with a frying pan before going on to kill two women. And yet it would be a mistake either to reduce *Maud Martha* to an inspirational social scientific allegory that switches out the pathological personality for the integrated one or to split the difference, as some critics have effectively done, by teasing out the indignant rage lurking beneath the character's placid surface.[12] Rather, as this chapter undertakes to demonstrate, the novel's juxtaposition of damaged and integrated personalities (and bitter and agreeable emotions), with perspective and proportion favoring the latter, speaks to Brooks's larger project of dramatizing the welfare state's unfinished business. During an era of political conservatism's resurgence and relentless hostility to liberal reform, Brooks draws positive attention to the institutional landscape that undergirds the welfare state.[13] She acknowledges the uneven development of this sociopolitical endeavor—indeed, its complicit perpetuation of injustice in its discriminatory treatment of the black population—while embracing its overall ambitions. In *Maud Martha* and elsewhere in her oeuvre, Brooks works up a defense of the welfare state by pointing to the contributions it makes to a person's manner of flourishing. As the political philosopher Thomas W. Pogge recently put it, "The idea of human flourishing is central not only to our personal and ethical reflections about our own lives and the lives of those around us, but also to our political discourse about our social institutions and policies."[14] In this context, Maud Martha's happiness becomes emblematic not only of the potential for ego integration on the South Side but also of the more or less functional adequacy—despite obvious deficiencies—of Chicago's public and private institutions. The scene at the University of Chicago already hints at this broader narrative ambition: the way Maud Martha avails herself of an opportunity to attend a public lecture there without feeling estranged by a need to belong to its core constituency attests to the novel's vision of the beneficial reciprocity, however limited and disproportionate, between disadvantaged persons and the surrounding institutional infrastructure. As a contrast to David, Maud Martha figures an orientation that accords with the welfare state's endeavor to facilitate the well-being of its populace. The narrative's cumulative progress, vignette by vignette, toward its jubilant, forward-looking conclusion serves at once to articulate and to justify the pursuit of happiness as a project of flourishing, which, sutured to the pursuit of socioeconomic justice, constitutes the horizon of midcentury liberalism.

One way that *Maud Martha* registers its commitment to the welfare state's idea of happiness as a project of flourishing is by enlisting this idea's grounding metaphors: the flower and the bloom. Whereas social science's vision of the integrated ego puts stress on the mechanics of mental-hygienic coordination, the floral trope evokes the temporal and developmental qualities of organic growth. We'll see, however, that Brooks importantly modifies this organicism and thereby differentiates her project of justifying happiness from the naturalism of one of the era's dominant social sciences, humanist psychology. Her model of integration as flourishing comes to resemble what midcentury political scientists called *incrementalism*, in reference to an operation of public decision-making that tethered an inductive method of preference selection to the American welfare state's grounding ethical values. The midcentury liberal activists Robert Dahl and Charles Lindblom developed this procedural theory as an alternative to conservative ideologues, leftist utopians, and social choice utilitarians.[15] *Maud Martha* discloses intimate points of contact between the incrementalist administrative procedure and personal development within the broader collective life-form afforded by the welfare state. Whereas African American criticism (and minority criticism more generally) typically constructs an axial dialectic of the *self* and an identitarian *community*—what Michael Omi and Howard Winant call "black collective subjectivity"—this chapter seeks to tease out the implications of Brooks's attunement to midcentury liberal activism by reading her semiautobiographical and formally *self*-centered *Maud Martha* against the backdrop of normative midcentury *institutions* of collectivity.[16] However inadequate these mediating institutions were in redressing socioeconomic injustice, their influence on African American experience and consciousness, Brooks reveals, was enormous.

Indeed, Brooks's two autobiographies suggest that she regarded her own life from the perspective of a midcentury liberal. The second section of the chapter thus extends the examination of Brooks's welfare-state liberalism to include her authorial career. It focuses on her evolving engagement, now as a renowned poet with social capital to invest in the prestige economy, with the post-*Brown* realities of de facto racial segregation and the emergence of the Black Power movement. I suggest that, during a period of deep ambivalence about African Americans' participation in integrationist politics, Brooks advances a Black Power politics from within—rather than apart from—the liberal vision of integration. Her stance reflects the semantic and conceptual resonance between *integration* as a midcentury social scientific ideal of personality or ego and *integration* as midcentury liberalism's ideal of racial order. Whereas critics tend to make much of her self-described turn away from the integrationist paradigm in 1967, I suggest that once we situate Brooks within the welfare state's project of flourishing we can see that ideological and aesthetic continuities between these two periods abound and that happiness is one of the central tropes through which Brooks makes these continuities visible.

But alongside these commitments to liberalism's political and cultural values, Brooks recognized the pull of charismatic alternatives to the liberal paradigm. The chapter's final section thus turns to her engagement with these alternatives—particularly as they crystallize in the form of what Lauren Berlant calls "cruel optimism."[17] With this phrase Berlant names the way liberal-capitalist promises of the good life generate desires and attachments whose very existence frustrate a person's progress toward fulfillment. For people inhabiting conditions of socioeconomic precarity, this psychology is particularly destabilizing. The predicament is so dire, Berlant implies, that it calls into question the entire project of liberalism. In Brooks's hands, however, a remarkably different implication emerges. Her poetic strategy of disclosing through figures of precarity the difficulty of sustaining happiness as a horizon of experience and value points not to the abandonment of the liberal vision but rather to the ethical necessity of imagining liberalism as a political and psychoinstitutional practice of vigilance. She thus legitimates the welfare state as the most viable alternative to free-market predation.

Flower Power

The object of David McKempster's intellectual and social desire, Parrington's *Main Currents in American Thought*, tends to be remembered in discussions of midcentury American history as the focus of Lionel Trilling's notorious attack in "Reality in America" (1940), whereby, as Thomas Hill Schaub puts it, Parrington "stood for those simplifications of reality which had produced the left's naive fascination with Stalinism."[18] Trilling played a central role in deflecting midcentury liberals' attention away from conservative assaults on the welfare state in part by critiquing the left and declaring liberalism's intellectual victory over a conservatism bereft of ideas.[19] He called on liberals, in the purported absence of a present-day conservative such as Samuel Taylor Coleridge to challenge their thought, to avoid becoming "prosaic" by attending to Coleridge's insight that "the world is a complex and unexpected and terrible place which is not always to be understood by the mind as we use it in our everyday tasks."[20] This more elevated mind needed to treat liberalism—and literature's relation to it as a political culture—as "a large tendency rather than a concise body of doctrine" so as to regain its "lively sense of contingency and possibility."[21] This disparagement of both actual doctrine and the everyday mental work that sustained it exemplifies what historian David L. Chappell has called "liberals' overweening self-assurance" and arguably "the most important single reason for their fall" in the ensuing decades.[22] Liberalism's leading intellectuals, in other words, ignored both the practical and philosophical ambitions of political conservatism at their peril.

The more likely source for Brooks's reference to Parrington, however, was an article that appeared in 1950 in *Phylon* titled "The Welfare State: Embattled Concept" by the black philosopher and journalist Marc Moreland. One of the era's leading periodicals in African American politics and culture,

Phylon had reviewed Brooks's work since the publication of her first book of poems in 1945, and in 1950 Brooks published a brief essay there.[23] Like Moreland, Brooks tended to dwell on the welfare state's broad institutional principles while only lightly addressing actually existing New Deal and Fair Deal programs. And yet both writers were decidedly more prepared than Trilling was to embrace the cause of everyday liberalism. Moreland mounts a vehement defense of the welfare state against contemporary conservative elites who prophesize "imminent doom" if America pursues this governmental idea.[24] Recognizing that "the assumptions and implications of this conflict" are not "far removed from the experiences of workaday living," he hopes liberals' "memory" of the conservative "cry of havoc against the idea of the welfare state" will "sharpen the wit and fortify the will of anyone who believes in the dignity of human life, and who wants to see established a context within which it can realize itself."[25] The specific occasion triggering Moreland's alarm was James F. Byrnes's denunciation of Truman's Fair Deal proposals in Truman's 1949 State of the Union address. A staunch segregationist and former senator from South Carolina during the New Deal era, Byrnes weighed in on what Moreland calls "the most roiling issue of our time." Byrnes was one of Roosevelt's key congressional allies who brought other southern Democrats to support New Deal legislation that also incorporated provisos ensuring the continuance of segregation in the South.[26] In 1949 he was Truman's estranged former secretary of state and in the process of building up his pro-business and firmly conservative credentials, such that by the 1960s he supported Barry Goldwater and Richard Nixon.

For Moreland, Byrnes seems to exemplify the conservative forces working to dismantle the welfare state tout court. He thus summons Parrington to remind readers of the way "economic" interests have thwarted the welfare-state ideal throughout American history and to bolster his argument (for which he also depends on Roger Williams and Spinoza) for the welfare state as the legitimate expression of popular sovereignty: "For what is the validity of the concept of sovereignty but the belief that the people have the right and the power to preserve themselves, in short, to insure their well being; and, conversely, what is the validity of the concept of welfare but the belief of the people in their inalienable right and power so to preserve and insure?"[27] Substantial quotations from Spinoza serve to validate the general idea of well-being and the liberal state's obligation to support it: "If liberty is the end of the state, then the function of the state is to promote the growth of the individual. Growth depends on the individual's finding freedom for his capacities. If the laws of the state should hinder growth, the laws are obviously unjust. For the highest function of the laws of the state is the welfare of the people." This "power of acting" in a manner that "maintain[s] one's being," he insists, again citing Spinoza, amounts to "man's *happiness*."[28] Here happiness is crucial, but it's crucially epiphenomenal, an index and justification of the state's operative liberal values. Moreland concludes the article by waxing poetic about this mode of happiness as it pertains to the "people" and their capacities for growth: "The people with their wants and aspirations, their desires and yearnings, their needs and satisfactions; the people with their errors and their corrections, with their muddy feet and their dreaming contemplation: these are they from which states derive and from which they have such authority as is properly theirs."[29] Less authorial indulgence than a sign of the welfare state's uncertain future, Moreland's rhetorical flight urges the reclamation of the liberal ideal in the idiom of universalism. It is a matter of "the people" and their "inalienable right."

On the matter of race, Moreland is entirely silent. But in the context of African Americans' progressive activism this silence spoke not only to the movement's universal idealists but also to its hands-on pragmatists. As the historians Dona Cooper Hamilton and Charles V. Hamilton explain, civil rights groups of the period (such as the NAACP and the National Urban League) developed a "dual agenda" whereby, in addition to advocating for race-specific policies and judicial decisions to end discrimination, they fought "for social welfare policies to help the poor" in general—that is, to help "all people."[30] In the promotion of social welfare as a universal value these activists' primary concern was to work toward a system that aimed for full employment, that operated on a federal level, and that did away with the invidious two-tier distinction between contributory social insurance and public relief (in which some looked like entitled beneficiaries while others were stigmatized as recipients of charity). Such a system would enable blacks to benefit alongside whites by eliminating the discriminatory practices of state and local authorities, especially in the South; it would also permit the federal government to "redistribute resources to poorer states" and thus accommodate a mobile society's needs to cross state lines with ease.³¹ Moreland's universalist orientation was thus in accord with midcentury efforts to advance the cause of black people's welfare without reference to race-specific needs.³²

But if Moreland's uninflected liberal idealism resonated with the era's African American reform activism, it also connected with Brooks's more intimate literary project. Resonant with the Spinozan idea of happiness that Moreland promotes, *Maud Martha* dwells on a protagonist whose "capacities" for "individual growth" give rise to a remarkably supple interiority. This appealing manner, Brooks implies, is also the result of Maud Martha's continuous engagement with the welfare state's institutional matrix. However much we may be invited to admire her as a concrete character with a specific personality—whether this admiration is for her mild manner and inward ways or for her demonstrations of fortitude in the face of what one critic calls "the triple jeopardy of racism, sexism, and classism"—Brooks also insists that we understand her as an emblematic figure of liberal subjectivity.³³ Maud Martha becomes Brooks's narrative vehicle for disclosing the potentiality for the black personality to benefit, like the white personality, from midcentury liberalism's broad infrastructural values and institutional temporalities. One of Brooks's working titles was *American Family Brown*, suggesting her interest in joining racial specificity with national universalism. Its middle term further anticipates what *Maud Martha* imagines to be the likely mediating agent of this project: the well-integrated nuclear family. While Brooks nods approvingly to happy kitchenette folks such as the childless couple, Oberto and Marie, and the fatherless only child Clement Lewy, whose mother barely scrapes by (*MM* 108–12, 114–16), she concentrates on Maud Martha's transition from her two-parent, three-child family to the start and expansion of her own nuclear family. Without being doctrinaire, the novel further suggests that this family unit holds the key to black people's accumulation of financial wealth in the form of home ownership and social wealth in the form of reined-in passions and appetites. As discussed later, this social theory, however aligned with the traditional middle-class ideal, turns out also to inform a more conspicuous work of 1950s social protest, *A Raisin in the Sun* (1959) by Lorraine Hansberry.³⁴ Both works depend on the viability of imagining midcentury black people as deeply invested in conventional desires and ambitions, even if this disposition entails ratcheting back righteous anger so as to accommodate meaningful goals that are within reach.

In *Maud Martha* Brooks unabashedly characterizes the protagonist as in sync with middle-class mores, although she lacks the resources to satisfy her material desires. What appears to matter more than actual fulfillment is that, like Moreland's people with their wants, aspirations, desires, yearnings, needs, and (occasional) satisfactions, Maud Martha is a person of many preferences. As a girl, we learn in the opening sentence, she "liked candy buttons, and books, and painted music ... and dandelions" (*MM* 1). We also learn that she "would have liked" more exotic flowers had they been available, such as "a lotus, or China asters or the Japanese Iris, or meadow lilies" (1). But she makes do with dandelions, as that "was what she chiefly saw" (2). If her logic here seems a bit circular—preferring what she has, having what she prefers—this style of exercising preference is both compounded and slightly altered in her next preference assertion, in which she considers the various qualities of the dandelion itself. She deems their "demure prettiness" to be "second to their everydayness," and she even has an explanation for this ranking: it is because "she saw a picture of herself" in their everyday quality, whereas her sister is widely acknowledged as the demurer and prettier one in the family (2). Here her preference style isn't so much circular as reflexive. Another of Brooks's working titles for this lyrical bildungsroman was *The Natural History of the Dandelion*, and this primal scene of self-preference helps to explain why.[35] She may suffer from envy toward her sister and later endure frequent injuries to her vanity on account of her plain features and dark skin, but ultimately she likes herself. In contrast to David McKempster, she does not want to throw up. In this originary preference we glimpse, in the book's opening pages, the baseline of Maud Martha's dignifying recognition of her self-worth. She obviously prefers being a self to not being a self.

Slightly less obviously, Maud Martha prefers being a self with preferences to being a self without them. Indeed, this personality streak is what sustains Brooks's novel. In the 1950s the African American scene of preference was dominated by Kenneth and Mamie Clark's infamous doll-testing scheme, in which the evidence of black girls' preference for white dolls over black dolls indicated the harm done by segregation and prejudice.[36] But in *Maud Martha*, Brooks engages the terms of welfare-statism by exploring first of all the broader political and existential significance of having preferences. As the midcentury political philosopher and liberal activist Harry K. Girvetz suggested, no matter which place one inhabits on the socioeconomic spectrum, "there is no substitute for the individual in the determination of his preferences."[37] In this context, having individual preferences is understood to be an index of liberal agency. As Maud Martha reflects on, compares, and evaluates almost everything she encounters on the South Side, she seems to derive as much satisfaction from the opportunity to have and contemplate her preferences as she does from experiencing their fulfillment. Over the course of the narrative she registers preferences for numerous things that she clearly won't get, or at least won't get frequently or soon. Among them: a husband who is responsive to her particular needs and endowments (*MM* 53), a kitchenette without cockroaches (63), movies in Technicolor (77), a chicken from the butcher that is already cleaned and cut up (152), a job that doesn't require putting up with the obnoxious attitudes of rich white women (161), and a department store Santa Claus who isn't mean to her child (173). The sustained poise—combined on occasion with righteous indignation—with which she reflects on such disappointing realities would suggest that even unfulfilled preferences make worthwhile claims on her being. These claims indicate an enlivened autonomy—what the philosopher John Stopford has recently described as "something exercised in the space between the consciousness of our situation on the one hand, and our wish to give shape to that situation on the other."[38]

Maud Martha's vignette seriality heightens the intensity of its protagonist's exertions of consciousness, as each discrete vignette typically settles on a spot of time and space. While maintaining the bildungsroman's convention of diachronic linearity, the serial structure diminishes conventional realism's stress on event- and character-induced causality. It seeks occasion for lyrical dilation on Maud Martha's experience of a range of interconnected situations and thus registers her contemplative, observational, wishful, and agential relation to her present and future. For scholars of modernist and experimental poetics, seriality tends to be associated with aleatory open-endedness and discontinuity—amounting, as Joseph Compte puts it, to a "serial process [of] accumulation" that signals "a distinct alternative to the organic sequence" of romanticism.[39] But, as Brent Hayes Edwards explains, seriality can encourage "the reader to discover points of connection and resonance," as its form of repetition generates backward-looking recursiveness.[40] He locates in one practitioner of seriality, Ed Roberson, an "episodic quality" and an "empiricism of surfacing and recording what you see" that seems to acknowledge normative epistemological and historical structures of experience.[41]

In Brooks's hands, the inflection of narrative realism with elements of avant-garde poetics functions to convey a sense of fertile mental life within—not apart from—the liberal regime. If, as suggested earlier, it is crucial to her liberal-activist ideology that the operations of enlivened consciousness are embodied even by an underprivileged black girl on Chicago's South Side, these operations arguably become that much more valuable to Maud Martha once she grows up and becomes a housewife in a smelly, overcrowded kitchenette building. Now immersed in the repetitive, tedious, and degrading chores that constitute South Side housekeeping—necessitated by the roaches, the mice, the smelly garbage, and the shabby furniture the landlord refuses to move—Brooks's protagonist figures a mode of subjectivity that departs from prevailing tropes of domestic femininity. Maud Martha has little in common with the Dilseys of the world whose destiny, effectively naturalized by William Faulkner, is to *endure* as noble martyrs the tragic burden of America's racial history. She also proves immune to the "mental gray-out" that Betty Friedan and other mainstream writers would soon diagnose in midcentury American housewives—an affliction engendered by the empty drudgery of routinized domestic labor.[42] Her episodic seriality thus bears no resemblance to the static temporality of repetition-compulsion that the feminist critic Jane Elliott observes in that grotesquely happy housekeeper, the Stepford wife, who emerges as Friedan's domestic misfits' gothic prosthesis.[43]

Instead, Brooks locates in Maud Martha's serial stillness a power of reflective and connective consciousness that enables keen attentiveness to the intricacies of the menial task, of the ordinary defeat. The vignette on the butcher's undressed chicken, for instance, recalls earlier episodes of quiet disgust in which Maud Martha takes stock of kitchenette conditions—noting, indeed, "a whole lot of grayness" (*MM* 64). Once again, the matter of intestinal fortitude is in play. Now, facing the "vomit-looking interior" of the carcass, she takes pride in her iron stomach and thinks back on "those happy, happy days" before the war when butchers themselves were "happy" to clean and cut up the fowl (151, 152). She also deems herself "lucky," however, in the present reality of shortages and dwindling ration stamps to have procured a chicken at all (152). She proceeds mentally to prepare herself for the "stomach-curving" steps of dressing the carcass—"cut a chicken open, take out the mess, with bare hands or a bread knife, pour water in, as in a bag, pour water out, shake the corpse by neck or by legs," and so forth (152)—before hatching a what-if scenario in which a human corpse takes the place of the fowl, "with no head or feet" and hair instead of feathers to pull out but with similarly "ooz[ing]" intestines and a "stench" to contend with (152–53). This macabre vision gives way to its reverse, to a consideration of the chicken as "a sort of person, a respectable individual, with its own kind of dignity" (153). These conspicuously liberal terms echo an earlier vignette in which Maud Martha successfully traps a mouse but ultimately releases it after seeing in it "a fine small dignity" and imagining its own familial and domestic needs (70). In the later vignette this recursive interplay cashes out in Maud Martha's formulation of an epistemological problem. "The difference was in the knowing," she surmises, as she thinks through our "unreal" relation to chickens—that is, the fact that we don't "live with them" the way we live with other humans and, as the earlier vignette suggests, with mice (153). We don't "know them, [or] see them loving their children" (153). The point here is not so much the specific ethical quandary that Brooks has her protagonist contemplate or whether she comes down on the side of vegetarians or carnivores. Rather, it is Brooks's figuration of a domestic laborer who manages to ward off mental gray-out without retreating into virtuous martyrdom or the romance of transcendent singularity. Brooks's housewife remains extraordinarily ordinary. Indeed, it turns out that identifying a troubling epistemological contingency that makes chickens available for slaughter and consumption does not interfere with Maud Martha's culinary prospects: "When the animal was ready for the oven Maud Martha smacked her lips at the thought of her meal" (153). This vignette's conclusion in lip-smacking anticipation, I suggest, indexes more than the protagonist's satisfaction with a repulsive household job well done. A sign of liberal happiness, the conclusion encodes the nonutilitarian value of enlivened consciousness for its own sake—of a mental episode well thought.

But if such demonstrations of individual consciousness seemed vital to midcentury liberalism's pursuit of justifiable happiness, they were hardly sufficient. As Girvetz insisted, there may be no substitute for the individual in the determination of personal preferences, but there was also no substitute for public institutions and the planning they entailed. The liberal "basis of discussion must be shifted from the psychological to the institutional level," he contended, inveighing against "orthodox economists" such as Lionel Robbins, who, like his utilitarian and neoclassical brethren, was "engrossed with man as a calculating animal who sets up a schedule of preferences and then governs himself by it."[44] Girvetz charged this traditional free-market approach with pursuing a "science of wealth" while allowing "the neglect of welfare."[45] The problem was not so much with orthodox economists' picture of the private individual's rational preferences but with their deductive (and ideological) assumption that these preferences in aggregation trumped all other ways to measure a polity's well-being. With happiness effectively defined by economic orthodoxy as preference satisfaction, these utilitarians arrived at the mistaken "guide to specific social policy" of "the greatest good [or happiness] to the greatest number." Although Girvetz accepted "happiness" as "the ultimate justification of policy," he did not accept the utilitarians' hedonic definition of happiness. Echoing Galbraith, he complained that current metrics of the standard of living, for instance, were "almost invariably limited" to the purchasing power of "private incomes," thereby ignoring "the contribution of social services and public amenities."[46] To remedy this situation, "as a matter of right and justice," he called for an end to social welfare's "subordinate" status and for the affirmative recognition of socioeconomic "interdependence" alongside personal "independence."[47]

The restrained urgency with which Girvetz lays out the case for political-economic reform captures the difficult two-step operation of postwar liberal activism. He appreciates the distinction between the conditions of "crisis" that, for instance, spurred the government into New Deal action during the Great Depression and the "routine" mechanics of party politics that usually "take over" in the aftermath of a crisis. The liberal activist must draw on but also step away from both crisis and routine. As Girvetz writes, "It took the spectacle of mass deprivation and mass unemployment to arouse Americans . . . to a high pitch of idealism. Out of this came a great forward thrust, a moral momentum that produced the Minimum Wage and Social Security laws." Not prepared, for obvious reasons, to advocate a return to conditions of mass unemployment and deprivation in order to restore "moral momentum," he equally resists accepting the mechanical, enervating conditions of "routine" party politics, which now prevail. In other words, he argues, the nation is in need of "what William James once called a 'moral equivalent to war.' We also need a moral equivalent to [economic] depression."[48] But he also implies that the intensity of political arousal he seeks should be something less than revolutionary. Following Locke, he appreciates as good luck the evident fact that the revolutionary spirit is extremely difficult to arouse in the populace even though the right to revolution is built into the liberal tradition.[49]

Girvetz concedes that the liberal activism he promotes is "essentially a fluid and frequently elusive doctrine," which is why it is "often regarded with suspicion by the Right and with contempt by the doctrinaire Left." But he also offers concrete indices of its relevance in the long history and recent practice of liberalism.[50] It is visible in the eighteenth-century institution of the constitutional amendment as a formal procedure, whose "cumbrous process" serves to dampen but not to quash a revolutionary "sense of outrage" and thus to enable significant political transformation without "explosive violence." It is also visible in the contemporary liberal figure of the "social frontiersman" who, in "contrast to the revolutionary," is willing to "pause at the brink of action" but also, in "contrast to the conservative . . . , is more hospitable to change, more willing to reexamine established institutions and accepted practices in the light of new problems and new needs."[51] Girvetz stresses the historical situatedness of contemporary liberalism's heightened moral vigilance. He does not appeal to the American Constitution's preamble per se—with its reference to the general welfare—to back up his insistence on socioeconomic justice. Rather, he builds his case on the recent legislative activism of the FDR administration. Its ability to work around the Supreme Court, which was reluctant to refer to the general welfare clause, by exploiting the "spending power in the form of federal grants-in-aid" (until the 1937 decision *Helvering v. Davis* validated Social Security benefits as constitutionally permissible) testifies to liberalism's evolving practices of goodwill and thereby to its ability to remain true to its fundamental principles.[52] Laying claim to this goodwill, Girvetz exemplifies the vigilant liberal whose activism operates in the interstices between the unacceptable alternatives of revolution and routine.

Like Girvetz, social scientists who were involved in the cause to end racial segregation understood themselves to be working "on the frontiers" of their fields.[53] In her 1972 autobiography Brooks herself described a black friend who in the 1940s bought a house on Drexel Avenue, a white street east of Cottage Grove, as a "pioneer."[54] This shared trope points to midcentury liberal activists' endeavor to imagine themselves as conscientiously advancing the possibilities of individual and social transformation within the welfare state. Brooks's Maud Martha, despite her inwardness, figures the "social frontiersman" as well. She may lack the financial resources of Brooks's friend to challenge residential restrictions, but she is an intrepid participant-observer of life on the South Side. Through her eyes we come to see the South Side's mixture of met and unmet institutional needs.⁵⁵ She carves out a space between revolution and routine in her way of examining closely the institutional options on offer, of acknowledging the welfare-state values embedded in them while calling attention to their manifest limitations if not outright violations of goodwill.

Whereas *Maud Martha*'s opening vignette does much to establish the protagonist's preference-possessing autonomy, the next several situate her within an array of familiar urban institutions: the school, the zoo, the hospital, the single-family home, the theater, and the church. The second vignette, "spring landscape: detail," reprises the first vignette's floral conceit, transferring the liberal theory of flourishing it commends for Maud Martha to a swath of children in a schoolyard. Befitting such intrinsic universalism, this second vignette takes a more distant third-person perspective, viewing Maud Martha as one among the many: "Up the street, mixed in the wind, blew the children . . . [into the school court]. It was wonderful. Bits of pink, of blue, white, yellow, green, purple, brown, black, carried by jerky little stems of brown or yellow or brown-black" (*MM* 5). Brooks thus foregrounds the children's equal yet unique status, presenting each as pieces in a mosaic of seemingly random cardinal colors: "pink . . . blue, white, yellow, green, purple, brown, black." Yet this stress on the value of their nonhierarchical and incommensurate uniqueness does not obscure the social contingency of race, which Brooks registers by attaching these unique beings to recognizably racial hues, to "stems of brown or yellow or brown-black."

Underscoring in this way the universal applicability of flourishing to a broad population of unnamed colored kids, Brooks keeps her finger on the midcentury liberal lesson. She noted in her autobiography that this scene combined elements from her childhood with her adult experience in the 1940s of waiting for her "kindergartener" to be released from school (*RPO* 191). In the novel she conveys sufficient confidence in this institution's functionality: "The school looked solid. Brownish-red brick, dirty cream stone trim. Massive chimney, candid, serious" (*MM* 4). Its 8:55 a.m. bell signals the concern that pupils arrive on time for their lessons (5). The scene evokes "little promises, just under cover; whether they would fulfill themselves was anybody's guess" (4). An aspiration derived from the foundational claim of human worth, the prospect of flourishing in this institution, Brooks implies, is what justifies its existence in the first place.

As the narrative chronicles Maud Martha's exemplary aspiration to flourish at school and elsewhere, its vignette seriality reinforces midcentury liberal activism's understanding that personality development involves a practice of experiential repetition and accumulation within a wide assemblage of more or less stable public and private institutions. Following the scene of the school, the next vignette makes reference to a zoo, which Maud Martha seems to have visited earlier and which now stimulates her pleasant sleep-dream of a gorilla's escape (*MM* 7–10). Next, there's the racially integrated hospital (probably Michael Reese) that tends adequately enough to her dying grandmother despite a shortage of nurses (11–15). Then there's the Regal Theatre, where at age sixteen she comes to see that she doesn't share the audience's taste for popular music and showy entertainment (19–22). After that she's in the church where her uncle's funeral is being held and where she contemplates his small but worthy life as judged by God but more decisively by Uncle Tim himself (25–26). Not least and not last, there's the lawyer's office that employs her, now seventeen, and her sister at paltry wages (34). By mapping out in one vignette after another the South Side's institutional geography—concretized through frequent allusions to actual street names—Brooks suggests the crucial role the institutional matrix cumulatively and recursively plays in her character's well-being. This social wealth, despite the Depression era's economic challenges, enables Maud Martha to fulfill her dandelion promise. While Trilling may not highly regard the liberal imagination of the "everyday," Brooks surely does.

The close interdependence of discrete private and public institutions in the welfare state becomes particularly vivid in the eighth vignette, in which the fate of the family residence—that prominent emblem of private life and personal economy—hangs in the balance. Titled "home," this vignette portrays Maud Martha waiting anxiously on the porch with her mother and sister for her father to return from "the office of the Home Owners' Loan" with news regarding his request for a loan extension on their single-family house of "more than fourteen years" (*MM* 29). The Home Owners' Loan Corporation (HOLC) was one of the emergency measures taken by the New Deal in 1933, as the nation reached a new height of foreclosures. Its mandate was to purchase and refinance mortgages on owner-occupied nonfarm homes that were in distress through no fault of the owner. President Roosevelt described the initiative as "protect[ing] home owners from inequitable enforced liquidation, in a time of general distress, [which] is a proper concern of the Government."[56] To qualified borrowers it offered longer amortization periods and lower interest rates than commercial banks, and its schedule of repayment enabled the borrower to pay down the principal month by month. Functioning as what Ira Katznelson and Barry R. Weingast would call a "distributive switchboard," the HOLC was an institution that rearranged individuals' and groups' "assets and possibilities."[57] Specifically, it rearranged temporal schedules while "tapping a new class of investors who were willing to invest in the HOLC and there[by] supply credit to borrowers." It was largely financed by the issuance of government-guaranteed bonds, which meant that "taxpayers were potentially on the hook to repay them" if borrowers defaulted on their loans en masse.[58] Along with the new amortization period these bonds, slated to mature between 1949 and 1951, introduced a new, more relaxed temporal structure. In this manner the HOLC enabled private lenders with short-term liquidity problems, now disencumbered of long-term toxic assets, to participate in financial "activities that generated cash flow sooner rather than later."[59] Like the HOLC's borrowers, the era's lenders and homebuilders and the real estate industry at large seemed ready to embrace a good new deal when they saw one.

The chronology of *Maud Martha* dates the vignette to around 1934, thus placing it in the three-year period in which the HOLC made loans. Technically, the HOLC didn't start granting loan *extensions* until 1939, when it changed the amortization period from fifteen to twenty-five years. For Maud Martha, in any case, the episode is extremely unpleasant, as the loan office is known to be "hard" (*MM* 29). In her autobiography, Brooks, suggesting another bout of stomach trouble, described the "fact-bound" episode as based on the "sickening reality" of her family's experience with the HOLC (*RPO* 191). Indeed, the HOLC rejected about 50 percent of its loan applications.[60] It also drew on and extended previous commercial practices of redlining, although it did refinance property inside red zones, such as the South Side.[61] Thus as a counterweight to the housing policies erected by state and local authorities, including the race-restrictive covenants that fueled the South Side's overcrowded, overpriced, and substandard housing conditions, the federal loan program in this instance achieves a minor miracle. It spares the Brown family the harder and more sickening prospect of foreclosure and eviction.

Notably, not even in this "sickening" situation does Maud Martha share

David McKempster's abnegating desire to throw up. To the contrary, unlike her mother and sister, who prepare psychologically for eviction by disavowing their affection for the house, Maud Martha refuses to deny her and her father's attachment to it (*MM* 29–31). (Only after the loan extension is secured do her mother and sister express pride in home ownership [32.]) Besides demonstrating emotional honesty and filial loyalty, Maud Martha mirrors the loan office's hardness; she possesses sufficient resilience to resist alienation from the institutional matrix she inhabits. Indeed, her defense of her father's "love for this old house" speaks to the novel's vigilant concern to promote the idea of flourishing within this matrix (37). This quotation significantly appears in the subsequent vignette; as it reiterates the father's love, it recursively links Maud Martha's respect for her father's domestic attachment to her respect for her father's occupational preference. For in this later vignette we learn of his "decision to remain" a janitor "for the rest of his days" rather than to seek a more remunerative, prestigious job, as other members of the family urge him to do (37). With Maud Martha's affirmation of this "decision," Brooks introduces a vital modification to the novel's picture of flourishing. Up to this point the floral conceit has done much to convey the magnificent loveliness of human beings in all their variety and potential for growth. Schoolchildren are not the only ones blessed in this way: near the end of the novel Maud Martha conceives everybody outside on Thirty-Fourth Street as "blooms," be they "in their undershirts, sundresses [or] diapers." She thus aligns the South Side population with simple organic beauty (164). But here in her father's house the act of cutting short—of deciding—is what matters.

In this manner Brooks avoids hypostatizing the idea of flourishing as nothing more than the cultivation of a natural telos. That is, individual flourishing could seem in complete accord with the logic of growth; in turn, an individual's growth could seem dependent on society's economic expansion. The kind of welfare state Girvetz promoted, for instance, generally looked to macroeconomic growth to solve problems of socioeconomic justice—to sustain full employment of a steadily increasing population in the face of increasing automation, to fund programs for the least advantaged who were in large part victims of urban crisis, and to extend aid to developing countries (and thus compete with the Soviet Union for influence).[62] But where Girvetz urged economic growth as a practical, ethical, and geopolitical necessity, Moreland's Spinozan vision of happiness, a function of the state-sponsored "growth of the individual," conformed more readily to a naturalist logic. Indeed, the existential cast of Moreland's political philosophy dovetailed with the work of a number of influential midcentury culture and personality theorists, particularly the neo-Freudian and humanist psychologists. For them, the teleological proposition of self-realization or self-actualization was existentially paramount. With the aim of supplanting the fatalistic and mechanistic theories of personhood advanced respectively by Freudianism and stimulus-response behaviorism, they typically incorporated a kind of growth idealism into their theories.[63] The most prominent of the humanist psychologists, Abraham Maslow, understood self-actualization explicitly in terms of biological essentialism: it "is intrinsic growth of what is already in the organism, or more accurately of what *is* the organism itself." He allowed that "paradoxically the highest motivation is to be unmotivated and nonstriving, that is, to behave purely expressively."[64] But only the highest achievers of self-actualization who discovered their "true bent" attained this state of "excellence." He had in mind exceptional figures—people such as "Einstein, Eleanor Roosevelt, Jane Addams, William James, and Spinoza"—not somebody, in other words, like Maud Martha's father.[65]

This model of growth, which collapsed personality formation into Aristotelian virtue ethics, had deep ties to the midcentury discourse of happiness.[66] In his intellectual history *The Idea of Happiness* (published in 1967 in a series of scholarly monographs on the great ideas of Western thought overseen by Mortimer Adler at the University of Chicago), V. J. McGill devoted the concluding chapter to these midcentury trends. He observed that "personality theory and psychotherapy" constitute "the most important current development of the theory of the good life."[67] He goes on to quote Maslow's view that inquiry into the good life belonged to natural science: "We may agree with Aristotle when he assumed that the good life consisted in living in accordance with the true nature of man, but we must add that he simply did not know enough about the true nature of man."[68] McGill's account rightly suggested that midcentury humanist psychologists and neo-Freudians were committed to identifying "true" human nature whose actualization ipso facto occasioned virtuous happiness, whether the focus was on expressive self-actualization (as with Maslow), holistic integration of the human organism (as with Kurt Goldstein), self-loving productivity (as with Erich Fromm), or functional autonomy and self-extension (as with Gordon Allport).

Yet even McGill, who clearly sympathized with the midcentury work he described, stopped short in the final pages of his book of declaring that "the end and justification of government" is "to *make* men happy" in this way. Ultimately he acknowledged the distinction between "the Platonic-Aristotelian tradition," with its "intention to promote morality," and the American constitutional system, whose "*program* of promoting general welfare" only "promises that the external means would be provided for citizens to pursue their happiness, each in his own way."[69] The perfectionist model of personality didn't just deprecate the lives of, say, the 99 percent who might not in fact enjoy the "external means" to achieve excellence. Perfectionism, conceived as a state pursuit, as John Stopford observes, also "fails to take seriously the distinction between persons," whose conceptions of the good might or might not prize excellence. Further, it commits the state "to some independent standard of human excellence that might conflict with their *still unknown* conceptions of the good."[70] This cognitive limitation doesn't derive from our deficient knowledge of human biology (as Maslow might have it) but from persons' ordinary relation to their future.

Such perfectionist ambitions of midcentury psychology and personality theory are conspicuously absent from Brooks's figuration of the potential to flourish. The "decision" Maud Martha's father makes not to pursue a better job hints at a model of flourishing in which this quality of the "still unknown" factors into the ethical and existential calculus. Presented as neither a predictable nor exactly a desirable development in the eyes of most family members, the decision is nonetheless one that Maud Martha deems worth defending. It also signals the father's ongoing exercise of situational autonomy; he too has his preferences. For Brooks, this is ultimately the meaning of "growth," even when it amounts to the family's material stagnation. Once again, the novel's vignette seriality underscores the liberal activist logic informing Brooks's intervention. Its temporal and causal gaps, made visible by not-quite-new beginnings every few pages, convey the sense that the father's decision amounts to an existential deflection of both revolutionary and routine futures. Embracing neither radical spontaneity nor naturalist teleology, the father seems to take his cue from the HOLC's even-keeled amortization schedule, opting to earn a predictable wage, month by month and year by year, and enjoying in his own way "the rest of his days." (As it happened, Brooks's father, on whom Maud Martha's father is modeled, died in 1959; he thus surpassed by only eight years what conceivably might have been his final mortgage payment to the HOLC, which ceased operations in 1951.) The liberal epistemology of growth, in Brooks's picture, depends as much on institutional temporality and personal decision as on floral analogy.

This vignette's intimate link between home life and work life thus makes visible the centrality of preference in what might be called liberalism's macrodynamic imagination of flourishing, that is, its vision of the reciprocal relation between a person's exercise of autonomous capacities and the welfare state's commitment to socioeconomic justice. But *Maud Martha* offers insights into the microdynamics of flourishing as well. It figures "frontier" agency as essentially an ongoing drama of circumstance—as involving both short-term and long-term commitments, as advancing both trivial and consequential projects (sometimes both at once), and as requiring its agents of change to operate on the margins of adjustment. This cloud of particulars, Brooks's novel suggests, makes it difficult although not impossible to glimpse the foundational ethical values anchoring the praxis of liberal activism.

Here too, in this realm of microdynamic flourishing on the margin, the father's "decision" proves illuminating. The very smallness of the decision, for one thing, is suggested in the incidental way we learn about it. The vignette in which it appears takes Maud Martha's sister Helen as its focus. Here Maud Martha reflects on feeling slighted by the attention her father showers on Helen and not on her, despite her many overt demonstrations of sympathy, such as her defense of his job decision (*MM* 37). This intrafamilial problem itself is on the small side—sibling rivalry is a common enough source of adolescent distress, and Maud Martha's experience is hurtful but not devastating. The discrepancy between the father's treatment of her and of Helen, the narrative suggests, may in fact be minimal. And it is this condition of minimal discrepancy that also informs the father's job decision, rendering it merely incidental to his flourishing. Although it is key, as suggested earlier, to Brooks's portrayal of a crucial alternative to the dominant discourse of growth, it is incidental to the father, because the difference between preferring a better job and preferring the job he has is trivial. Had he in fact decided to pursue a better job, this decision too would have been consistent with his fundamental preference to flourish, albeit in a more predictable way. Brooks presents him as one who recognizes his margin of maneuverability within the liberal regime.

But the implications of recognizing this margin are perhaps best clarified by the negative example. What the father does not decide to do, after all, is go on a bender, abandon his job, prod his son into having implausibly big dreams, and squander the family money on a crooked business scheme. These are the decisions Walter Lee Younger makes in Lorraine Hansberry's 1959 classic play, *A Raisin in the Sun*. They are what bring him—as father, son, husband, and brother—along with the rest of the household to the brink of mental and material ruin. The play stages in effect a series of lessons on how not to flourish. Taking place in an overcrowded kitchenette apartment on the South Side, its central prop is "*a feeble little plant growing doggedly in a small pot on the window sill.*"[71] At first, the play seems to operate in the vein of *Native Son*'s naturalism more than in that of *Maud Martha*'s liberalism, with the volatile and big dreamer Walter Lee functioning as the symbolic symptom of an oppressive world. The title comes from a line in Langston Hughes's famous poem, "Harlem" (1948), which serves as the play's epigraph: "What happens to a dream deferred? / Does it dry up / Like a raisin in the sun? / . . . *Or does it explode?*" (*RS* 473). As these alternatives of drying up or exploding appear to frame the play, they suggest in advance the profound shortage of opportunities for African Americans to flourish on the South Side.

Even when resources arrive, in the form of ten thousand dollars (the insurance money resulting from the death of Walter Lee Younger Sr.), the many mistakes made regarding preferences and decisions imply that the family, as a unit of decision-making, is insufficiently equipped with the cognitive and emotional funds to act in ways that enable its well-being. Only after Walter Lee curbs his "hysterical" tendencies (*RS* 510), lowers his career ambitions, and recovers his dignity does the family follow through with the plan to move into a house in a white neighborhood. They know full well that this move will spoil the "happiness" of the white community, whose representative attempts to bribe them not to move in (514). But they can justify this consequence because they have also learned the lesson spoken by the family matriarch: "Son—I come from five generations of people who was slaves and sharecroppers—but ain't nobody in my family never let nobody pay 'em no money that was a way of telling us we wasn't fit to walk the earth. We ain't never been that poor. . . . We ain't never been that dead inside" (526). Having turned the corner—away from inner deadness and toward practical, dignified decision-making—the family is now on the brink of flourishing. Here, then, is a drama of rescue: an angry youngish man is encouraged to abandon his own will to destruction and instead to tether himself to the goals of developing familial wealth and stability over generations. His retreat further spares his wife, Ruth, an unwanted abortion. But Hansberry strongly implies that without a network of social, civic, and legal institutions to sustain their commitment to buying property, the family has little chance of being integrated into the welfare state. Indeed, the bravery this family has collectively summoned to mount their incursion into a white neighborhood stamps them as liberal activists who insist these conditions be met. They've joined, as it were, the club of "social frontiersmen," much as Hansberry's actual family had.[72] Fittingly, the play ends with Mama rushing back into the kitchenette apartment one last time, having decided to take her feeble plant to the new place (530).

If the Younger family ultimately operates, like the Brown family, within a margin of activist maneuverability that is conducive to microdynamic flourishing, the decision-making process of both families turns out to resemble, in its incipient form, what certain midcentury liberal activists were keen to promote as a full-blown method for public decision-making. In their 1953 book, *Politics, Economics, and Welfare*, the political scientists Robert A. Dahl and Charles E. Lindblom advanced the merits of a pragmatist orientation to formulating public policy. They called their method "incrementalism." A few years later Lindblom published a landmark essay, "The Science of 'Muddling Through'" (1959), in which he sought "to clarify and formalize" this method.[73] Instead of regarding contemporary (nontotalitarian) political systems as "grand alternatives," Dahl and Lindblom argued that, for instance, the US capitalist system and the UK socialist system were not radically distinct. Both depended on policy plans, and both thus required "social techniques" to aid action. An incrementalist method, they argued, appreciated the fact that a society, like a person, had many frequently conflicting goals that "require[d] a delicate and changing compromise"; their step-by-step method built more predictability and hence less risk into a system's policy options than did revolutionary or utopian calls for dramatic comprehensive change. It enabled easier recovery from mistakes and reinforced the durability of the social organization in question.[74]

Incrementalism, they suggested, could function only when alternative policy preferences were nearby and plausible; it was "a method of social action that takes existing reality as one alternative and compares the probable gains and losses of closely related alternatives by making relatively small adjustments in existing reality, or making larger adjustments" when the consequences are proportionately more predictable. Such alternatives were generated by and predicated on the fact that in a place like the United States "widespread agreement exists on basic issues," by which they meant fundamental goals and values.[75] Lindblom cited the example of the Chicago Housing Authority, which accepted the "clear objective of providing a certain number of public housing units in the city" but had to deal with internal disagreement over location alternatives.[76] In other words, Dahl and Lindblom's mode of pragmatist incrementalism eschewed polarized ideological debates and metaphysics, but it didn't subscribe to antifoundational relativism. The observable claims of "social habituation" on persons—norms, codes, ethical systems, indoctrination—allowed them to proceed inductively, to enumerate with some confidence contemporary liberalism's moral entailments as "basic ends for social action": "freedom, rationality, democracy, subjective equality, security, progress, and appropriate inclusion."[77] Building these values into the incrementalist calculus is what distinguished the method from the microeconomic cost-benefit analysis of social choice theorists. And the conservatives and radicals who didn't accept these values, Dahl and Lindblom implied, would also have difficulty accepting incrementalist alternatives as relevant because any operation on the fluctuating margins of possibility would amount to much-too-small potatoes. Meanwhile, the overwhelming majority of people who did endorse these values could recognize themselves in systemic but unsystematic processes of social action. They could look forward to what Lindblom described as a multilateral series of "successive limited comparisons." Through this conventional cognitive practice, "[p]eople discover what they want by living; wants grow and change with experience."[78] Such "wants" could claim legitimacy only insofar as they conformed to the system's macroethical conditions.

The political scientists were of course primarily interested in this method's applicability to policy-making in public administration, but they also acknowledged its relevance to "personal problem-solving." Furthermore, they acknowledged—referencing Freud and contemporary "interest in psychiatry, psychoanalysis, psychology, and anthropology"—the limited capacities of most human beings for rational calculation.[79] But they did not concede, for all that, the method's irrelevance:

Man's limited mental capacity, lack of emotional integration, inhibited foresight, and need for uncalculated actions—all this we take for granted. But to accept these premises is not to adopt certain irrelevant conclusions inferred from them: . . . That to postulate rationality as a goal (among others) is to exaggerate man's capacity for rational calculation. This proposition is no more valid than to say that to postulate freedom as a goal (among others) is to deny man's capacity for unfreedom and to exaggerate his capacity for freedom.

As long as it remains plausible to imagine a moral horizon, they argue, it's also plausible to imagine an inductive methodology that keeps that horizon in view. They go on to defend rational calculation as in fact compatible with "unconscious or impulsive actions," when such actions facilitate the attainment of goals; they further suggest that incrementalism hinges more on an agent's pragmatist orientation toward—and loosely knit range of—goals than on a specific psychology.[80]

In *Maud Martha* it is not the family unit but the protagonist who becomes the central vehicle for dramatizing the virtues of this method over time and in continuous action. The sequence of vignettes in which Maud Martha considers men as marriage material renders particularly vivid the merits of thinking through proximate alternatives and observing the bilateral operations and compromises that enter into the incrementalist calculation, while other vignettes that portray her encounters with the white world indicate the psychoinstitutional merits of being open to evolving priorities and contingent desires. Altogether Brooks suggests that for black people especially, who possibly face a lifetime of dispiritingly routine work and poverty and yet may be compelled at midcentury to navigate an uncertain social landscape on the cusp of Jim Crow's legal demise, this liberal activist footwork may be worth the trouble.

In the personal realm of husband hunting, Maud Martha demonstrates her incrementalist chops. What becomes clear in a sequence of four contiguous vignettes—over the course of which Maud Martha attains her long-term goal, a marriage proposal—is that she is quite adept at making successive comparisons of close alternatives and managing her fantasy desires. Similar to Goldilocks but facing a much more complicated set of variables, Maud Martha peruses her South Side options. In the tenth vignette, "first beau," we meet the dandified Russell, whose "technique" with other girls she has observed for some time and with some suspicion (*MM* 40). When he trains his sights on her, she discovers that she likes him more than she expected but ultimately deems him a self-aggrandizing "flourish"—too "decorated inside and out" for her taste (41). In the next vignette, "second beau," we meet the more thoughtful but, as discussed earlier, psychically hobbled David McKempster. Although his intellectual interests are more appealing than Russell's stylishness, she seems to think that his racial wounds are largely self-inflicted, a function of allowing his upper-class dreams to belittle him and everybody else west of Cottage Grove. "[D]on't laugh" at him, she asks us, for wanting the purebred dog, indicating her own mixed attitude of pity and contempt (42).

Brooks underscores the value of adopting a more dignifying incrementalist orientation by juxtaposing in the very next vignette Maud Martha's prudent management of her own big dreams. In "Maud Martha and New York," she indulges in magazine-induced fantasies of the luxurious ease and beauty that wealthy New Yorkers enjoy. While entertaining visions of Russian caviar, Chinese boxes, Persian rugs, and the like, her attachment is indeed so strong that "her whole body became a hunger" (*MM*, 48). But crucially, she reins in this vision of New York by converting it into a "symbol" of how "life" in general "ought to be": "Jeweled. Polished. Smiling. Poised" (49–50). Maud Martha does not confuse this aesthetic utopia with how life actually is or with how she might expect it to be. Her capacity to think symbolically thus enables her to experience fantasy as a source of pleasure rather than of self-abnegation: "What she wanted to dream, and dreamed, was her affair. It pleased her to dwell upon color and soft bready textures and light, on a complex beauty, on gemlike surfaces. What was the matter with that?" (51). Here the utopian impulse functions in the manner Dahl and Lindblom considered valuable—not as a perfectionist model of planning that negates piecemeal incrementalism but as a stimulus to the imagination that prevents incrementalism from "degenerat[ing] into petty change, fear of the future, [or] a placid tolerance of existing distress."[81] As noted earlier, Maud Martha experiences over the course of her life the unfulfillment of many dreams, including less fantastic ones. Here Brooks offers a condensed version of how both cognitive abstraction and hedonic aesthetics—symbol and pleasure—combine to deepen Maud Martha's autonomy and resilience and thus to prepare her for marital compromise, as depicted in the next vignette, "low yellow."

A grand alternative neither to Russell nor to David, her third beau, Paul

Phillips, is the one she's confident she'll "hook" (*MM* 55). Somewhat like Russell, he likes "the gay life [and] spiffy clothes" (55). But unlike both previous beaus, he recognizes and is seemingly at ease with his strengths and weaknesses—light skin color but "not handsome" (54). Moreover, he recognizes that Maud Martha "will do." She "is not what he would call pretty," she thinks, but is "what he would call—sweet" (52). To cap off the courtship, Paul entertains the proposition of having children with her (54). Within this one brief vignette Brooks shows how two individuals make incremental adjustments to their expectations, desires, and plans. They engage in Dahl and Lindblom's process of "delicate and changing compromise." The novel goes on to show that Maud Martha and Paul are in fact not perfectly compatible, but it also suggests that a lasting marriage such as theirs is properly understood as a work in incremental progress.

Mark McGurl has compellingly argued that the long tradition of the marriage plot in realist fiction dovetails with a strain in neoclassical economics that frames such choices as whom to marry using a consumerist ideology fixated on opportunity costs. The choice of one spouse over another gives rise to the counterfactual or novelistic narrative of how things might have been, of what other pleasures might have been enjoyed and other downstream preferences satisfied. McGurl notes that more than a little hopelessness enters into this consumerist calculus by virtue of the very real consequences of choice. What Brooks's marriage plot helps us to see, however, when framed by incrementalist decision theory, is that such costs may be offset by the dividends paid out not so much by the actual spouse chosen but by the method informing the choice, guided as it is by a commitment to flourishing—a flourishing defined, that is, less by specific acts of consumption than by a liberal system that enables preferences to be imagined and concretized.[82]

There's an additional political dimension to consider. As the vignette sequence tracks Maud Martha's serial interactions with a few men who are not drastically dissimilar, she comes to resemble those "people" who "discover what they want by living; wants grow and change with experience." The cumulative quality of this seriality reveals as well how the habitual practice of personal incrementalism contributes to her capacity as a South Side "pioneer" who confronts the everyday politics of race. While Maud Martha can't do much about the slumlord who won't permit her to switch out the furniture in the kitchenette apartment, she can choose the circumstances under which she challenges de facto segregation. Brooks suggests that one advantage of the incrementalist ethos is that it encourages a person largely to choose her battles, because they don't usually involve all-or-nothing ultimatums. In the vignette, "we're the only colored people here," Maud Martha persuades her husband to venture out with her into a white neighborhood to see a movie. She may well prefer not to witness the way the white "people in the lobby tried to avoid looking curiously at two shy Negroes wanting desperately not to seem shy" (*MM* 76). But she also takes seriously her preference to see a movie in Technicolor and in a fancy theater. The critic Tyler T. Schmidt insightfully describes this scene as one of "tentative integration [that] deftly captures the tensions between public space and private desire . . . and the delicate balance between public pride and personal shame."[83] The psychosocial stakes are a bit higher when Maud Martha verbally confronts (rather than jabs with scissors, as she fantasizes doing) a department store Santa who snubs her young daughter (173–75) or when she decides to leave after one day and without explanation a well-paying domestic job for an unbearably condescending white woman. In acting on her preference neither to voice her reasons for quitting nor to lash out at her employer, she breaks the routine of subservient courtesy while forbearing violent trouble. This silent but decisive revolt amounts to Maud Martha's highest watermark of frontier activism. But the incrementalist paradigm also validates Maud Martha's decision not to revolt at all, as when she goes along with her hairdresser in overlooking a white saleswoman's racist remark. "I'm too relaxed to fight today," Maud Martha thinks to herself, going on to justify her inaction: "Sometimes fighting is interesting. Today, it would have been just plain old ugly duty" (140). As Brooks presents Maud Martha in vignette after vignette in which (to borrow Dahl and Lindblom's phrase) "closely related alternatives" obtain, she discloses a process through which the preference chosen, for better or worse, provides an occasion for her to test out and make public her claims to institutional dignity. She thus illustrates a formidable attachment to the everyday ethos of the liberal imagination as it operates in and on the welfare state.

The New Integrationism

By midcentury social scientific measures, then, Maud Martha exemplifies the well-integrated personality or character. From the standpoint of critics such as Theodor Adorno and his colleagues, who sought in *The Authoritarian*

Personality (1950) to define the democratic or "genuine liberal" personality over and against the submissive, authoritarian one, she meets this personality's key qualifications. To borrow the historian Robert Genter's recent summary of Adorno's account, she is "an emotionally secure individual capable of weathering frustrations without producing an unraveling of ego integration." She exhibits "'a strong sense of personal autonomy and independence'" and is immune to "compulsive identification with others." She is tolerant of others and "possess[es] the ability to stop from immediately gratifying every id impulse but also to avoid the compulsive repression of those impulses."[84] From the standpoint of structural sociologists such as Hans Gerth and C. Wright Mills, who coauthored *Character and Social Structure: The Psychology of Social Institutions* (1953), Maud Martha also exhibits the traits indicative of a healthy character structure, which, to borrow again from Genter, "was a complicated integration of [a person's] individual psychic structure with the pattern of desires and expectations instilled by [her] personal upbringing and the various social roles [she] inhabited over [her] lifetime."[85]

If Maud Martha thus looks nothing like Bigger Thomas, she distinctly resembles Gwendolyn Brooks, who indeed described her novel as partly autobiographical (*RPO* 162). Moreover, the author of *Maud Martha* has a good deal in common with the author of *Native Son*. Although never handed the Pulitzer, Richard Wright also rose to national prominence early in his writing career and in fact reviewed for the publisher Brooks's first book of poems.[86] In other words, they both flourished. Both were more or less successfully integrated into available networks of public literary culture. As Ralph Ellison would say of Wright and James Baldwin in his famous response to Irving Howe's celebration of Wright's purported assault on American values, "Both are true Negro Americans, and both affirm the broad possibility of personal realization which I see as a saving aspect of American life."[87] In Brooks's hands, as we've seen, the commitment to the idea of "personal realization" mirrors the commitment to the welfare state's institutional matrix. But it also serves as Brooks's warrant for a commitment to a certain form of racial integration in a period of widespread ambivalence toward, if not outright repudiation of, this liberal ideal. While midcentury literary critics such as Arthur P. Davis and Irving Howe saw the integrationist ethos as an abandonment of the literature of protest, later critics such as Houston A. Baker Jr. objected vehemently to "integrationist poetics" on the grounds that it excluded blackness—specifically, the black vernacular—as an aesthetic and social category. Integrationists who took "democratic pluralism" as their model, he argued, made a raceless, classless, homogeneous society the "implicit goal" of America. As Baker put it, "The integrationist assumed as a first principle that art was an American area of achievement in which race and class were not significant variables."[88] What all these perspectives fail to acknowledge, however, is that the welfare state's ongoing endeavor to advance the institutional praxis of integration has had enormous consequences for aesthetic production. And this is what the example of Brooks's authorial career reveals.

By 1972, the year Gwendolyn Brooks's first autobiography appeared, the author had received all kinds of institutional accolades and honors: the Pulitzer Prize, the state poet laureate appointment, two Guggenheim fellowships, multiple honorary doctorates, and an invitation to the White House, to name only the most prominent. This wealth of public recognition helped, among other functions in the economy of prestige, to sustain the aspirations of midcentury integrationists who looked to Brooks as one of their own and who could see in her achievements the propitiousness of an American ideal. No one less than Paul Engle, then director of the Iowa Writers' Workshop and champion of minority writers such as Margaret Walker, was the first to review her debut collection, *A Street in Bronzeville*, in 1945. He insisted that it wasn't so much a collection of "Negro poetry" written for blacks only but a book "by a civilized American citizen . . . for all men."[89] With similar enthusiasm the critic Dan Jaffe likened her in 1969 to Robert Frost and William Carlos Williams in being "attuned to the voicebox of the people." He went on to celebrate her artful representation of both blackness and Americanness: "The history of American literature it has been said is the history of a search for a definition of *American*. . . . Brooks leads us to a sense of the ghetto and the black man. She leads us also to a sense of the American dilemma, one hopes toward some resolution."[90] In Jaffe's gesture here to Gunnar Myrdal's 1944 book, he aligns Brooks with the era's dominant model of integration, one that drew on the ethnicity paradigm to advance a theory of blacks' eventual assimilation into mainstream America.[91] Brooks's cultural work, so the "hope" went, would help make this happen.

But by this point in her career Brooks's racial politics had evolved considerably, such that she understood herself as leaving behind the integrationist paradigm of the 1940s and 1950s. Early in the first autobiography, she sounds the valedictory note. After several pages detailing her poor but "happy" childhood (*RPO* 41), one warmed by "welcoming, enveloping" parents (39) and punctuated by a nearly endless series of Fourth of July, Christmas, Easter, Thanksgiving, and birthday celebrations (39–44), she turns to matters that have required a different kind of affection ever since the 1967 Black Writers' Conference at Fisk University opened her eyes. Her childhood happiness may have had its merits, but she now regards it as propped up by white convention: "Not one celebration in my black household or in any black household that I knew featured any black glory or greatness or grandeur" (44). Whereas previous decades of holiday celebrations ritualized her family's commitment to assimilation, now, at the start of the 1970s, she lays claim to a different set of "fertile facts" or "know-nows" (45). Foremost among them is Brooks's new knowledge of institutional, national, and geographical affiliation. Deeming that only "the Indian is the authentic American," she now identifies as "an essential African, in occupancy here because of an indeed 'peculiar' institution" (45). Two generations removed from slavery—her father's father (whom she did not know), we learn a few pages later, escaped slavery and fought in the Civil War (50)—the horizon of her personal history now goes many generations back, reflective of the long geopolitical term of modernity. She thus calls for a new kind of holiday, "a Black World Day, with black excitement and black trimmings in honor of the astounding strength and achievement of black people" (45–46). She also voices a dim view of the integrationist paradigm: she now "know[s] that the black-and-white integration concept . . . has wound down to farce" (45). In a 1971 interview, Brooks similarly minces no words on the subject. She describes how she "thought [she] was happy" mixing with white writers, speaking the integrationist idiom, and throwing "big literary parties"; but after her transformation, she no longer associated much with white people: "You see, I couldn't. That would be impossible. I just don't think 'that way' anymore" (177).

Brooks's renunciation of "that way" of thinking and the embrace of another way may create the impression that she fully succeeded—and wanted to succeed—in repudiating what George E. Kent calls "the standard script inscribed by the white liberal critical consensus."[92] Kent certainly advances this narrative in his 1990 biography, as does Brooks's protégé, Don L. Lee (Haki R. Madhubuti), in the preface to Brooks's autobiography. There Lee refers to Brooks as "an African poet" who, "by acknowledging her Africanness, her blackness, . . . reverses the trend of being defined by the negative to her own definition in the positive" (*RPO* 27). But certain details about Brooks's career, if nothing else, should encourage critics not to draw too bright a line between her pre-1967 and post-1967 commitments. For one thing, Brooks doesn't renounce the accolades and awards bestowed on her by the white critical establishment—neither in the 1972 autobiography nor in the 1996 sequel, *Report from Part Two*. For another, despite her parents' neglect of "black glory," her deep affection for them and for her childhood happiness hardly faltered (as both autobiographies plainly demonstrate). It is not surprising, then, that for every critic invested in aligning Brooks with the politics of rage and radicalization, another sees her as committed to affirming the lives of ordinary, moderate black folk who, against America's racist odds, stand for understated heroic resilience; calm self-determination; and cheerful, near-poor, lower-middle-class dignity—all of which square with the American value system.[93]

In a remarkably conciliatory essay from 1972 (evidently before he turned against integrationist poetics), Baker himself seeks in a sense to resolve this tension. First, he argues that Brooks exemplifies a double consciousness in the mode of Du Bois, a duality of white style and black content that generates her dynamic poetics of realism and imaginative expansion. Second, he insists that through this dual insight, Brooks portrays the "truth" of modern life: "Brooks's protagonists, personae, and speakers, in short, capture all of life's complexities, particularly the complexity of an industrialized age."[94] This picture of Brooks's literary complexity is in many ways persuasive. But if we accept the method of Baker's reconciliation through complexity and difficulty, we then also need to acknowledge the striking resemblance between Baker's argument and the sort advanced by Lionel Trilling, that quintessential midcentury white liberal intellectual. His 1949 preface to *The Liberal Imagination* famously called on critics to attend to literature as "the human activity that takes the fullest and most precise account of variousness, possibility, complexity, and difficulty."[95] Furthermore, Baker echoes the liberal versions of appreciation proffered by Paul Engle and Dan Jaffe when he goes on to claim that Brooks's pursuit of truth allows her to transcend ideological consistency—for "truth, one likes to feel, always lies beyond the boundaries of any one ideology"—and appraises her work as "equal[ing] the best in the black and white literary traditions."[96] This aesthetic judgment effectively locates Brooks's transcendence within the liberal integrationist framework. The truth he appeals to may erase the boundaries of racial ideology, but its predication on attentiveness to empirical realities and complexities as well as on what he calls "the imaginative intellect" draws this idea of truth deep into the operations of liberal epistemology.[97]

Baker thus exemplifies one version of the general predicament that Kenneth W. Warren describes as marking the postwar period's racial-literary discourse, namely, of attempting simultaneously to argue for African American writing's racial particularity and its aesthetic excellence. An assertion of the latter quality invariably reinscribes the terms and conditions of the white literary aesthetic that the critic had hoped to transcend. As Warren sees it, African American literature in this period was practically defined by this duality: it "was a literature in which claiming to be *different from* and claiming to be *the same as* the dominant society could appear to have equal critical force."[98] He further explains how this duality has evolved within mainstream institutions over more recent decades. Since the 1970s, university programs in African American studies have been designed to promote desegregation and integration and thus to "mirror" on the curricular level the Supreme Court's mandate to desegregate public schools. "That the major centers of black studies today are in places like Harvard, Princeton, and Yale rather than, say, the Atlanta University Center" speaks to the success of this integrationist vision.[99] In the postwar era of welfare-state institutionalism and even in the ensuing decades, the integrationist ideology has proven remarkably difficult to throw off.

This insight that Baker at once proffers and sidesteps and that Warren confirms should form the basis for considering Brooks's place in literary and cultural history. Brooks's very formation as a writer was indebted to dominant institutions and integrationist politics. As she recounts with gratitude in her 1996 autobiography, she grew up in a household devoted to that icon of liberal humanism, the five-foot shelf of Harvard Classics—her "father's wedding gift to [her] mother."[100] Two of the three high schools she attended were racially mixed (*RPO* 172). She obtained her first job after junior college through the Illinois State Employment Service (162). Arguably more germane to her literary career, the formative poetry workshop she attended in the early 1940s was integrated under the direction of the white editor of *Poetry* magazine, Inez Cunningham Stark. Indeed, the South Side Community Center in which the workshop took place was an integrated WPA project, dedicated by

Eleanor Roosevelt in 1941.[101] In the key of integrationist irony, Brooks concludes her first autobiography with an anecdote about her young daughter's selection, from the animal welfare shelter, of the family's beloved and presumably race-blind dog, Fluffy. It had "off-gold . . . off-white" fur and was so "excitedly" and "happily" chosen that it "planted" its paws "firmly on the backs of little twin black dogs" (215). Here Brooks seems to channel Maud Martha, running into David McKempster yet again.

With the postwar integrationist paradigm thus effectively baked in, Brooks applied her "imaginative intellect" to affirming the relevance, rather than the inapplicability, of the welfare state's core values to African American life and literature. Indeed, she can be seen to challenge the cultural logic Arthur P. Davis invoked in his 1956 essay, "Integration and Race Literature," when he disparaged "surface integration and token integration" over and against "actual" integration.[102] Whereas Davis doesn't name the Pulitzer (or anything else for that matter) as an example of token integration, his attention to Brooks in the essay seems partly due to the fact that she was the first African American to win the award (in 1950). Further, his dichotomous taxonomy implies that "token" integration functions in a zero-sum way to cancel "actual" integration, that it somehow masks or prevents people from seeing the glaring facts of everyday racial discrimination. By this logic token integration becomes inherently suspect. Brooks, however, exemplifies the operative possibility of a different racial-political math, one that is additive rather than subtractive. Both autobiographies contain lengthy passages (some are pages long) in which Brooks recounts the plethora of honors and awards she has received, the schools and centers that have been named after her, the speeches she's been invited to give, and so forth. Her tone in these passages is neither boastful nor humble but deeply appreciative, acknowledging in a manner that stresses reciprocity what she's brought to black and American literary arts and what she's received in return. Describing her work as poetry consultant at the Library of Congress, for instance, she delights in the way "everyone" in the office "treated my work, my ideas, my preferences with respect, concern and warm enthusiasm."[103]

More important, Brooks deploys her recognition capital in a manner that makes hash of Davis's taxonomy. She shows how various practices of integration may flow through mutually reinforcing, rather than rivalrous, circuits of influence. Her possession of sufficient celebrity to warrant the publication of an autobiography allows her to exploit this venue to promote the black activist Don L. Lee's revisionist view of integration, as she quotes his poem, one word per line, titled "The New Integrationist": "I / seek / integration / of / negroes / with / black / people" (*RPO* 45). In this poem, integration isn't disavowed but rather reconceived as leveraging a politics of race solidarity. It recognizes strength in numbers and cohesion. One takeaway for Brooks from the Fisk conference was that there was no shortage of black people who were now prepared to repeat "the Baraka shout," the "substance" of which was "Up against the wall, white man!" (45). Brooks stressed, however, that the more important lesson was not being "*against white*, but FOR *black*" (85). This reorientation entailed Brooks's heightened engagement as an institution builder: for instance, by leaving Harper and Row to publish with black-owned presses (Broadside, Third World, and eventually her own, David Press, named after her father); developing a writers' workshop—not unlike Inez Cunningham Stark's—for the Blackstone Rangers, a "teenage gang in Chicago" (168); and sponsoring literary contests for elementary and high-school students (141).[104] In other words, Brooks's "new integrationist" ambitions were animated by the same liberal values that animated the old integrationist paradigm. Her investment in black institutions, in which various modes of black solidarity combined to expand the black literary economy, had everything to do with helping people flourish. Her activism stemmed less from what Michael Omi and Howard Winant consider the Black Power movement's "politicization of black identity [or] *the rearticulation of black collective subjectivity*" than from the welfare state's idea of well-being.[105] It isn't black ontology she cares about but rather socioeconomic justice for blacks. She need not burn her Pulitzer.

Toward the end of *Report from Part One* Brooks pauses to relate an anecdote redolent of this new integrationist activism, one that speaks not only to the intimate circuitry of various integrationist practices but also to the additive happiness effects of her institution-building project. After having visited one of Chicago's schools to give a poetry reading—one of her methods of simultaneously exploiting and increasing her recognition capital—she received some good news about a sixteen-year-old boy named Placido Tugo who was in attendance. He was so struck by her poem "We Real Cool" that he reversed his clearly nonincrementalist decision to drop out of school. Brooks was inspired to send the boy a follow-up note: "What a happiness to know that words of mine could influence one of the largest decisions you will ever make ... For this alone, I am most happy that I could come to read to you. . . . I am sure your teachers and principal will do everything possible to help you. They are excited and happy that you are determined to continue" (214). Here Brooks locates—and implies the legitimacy of—her and the school agents' happiness deep in the institutional matrix of the welfare state. Not unlike Philip Roth's Neil Klugman at his job in the public library, the adults in Brooks's classroom justifiably thrive by collaborating with an underprivileged kid to talk him off the ledge of socioeconomic doom.

Near-Cruel Optimism

In the Placido anecdote one may detect Brooks's simultaneously circular and reflexive deployment of the happiness trope, whereby the teenager is glad to learn Brooks's "good lesson" about staying in school and Brooks as social worker is glad to nudge him toward his newfound preference (*RPO* 214). It thus recalls Maud Martha's circular way of preferring what she has and having what she prefers, along with her reflexive way of analogically liking herself. This reflexive circularity, Brooks implies, is built into the logic of midcentury liberalism. It figures the structural dynamic through which its legal and social institutions legitimate themselves—that is, by referring to the new liberalism's predicative values rather than to divine truth or to natural law. The anecdote thus allegorizes the intrinsic universalism informing Brooks's new integrationist project, insisting as it does on the applicability of happiness's conditions of possibility even to those whom the system appears devastatingly to fail, such as young black men.

This integrationist project stands out against the countercultural trend in the 1960s and 1970s, when confidence in universal applicability was on the wane and the reflexive welfare state became more susceptible to attacks by opponents from within. Alongside the rise of black nationalism and the increasing authenticity of black rage, the New Left generated fresh suspicion of the welfare state. As historian Howard Brick puts it, the counterculture "understood [the welfare state] as a hierarchical, repressive order of 'corporate liberalism.'"[106] Such perspectives led among other things to a bifurcation of temporal values—whereas liberalism's commitment to "long-range needs was perforce focused on central, national institutions," New Left radicals turned to "an antinomian dynamic of self-gratification that undermined the communal ethos needed for society" to work out long-term solutions to systemic problems.¹⁰⁷ This charismatic alternative to the system deeply informs Brooks's most famous poem, "We Real Cool" (1960), which ventriloquizes the Black English of seven South Side pool players' enumeration of immediately gratifying alternatives to school while intimating the palpable seduction of antinomian insurgence:

> We real cool. We
> Left school. We
>
> Lurk late. We
> Strike straight. We
>
> Sing sin. We
> Thin gin. We
>
> Jazz June. We
> Die soon.¹⁰⁸

Although the poem succeeded as a cautionary tale for Placido when read aloud by its author at his school, the fatalist alacrity of its final declarative underscores the countercultural compulsion to resist the "strong measure of optimism" that animated midcentury liberal activism.¹⁰⁹

To put it another way, the hipster bravado visible in each of the poem's declaratives captures the overdetermined spirit of what Lauren Berlant calls the "cruel optimism" of the good life as hegemonic aspiration. Functioning as both a description of late capitalism's affective structure and a diagnostic theory of this structure's effects on subjectivity, cruel optimism identifies an affliction that fills the vacuum created by liberal capitalism's undelivered promises. Hegemonic optimism elicits attachments to things that bring about "the attrition of the very thriving that is supposed to be made possible in the work of attachment in the first place."¹¹⁰ Under conditions of socioeconomic precarity, such attachments are particularly troubling in that they entice those whose heads are barely above water to drift into further depths of desire, thereby weakening their capacity to latch onto whatever practical support may be available. Drawing explicitly on Eve Sedgwick's work but without that critic's commitment to a "reparative" dialectic, Berlant predicates the theory of cruel optimism on the psychopolitical truth claim of misrecognition. This is the "process by which fantasy recalibrates what we encounter so that we can imagine that something or someone can fulfill our desire[.] ... To misrecognize is not to err, but to project qualities onto something so that we can love, hate, and manipulate it for having those qualities—which it might or might not have."[111]

Among the many recent works of cultural theory that enjoin us to reexamine more skeptically the value of liberalism, Berlant's is one of the most elaborate and insightful and is arguably the most relevant to this chapter's effort to unpack Brooks's idea of happiness. There are surprising similarities between Berlant's archival method of gathering subjects (from works of literature and film by diverse contemporary artists including John Ashbery, Charles Johnson, Mary Gaitskill, and the Dardenne brothers) who suffer pronounced deprivation and abuse—from unemployment and overwork to incest, fat shame, and suburban tedium—and Brooks's literary method of assembling casts of socioeconomically injured South Side figures (in books of poems such as *A Street in Bronzeville* [1945] and *The Bean Eaters* [1960] and in a single long poem like "In the Mecca" [1968]). Both methods amount to a kind of selective sampling, which enables both poet and critic to develop psychosocial insights into what Berlant calls "genres" of damaged being, suggesting their representative status. As we'll see, however, the similarities between their approaches to these samples do not go all the way down. Brooks descends into the netherworld of cruel optimism not in order to embrace the totality of its truth claims but rather to become intimately familiar with its charismatic logic and thereby defeat its claims on its own ground.

To return to Brooks's seven pool players, for instance, Berlant's theory helps to make sense of their brisk alliteration and monosyllabic diction. While conveying lively buoyancy, the verbal style also suggests a scene of misrecognition in which their enunciation of self-gratifying alternatives to school—a grotesque parody of the free market's phantasmagoria of choice—discloses the stammering, fragmented, terminal voices beneath a sheen of unanimity. The poem's enjambments—seven "We's" for seven brothers, each an assertive air punch at the end of a broken line—render the final line, "Die soon," both punch-drunk jokey and painfully fatalist. The dropouts, no longer boys but not yet adults, are encircled by their uniting chant of misrecognition, "We," and thus left to circle the drain of their own hedonic preferences. "Soon" names the not quite now of being at cruel optimism's drowning point. Berlant's interpretive paradigm also helps to identify confreres of cruel optimism elsewhere in Brooks's work—in the eponymous figure of "The Sundays of Satin-Legs Smith" (1945), for instance, or the pretentious fellows belonging to the Foxy Cats Club in *Maud Martha*, or virtually everybody nursing an attachment to life in the notoriously decrepit apartment building, the Mecca, in her long poem "In the Mecca." As the moniker suggests, Satin-Legs Smith's mental resources—with his attachment to colorful zoot suits and to equally tacky "vivid" women, with his devotion to a Sunday routine of movies, dates, and diner comfort food—amount to a psychic deflection of his world's entrapping poverty. He is incapable of acknowledging his "old intimacy with alleys [and] garbage pails" or that he is one of those "people" who "want so much that they do not know" how "promise piled over and betrayed" them (*WGB* 27, 28).

The speaker in this poem appears at first glance to adopt the position of expert authority that Berlant indicates the diagnostic "analyst" holds, as she "more easily perceive[s]" than the subjects themselves "the cruelty of optimistic attachment." Such pathetic beings can't see that their lives are little more than an endurance of "merely living" or "wearing out" under "capitalized time's shortened circuit."[112] From this knowing critical perspective it's possible to draw a through line from the speaker of "Satin-Legs" to the speaker of "In the Mecca," in which the poet hovers sympathetically near but cognitively above the inhabitants of the dilapidated, squalid tenement—once an architectural gem and tourist attraction and later a sort of miniature Cabrini-Green.[113] In the manner of reporter-analyst, the poem's speaker simultaneously documents the dismal straits of the building's multitudinous residents and shadows the slow-motion desperation of the search through the building by one woman, Mrs. Sallie, for her missing daughter, Pepita. The speaker appears to view doubtfully these damaged residents' psychic mechanisms for sustaining attachment—for instance, one kid's identification with the mythic heroics of Johnny Appleseed (*WGB* 384) and another's attempt to imitate his cat, which is "happier than people" because it stays detached from them and doesn't read newspapers (383).

Such figures of quiet misrecognition prepare the poem's ground for its portrayal of the cruelty of normative optimism for taking the nuclear family itself as an object of attachment. Mrs. Sallie shares Satin-Legs's surname, Smith, which suggests a similarity in their psychic modalities despite vast differences in life experience and situation. As she conducts her dogged search, apartment by apartment, for her precious ninth child, she exemplifies what Berlant calls adults' "fantasy" of "want[ing] to pass the promise of the promise [of familial love] on to their children."[114] In this manner, Mrs. Sallie's belated and futile attempt to protect her child from harm—an attempt formally stalled and strung out by the speaker's dilative stops at the neighbors' doors—draws the poem into the genre Berlant calls "situation tragedy." Here "people are fated to express their flaws episodically, over and over, without learning, changing, being relieved, becoming better, or dying."[115] From this standpoint, Mecca residents gain as little from loving their children as from killing them, which it turns out one of them has done. When Pepita's body is discovered under the cot of the murderer, "in dust with cockroaches," her mother recalls in grief how the girl once "wriggled, like a robin" (*WGB* 403). This analogy effectively inscribes the convulsive logic of cruel optimism. Its theory of psychic necessity reduces human aspiration to the status of animal impulse. Indeed these "little wrigglings," which Brooks invokes again in the poem's penultimate line (403), may serve as cruel optimism's presiding diagnostic metaphor.

With a preponderance of evidence pointing toward the conditions of cruel optimism, both in Brooks's poems and on the South Side, it may thus be tempting to read her as Berlant reads her contemporary Herbert Marcuse, namely, as a prophet of this psychosocial theory; his "prophetic description of postwar U.S. society charts it [the logic of optimistic attachment] out: while people comfort themselves with stories about beating the system or being defeated by it, they 'continue the struggle for existence in painful, costly and obsolete forms.'"[116] Berlant might have just as easily named C. Wright Mills of *White Collar*, Arthur Miller of *Death of a Salesman*, or any number of midcentury critics of American liberal-capitalist mass culture. And yet to add Brooks to the list would require filtering out the distinctive sounds of her foundational commitments. It would require, for instance, overlooking the lines in "Satin-Legs" that, dripping with sarcasm, map out a strategy for leaving this figure in the lurch of cruel optimism:

> Ah, there is little hope. You might as well—
> Unless you care to set the world a-boil
> And do a lot of equalizing things,
> Remove a little ermine, say, from kings,
> Shake hands with paupers and appoint them men,

> For instance—certainly you might as well
> Leave him his lotion, lavender and oil. (*WGB* 27)

In these lines Brooks nods to—while rhetorically daring the reader to ignore—the ethical scaffolding that would keep Satin-Legs within the purview of the welfare state. She imagines the reformist imperatives of redistribution (wealth from kings) and reciprocal recognition (equalizing identities) as conditions of possibility—or, more precisely, of moral and political necessity—even for figures so nearly fallen to cruel optimism's depredations as Satin-Legs. As the critic R. Baxter Miller argues, "For Brooks's narrator and the [implied] reader to 'shake hands with paupers and appoint them men' is to perceive that worth and happiness are human rights, not social privileges."[117] Further, Brooks introduces conditions of judgment that invite reflexive doubt about the speaker's assessment of Satin-Legs as a profligate. However sincere her disapproval of his ways of pursuing happiness, her recognition of his status as a man deserving respect entails her recognition of his capacity to have and express preferences, even tacky, unedifying ones. Since this ethical recognition is abstract, it remains conceptually distinct from the social and psychological mechanics of misrecognition that give rise to cruel optimism. In other words, the speaker's third-person judgment runs up against Satin-Legs's first-person presence. Enjoined to consider this presence, we must now see that the poem's figure of a handshake all but asks Satin-Legs himself what he thinks about his pursuits.

This near-colloquy brings us back to "We Real Cool," in which we do hear directly from the dropouts themselves. Whether understood as a compressed cautionary tale; a revelry song that, in Hortense J. Spillers's view, "subvert[s] the romance of sociological pathos"; or a proleptic elegy that protests the limited career options of young black men, the poem's concluding reference to fatality would suggest its plural speakers' antithetical relation to the proposition of living.[118] Yet Brooks encourages us to regard these fellows as aesthetically interested in themselves and as possibly harboring deep down a mode of normative optimism that is less cruel than it is usual. For one thing, the concluding line's speculative declaration displaces the previous lines' descriptive declarations, which allows for the faint but genuine possibility that they know not of what they speak, that they might be selling themselves short and "soon" find a way, like the student Placido, to turn themselves around.

For another, Brooks aligned this herd of cool cats on more than one occasion with that ubiquitous postwar legend, Kilroy. "The ending WEs in 'We Real Cool,'" she explained, "are tiny, wispy, weakly argumentative 'Kilroy-is-here' announcements. The boys have no accented sense of themselves, yet they are aware of a semi-defined personal importance" (*RPO* 185). In other words, despite her obvious preference for the Placido-style turnaround, Brooks imbues her dropouts with the disembodied yet lively presence of old-style graffiti expression—a kind of street-culture version of a line that Third World Press included in their 1993 reissue of *Maud Martha* as a quasi-epigraph: "Maud Martha is still alive" (*MM* n.p.).[119] Brooks does what she can to suggest that the boys too need to be imagined as worthy of recognition.[120] Indeed they retain the kernel of potential that Maud Martha observes in Clement, the little boy who lives in a nearby kitchenette and invariably appears "happy" and "spirited." After school, when he would see his mother coming around the corner, "he would run to [her] and almost throw his little body at her. 'Here I am, mother! Here I am!'" (116). This intertextual echo suggests that the later poem draws on the same kind of conceptual "hope" that Brooks refers to in "Satin-Legs," which isn't so much a matter of having a positive feeling or a sunny disposition as it is of insisting on liberalism's ethical and cognitive perspective—of seeing, as it were, a remediable duck subject to the equalizing logic of reciprocity rather than a pathologized rabbit subject to cruel misrecognition.

Brooks's poems of what we might call near-cruel optimism register the reflexive circularity of a midcentury writer who, testing the ethical and cognitive limits of liberal possibility, reveals a deep sensitivity to the pressure that racial and socioeconomic injury puts on her ingrained commitments. They shed light on the massive aesthetic and conceptual resources Brooks marshals to weather this pressure's colonization of her mind. In turn, her poems of near-cruel optimism may be understood to put pressure on postwar liberals' overweening confidence in their ideological triumph—on those, say, who turned away from everyday politics because they believed arguments for equal job opportunities and equitable housing and educational facilities didn't require the liberal imagination. Although the demolition of the Mecca in 1952 was supposed to testify, along with other urban renewal projects, to the efficacy of the welfare state's goodwill, the fact that Brooks revisits this building as an emblem of social collapse in 1968 indicates the political and poetic necessity of vigilant pressure. Things don't always get better. Finally and most powerfully, however, Brooks's poems of near-cruel optimism enjoin those who simplify, give up on, or defiantly reject liberalism to lean away from the charismatic logic of misrecognition and to recall the human potential for something more than robin-like wriggling.

What prevented Brooks from participating in the antiliberal demolition crusade was her ability to lean into the 1960s and 1970s counterculture without abandoning her 1940s and 1950s "voice." For her, this tether amounted to a kind of existential rule of thumb: "My newish voice," she declared in her 1972 autobiography, "will not be an imitation of the contemporary young black voice, which I so admire, but an extending adaptation of today's G. B. voice" (*RPO* 183). This adaptive orientation is on view a few years earlier as well, when she ends her volume *In the Mecca* with two brief but majestic hortatory poems, "The Sermon on the Warpland" and "The Second Sermon on the Warpland." The second poem concludes with the oft-cited line, "Conduct your blooming in the noise and whip of the whirlwind" (*WGB* 426), an instruction that critics generally take to reflect her post-1967 embrace of the tempestuous conditions of black radical politics. What tends to be overlooked, however, is that in Brooks's lexicon, "blooming" is the whole point of welfare-state liberalism.

Queer Consumerism, Straight Happiness
Patricia Highsmith's "Right Economy"

The Price of Salt (1952) is often touted as the first lesbian novel with a happy ending. In the afterword to its 1990 reissue, Patricia Highsmith explains that she first published it under a pseudonym to avoid being "labelled a lesbian-book writer"; she also draws attention to the fact that the novel first appeared in hardcover and received "some serious and respectable reviews" before being marketed as lesbian pulp and selling a million copies.[1] Defensive vanity gives way to more dignified pride when Highsmith describes the stream of fan letters, from men as well as women, thanking her for telling a story in which homosexuals did not have "to pay for their deviation by cutting their wrists, drowning themselves in a swimming pool, or . . . switching to heterosexuality . . . or by collapsing—alone and miserable and shunned—into a depression equal to hell" (*PS* 261). Readers liked the fact that her main characters, Therese and Carol, "were going to try to have a future together" (261). Highsmith also tells of replying to some of these fans, encouraging the lonely ones to seek similarly inclined people in "a larger town" (262). There is agreeable irony in this image of Highsmith—whom biographers portray as orneriness incarnate and as a sexual predator, misanthrope, and habitual racist—embracing the novel's therapeutic and educative effects. Like any good liberal, she not only affirms the interpretation of the novel's happy ending but also accepts as legitimate the values this ending reflects.

One may infer from her account that these fans were also good liberals—at least in their manner of reading. Steven Knapp explains that the paradigmatic liberal reader "discovers, by reading literature, the conflicts, inconsistencies, and overdeterminations among her own dispositions" and is thus able to "read *herself* as an instance of descriptive representation." When literature is subject to a reader's dialectic of identification and disinterest, of involvement and self-awareness, it doesn't so much dictate values to readers as it "helps us find out what our evaluative dispositions *are*."[2] Such readers evidently took away from *The Price of Salt* valuable self-confirmation, and perhaps even inspiration or courage to pursue same-sex desire, without confusing their lives with those of Highsmith's characters. A distilled formulation of this ambidexterity appears in one of the letters Highsmith quotes from, in which the reader thanks her for the "story. It is a little like my own story" (*PS* 262). The unassuming analogical phrase here, "a little like," allows for capacious differences between the author's and the reader's worlds, even as the reader revels in their likeness.

In the postwar era this queer-liberal reading style played a crucial role in the birth of a vibrant lesbian subculture. Jennifer Worley has shown how lesbian pulp fiction, despite its general aim to gratify heterosexual male prurience and despite the era's oppressive policing of homosexuality, functioned to render queer female identity fathomable: "The pulps offered [these] readers a vocabulary of dress, language, gesture, sexual practice, and public behavior from which they could both forge their own performance of sexual identity and 'read' the performances of others." Anecdotal evidence confirms the pulps' facilitation—"as physical objects of exchange [among friends], as conduits to a shared pleasure"—of women's emergent but still uncertain sense of same-sex desire.[3] Here readerly agency and consumerist agency dovetail to the benefit of self-inquiring, socially forming subjects. This history supports Michael Warner's contention that "variant desires," like any "deep pleasure," may involve "discovering" something previously undetected, which is to say that these desires need not be considered "legitimate only if they can be shown to be immutable, natural, and innate."[4] (This does not deny the possibility but only the necessity of innate desire.) This is part of his broader critique of the way majoritarian culture, in privileging the normal, stigmatizes deviant sex practices and drives them from public view. Worley's account reminds us, however, that majoritarian culture's economic structure—particularly its consumerist focus and its knack for market segmentation—has for decades contributed importantly to the production of queer knowledge.

Furthermore, in keying queer desire enhanced by liberal agency to personal discovery as well as addressing the question of legitimacy, these accounts gesture to one of liberalism's intractable values: the development or flourishing of persons according to their varying conceptions of the good. Promoted since the eighteenth century in the United States as "the pursuit of happiness," this core tenet was enshrined in the postwar era by the United Nations' (UN) 1948 Universal Declaration of Human Rights (UDHR) as "the full development of the human personality."[5] The premium the post-Holocaust era placed on self-realization testified to—indeed it was the practical extension of—the premium it placed on the equal "dignity and worth of the human person," to cite the UDHR again.[6] At once chastening and enabling, these abstract ideals formed the basis of midcentury liberalism's self-legitimating project. They constituted a secular and cognitive ethical framework within which a polity's specific social, cultural, and economic practices could evolve.[7]

Historical propinquity alone invites consideration of Highsmith's legitimation strategies in light of this heightened human rights consciousness. But there are closer ties. In what follows I argue that UDHR liberalism, besides circulating in the penumbra of *The Price of Salt*'s reception, enjoys a lively presence within the novel. As the novel's celebrated ending suggests, the sign under which the values of human worth and self-fulfillment operate is happiness. We shall see, however, that the trope of happiness in *The Price of Salt* does much more than help to legitimate Therese's project of self-development, important as that project is. I suggest that it also functions to draw into intimate proximity two sources of postwar American consternation: the question of same-sex desire's legitimacy and the question of postwar consumer society's legitimacy. Highsmith enlists the ideology of consumerism to legitimate same-sex desire, and as a conduit to personal discovery and a mode of defending homosexual pleasure, that feature of postwar society accomplishes much. But like the ideology it mirrors—namely, democratic pluralism—it also bears liabilities. Thus only by reversing course, by enlisting same-sex desire to legitimate consumerism, does Highsmith manage to figure her characters as liberals in pursuit of their own flourishing.[8]

Eleanor Roosevelt, who chaired the UN Human Rights Commission responsible for drafting the UDHR, evidently liked the book *Strangers on a Train* (1948).[9] In this novel Highsmith effectively honors UDHR values in the breach: Bruno recognizes the "priceless[ness]" of Miriam's life after taking it; her husband Guy, too, concedes that she may not have been "worth a great deal as a person . . . by [his second wife] Anne's standards or by anyone's. But she had been a human being," implying her worthiness of at least some life.[10] By 1955 Highsmith seemed to enjoy parodying these values. One of Tom Ripley's favorite impersonation "skits" is of "Mrs. Roosevelt writing 'My Day' after a visit to a clinic for unmarried mothers."[11] He clearly does not take very seriously this champion of liberal universalism, who wrote frequently about her work on the HRC in her syndicated column. And yet Tom's parodic attitude is at least partly undone by the travesty of his career as killer-gentleman of leisure. Tom may have the capacity, as Michael Trask has trenchantly argued, to align his "method" of impersonation with liberalism's prized ontology of autonomy, but that achievement has little going for it, Highsmith implies, without a supplemental respect for human pricelessness—not only others' but his own.[12] He and his wife are what Grey Gowrie calls "living-dead people," for whom material comfort and convenience fill the moral vacuum.[13] This condition arguably finds its fullest figuration in the scene in which Tom is buried alive in *Ripley Under Ground* (1970). The episode is brief enough to spare him the fate of the Guanajuato mummy that Theodore contemplates in *A Game for the Living* (1958).

Between Bruno and Guy's honoring breach and Tom and Heloise's deadening crypt, Carol and Therese's happy end crops up. Tapping the literary tradition most congenial to imagining self-realization as a good thing, the bildungsroman, the conclusion of *The Price of Salt* signals Therese's happy reversal of the "hopelessness" she suffers at the start of the narrative "of ever being the person she wanted to be" (*PS* 14).[14] Along the way, by my casual count, she and other characters experience or assess their happiness more than three dozen times. As a discursive trope, happiness conventionally involves not only feelings but also cognitive and evaluative faculties. Indeed, happiness could not maintain its cultural prominence without its capacity to signify something other (or more) than sentient feeling. As the cultural critic Sara Ahmed observes, it "mediates between individual and social, private and public, affective and evaluative, mind and body, as well as norms, rules and ideals and ways of being in the world."[15] In *The Price of Salt* happiness is often invoked to indicate Therese's bumpy progress toward a sexual orientation that satisfies, but it also becomes Highsmith's means for testing the limits of liberal normativity, as when Therese entertains the idea that "love" may be less a matter of the "warm and happy" feelings she sometimes has for her boyfriend Richard than of the "blissful insanity" that Carol provokes (23, 43).[16]

Within Highsmith's intellectual orbit, the *Partisan Review*'s 1948 publication of Lionel Trilling's essay on the Kinsey Report (to which I return later) and of Leslie Fiedler's landmark essay on Huck and Jim reflects midcentury liberalism's growing concern to engage seriously with the question of homosexuality.[17] Ironically, however, in Highsmith's novel the homosexual theme commands so much attention that critics generally overlook its trenchant engagement with the era's more pervasive concern to grasp the implications of consumer society. Briefly, as the United States shifted from a wartime economy of scarcity to a consumer economy of abundance, American society was beset with a crisis of legitimacy. Some critics decried Americans' ostensibly insatiable appetite for material goods as the ruin of genuine goodness—what Christian existentialist Joseph Haroutunian called "living according to truth and right."[18] For him and his ilk, happiness itself was no longer legitimate because it reflected the triumph of "a new infinite," provided by comfort-producing machines, over "the old eternal" of transcendent good, which an economy of scarcity and its attendant sense of "man's finitude" had managed to preserve.[19] As the historian Howard Mumford Jones memorably intoned in 1953, the fully privatized right to pursue happiness now "guarantee[d] the American citizen the ghastly privilege of pursuing a phantom and embracing a delusion."[20]

Others worried instead that the onset of prosperity after World War II had, as David Riesman put it, "depleted" Americans' "stockpile of new and exhilarating wants"; they were now facing a troubling "wantlessness." This is why, according to journalist and editor Eric Larrabee, abundance "has not necessarily made people happier": "We seem to have constructed a machine which can satisfy wants faster than it can create them, yet is dependent on wants in order to keep going. We are running low on our supply of utopian dreams[.] . . . We are so doubtful about the national aims that the President has appointed a commission to find out what they are."[21] For all its devotion to self-examination, Larrabee muses, the nation can't seem to parlay its material and intellectual resources into anything it can strongly believe in or be committed to. Here the absence of new value and meaning amounted to a failure of applied political-economic imagination. Americans risked delegitimation, in other words, by failing to flourish. Either way, postwar prosperity threatened to render American liberalism a casualty of its own success.

The Price of Salt, I argue, splits the difference in this debate. As the novel's beginning indicates—both its title and its opening scene of Therese's employment in a Manhattan department store during Christmas rush—the world Therese and Carol inhabit is pervaded by commerce and consumerism, by institutions of private enterprise and private life.²² Besides the department store, its emblematic locations are the suburban home Carol lives in and the comfortable sedan she and Therese tour the country in. Therese may loathe the working conditions of the Frankenberg "prison" (*PS* 4), but she's not averse to buying its merchandise, such as the book of Degas reproductions that "Richard wanted and hadn't been able to find anywhere" (93). One of her and Carol's early dates leads them to Chinatown, where they "ducked from one shop to another, looking at things and buying things" (94). On their road trip, they buy things at every turn—from homemade sausages in Pennsylvania for Therese's former coworker Mrs. Robichek to suede shirts in Estes Park for Carol's daughter and for Therese herself (157, 187). Indeed, this cross-country tour is an extension of, rather than an escape from (as some critics suggest), the comfortable life in the suburbs that Carol's estranged husband funds. Consumer agency, as we'll see, becomes the central means by which Therese and Carol signal their mutual interests, probe their desires, and think through a philosophy of happiness. To be sure, their consumerist ethos has some troubling strings attached; it proves both to enable and to obstruct their ambition of self-fulfillment. Still, they take advantage of what historian Joyce Appleby identifies as consumerism's key social and personal value. "It's not that our humanity requires commerce for its fulfilment," she explains, "but rather that in a commercial society, a whole battery of new cultural means has been created to articulate a broader range of human intentions."²³ On balance, Carol and Therese participate in the broadening and validating of this range.

Ice-Cream Cones and Gooey Fudge Sundaes

Critics tend to view *The Price of Salt*'s titular metaphors as signs of the disciplinary penalties that Cold War homophobia imposed on persons who acted on their same-sex desires. Carol and Therese do not, to recall Highsmith's afterword, "pay for" their romance in suicide or mental collapse, but Carol does lose custody of her daughter and Therese is subject to her former boyfriend's epistolary verbal abuse. Yet reading *price* as exclusively sacrificial or punitive and *salt* as exclusively sexual occludes the homologies that Highsmith labors to establish between amorous and consumer economies, wherein price functions to register potential exchangeability or substitutability and to calibrate desire to the availability of goods or persons. Highsmith keeps a healthy distance from the seductive but radically antisocial vision of the market economy that Michael W. Clune identifies in certain midcentury writers. For William Gaddis, Frank O'Hara, and others, "the price system structures subjectivity" in that "interest and desire play across an environment already organized by price." An "object of cultural fascination," this "purely economic world" allows them to imagine economic activity such as price comparison and consumer choice as being entirely independent of social or intersubjective relations.[24] In fact, that is this world's raison d'être: the writers Clune examines promote an aesthetic alternative to realism's representation of actually existing conditions. They want us to accept "that literature's value is not always a social value." Its value might be instead to advance the idea of an aesthetic world elsewhere.[25]

By contrast, Highsmith adheres closely to the realist literary tradition, which more readily accommodates authorial ambitions to reflect, revalue, and potentially transform the social world. In her exploration of the relays between amorous and consumer economies, however, Highsmith does not assume that these psychosocial structures entirely organize midcentury experience and value. Crucially, she suggests, not everything valued can be priced—specifically, not UDHR ideas of human dignity and worth—even if the priceless status of the human being often appears overshadowed by a market logic of rarity. The novel poses in effect the following questions: When is the happiness derived from choosing a same-sex love partner a lot like the pleasure derived from choosing an expensive leather handbag (such as the one Therese buys for Carol)? Conversely, when is the happiness derived from a leather handbag a lot like the pleasure derived from a love partner? When are these choices and conceptions of the good not at all similar, and why not? The ethical stakes of *The Price of Salt* ultimately depend on the viability and the intelligibility of these questions.

On the one hand, for the purposes of legitimating same-sex desire, the novel imagines amorous and consumerist modes of desire as practically identical. The homology underwrites Carol's righteous (if unsuccessful) defense against the family court's accusations of her "vice and degeneration" (*PS* 229). Erotic intimacy, she insists, "is a question of pleasure after all, and what's the use debating the pleasure of an ice-cream cone versus a football game—or a Beethoven quartet versus the *Mona Lisa*" (229). Here she banks on the moral triviality of consumer choice and the subjective principle of aesthetic taste to challenge traditional homophobic prejudice. Her consumerist ethos thus avoids the pitfalls and inconsistencies that Lionel Trilling discovers in Alfred Kinsey's scientific arguments in *Sexual Behavior in the Human Male* (1948). Trilling observes that not without disingenuousness does the Kinsey Report reserve its "harshest language" for criticizing "the idea of the Normal" while "letting the idea of the Natural develop quietly into the idea of the Normal." He allows that for liberal Americans committed to tolerance the beneficent effects of establishing "a democratic pluralism of sexuality" are many.[26] For one thing, the pluralist ideology helps to expose the narrow-mindedness of the pervasive tendency to imagine the homosexual as a neurotic, degenerate psychopath. But the Kinsey Report's mission of tolerance hinges on unacknowledged and dubious methodological biases. For instance, it defines male potency in terms of frequency of orgasm rather than in terms of, say, "the ability to withhold orgasm long enough to bring the woman to climax." It also problematically reduces human sexuality to animalistic behavior "by encouraging people in their commitment to mechanical attitudes toward life."[27] As mechanization takes command, Trilling fears (not entirely unlike Haroutunian), people may detach sex from important emotional, social, and moral aspects of their lives.

From Trilling's standpoint, then, Carol's consumerist argument for sexual preference can look like a less fraught form of "democratic pluralism." At least it takes the human subject's pleasure into consideration, whereas Kinsey's methodology neglects to ascertain whether a sex practice "is actually enjoyable."[28] On the other hand, however, although Carol's defense of same-sex desire doesn't rely on scientific authority, her invocation of an aesthetic principle so subjective that it has no "use" for debate introduces pitfalls of its own. One pitfall is indeed the triviality of consumer choice. Carol's indiscriminate array of goods—her analogical slide from the alimentary to the athletic before rendering these pleasures indistinguishable from aural and visual fine arts—certainly provides tolerant liberals such as Kinsey and Trilling a line of defense against conservative moralists. But this blur of consumerist analogies also subjects interpersonal intimacy—more precisely, intimate persons—to the vicissitudes of what social theorists call the overspiritualization and underspiritualization of consumer goods. As Michael Schudson explains, some theorists, such as Raymond Williams, worry about the undervaluation of goods in and of themselves as well as about the overspiritualization of goods via advertising, which "is magic, and it magically associates extra, non-essential meaning with perfectly ordinary, serviceable goods." Meanwhile others, such as Christopher Lasch, worry that "people underspiritualize goods," particularly handcrafted ones that might serve as transitional objects and thus help children develop autonomy. Such volatility forces the question Schudson poses: "What is the appropriate level of aesthetic interest a consumer good should evoke?"[29] He identifies numerous social and personal variables that make the question difficult to answer (labor cost, environmental impact, and so forth), whereas Carol's conflation of wide-ranging consumer pleasures renders her entirely unable to field the question. The implied substitutability of one analogy for another too easily elevates ice-cream consumption to the experiential status of interpersonal intimacy just as it too readily demotes an enduring work of art to the status of something as fleeting as sex.

A related yet greater liability of Carol's consumerist defense is what I'll call the Humbert Humbert syndrome of converting politically sanctioned privacy into solipsistic—and, in his case, criminal—subjectivity. Terry Castle has written provocatively about the resemblance between Nabokov's *Lolita* (1955) and *The Price of Salt*—the "transgressive sex," the detective-trailed road trip, and the "frenzied bid for freedom."[30] The comparison is instructive, although I want here to suggest that it is less because of the novels' similarly dramatic adventures than because of their differently calibrated relays between sex, consumerism, and happiness. As many critics have noted, American consumer culture is both the object of Humbert's bitingly witty contempt and his explanation for handling Lolita as a delectable object of consumption. The girl he describes as the "ideal consumer"—one who "believed, with a kind of celestial trust, any advertisement or advice that appeared in *Movie Love* or *Screen Land*"—is the girl he plies with an endless array of goods—clothes, magazines, tourist souvenirs, and "gooey fudge sundaes."[31] Such gifts are compensation as well as preparation for Humbert's sexual indulgences. The self-described nympholept discerns in Lolita's consumerism a narcissistic self-awareness, and hence cultivation, of her sexual attractiveness but without a corresponding self-awareness of the intersubjective position she might occupy. In the novel's notoriously titillating scene of Humbert's initial orgasmic encounter with her, he counts on her being "safely solipsized": the "child knew nothing."[32] Nabokov reveals, in effect, the conditions necessary for making the happiness (Humbert's) derived from an underage sex partner look a lot like the happiness (Lolita's) derived from a gooey fudge sundae. He also reveals, it should go without saying, the insufficiency of "democratic pluralism" as grounds for legitimating a sexual preference.

But Humbert Humbert hardly need worry about his moral and legal dereliction, because the consumerist logic he embraces also supplies the terms for *exceeding* socially legitimate happiness, for accessing the transcendent realm of religious bliss:

> [The reader] must understand that in the possession and thralldom of a nymphet the enchanted traveler stands, as it were, *beyond happiness*. For there is no other bliss on earth comparable to that of fondling a nymphet. It is *hors concours*, that bliss, it belongs to another class, another plane of sensitivity. Despite . . . the horrible hopelessness of it all, I still dwelled deep in my elected paradise—a paradise whose skies were the color of hell-flames—but still a paradise.[33]

Nabokov suggests that the price Humbert pays for his theosexual consumerism is high—not merely because it involves child abuse and even a murder that Humbert all but overlooks or because it results in his incarceration. Humbert has also forfeited his capacity to validate his happiness; he can merely observe and confirm it. "I have but followed nature," he declares. "I am nature's faithful hound." Earlier he attributes his nymphet addiction to the trauma of having been caught in an "unsuccessful first tryst" with his childhood love Annabel, of never having been able to consummate this love.[34] This etiology serves to attach his sexuality to the very core of his being, rendering him, not Lolita, the novel's true emblem of solipsism.

By conflating happiness and naturalized appetite and by converting both into a ticket to personal salvation in bliss, Humbert pursues a radically subjective conception of the good. This is why he can imagine "horrible hopelessness" as something not to overcome but instead to equate with self-fulfillment. The combination of aesthetic masochism and sexual religiosity (the blessedness of bliss) absolves Humbert not so much of his crime of child abuse—which he recognizes—but of his reckoning with liberal selfhood. That is, in addition to the absence, in his amorous economy, of an acknowledgment of Lolita's inherent worth—her pricelessness—is the absence of an acknowledgment of his own pricelessness. By understanding himself as nature's faithful hound, Humbert forecloses on the possibility of endorsing—or, for that matter, reproaching—his actions. He is unable to see himself, to borrow from the philosopher Christine Korsgaard, "as having a will, as having the kind of *self-conscious* causality that *is* a rational will."[35] This condition of causality drives a wedge between Humbert's self-styled naturalism and liberal self-constitution: "If I am to constitute *myself* as the cause of an action, then I must be able to distinguish between *my* causing the action and some desire or impulse that is 'in me' causing my body to act." This kind of self-claiming understands the self as a necessary value, as priceless; it entails the conversion of historical contingency and personal will into necessity by virtue of "valuing the humanity that is their source."[36] Korsgaard's concern here with the "sources of normativity" is not the familiar moralistic one of theorizing the kind of person who must lay claim to her actions and thus be accountable for them. Rather, she theorizes the kind of person who might change her mind or who might see herself as mistaken. "There is no normativity if you cannot be wrong" in your evaluation of your dispositions and desires.[37] Humbert Humbert is nothing if not confident in being unmistakably and indeed existentially right about his.

In *The Price of Salt* Carol offers no comparable description of herself as hopeless or as nature's hound. But when she asserts the pointlessness of debating subjective taste, she exhibits a kind of contempt for the proposition of mind-changing, which is often the point of debate. Her designation of love partners, alongside works of art, as sources of hedonistic "pleasure" renders them unworthy of interpretative scrutiny or evaluative judgment; she thus severely restricts the significance of choosing one potential partner over another. Although it hardly makes sense to debate a preference for one ice cream flavor over another or even for eating ice cream over watching football (since such preferences have more or less psychophysiological causes and are trivial), when it comes to choosing love partners, UDHR liberalism's commitment to human dignity and fulfillment encourages the engagement of normative, willed mindfulness. Indeed, the novel's overarching portrayal of Carol's slow and rather careful consideration of Therese as a love partner indicates a happy inability to abide by her own pernicious proposition.

Mistaking the Right Economy

In *The Price of Salt*, Therese bears the narrative burden of disclosing the fuller implications of this proposition. She is only nineteen and at stake in her youth is not so much the frisson of her becoming an underage sex victim (Richard complains that since she is not "a child" he can't "report . . . to somebody" that Carol is "committing a crime against" her [PS 136]); rather, it is her relatively unformed personality. Through her, Highsmith stages not only the difficulty of making up one's mind and of building mistake and error into one's constitution but also the perils of deserting this capacity. One might reasonably presume that the novel's most prominent example of a mistake is Therese's fumbling relationship with Richard; certainly, Therese's transformation from a muddled, awkward heterosexual into an ardent, self-aware lesbian indicates her initially mistaken sexual orientation, which gets cleared up once she and Carol find each other. As Alfred Kinsey stated in his second report, *The Sexual Behavior of the Human Female* (1953), new knowledge about all modes of sexual behavior "has increased man's capacity to live happily with himself and his fellow men."[38] But although knowledge may be happiness, I suggest that Highsmith mobilizes Therese's error in sexual orientation less to convey the importance of epistemological self-correction than to disclose the possibility of legitimating amorous attachment. This possibility receives narrative treatment in Therese's halting and mistake-prone process of self-development and culminates in her rapid mind-changing when she meets another woman. Thus things don't get cleared up until the very end of the novel.

Though only a visitor to the suburb, Therese embodies certain dimensions of its ethos, ones that resonate with the potential for making mistakes. Earlier I alluded to the similarity in *The Price of Salt* between the suburban and highway worlds as sites of her and Carol's eager consumerism. But David Riesman's 1952 comments on the suburb suggest that the era's consumerism is significant as a phenomenon of not just alacrity but also awkwardness. Ever the counterintuitionist, he encourages people to think of suburban residents as "explorers" of new "frontiers of consumption" who are thus "opening up new forms of interpersonal understanding [and] new ways of using" private and public institutions such as the home, school, community center, and chapel.[39] Indeed, they can be seen as early adapters to what Article 24 of the UDHR identifies as the right to "rest and leisure." Having served in the early 1940s on an international committee tasked with "drawing up a Bill of Rights," to which he contributed the idea of "reasonable leisure," Riesman understands suburbanites as subject to their own "awkward" behavior, as "likely to pay a price in loneliness and discomfort" for their choices. He thus implies that what the postwar world of abundance really needs are new ways of appreciating the legitimacy of leisure opportunities and that as the site of postwar society's "research and development" the suburb might find legitimacy in the very way its denizens make mistakes as they come to terms with their new rights.[40]

Taking advantage of consumer society's suburb and sedan, Therese figures Americans' inarticulate, clumsy, and even perilous effort to legitimate new opportunities derived from postwar prosperity. She dramatizes the challenge of reading and evaluating one's nontrivial consumerist experiences. Like Carol, she addresses the question of subjective taste's applicability to amorous desire, but she articulates a more adequate response to the "should" in Schudson's question: "What is the appropriate level of aesthetic interest a consumer good should evoke?" It all depends on locating the ground of legitimation, Highsmith suggests, in the conditions of liberal agency. Therese doesn't have lesbian pulps at her disposal to help her find out what her sexual disposition might be. Instead she has random items of consumption—things like a pair of "green woolen gloves" given to her by Sister Alicia when she was a child in an orphanage: only after Carol enters her life and she begins to wonder about her impulses and patterns of desire does she come to understand why she has held onto these gloves without ever wearing them. They seem to function for her as a kind of inert transitional object, providing cold comfort at best and little to no psychic security; by the end of the narrative she is prepared "to throw them away" (*PS* 249). Her hoarding impulse is thus retrospectively recognized as a sign of attachment—possibly oedipal, possibly more straightforwardly erotic—that had been too powerful to ignore but too confusingly encrypted to grasp. With similarly clouded intuition, she resists a Christmas gift from Richard's mother—a handmade dress—while insisting that Carol accept her Christmas gift—an expensive leather handbag. Pawning a necklace Richard gave her and still nearly emptying her bank account in order to purchase the handbag, Therese witnesses herself mapping out locations of pleasure, attraction, anxiety, obligation, and expenditure, some of which she wants to avoid and others of which she wants to visit.

Highsmith employs a focalizing technique to underscore Therese's evolving self-awareness. Her inwardness and narrow social horizon seem to make her less susceptible than others of her generation to what Riesman in 1953 called the era's "Veblenism," which regards consumption choices—whether conspicuous, studiously nonconspicuous, or even anticonsumerist—as "determined mainly by the desire to impress others."[41] Her self-awareness, then, isn't the sort Riesman worries about in his college students who, in absorbing Veblen's critique, have themselves become unable to appreciate "whimsical and idiosyncratic" elements in their own "consumer behavior."[42] They too readily accept Veblen's social theory in which, as Colin Campbell more recently put it, "consumption is a form of communication in which 'signals' concerning wealth (and thus, it is argued, social status) of the consumer are telegraphed to others."[43] Instead, Therese forms a kind of internal telegraph system, which is organized around her reflections on the symbolic or analogical signals that she creates from items of consumption and her actions involving them. When, for instance, Therese first hears Carol's voice—soon after "their eyes met at the same instant" (*PS* 28)—she responds to it analogically: it "was like her coat, rich and supple, and somehow full of secrets" (28). Therese's activity of analogy making and exegetic elaboration alerts her to her own desire; it gives her "heart" time to "stumble" and "catch up with the moment it had let pass" (28). To come back to Schudson's question, here the aesthetic interest in a consumer good seems appropriately balanced with Therese's romantic interest in a person. This is how the novel imagines readerly agency and consumer agency combining to create occasions for mindful attentiveness, on which mind-changing is predicated.

Tellingly, when Therese does exhibit Veblenist tendencies, when she tries comparing her status to others, her capacity for crisp analogy—one crucial indication of her mindfulness—falters. The scene of Christmas Day at the home of Richard's family in which she struggles to make sense of Richard's beautiful kite discloses this tension between reading herself in relation to things and persons and ranking her experience in relation to that of others. By this point Carol's coat-person veritably overflows with secrets: Therese has the sense that "Carol was like a secret spreading through her, spreading through this house, too, like a light invisible to everyone but her" (*PS* 78). Reveling in this figural emanation, she feels "immensely superior to [Richard] suddenly, to all the people below stairs. She was happier than any of them" (79). She further likens the effect of Carol's "invisible" presence to a happy kite: "Happiness was a little like flying, she thought, like being a kite" (79)—even more so when the actual kite she and Richard fly in the nearby park becomes "all but invisible" in the sky (83). This optical perception leads her to imagine the kite as a "delicious and buoyant" force, "as if the kite might really take her up if it got all its strength together" (83). The intensity of her attachment to this figural cluster and the desire to sustain the happiness it yields are so strong that when Richard, in a moment of sophomoric exuberance, cuts the line to the actual kite, Therese is "speechless with anger" and "fear" (84). Here Therese's analogy fails to sustain the dialectic of identification *and* disinterest. More precisely, Therese fails her analogy both by losing sight of its figurativeness and by measuring her affective response to it against those who have no access to it (since she has kept it secret). This is why, in response to Therese's "shrill" assertion that Richard's action is "crazy" and "insane," he justifiably pushes back: "'It's only a kite!' Richard repeated, 'I can make another kite!'" (84). She has effectively converted Carol's coat-person into a causal principle over which she has no will. In this instance, only we readers, privy as we are to Therese's absorption in her all-too-consuming figures, are left to observe the glitches in her method of self-discovery and to observe how near the brink of solipsism she hovers.

Indeed, for much of the narrative Therese's personality development is hampered by solipsistic absorption that compromises the legitimacy of her actions and passions. She has a tendency to envelop her experience of Carol in what Carol calls her "private conception of everything" (*PS* 156). Their romance's oft-noted oedipal coloration (in which Carol substitutes for the loving mother Therese never had and Therese for the devoted daughter Carol is about to lose) gains structural reinforcement in Therese's seeming desire to eliminate mistake from the conditions of its possibility. This is where consumer culture's methods of spiritualizing goods prove most hazardous to the same-sex romance's legitimacy. In the kite scene we saw that Therese's fantasy of Carol as her special invisible secret arises from an overspiritualization of Carol's coat and Richard's kite. Now we see that a fantasy of Carol's absolute specialness arises from her transfer of this logic of overspiritualization to Carol's personhood. Denying in effect Carol's mortal finitude, this scenario violates UDHR principles of secular dignity.

Innocuously enough, Therese imagines the perfume Carol wears as only an advertising department could hope: the scent "was hers alone, like the smell of a special flower" (*PS* 39). Yet the toxicity of consumerist aura becomes apparent when Therese imagines Carol's specialness as so exquisite as to isolate her from human relations. She finds it "strange to think of" Carol as having parents or siblings, "'because I just think of you as you. *Sui generis*'" (155). She combines the thought of Carol's autogenesis with similarly isolating visions of the couple's location in time, imagining their excursions into the Rockies as "without past or future," as "suspended somewhere in the heart or in the memory, intact and absolute" (190). This envelopment in singularity and twosomeness brings Therese to the pinnacle of happiness—indeed, to "a complete happiness that must be . . . so rare that very few people ever knew it" (191). Flirting once again with Veblenism here, Therese derives her sense of Carol's and her own worth not from the principle of human pricelessness but from the market logic of supply and demand, whose psychosocial principle is *the rarer the better*. Not unlike Humbert Humbert, then, Therese's happiness in such instances becomes a conduit to something "beyond": "If it was merely happiness, then it had gone beyond the ordinary bounds and become something else"—something that is "more often painful than pleasant" (191). Also like Humbert, Therese seeks at times to draw her romance into the orbit of religiosity and fate. More than once she invokes her "lucky" fortune in having "found" Carol (136, 179); and she considers what they "possess" to be a kind of "miracle" (186). These appeals to otherworldliness are symptomatic of her fetish-like fixation on Carol; they serve to reinforce and to explain why "she could not imagine ever leaving Carol" (171).

This consumerist mediation of Therese's desire threatens, in effect, to convert Therese's *homo*sexual desire for Carol into something like *idio*sexual desire, that is, into an absolutely Carol-specific desire. This is problematic, the novel suggests, because it denies the persons involved the possibility of being mistaken about their love for each other, of having mindfully chosen each other. This threat culminates in a moment of consumerist epiphany, which strikingly resembles her love at first sight in the department store. It occurs near the end of the novel, when Therese finds herself alone in Sioux Falls after Carol has flown back to New Jersey to deal with the divorce and custody battle. Wandering about the town, contemplating Carol, she comes across a shop display: "And there was the beautiful thing, transfixing the heart and the eyes at once, in the dark window of an antique shop in a street where she had never been. Therese stared at it, feeling it quench some forgotten and nameless thirst inside her." Highsmith has Therese optically revel in all the precious and erotic uniqueness of this object, "a tiny candlestick holder": "Most of its porcelain surface was painted with small bright lozenges of coloured enamel, royal blue and deep red and green, outlined with coin gold as shiny as silk embroidery, even under its film of dust. There was a gold ring at the rim for the finger" (*PS* 222). When she later gives this totem to Carol, Carol's response meets and raises the stakes of their amorous gamble. "'I think it's charming,' Carol said. 'It looks just like you.'" Therese's response: "Thank you. I thought it looked like you" (247). This specular mirroring of selves and "charming" thing takes Highsmith's couple to the brink of Humbert Humbert's solipsistic abyss. While their adult status exempts them from tolerant liberalism's full condemnation, their romance appears beholden to a market logic of idiosexual specialness and miraculous discovery—expensive, indeed, but not priceless.[44]

Indeed, Highsmith stages here the seductiveness of a licit—that is, socially tolerable—but not exactly legitimate amorous economy. Earlier in the novel, however, she discloses its more insidious aspects. This takes place in Manhattan, where Therese has a pensive conversation about the meaning of happiness with her friend Dannie, a graduate student in physics. She feels closer to him than to her boyfriend, Richard. Dannie is a personable character; he's attracted to Therese yet, unlike Richard, not angry or repulsed by her possible homosexuality. At age twenty-five he's smart, mature, and wise; he smokes a pipe. In this conversation he advances a kind of existential physics in which happiness amounts to accepting a "right economy of living and of using and using up." He proceeds by way of anecdote:

> "It's like a feeling I had once riding up a hill on a horse. . . . I didn't know how to ride very well then, and I remember the horse turning his head and seeing the hill, and deciding by himself to run up it, his hind legs sank before we took off, and suddenly we were going like blazes and I wasn't afraid at all. I felt completely in harmony with the horse and the land, as if we were a whole tree simply being stirred by the wind in its branches. I remember being sure that nothing would happen to me then, but some other time, yes, eventually. And it made me very happy. I thought of all the people who are afraid and hoard things, and themselves, and I thought, when everybody in the world comes to realize what I felt going up the hill, then there'll be a kind of right economy of living and of using and using up. Do you know what I mean?" Dannie had clenched his fist, but his eyes were bright as if he still laughed at himself. "Did you ever wear out a sweater you particularly liked, and throw it away finally?" [. . .] "Well, that's all I mean. And the lambs who didn't realize how much wool they were losing when somebody

sheared them to make the sweater, because they could grow more wool. It's very simple." (*PS* 105–6)

At first blush this "right economy" looks like the salutary antidote to Therese and Carol's mutual fixation. It exudes tolerant acceptance of all things as they thrive and pass. It also resonates with postwar rebuttals of American acquisitiveness. As Larrabee suggested, "Belief in consumption, in addition, requires belief in waste. If it is desirable, in itself, for more people continually to consume more things, then it is also desirable for those things to be worn out and thrown away as rapidly as possible."[45]

More important, Dannie illustrates his philosophy's relevance to interpersonal intimacy by kissing Therese, which she experiences as having "mingled" qualities of "tenderness and roughness," as though the kiss were an objective correlative of the philosophy itself (*PS* 106). According to Dannie's algorithm of affection, kisses shared between him and Therese need not imply kisses lost between her and Richard (or, as the case will be later, Carol). Such is its "tenderness." But Highsmith suggests that there is troubling "roughness" in such an algorithm's idea of persons' endless availability for "using and using up." It makes individual lives seem all too cheap; it denigrates both self-preservation—as though fear could never be rational or appropriate—and monogamy—as though the happiness obtained from interpersonal intimacy hinged on the ready abundance and casual equivalence of substitutes.

In the homology between persons and unhoarded sweaters, Dannie reproduces Therese and Carol's neglect of the distinction between things and persons when they bond over and with the candlestick holder. In the novel's representation both of indiscriminate promiscuity and hyperrefined selectivity, then, the line between choosing an amorous partner and choosing a handbag or sweater or ice-cream cone threatens to lose its brightness. During the scene of Therese and Carol's sexual consummation in Waterloo, Therese recalls the terms of her conversation with Dannie to make sense of their ecstatic intimacy. Similar to Dannie with his horse, she likens herself to "a long arrow" in flight, a flying arrow attached to Carol: "She realized that she still clung to Carol . . . , and she did not have to ask if this was right, no one had to tell her, because this could not have been more right or perfect" (*PS* 168). Just as Dannie's psychophysics of harmony brooks no mistake, here too there's no possibility of questioning the rightness or perfection of their togetherness.

We are now in a position to appreciate the ending's crucial function of restoring the novel's liberal vision and thus legitimating Therese and Carol's romance. All along in their growing intimacy Carol has served to check Therese's solipsistic inclinations by interjecting a self-consciously rational and at times pedagogical will. When Therese wants to do away with the temporality of "past history," Carol cautions that a "duller" alternative might be "futures" such as theirs "that won't have any history" (*PS* 39). When Therese wants to revel in her sense of feeling "happy" ever since they met, Carol expresses concern that Therese's youth and inexperience make her unable to "judge" this feeling adequately (170). Thus despite Carol's flawed account of subjective taste and her complicity in their mutual fixation, the burden is really Therese's to meet the crisis of legitimation. This takes place just before her final reconciliation with Carol, when Therese attends a party in Manhattan in hopes of making career-related connections. There she is introduced to and later hit on by the sexy actress Genevieve Cranell. In turn, Therese is captivated; she experiences "shock" and "heat"—a "rush inside her that was neither quite her blood nor her thoughts alone" (253). Here Highsmith notably supplements pleasure ("blood") with self-conscious mindfulness ("thoughts"). Both start out in a "rush," but her mind takes over and slows to a standstill: "Her consciousness had stopped in a tangle"; "her mind was caught at the intersection" of conflicting desires (255, 256). Highsmith's emphatic repetition indicates not that Therese's mind is shutting down but that she struggles to make sense of her desires and to prioritize her options.

What signals Therese's ultimate success in this struggle is her courteous but confident decline of the actress's invitation to hook up later at a more exclusive party—not because, as the actress thinks, something is "wrong" but because Therese has willed a change of mind. Her brief spell of confusion has led her both to discover and to claim that Carol is right for her after all—or, more precisely, that she is right about her love for Carol.[46] While still contemplating her options, she thinks, "This woman [Genevieve] was like Carol" (*PS* 253). Therese has recovered her command of analogical thinking: here being *like* proposes similarity without necessitating homologous identity. Approximate substitutability becomes Highsmith's means of neutralizing idiosexual desire and installing homosexual desire. We now see that the happiness derived from the prospect of same-sex monogamy or imperfect substitutability is predicated on the very possibility of substitutability—not Dannie's version of cosmic promiscuity but Therese's normative albeit queered version of an intersubjective attachment that recognizes the constitutive pricelessness of the persons involved (herself as well as Carol and Genevieve). From the vantage point of this concluding episode, the tiny candlestick holder with its golden ring thus begins to look less like an erotic fetish marking the two women as narcissistic extensions of each other and more like the golden bands that get exchanged during nuptials, marking intersubjective happiness as something humanly willed rather than miraculously caused.

It turns out, then, that the novel's exalted happy ending of reconciliation is, strictly speaking, irrelevant to its narrative trajectory. According to biographer Andrew Wilson, Highsmith initially planned to end the novel on an "unhappy, tragic note, with Therese and Carol going their separate ways," but her editor persuaded her "to choose the more optimistic version."[47] I'm suggesting that the choice hardly mattered. The optimistic version merely tenders confirmation that Therese is right, or at least thinks she is for now, about her amorous attachment. She self-consciously affirms that she loves Carol, not Genevieve and not Dannie. The tragic version would have indicated her error about Carol, but it would have also suggested the self-conscious rightness of adopting a more "deviant" practice of promiscuity. It is in the very perplexity and subsequent assessment and claiming of her desire that Therese exemplifies liberal agency, not in her specific choice of future monogamy over promiscuity. Both scenarios involve an ongoing commitment to liberalism's values of human worth and self-development. It is thus not going too far to say that the novel exemplifies what Stanley Cavell argues is the contribution made by 1940s romantic comedies of remarriage to our understanding of "the achievement of human happiness": that it "requires not the perennial and fuller satisfaction of our needs as they stand but the examination and transformation of those needs."[48] If only Hitchcock had elected to film *The Price of Salt* instead of *Strangers on a Train*.

The Trouble with Suspense Fiction

In ventilating *The Price of Salt*'s queer-liberal investments, I want to suggest finally that Highsmith offers us a helpful model for rethinking what Michael Warner calls "the trouble with normal." He argues that the policing and internalization of sexual-political norms have stacked the deck against practices of sexual deviance, which in turn generates the doubly corrosive effect of reducing the gay movement to a desexualized politics of identity and exacerbating deviant sex practitioners' experience of shame.⁴⁹ Although this claim is empirically verifiable in many cases—and Warner provides ample compelling evidence of the state's collusion with majoritarian culture's aversion to deviance—his theoretical basis for it excludes too many equally verifiable alternatives. The underlying theory is not unfamiliar: modern sexual politics is propped up by mass culture's dissemination of a "consciousness" imbued with the statistical majority's imagined commonality, which "make[s] us aspire to be normal." In other words, sexual politics is largely if not entirely a matter of social psychology. He summons the example of *Newsweek*, whose mass-mediating magnetic "gravity" teaches us how to measure and guard our normality against "deviations and extremes."⁵⁰ Majoritarian culture is by definition oppressive and impoverished, then, since its formation is no more than a symptom of anxious conformity.

This mass-cultural theory, however, occludes much. Not least, it occludes certain social histories that reveal the dialogical function of mass-niche commodities: as Worley's account of lesbian pulp would indicate, opportunities continually ripen for queer-liberal readers' participation in mass markets of deviance while eluding "normal" culture's stigmatizing apparatus. More generally, then, it occludes the dialectical propensities of readers that Knapp maps out. Finally, Warner's theory of "normal" occludes Korsgaard's theory of "normativity," which entails acknowledging the capacity not only to observe the anthropological fact that values inform the modern world but also to "recognize value itself."⁵¹ This recognition, however imperfectly accommodated by persons, becomes the operative condition of liberalism's possibility; it secures liberalism's idea of universal human dignity and worth. With normativity installed as a guiding principle, Korsgaard's approach allows for the distinction between commendable and reproachable practices of a statistical majority as well as those of a deviant; it isn't clear, though, how Warner's theory would commend any majority or reproach any deviant.⁵² Like Warner's theory, Korsgaard's involves separating innate desire from the grounds of legitimation. She arrives at this claim, however, not by routing desire through society's mediating mechanisms but by considering the human being to be a self-justifying and self-endorsing—rather than merely self-explaining—agent.

I've argued in this essay that Highsmith's ambition in *The Price of Salt* to justify a queer amorous pursuit proceeds by dramatizing the distinction between the main characters' commendable and reproachable intersubjective practices—a distinction that she shows is equally applicable to the novel's resolutely straight characters such as Dannie and Richard. While this salute to liberal normativity may well make the novel an exception in Highsmith's oeuvre—populated as this oeuvre is by misanthropic, criminal deviants—it is worth noting the way it chimes with her comments about her own work and career in her handbook, *Plotting and Writing Suspense Fiction* (1983). In that book she imparts her views on the formal and commercial relays between her signature genre, suspense, and what she calls the "straight novel"—by which she means "just 'a novel'" that is either "good" or "bad."[53] She takes herself seriously as a fiction writer—indeed as a member of the "classless" class of "creative people"—and predictably dislikes being categorized according to genre. She complains that "critics and reviewers in America consider the mystery novel as superficial and inferior to the straight novel, which is automatically assumed to be more serious, important, and worthwhile because it *is* a straight novel and because the author is assumed to have a serious intent in writing it."[54] What I earlier described as Highsmith's defensive vanity might here be redescribed, borrowing from Warner, as vocational shame derived from the maligned status of her chosen line of creativity.

Yet rather than repudiating this shame by championing suspense fiction's deviation from "straight" fiction—which would be the literary-political equivalent of Warner's championing of "queer" over "normal" sex practices—Highsmith seeks to reframe the trouble with her vocation by displacing categories of identity (straight fiction, suspense fiction) with categories of practice (good writing, bad writing). As though to redress Carol's consummate inability to debate matters of aesthetic taste, Highsmith supplies numerous criteria by which to assess the goodness or badness of a literary work. Hack suspense writing is bad not simply because it's done for money—after all, she writes for money, having "no private income"—but because it uses "gimmicks" and "trick ideas" such as surprise endings, expert knowledge of forensics, and withholding information from the reader.[55] Good writing, though, has "insight, character, [and] an opening of new horizons for the imagination of the reader," all of which are qualities available to the "suspense writer" who wants to "improve his lot and the reputation of the suspense novel." Indeed, since every "story with a beginning, middle, and end" has "suspense," she is confident that "the intellectual as well as the mystery and suspense fan" will "enjoy" her work as long as it's "good."[56] Less important here than the specific criteria she proposes is the fact that she imagines aesthetic criteria as an alternative to the genre labels that reinforce prejudice. Such is Highsmith's way of reproaching and commending the various options available to writers of fiction, of supplanting dubious distinctions with more justifiable ones.

From Highsmith's perspective, then, the suspense genre is best understood as one among many available venues that allow the talented writer "to advertise his talent." As this brush with Mailerism intimates, she recognizes in writing suspense fiction the possibility of preserving her authorial "personality" and "individuality," in which she locates a "kind of [organized] freedom"—what we might call her own queer writerly specificity—while fully assimilating herself to the economic and aesthetic contingencies of the mid-century literary sphere. Not unsurprisingly, Highsmith ends her handbook on a personal note: she has the "feeling" that she has "left something out, something vital," namely, "the joy of writing, which cannot really be described, cannot be captured in words and handed to someone else to share or to make use of."[57] In other words, writing suspense fiction is for her the closest thing to self-fulfillment. At once deviant and straight, it becomes her source of normativity.

4 Countries of Health

It is well known that Sylvia Plath's 1961 poem "Tulips" was occasioned by an appendectomy. The setting is a hospital that, in its clean and peaceful whiteness, is a paragon of functional order; it bears none of the contagiousness that menaces the hospital in that other famous poem of resuscitation, William Carlos Williams's "Spring and All." As Plath's nurses, along with the surgeons and anesthetist, do their work, "they are no trouble"; they tend to her body "as water / Tends to the pebbles it must run over, smoothing them gently."[1] Institutional and vocational purpose guide their actions; restoring the patient's health is habitual, as coordinated and efficient as hydraulic physics. If these professionals stir any trouble at all, it's by permitting someone to leave in the room a bouquet of tulips whose "redness talks to [her] wound," "hurt[s]" her, and "eat[s her] oxygen" (39, 36, 49). Before the flowers arrive and hold her concentrated "attention," she "was happy / Playing and resting without committing" herself (55, 56). She was happy, in other words, in her role as passive patient, allowing her convalescence to proceed according to hospital protocol. In this context, happiness's connotation of fitness, of appropriateness to the occasion, steers the affective claim.

But affirming hospital happiness is hardly the point of "Tulips." Critics have observed that Plath harbored considerable hostility toward hospitals, particularly psychiatric ones. Encoded in the speaker's difficulty coping with tulips is what Abigail Cheever has shown preoccupies Plath in her 1963 antipsychiatry novel, *The Bell Jar*: the way "'authentic versions' of freedom, power, and creativity . . . might be lost through institutionalized cures."[2] In this light the hospital looks like a seducer who has coaxed the patient—echoing Lady Lazarus—into stripping off one by one her "name" and "dayclothes" and her "history" and "body" (6, 7). Now we see that access to happy tranquility involves forgetting the "wound" not of surgery but of something like institutional assault. However successful the surgery, the "country" that permits such treatment in the name of "health" is indeed "far away" from its patient's authentic being (63). The monstrous tulips thus turn out to be agents of deliverance. They may be disagreeable, but they stir the patient back into the world of "snags and eddies," of imaginative fertility and contrarian complaint (54).

Or, to borrow the terms of cultural studies critic Sara Ahmed, the hospital looks contagious after all, although not because it spreads infectious disease. In its mission to cure what ails, prevent disease, bring babies into the world, and the like, it functions instead as a "happy object," a coercive icon that spreads happiness.[3] Ahmed examines the way such objects as nations for immigrants and wedding days for brides—and let me add hospitals for poets—become "contagious" or "sticky" with happiness; their "proximity" promises happiness: "So the promise of happiness—if you do this, then happiness is what follows—is what makes things seem 'promising,' which means that the promise of happiness is not in the thing itself" but rather in society. "Happiness involves the sociality of passing things around," Ahmed writes.[4] This psychosocial fabrication is how feeling good, along with the very desire to feel good, proliferates. And how it concomitantly drives down the value of feeling bad: Ahmed wants, among other things, to rescue the endangered species of bad affect so as to redeem the social value of its carriers. In Plath's poem, the speaker's disagreeable feelings of hurt effectively immunize her against the contagions of the promising hospital; she becomes the kind of "affect alien" that Ahmed champions.[5]

Ahmed's argument extends in part from Foucault's disenchanted account of the postwar welfare state, including its commitment to health care. In his view the postwar state apparatus is essentially no different from the eighteenth-century police state, in which happiness is pursued (as quoted by Ahmed) "as a 'requirement for the survival and development of the state. It is a condition, it is an instrument, and not simply a consequence. People's happiness becomes an element of state strength.'"[6] In Foucault's historiography, the biopolitical mandate is clear-cut: modern states carried out their duty to sustain the health of their populations by creating "great welfare, public health, and medical assistance programs" while also conducting military campaigns that necessitated "huge mass slaughters" of these populations. With his flair for grim melodrama, Foucault devises a "slogan" to "symbolize" the subsumption of state benevolence under malevolence: "Go get slaughtered and we promise you a long and pleasant life. Life insurance is connected with a death command."[7] By Ahmed's and Foucault's political calculus, then, midcentury Americans—including the poor and uninsured—had every reason to cheer the US Congress and the medical establishment for derailing liberal activists' repeated efforts to reform the distribution of medical care and to universalize health insurance. With a paucity of health-care objects in the vicinity, Americans might perish by the mere dozens—as in Morton Thompson's middlebrow saga, *Not as a Stranger* (1954)—of typhoid due to a corrupt water system. Read through the prism of welfare-state suspicion, the novel's withering portrayal of the town of Greenville's failure of political will to modernize its water system emerges as an unwitting allegory of populist triumph over welfare-state machinations. Or if they might perish singly—as in Lionel Trilling's political novel, *The Middle of the Journey* (1947)—in rural Connecticut due to a weak heart, they might consider themselves mercifully distant from the welfare institutions of urban centers. Discussed more fully later, the novel presents this death, a child's, as largely the result of familial circumstance, for which the welfare-state critic need not answer. For someone like Plath's speaker in "Tulips," who appears unable to avoid the restoration of physical health, a modicum of cold comfort may be extracted from her subsequent pangs of psychic agony.

Midcentury liberal activists, however, had little truck with Foucauldian disenchantment; and from their standpoint Americans had every reason to be dismayed by the seemingly intractable problem of health-care injustice. President Roosevelt's "Second Bill of Rights" of 1944 had invoked a "right to adequate medical care and the opportunity to achieve and enjoy good health," which the United Nations (UN) formalized in 1948 as the "right to a standard of living adequate for the health and well-being of himself and of his family, including food, clothing, housing and medical care and necessary social services."[8] But in a country in which the doctor-patient relationship was sovereign, opposition to government involvement in medical care and health insurance was formidable. Still, the postwar era witnessed a persistent if uneven effort to legitimate government's interventionist role in effecting the equitable distribution of social goods and services such as education, consumer protection, and health care while advancing ever more individualized conceptions of the good. With respect specifically to health care, what made this development possible was increased understanding and acceptance that health was an asset—a "critical background condition," as Norman Daniels put it in 1979, whose "justification" derived from a "theory of distributive justice."[9] As such it could be seen to contribute to one's overall ability to pursue one's interests. "Man does not live by good health care alone," Daniels maintained, "nor is it what makes life worth living."[10] But it is one of many high-ranking goods that modern society should seek to distribute equitably. Around the same time, Bruce Ackerman succinctly clarified the broader stakes of this liberal project: "Once we are prepared to affirm the value of fulfilling our own life plan, we may use this initial affirmation as the foundation of a public dialogue of right."[11] Within this framework, the idea that health is an asset, as Brian Barry elaborates, becomes eminently justifiable:

> "Eliminating health inequities is important as a matter of social justice because health is an asset and a resource critical to human development" and because of "scientific evidence that health inequalities are the outcome of causal chains which run back into and from the basic structures of society." Of course, public policy can't determine how healthy or long-lived any given individual will be. But public policy does not determine individual educational attainments or earnings either, and this does not stop its making all the difference to the justice or injustice of their distribution.[12]

This passage's inclusion of quotations from health professionals who justify governmental intervention on the grounds of self-development and fairness indicates a broadly shared sense of the virtues of state-organized health-care policy. Incipient versions of this view gained traction in the 1940s when the Wagner-Murray-Dingell Bill called for compulsory national health insurance funded by a payroll tax and when Truman proposed in 1948 a single universal health-care plan. Both legislative efforts were defeated, due in no small part to the American Medical Association's (AMA) and conservative Republicans' specter of "socialized medicine." Yet the articulation of universalist claims in the debate signaled a midcentury commitment to viewing health care as a right rather than as a free-market commodity or discretionary charity.

Moreover, as Barry clarifies, such claims derived from a long history of even more basic health-care concerns. In the discussion cited earlier he goes on to chide Richard Dworkin for misrepresenting Descartes as one who declared health *care*, rather than health, as chief among all goods. This confusion is not benign, for it obscures the fact of the "relative insignificance of [personal] health care" when compared to public-health measures.[13] He points to the eradication of typhoid fever and cholera in nineteenth-century Britain "by the provision of pure drinking water and the safe disposal of human wastes" and to the dramatic reduction in New York of tuberculosis by creating housing codes that mandated ventilation and prohibited overcrowding as examples of public-policy efforts to improve the health of citizens in wider-reaching ways than those that came out of recent efforts to improve the delivery of hospital care and distribution of insurance.[14] What matters here is less his argument for the merits of one kind of health provision over another than his way of conceptualizing health as a political issue. For Barry, health may be an asset, but it is best understood as an inexchangeable one—not so much in the Cartesian sense of its superlative status among goods (an arguable claim in any case) but in the sense of its status as a public good, whereby it becomes more or less inalienable. As it gets built into the literal infrastructure, the health-care asset also becomes part of the political-conceptual architecture. Whether good health intrinsically (neurochemically, sociobiologically) makes us happy—as legions of contemporary happiness studies would have it—or incidentally makes us happy, far more pertinent is the fact that widening the distribution of good health helps to level the playing field and allows us to pursue our own versions of happiness.

From the standpoint, then, of midcentury liberal activists pursuing health-care justice, Plath's speaker makes a category mistake about her affect-laden objects. She needn't get far away from health in order to get rid of happiness. She need only attach her happiness to a different object and then get rid of it. Thinking of health as an object of justice rather than as an object of happiness would allow her to stay in the country and be as unhappy and alienated as she pleases. Since the country Plath resided in at the time of the poem's composition was the United Kingdom, this object reorientation would have been even easier than in the United States. As medical historian Rosemary Stevens explains, after World War II "hospitals were nationalized and grouped into regional and local consortia; consultants and specialists put on salary and given specific assignments . . . , [and] virtually the whole population signed up with general practitioners. . . . The middle-class population rapidly came to accept medical care as a right, as natural a privilege as free education."[15] In other words, the basics of publicly administered health included not only things like clean air and clean water but also things like nurses and appendectomies.

The problem for Plath's speaker is that she takes her health personally and wants to treat it as an exclusively private matter. She imagines health to be something she's indeed entitled to get far from, as though it were an alienable object rather than an inalienable asset. This is how she lays the groundwork for getting some sort of emotional rise from her health, for crafting what Deborah Nelson calls a "deliberately intense" poetic experience.[16] To put the problem another way, for Plath, health happiness doesn't feel enough like a feeling. It feels instead like a standard-issue steady state, an ersatz affect that the hospital supplies along with the pillows that prop up her head. Health happiness isn't so much felt by Plath as it is built into the hospital's white walls. It forces her into the near stasis of "playing and resting without committing" herself to anything (56). The string of progressive-present participles implies hospital time's bland ongoingness. Happiness is too uniform both in the way Cheever elucidates it (pertaining to Plath's desire for identitarian uniqueness) and in the temporal sense of constancy. The poem argues in effect that as health care recedes into the institutional architecture, its correlative happiness loses its status as a meaningful, feeling experience. Her solution is to reverse course by committing her attention to the "too excitable" and "upsetting" tulips (1, 41). Getting rid of hospital happiness and getting upset by flowers thus become affective proxies for restoring (mental) health's alienability. In effect she claws the health asset back from the public domain.

Plath's poem crystallizes the way midcentury American writing could become entangled not only in what Susan Sontag described as a mystification of illness through "lurid metaphor" but also in the politics of actually existing health care. Her 1978 book, *Illness as Metaphor*, critiques the long tradition and mental habit, intensified by romanticism, of reaching for figures of illness to express a range of heightened states, some of which were deplored and others of which were styled as glamorous. Tuberculosis, for instance, becomes in the nineteenth century a badge of antibourgeois poetic sensitivity. In the twentieth century, mental illness displaces this bacterial disease as the sign of an exceptional being. In these scenarios, "health becomes banal, even vulgar."[17] Meanwhile, cancer and epidemic disease become the preferred metaphors for a disordered, corrupt, blighted, and totalitarian society. Sontag's cultural critique seeks to defuse the moral anxiety aroused by the habitual deployment of such "lurid metaphors."[18] She describes everyone as possessing "dual citizenship, in the kingdom of the well and in the kingdom of the sick" and envisions her work as effecting a kind of "liberation" from this linguistic tyranny.[19] But apart from the occasional glance—such as at the 1971 National Cancer Act's obsession with "the cure" rather than with "near-to-hand decisions"[20]—Sontag has little to say about how or if this metaphorical excess affected the practical politics of medicine and health care. The linguistic turn in her mode of criticism seems to organize itself more easily around metaphorical citizenry than around empirical persons and their health-care jurisdictions.

The present chapter examines a series of midcentury works of fiction—primarily Trilling's *The Middle of the Journey*, Mary McCarthy's *The Group* (1963), James Gunn's *The Joy Makers* (1961), and Paula Fox's *Poor George* (1967) and *Desperate Characters* (1970)—whose literary force depends considerably on their representations of health-care systems and value structures through which illness and health are refracted. Taken together, these works help explain why welfare-state provisions, especially health care, have always been such a hard sell in the United States. They register the difficulty of displacing the lurid metaphor with the "symbols of happiness" that, as discussed in the introduction, John Kenneth Galbraith called for to encourage a more civic-minded orientation toward the country's wealth and public-policy ambitions.[21] From his perspective, Plath's desire to preserve health's alienability looks like a precise symptom of American affluence. Preoccupied with production, which economists calculate almost exclusively in terms of private wealth, postwar America has created a "disparity between our flow of private and public goods and services," including public health.[22]

Galbraith faulted both recent and traditional utilitarian praxis for this dismal irony of "private opulence and public squalor."[23] On the one hand, a lingering Keynesian imperative to stimulate consumer demand dominated midcentury liberal economic policy. On the other hand, ever since the "Benthamite test of public policy was 'what serves the greatest happiness of the greatest number,' and happiness was more or less implicitly identified with productivity," modern society has misdirected its economic and ethical energies away from those who need and deserve it most, namely, the poor.[24] As earlier chapters of this book suggest, midcentury liberal activism's concern to rope in the utilitarian creed without choking off the happiness-seeking subject—who was central to both creeds—proved difficult for the era's literary practitioners to articulate. As we'll see in this chapter, when it came specifically to health care, the gravitational pull of utilitarian logic was particularly powerful, drawing into its orbit such liberal-leftist worlds as the New York intellectuals populating Trilling's political novel and the World Health Organization that Gunn seems to parody in his work of dystopian science fiction. The trope of personal happiness circulates in these works to organize utilitarian achievement. And yet, both McCarthy and Fox manage to give voice to liberal activism's alternative vision of rights-based health care, although in McCarthy's novel that voice is arguably reduced by its satire to a kind of muffled croak. For Fox's part, the grim realism of her two early novels lowers the bar of narrative hope, which ironically enables her to eke out chastened affirmations of distributive health-care justice amid New York's confused population and crumbling hospital and insurance system in the 1960s. Fox's novels, I suggest, convey serious apprehensions about the ready availability of health-care happiness legitimated by the welfare state, but they nevertheless operate under the sign of Galbraith's symbolic ethos.

Trailing Clouds of Mortality

Paul Starr's esteemed longitudinal history, *The Social Transformation of American Medicine* (1982), makes clear that midcentury liberal activists concerned to improve the American health-care system could hardly count on the dominant paradigms of social science for guidance or support. Although, for instance, "the most influential schema in the sociology of medicine," that of Talcott Parsons, yielded a hefty tenth chapter in his 1951 tome, *The Social System*, the chapter focused almost exclusively on the doctor-patient relationship and social role expectations.[25] Parsons's functionalist approach would shed new light on "motivational mechanisms" and patterns of "value-orientation" within institutionalized medicine.[26] But he largely reproduced the AMA's version of the medical system as one organized around interpersonal attentiveness:

> [He] concentrates almost entirely upon the system of norms in purely voluntary doctor-patient relations. . . . The distribution of power, control of markets, and so on do not enter significantly into his analysis. Parsons also neglects other

relations important to medical practice, such as those among doctors and between doctors and organizations. The more important these collegial and bureaucratic relations become, the less useful Parsons' approach appears. (STAM 21)

Parsons certainly recognized that midcentury medicine was evolving away from the independent private practitioner and toward "the complex cooperation of several different kinds of physicians as well as of auxiliary personnel," along with more complex hospital facilities.[27] But this observation did little to distract him from his objective of disclosing the psychosocial dynamics between the person in the "sick role" and the medical expert.[28] If the "effect" of Parsons's style of inquiry, as one critic notes, "was to help transform sociology into an insular discipline disconnected from public discourse," it also helped to sustain the fantasy that the medical system was similarly insulated.[29]

Perhaps more remarkable than Parsons's blind eye to the political implications of the postwar era's increasingly organized medical system is that his exact contemporary and a more self-conscious public intellectual, Lionel Trilling, leaned heavily on this insular view of medical practice for the construction of his one novel, *The Middle of the Journey*. The novel depicts two phases of the protagonist John Laskell's summer-long convalescence following a near-fatal bout of scarlet fever. He is a young urban professional whose New York residence ensures ready access to medical care and whose independent wealth seems to free him from concern about medical expenses. Casting the interpersonal medical scenario in deeply attractive light, Laskell's focalized perspective eclipses but doesn't entirely expunge references to the broader systemic conditions on which this scenario depends. Particularly significant are the glimpses the novel affords of the considerably less robust medical care available to an underprivileged young girl in rural Connecticut whose chronic ailment of a "weak heart" goes untreated. But rather than probing the sociomedical conditions that enable the discursive circulation of this vague and romantic phrase alongside the do-nothing approach recommended by doctors in Hartford, the novel capitalizes on the girl's affliction to drive the plot toward its conclusion of revelatory existentialism. Indeed, Trilling seems to require the diagnosis—a contrivance of sentimental fiction and negligent medicine alike—to elevate his moral and political themes above existing political actualities such as the pursuit of health-care justice.

Set in the late 1930s, the novel is equipped with a solid alibi for not addressing the dramatic transformations in the American health-care system at the time of its 1947 publication. These transformations lay predominantly in the direction of the privatization of middle-class benefits, thanks to employers' fringe packages, labor unions' bargaining influence, and conservatism's resurgence in legislative politics. But the cataclysmic 1930s also witnessed major developments in health-care insurance and delivery, among them the introduction, for the middle class, of Blue Cross prepayment plans to cover nonprofit hospital expenses; the expanded role of municipal and county hospitals in treating the indigent population; efforts on the part of rural populists and Roosevelt's Farm Security Administration to establish small-town medical cooperatives; and the AMA's highly consequential legal wrangling with the Department of Justice over the formation of urban health-care cooperatives. Most of these trends reinforced a two-tier system of parsimonious charity for some and generous insurance and hospital care for others.[30]

None of these developments draws Trilling's attention. Instead he dwells on John Laskell's recovery in the comfort of his own city apartment (in the first phase) under the capable care of Dr. Graf—the highly regarded physician of his close friends—and a pair of alternating private nurses. These conscientious and affluent friends, Nancy and Arthur Croom, also supply extra bedsheets, pajamas, and a crate of oranges.[31] Even the New York Board of Health is on his side. Its quarantine of his apartment turns out to ensure the social isolation he desires. It permits him to contemplate almost endlessly a yet more profound isolation: the hard truth of mortality. A forerunner of Plath's tulips-watcher, Laskell practically revels in convalescent passivity and the sociomedical situation that permits it. He is captivated by "the white empty peace of illness" and the ample opportunity it affords him "to stare at a rose" at length, until he is "lost in its perfection" (*MJ* 14, 15). Likened to an unborn fetus in the womb (26), the perfect rose projects for him an image of "non-existence" (25).

Laskell's literal and then imagined brushes with death become the novel's organizing trope, through which it promotes the value and necessity of tragic consciousness. Regarding the plot, the experiences also become the source of Laskell's gradual estrangement from his left-liberal friends. The Crooms' unwillingness to let Laskell talk about being near death exemplifies the sort of liberalism Trilling made a postwar career of disparaging—the kind that negates the truth of tragic reality and thus reflexively banishes moral ambivalence, aesthetic difficulty, and psychological complexity. Such liberals are too simple and naïve, too attached to doing good. They lack what Trilling deemed the struggling "dignity" of "the Freudian man" who had "a kind of hell within him from which rise everlastingly the impulses which threaten his civilization" but who was redeemed by also being "a creature of love."[32] As Trilling saw things, such liberals were particularly ill-suited to meet the demands of the postwar world.

By contrast, Laskell in the late 1930s seems "prescient" in the way that Trilling finds Henry James to be in his political novel, *The Princess Casamassima* (*LI* 60). In his introduction to a reissue of this work, published the year after the appearance of *The Middle of the Journey*, Trilling salutes James's "imagination of disaster" for its "grainy and knotted" portrayal of "society as crowds and police, as a field of justice and injustice, reform and revolution" (60).[33] James exhibits a dialectical sensibility that is both astringent and sympathetic; opening himself to the vagaries of social catastrophe, James cultivates a sensibility of which the contemporary world, after "wars and concentration camps," has dire need (60). James's scrupulous eye beholds the violence of programmatic virtue and the guilt of both revolutionary and aesthetic passions; he thus offers future modernists "one of the keys to truth" (60). This probing introduction serves as a key to Trilling's own preoccupations in *The Middle of the Journey*. Laskell, the character who most closely figures the Jamesian disposition, emerges by the end of the novel an emotionally weathered yet tenacious hero-in-waiting. He is not sacrificed in the way Trilling sees James sacrificing Hyacinth Robinson for recognizing both his "sense of the social horror of the world" and "his newer sense of the [aesthetic] glory of the world" (85)—and for thus being "implicated" in the "guilt" of "civilization" (86). Falling mercifully short of actual death, Laskell's trial by fever in the late 1930s readies him, Trilling implies, for the daunting existential, aesthetic, and political truths of a postwar world.

Laskell spends the second phase of his convalescence at the Crooms' country place in Connecticut, where he arrives in precarious physical and mental health (one consequence of the debilitating bacterial infection is that he now experiences occasional bouts of near-paralyzing terror). He is also profoundly disturbed by the defection from the Communist Party and subsequent turn to Christianity of his and the Crooms' mutual friend Gifford Maxim. Modeled on Whittaker Chambers, this character now fears the

Party's lethal retaliation. He too thus seems to know what a death sentence feels like, although Laskell questions the rationality of Maxim's fear. Still, it is partly through Laskell's close encounters with this dubious if not indecent rival that Trilling asks us to appreciate the dignity of adopting both astringent distance and sympathetic intimacy vis-à-vis one's ideological and existential opponents. Structured as a pastoral interlude that is both bucolic and fraught with inner, interpersonal, and class conflict, Laskell's summer weeks in Connecticut lead him to several discomfiting but necessary insights. For one thing, the left-liberalism exemplified by the Crooms has enfeebled itself not only by the existential evasiveness mentioned earlier but also by fantasies of lower-class authenticity and the inability to wean itself from what Robert Warshow, in his 1948 review of Trilling's novel, called "the orthodoxy of Stalinist liberalism, which holds that man is the creature of his environment and thus free of moral responsibility."[34] For another thing, he sees that the conversion of a CPUSA member such as Maxim to an immoderate form of Christianity, radical Calvinism, should not surprise, as both commitments derive from the militancy and psychic needs of a reactionary. Also, Laskell discovers that the erotic reciprocity he enjoys with one of the local married women, Emily Caldwell, which lacks the element of "futurity" and the "promise" of enduring "love" (*MJ* 205), has nevertheless much to commend it, not least its revelation of his intimate partner's "simple sexual dignity" and "the cloud of mortality in which she walked" (205). The novel thus asks us to follow close by while Laskell renegotiates the terms and expectations of left-liberal bourgeois life.

Above all—and in conjunction with these new intuitions—Laskell arrives at the conclusive insight that the necessary disposition for the modern liberal is the very one his doctrinaire friends lack, namely, the capacity to embrace "an idea in modulation" (*MJ* 302). Under this sign, as the critic Anthony Hutchison recently put it, liberalism remains "continually reinterrogated" and thus avoids being "fossilize[d] into an extension of the will."[35] It is a heady moment in the narrative when Laskell's commitment to this proposition surfaces. During a set of tense and increasingly angry exchanges among these friends, Maxim—the new radical Christian—seizes on Laskell's unpremeditated formulation, declaring that it "showed [Laskell's] moment of happiness" (303). For Maxim, this exposure amounts to incrimination. But slightly earlier in the narrative (in terms both of days and pages), Trilling depicts Laskell reflecting on the meaning and value of happiness. There he concedes that his sexual encounter with Emily, exhilarating as it was, "had [not] made him happy"; but the concession also leaves him unsure "what the word 'happy' meant" (289). Now, in this later scene, we are encouraged to see that Maxim has accurately identified the proximate source of Laskell's genuine happiness, even if he has misattributed its etiology, in his Christian way, to Laskell's sense of being forgiven by Emily. The novel can be read, in other words, as an endeavor to identify and justify the happiness of a chastened liberal as the existential and political embrace of ideas in modulation.

Some of these modulating ideas are political and others are existential, erotic, or aesthetic, but none draws into its orbit the midcentury liberal activist's reckoning with distributive justice. As Amanda Anderson understands the novel—and Trilling's more general project of "privileg[ing] hesitation over commitment, appreciat[ing] . . . complexity over action"—Laskell figures "the necessary precondition," in a post-Holocaust world, "for any renewed or appropriate political engagement."[36] In her critical framework, he represents the ambivalent liberal whose vacillation resonates with but doesn't completely subscribe to the "bleak radicalism" of more disenchanted Marxists such as Adorno and Foucault.[37] The novel ends with Laskell on the train back to New York, prepared to resume his work in public housing, although presumably with a more circumspect view of progressive policy and planning. His accommodating but wary mode of engagement is what Trilling advances as prescient. In contrast to the Crooms—who exhibit what Trilling, in his essay on *Princess Casamassima*, calls "the modern will which masks itself in virtue . . . and despises the variety and modulations of the human story and longs for an absolute humanity" (*LI* 91–92)—Laskell backs away from the claims of the righteous.

For the politics of distributive justice, however, Laskell's mode of prescience is not entirely benign. As Anderson observes, Laskell's professional identity is predicated on liberalism's commitment to the incremental reform of "urban social policy linked to basic welfare and melioration . . . and also to the conditions of daily existence."[38] But as she also suggests, the novel's telos effectively disallows an endorsement of this kind of everyday liberalism: "Even such liberal progressivism is shown to be *irrelevant* to the primal experience of life-threatening illness and the changes it brings."[39] And there is precisely the rub. Midcentury liberal reformers may have operated in incremental fashion, but they still had to commit to decisions. The novel ends before Laskell faces too closely the knot that his alternating investments—in his professional vocation on the one hand and his newfound politicoexistential disposition on the other—have created for him.

A related and, from the standpoint of liberal activism, more troublesome narratological knot emerges long before the novel's conclusion. The novel seems unable to acknowledge the deep *relevance* of the political-economic "conditions of daily existence" to Laskell's journey toward his insight of modulation. Specifically, what the novel ignores is the relevance of the kind of medical care Laskell receives—and the stark contrast between it and the kind of medical inattention experienced by Susan Caldwell, the lovely young daughter of Emily and her husband, Duck. For all of Laskell's existential and ideological prescience, his narrow and complacent vision of the medical care he receives is decidedly behind the curve. In the first phase of Laskell's convalescence, as though he were supplying Parsons's study with the sociological evidence it requires, what he contemplates almost as deeply as the singularly perfect rose is the way he performs the "sick role." Indeed, however much he revels in the passivity of illness—observing that "for quite a time now his everyday life had been beautifully taken care of by someone else" (*MJ* 4)—he's also sensitive to the impropriety of extending this passivity indefinitely. His "retreat" into illness, he reasons, "was nothing to be ashamed of, not unless it were allowed to go beyond its proper term" (4). As befits this sense of obligation to get well, he also has high regard for his British nurse, the matronly Miss Paine, who naturally disapproves of his "love affair with that flower" (25). In her "admiration for manhood that followed tradition and built empire," she expects him to want to make a full and robust recovery (47). Her gentle yet firm ministrations elicit in Laskell the sort of emotion usually reserved for intimate members of a private household; he envisions her as "the family nurse or housekeeper . . . the nanny or the governess" (47). The "loyal[ty]" he imagines informing their rapport makes it difficult but not impossible for Laskell to acknowledge that she is merely performing her professional "function" and that she will soon move on to another patient (47, 57). This interpersonal connection is so strong on his side that he has "daydreams" of remaining in friendly contact over the years ahead (52), even though she draws attention to the transactional structure of their relationship by reminding him of how expensive her services are (57).

Thus modulating between Laskell's personalizing perspective and Nurse Paine's functionalist performance, the novel privileges what Parsons described as the "set of institutionalized expectations and corresponding sentiments and sanctions" that govern the modern patient-physician relationship. In addition to "the obligation to want to 'get well'" and to "cooperate" with the medical professional, the patient enters a relationship of "mutual 'trust'" and is permitted to feel helpless in the face of expert knowledge and technical competence.[40] For their part, medical professionals adhere to an interpersonal protocol that is sensitive to the "peculiarly 'private'" status of the patient's body—leaving the room, for instance, when the patient disrobes—and that avoids emotional "reciprocities."[41] To recall Starr's critique, however accurate Parsons's descriptive sociology may be, such close attention to persons' interactive behavior within the social system—which Trilling's novel reproduces—serves to occlude the political-economic machinations supporting it. To be sure, Parsons widens his lens enough to observe medical professionals' techniques for differentiating medical practice from profit-making endeavors and "jealous[ly] guarding ... their independence," particularly "vis-à-vis the state."[42] But even these details are presented more as evidence of the profession's insulating group behavior than as an invitation to situate the profession within a broader sociopolitical order.

Meanwhile, Trilling appears content to ignore the bruising friction of midcentury health-care politics—which was particularly visible in the acrimonious relations between the AMA and New Deal liberals—and yet almost blithely to imagine welfare-state medical care a fait accompli. Michael Szalay has recently argued that the scene of Laskell's illness organizes the novel's vision of a "new liberal polity."[43] This vision appreciates the welfare state's actuarial mechanisms for absorbing risk and contingency while still acknowledging the individual's "need for institutional assistance." In this view, "Paine's care stands in for the bureaucratizing of intimacy accomplished by modern health care" but also mitigates modern bureaucracy's tendency to stifle new experience, which in Laskell's case entails pursuing "questions of his own existence."[44] This account sheds light on the way Laskell's cultivated passivity indexes the largesse of modern institutional assistance. But it elides crucial distinctions between various welfare-state models and traditions while also overlooking similarities between the privatized system promoted by the AMA and the utilitarian welfare state. Indeed, it reinforces Trilling's erasure of liberal activists' laborious involvement in health-care politics and thus has the uncanny effect of rendering welfare-state assistance virtually indistinguishable from a fully privatized medical system. Szalay aligns Paine—and consequently Laskell's new liberalism—with a "new Rights of Man" discourse, but her functionalist performance conforms much more closely to the British utilitarian structure of the welfare state as well as to the American privatized system.[45] The AMA's pricing practice of a sliding scale fee-for-service functioned as a rudimentary actuarial system, absorbing risk and contingency on an ad hoc basis; like the utilitarian state, though, it was not beholden to principles of distributive justice, operating instead according to a paternalistic system of discretionary charity.[46]

Just as Nurse Paine likes to joke about having a "dreadful name for a nurse" (*MJ* 57), her having the same name as the renowned eighteenth-century sponsor of the *Rights of Man* is something of a lame joke. For in the realm of institutional medical ethics, as the bioethicist Laurence B. McCullough has clarified, the various state praxes emerging in eighteenth-century Britain, Germany, and France arose from quite distinct starting points. In Britain, patients' rights, such as they were, derived from the vocational duties of the physician and hospital, much as, in the nineteenth century, the AMA would define its vocational ethos. In both instances, the patient's passivity betokens the system's paternalistic structure.[47] In Germany (as perhaps only Foucault could fully appreciate), the hierarchy was yet more extreme: the state itself, in the form of the monarch, possessed "the right to a large, sturdy population" for the purposes of maintaining its armies. In contrast to these models, revolutionary France insisted on a natural right to health care "simply in virtue of being human," which did away with the British and American system of paternalistic charity—whether state-sponsored or private—and Germany's autocracy.[48]

In Trilling's novel, a similar delineation between the British and French models emerges in the contrast drawn between Laskell's two private nurses. Alternating with the night nurse Miss Paine, who clearly exemplifies the favored British tradition, is the bothersome day nurse Miss Debry, who hails from Quebec—*la belle province* of Canada, once part of the territory of New France, grounded in eighteenth-century French civil law, and long resolved to sustain France's political-cultural mores. These mores include France's socially conservative Catholicism—strains of which dominated Quebec in the late 1930s and the early postwar years under the governance of Maurice Duplessis—but they also include liberal-democratic idealism, which was held in abeyance until the Quiet Revolution of the 1960s, when the province's commitment to social democracy surged.

Trilling depicts Nurse Debry as a mixture of both lineages. For better or worse, she is far more prepared than Nurse Paine to treat the patient as a social equal rather than as a child. Specifically, she treats him as one whose adult heterosexual interests might match her own. She takes advantage of institutional correctness by decking herself out in the starched white uniform that enhances her dark beauty and by lightly transgressing mutually recognized interpersonal boundaries in ways that sexualize her attractiveness. Her "naughty" banter (*MJ* 46) and bedside manner of literally sitting on Laskell's bed, which allows her to show off her sizable bosom, turn institutional medicine's "rules" (50) and "elaborate technique[s] that preserved modesty" (46) into opportunities for flirtatious interaction. That Nurse Debry's name is a homophone of *debris* makes novelistic sense: with Nurse Paine scoffing at her colleague's "ill-conditioned Canadian" training (50) and Laskell blaming "provincial schools and hospitals" for her "foolish" mind (50), Trilling registers disapproval of the French-inflected alternative to the British way. When Laskell chooses Paine over Debry to be his only daytime nurse (no longer needing a nurse at night), he demonstrates discerning practical wisdom. The competent Paine would never destabilize his role as convalescing existentialist. His personal mission of high-minded inquiry depends on nestling into the de-eroticized arms of the mother country. This foreclosure on erotic disturbance—a mode of disturbance, to recall, that Plath's hospitalized patient ultimately comes to welcome—signals Laskell's contentment with a system of medical care that, in its insular distance from the era's politics of distributive justice, is in turn imagined as undisturbed.

If Laskell's insularity from the political "conditions of daily existence" thus amounts to a kind of ideological casualty through dismissal—that is, of activist liberalism—the life-or-death implications of the medical correlative of this dismissal become faintly visible in the surface details surrounding the novel's human casualty, Susan Caldwell. In other words, the novel's commitment to realist verisimilitude is sufficiently robust to sketch out the situation of the girl's chronic ailment and medical treatment. But these details are largely occluded, in terms of signifying power, by the novel's higher aim to convey the revelatory drama of embracing ideas in modulation. As though incapable of recognizing the scandal of its own realist evidence—that Susan's death is due in part to the inattention of medical experts—the novel parlays the incident into an ambiguity-rich existential meditation on tragic truth and beauty. This admixture of realism and sentimental romance discloses the soft violence of systemic inattention to be as consequential as a father's physical blows.

Notably, Susan's death is not the only literal death in the novel. A few years before its diegetic action begins, Laskell's cherished girlfriend died of pneumonia in New York. This sad event occurred despite "the best doctors, the best pneumonia nurses, the best equipment that the money of her comfortable parents could provide" (*MJ* 34). In the 1930s the viral and bacterial sources of pneumonia were well understood by medical science, although it would be another ten or fifteen years before antibiotics were introduced to treat such infections, lowering the death rate considerably. There seems nothing lurid or even metaphorically suggestive in this episode of the novel. By contrast, Susan's affliction, a "weak heart," is tinged with romantic obscurity—in the way, for instance, "pediatric cardiomyopathy" is not—and, in medicine's idiom, is lucid enough. The phrase, however, is invoked repeatedly by those who know of her condition, which include at first only two Hartford doctors and her mother, later Laskell, and then, after the death blows delivered by her father, everybody. No one seeks more precise medical information from the doctors. Instead, through repetition, the pat phrase renders Susan's ailment dimly sacred. Like Harriet Beecher Stowe's Little Eva, Susan's innocent charm and enigmatic condition spell her inevitable destiny. As one character puts it after her death, her father is merely "the agent of fate" (295).

On the one hand Susan's fate can be attributed to Trilling's knowing deployment of "melodramatic incident" and romantic "contrivance," for which even Warshow largely forgave him.[49] Viewed this way, Susan's function in the novel is but a pale shadow of Little Eva's: whereas Stowe's evangelical child is sacrificed to the noble cause of abolishing slavery, Trilling's rural urchin is sacrificed to the intellectual stoicism of modulating ideas. But on the other hand, alongside this romanticism (to which I return shortly), Susan's status as a sacrificial lamb gives voice to the reality of a deeply inattentive medical system. It resonates, for instance, with the way Emily exemplifies the trusting attitude Parsons describes, assuring Laskell that the Hartford doctors are "very good men" (*MJ* 204). In turn, Laskell, with his "city man's lack of faith in country doctors" (204), raises questions about the competence of these medical practitioners, but his skepticism targets them only as individual professionals and thus typifies the limited extent to which the traditional medical system faced scrutiny by the middle class. Neither before nor after Susan's death does Laskell or anyone else ask whether there should have been, say, a local clinic in place to monitor her regularly. Neither is Laskell stirred to question the broader socioeconomic relations that likely shape city doctors' treatment of the rural poor: their noninterventionist approach extends to their unawareness of—and perhaps outright indifference to—the fact that one parent was uninformed of the child's precarious health. This appalling failure to transmit key information proves disastrous for Susan, yet no one stops to wonder if the prevailing medical system—centered on urban hospitals and the delivery of acute care to the middle class—might have stacked the deck against a girl with a chronic disorder from an "underprivileged" family in rural Connecticut (223).[50] No one protests too much. More to the point, the novel leaves the impression that, in the realm of medicine, there is nothing to protest.

Trilling notoriously thought there was a special place in hell for writers of social-protest fiction. He viewed Henry James as one of the "few" novelists who is "able to write about the poor so as to make them something more than the pitied objects of our facile sociological minds" (*LI* 87). Hordes of other novelists contribute to a "literature of liberal democracy that pets and dandles its underprivileged characters" and then condescendingly "forgives them" their "faults" (87). In *The Middle of the Journey*, Trilling attacks this middle-class indulgence through his portrayal of Nancy Croom's attachment to Duck's authenticity—"he is so *real*" (*MJ* 19)—and her willingness to forgive the unreliability, crudeness, and inebriety of this unenterprising "odd-job man" (10). But as the narrative unfolds it becomes clear that more important than Trilling's desire to expose liberal democrats' (such as Nancy's) operations of bad faith regarding the lower class is his reluctance to endorse liberal democrats' commitment to goodwill, which was the founding impulse of midcentury liberal activism's pursuit of distributive justice.

In this respect, Trilling resembles the countercultural philosopher Herbert Marcuse, usually cast as Trilling's opposite number on the midcentury landscape. Marcuse ended his 1955 treatise, *Eros and Civilization*, with an extended attack on the neo-Freudian revisionist Erich Fromm for negating Freud's theory of the unconscious in favor of a consciousness psychology predicated on ethical idealism. Marcuse mockingly quoted the invocation by another neo-Freudian, Clara Thompson, of the human capacity for "justice, equality and cooperation" while scoffing at Fromm's description of love as involving "care, responsibility, respect, and knowledge."[51] Besides assailing neo-Freudian concepts, Marcuse mocked the neo-Freudian manner of writing. He contended that the neo-Freudians adopted a "*style*" of writing that "betrays the attitude." Like a "sermon" or the writing of a "social worker," their writing "is elevated and yet clear, permeated with good-will and tolerance and yet moved by an *esprit de sérieux* which makes transcendental values into facts of everyday life. . . . In contrast, there is a strong undertone of irony in Freud's usage of 'freedom,' 'happiness,' [and] 'personality'"—a bleak irony that seeks to drive home the illusoriness of such normative propositions.[52]

Trilling's similar commitment to a Freud-inflected tragic consciousness renders him averse to most things hinting of socioeconomic goodwill, be it encoded as style or substance. In *The Middle of the Journey*, this aversion leads him to frame the issue of class as primarily a long-standing problem of conflicting personalities and social manners rather than as a recent phenomenon of distributive politics predicated on equity justice. Class-based tensions come to a head when Laskell and his intellectual friends are awkwardly gathered around Duck, exchanging comments about the new custom-designed trailer that one friend, Kermit Simpson, has just arrived in. They are restrained by a Jamesian undercurrent of unspoken recognition that their chances of connecting with this social other are nil: "He was so apart from them all. . . . Their good will was not enough to overcome their superiority" (*MJ* 223). As the scene teases out the effect of class on character and personality, it steers Trilling's social analysis toward interpersonal psychology and away from considerations of equity. It is as though justice is too real an ideal, too goodwill driven, to be taken seriously by the aesthetic logic of the novel. Depicting the challenge of maintaining friendly relations in a class-fissured world becomes Trilling's way of addressing class while avoiding scenes of social protest informed by earnest goodwill. In the same vein, making an underprivileged man with very poor interpersonal skills the inadvertent agent of Susan's fatal collapse becomes Trilling's way of addressing the fact of socioeconomic difference while avoiding value-laden talk of sociomedical inequity or health-care politics more generally.

The novel's avoidance of health-care politics thus turns out to be crucial to its design. It enables the obscurity of Susan's weak heart to serve Trilling's higher—that is, existential-romantic—purpose of illuminating both the postwar significance and aesthetic necessity of dwelling in a cloud of mortality. The details of Susan's situation, which extend the novel's realism but also emphatically back Trilling's romantic existentialism, emerge when Emily discloses her secret to Laskell, who insists on routing this new information through a suitably romantic filter. At first, he strongly disbelieves Emily, despite recalling her surreptitious ways of protecting her daughter from, for instance, "walking too fast up the hill" (*MJ* 203). He suspects Emily of being the sort of woman who could "make up elaborate and romantic lies" about her life so as to confer on it alluringly tragic significance. But the more details she provides the more he comes to accept her account as truth: "He had to believe it now, he did believe it" (205). Believing, however, turns out to be the precondition not of medical evidence-gathering but of his own fanciful thinking. For as he goes on to qualify, "somehow he saw it as a fantasy, a thing that he could believe only for its own kind of truth. If it was a fact at all, it was not so much a fact in life as a fact in a poem" (205). The novel encourages us to regard this transmutation of real fact into poetic fact as an achievement of profound insight. For it is on account of this special factual status that Susan's illness redounds favorably to Emily's social status. It is what reveals her "great dignity" as she walks in what we now see is a genuinely tragic "cloud of mortality" (205). Possessing gravitas by virtue of her daughter's "precarious existence" (206), Emily earns the honor of being drawn into Laskell's personalized circle of existential truth. In this manner, ambient clouds of sociomedical unknowing succeed in preventing loftier clouds of existential truth from drifting back into the low-lying fog of everyday welfare-state politics and consternation.

In this scene of revelatory transformation, Trilling's subtle narratorial presence also works to reinforce the novel's central message that the possession of an active aesthetic imagination has political-existential value. Trilling's technique of focalization keeps Laskell's consciousness in the foreground, but Trilling supplements this perspective with a crafty intelligence that heightens the novel's literariness. Specifically, he embellishes this scene of Emily's medical truth-telling and Laskell's poetic truth-making with a foreshadowing pun of death. Amid the details recalled by Laskell of Emily's recent interactions with Susan—details that corroborate Emily's story—is Emily's gentle reaction to the child's excessive use of force when they were playing in the river: "He understood why it was that Susan could violently tumble Emily into the water with only the gentlest retaliation from her mother. There would have to be retaliation, Susan would have to be *ducked in revenge*, but only, as it were, in token form" (*MJ* 203, emphasis added). This verbal weaponization of the father's name exploits dramatic irony with such elegant violence as to flag Trilling's bid to meet the high standard of Jamesian artfulness. Later, when Duck's seemingly vengeful blows become the proximate cause of Susan's death, the displacement of the "token" by the actual stings, of course, but it also registers Trilling's commitment to combining existential truth and aesthetic play. He accomplishes what he once praised Allen Tate's one novel, *The Fathers*, for: "The strong tension of [Tate's] style which comes from the brutality of the 'abyss' being set against the narrative's delicacy and control."[53]

In *The Middle of the Journey*, Trilling explicitly thematizes this combinatory value, applying it even to works of art that exhibit an "ineptness" of "design" such as the painted wooden bowls Emily produces for sale at the local fair (*MJ* 294). Conspicuously not golden or exquisite, indeed earlier deemed "bad and silly and derivative" (240), the bowl Laskell has purchased "now" proves alluring in its "depths" of expression (293). Having been privy to Emily's cloud of mortality, her bowl now registers her profound "awareness of nullity, her knowledge of darkness" (294). Trilling presents this revaluation as the salutary consequence of Laskell's period of convalescence, as the achievement of his personalized yet distanced aesthetic and existential sensibility. Anderson argues that, Trilling, like Adorno, "turn[s] toward art as a kind of dynamic refuge from formal politics, invoking specific aesthetic energies ... to reorient moral and political thought."[54] However salutary this turn away from the "bleak radicalism" of Foucault's political historiography may be for contemporary theory, it is incumbent on us not to overlook the troublesome implications of this reorientation for midcentury political life. Although the rise of the aesthetic in Trilling's framework does not entail either a nullification of the political or a mutual exclusivity, his aestheticizing compass does point toward an idea of the political that operates almost exclusively in the lofty clouds of existential ideology. A literary realism that addresses welfare-state politics on the ground appears to be a bridge too near.

This reorientation, I've suggested, does much to keep the utilitarian tradition in place, a tradition that in midcentury America took little interest in destigmatizing poverty and disadvantage, that left distributive justice out of account, and that generally looked first to the marketplace for solutions to socioeconomic problems. In *The Middle of the Journey*, the 1930s setting and Laskell's professional vocation necessitate an acknowledgement of this dominant paradigm. But what's notable is how comfortable Laskell is with it. He counts among the class that historian Michael Lind describes as the "public service mandarinate," which is to say, an extension of "the patrician northeastern establishment" that prevailed in the Progressive Era.[55] It should come as no surprise, then, that Laskell understands his work in public housing as helping to meet the "basic needs of poor people" rather than helping to fulfill their rights on account of their being persons (*MJ* 31). Indeed, despite his "commitment" to this work (17), his attraction to free-market housing remains undiminished. This partiality becomes manifest in his admiration for the Crooms' country home, which veritably oozes "comfort and casualness," "elegance and neatness," "brightness and cheerfulness," and "compact privacy" (17). In its not "quite finished" picturesqueness, the house expresses the owners' "interest" and "feeling"—a stark contrast to public housing, which Laskell views as "at best poor makeshifts" (17). This is a public servant whose political-ethical ideas can't help but modulate in the direction of utilitarian preference satisfaction and patrician condescension.

Perhaps no episode discloses more vividly the implications of the novel's utilitarian slant than one near its conclusion in which Laskell comes precipitously close to embracing the goodwill stance of midcentury liberal activism. After Susan's death the issue of funeral expenses arises. As a gesture of personal affection for both mother and daughter, Laskell wants to lend a financial hand, but because of the illicit nature of his liaison with Emily, he wants to do this without drawing attention to himself. Laskell thus joins his wealthy and unwitting friend Kermit Simpson in covering these expenses, which includes buying real estate in the form of a cemetery plot for four and deeding it to Emily. When Emily's distant relative Miss Walker objects, Laskell resorts to New Deal ideology, asserting that she "has no more reason to be disturbed about this than Mrs. Caldwell's taking relief money. It's just as impersonal" (*MJ* 280). Aside from the irony that only in death does Susan's sociomedical fate precipitate Laskell's use of the language of distributive justice, it is worth remarking how close the novel comes here to articulating liberal activism's hostility to the distinction between deserving and undeserving welfare recipients, a distinction that allowed utilitarian welfare policy to align itself with traditional charity. And yet this moment of righteous hostility is fatally compromised by Laskell's deeply personal, deeply discretionary, and deeply buried motivation. Tellingly, the novel backs away from even this simulated endorsement of impersonal distributive justice. After all is said and done regarding the funeral arrangement, Emily meets up with Laskell and goes to considerable lengths to justify his charitable deed in the name of a personalized claim. "I'm happy [Susan] liked you so much," Emily declares, remonstrating against his sense of complicity in her death. "She was happy when she was with you. And I'm glad you paid for the funeral. You had a right to" (296). It isn't quite clear if Emily's gladness or Susan's happiness is supposed to matter more here, but it is very clear that Laskell's "right" hinges on their positive feelings toward him and his deeds. In other words, a utilitarian commitment to preference satisfaction guides the novel's conclusion. It ensures that the very idea of having a right is not uncoupled from the proposition of personalized or utilitarian happiness. Such is the novel's answer to being born with a weak heart.

A Classic in Sociology

An illuminating contrast to Trilling's occlusive picture of health-care politics in the 1930s can be found in his fellow New York intellectual Mary McCarthy's novel *The Group* (1963). When, for instance, the character Kay Petersen is persuaded to go to the hospital after an emotionally and physically violent altercation with her husband, we learn that she is motivated in part by her Blue Cross plan. Employed by Macy's, she envisions the kind of refuge that Plath's affect alien abhors—a place to "just rest and read and listen to the radio"—in one of New York Hospital's private rooms, for which she may use her insurance if she "[pays] the difference."[56] Although she ends up being surreptitiously committed by her husband to the "drab" Payne Whitney (G 315), which the novel informs us is "a private mental hospital, attached to Cornell Medical Center" (310), it turns out that the prospect of staying there, where she can receive hydrotherapy and a medical exam, see a gynecologist, have regular talks with a psychiatrist, play bridge and Ping-Pong, drink hot chocolate, and watch movies, becomes very appealing once she learns that "Blue Cross covers psychiatric hospitals" (331). This privileged Vassar girl, "trained," as literary critic Brenda Murphy puts it, "to believe in the efficacy of the New Deal," knows a good health-care deal when she sees one.[57] The novel ironically leaves it to her execrable husband Harald to fill in the objectionable detail, from the standpoint of New Deal liberalism, that "everybody doesn't have Blue Cross" (331).

McCarthy's only bestseller, *The Group* is generally understood to conform to her usual satirical style, whose mission is to expose the pretentious facades and shallowness of mass culture, including what Murphy calls the "false values and inadequate social theories" of the educated middle class, exemplified by the handful of recent Vassar graduates populating the novel.[58] Mocking one posture after another, the novel may thus appear to participate in the turn away from political judgment and toward culture and psychology that Thomas Hill Schaub argues marks postwar liberalism's refashioning of literary realism.[59] But the novel isn't entirely bereft of overt political reckoning. For one thing, there is its gender politics: feminist historian Nancy K. Miller has discussed "the sheer mass of detailed information" the novel provided "about the thirties and women's domestic lives."[60] *The Group* is particularly notorious for its early chapter, initially appearing in the *Partisan Review* in 1954, that portrays at length and in clinical detail the character Dottie Renfrew's pursuit of and fitting for a "diaphragm pessary" in Margaret Sanger's birth control clinic (G 51). Whereas such episodes prompted Norman Mailer to denigrate the book as "a classic in sociology," Miller locates its value precisely in this mode of "female realism."[61] Its delivery of crucial health-care information to women hampered by midcentury society's censorious attitude toward "the mysteries of sexual technology," Miller argues, amounts to an emancipatory project whereby women gain contraceptive knowledge about—and hence power over—their reproductive bodies.[62] In recuperating the novel's reception history (similar to critics' recent recuperation of lesbian pulp fiction's reception history, discussed in chapter 3), Miller fleshes out an episode in midcentury American history of distinctly feminist political progress.

But a historiography that promotes the value of McCarthy's novel primarily for its feminist effects in the 1950s and 1960s risks aligning it with the era's shifting liberal priorities—away from "working-class standard-of-living issues" to "quality of life [issues] reflecting the values and interests of the college-educated elite."[63] A closer look at some of the novel's less sensational aspects reveals McCarthy's sensitivity to this shift and a lingering commitment to class-based political diagnosis. The pessary episode itself illustrates this double investment. On the one hand, it portrays (with only mildly backhanded irony) the bravery of Dottie's pursuit of the birth control device. As a paying customer admitted to the doctor's "private practice," Dottie is invited into a lengthy, confiding conversation about her "right" to sexual satisfaction and pleasure (G 68); earlier the doctor's nurse assistant also expressed full confidence in Dottie's ability to follow instructions in using the device (68). Altogether the ordeal is shown to be interiority enriching and confidence building.

On the other hand, McCarthy widens her sociological lens to include underprivileged women in the picture—those who are "far from well-to-do" (G 59). These are the nonpaying "clinic patients" whom Dottie and Kay encounter in the waiting room. In their cheap, worn-out clothing and seeming timidity, they appear (at least to Dottie and Kay) to be latter-day living embodiments of the slum populations pictured in etchings and lithographs on the wall. One print is "of an early hospital ward in which untended young women, with babies at their side, were dying—of puerperal fever" (59). To be sure, a chain of elisions blurs the distinction between a pair of silent but extant beings and a multitude of women imprinted on two-dimensional images; in this manner the scene vaguely discloses the perceptual and cognitive operations by which the privileged class empties the underprivileged class of their living subjectivity. Still, Dottie and Kay demonstrate the moral wherewithal to recognize that these are the women the doctor is really concerned to help. "Private practice must be rather a letdown," says Dottie to the doctor (67), while Kay observes that "she and Dottie were just the frills on the doctor's practice"—mere girls with lifestyle choices to make (59). In her mind's ear, Kay can hear her jaded husband Harald pontificating on the middle-class's self-interested "birth-control crusade, whose real aim was to limit the families of the poor" (63). But the novel doesn't endorse his armchair declamations. Through the portrayal of the Kay and Dottie's firsthand encounter with the "dark, stately woman" doctor who has suffered police raids and even arrest for her "lifelong mission" (67), McCarthy conveys sincere respect for the clinic as a health-care institution. There may be less risk than in the past that impoverished women will die in childbirth, but the need to "limit their families" to mitigate poverty and women's chronic exhaustion is genuine (68).[64] These sociomedical afflictions are ones that economically comfortable and educated women such as Dottie and Kay need not personally fear. But the novel's intimate juxtaposition of class difference makes clear that they, as members of the class in charge of building the welfare state, would do well to become much more knowledgeable about such sociopolitical conditions of daily existence.

More journalistic metonym than lurid or romantic metaphor, then, *The Group*'s invocation of "puerperal fever" betokens the novel's commitment to a sociological realism that is reducible neither to its satirical exposure of facade, self-deception, and bad faith nor (as per Michael Trask's analysis) to its construction of authorial authenticity. To be more specific, the kind of sociology McCarthy aligns herself with in this novel is not so much the Cold War era's instrumental social science advanced by the likes of Talcott Parsons and Edward Shils, which Stephen Schryer has compellingly shown inflects McCarthy's late 1960s works on Vietnam, modernization, and globalization.[65] Rather, it is the kind of empirical-speculative sociology exemplified and defended by David Riesman and Eric Larrabee. Both political and characterological, this sociological style aimed, as Riesman explained in his sequel to *The Lonely Crowd*, to parlay empirical evidence into "illustrations, not . . . demonstration."[66] The method he and his colleagues employed involved conducting extensive interviews with individual Americans, thus compiling firsthand material from which they could test out sociological claims about contemporary American life: "Whatever realism the 'faces' possess," he maintained, "is abstract, not documentary."[67] The ambition, Larrabee added, is "to place less emphasis on prediction, manipulation, and control," in the manner of behavioral social science, "and more on understanding for its own sake."[68] Elsewhere, Riesman drew direct parallels between this kind of sociological knowledge and novelistic knowledge, clarifying that the pursuit of empirical-speculative understanding is intimately bound up with a society's reflexive self-examination, self-correction, and self-defense, "just as many novels and short stories today have writers as protagonists" to signify awareness of the endeavor's constructs. He leans on Trilling to back up these claims: "Not only must we all, as Trilling has said, become amateur sociologists to defend ourselves, perhaps against manipulation and certainly against misinterpretation, but we may all do so in order to share in a form of self-exploration which, among its other functions, has taken its place alongside the novel."[69] This relaxation of discursive borders gave credence to both Trilling's and McCarthy's styles of realism.

As critics have noted, McCarthy's employment in *The Group* of *le style indirect libre* along with copious use of direct speech effects an erasure of authorial personality—what McCarthy called ventriloquism—while enabling her projection of detached, ironic authority.[70] But however distant McCarthy may stand from her subject matter, the novel indexes the author's formidable retention of loads of specific 1930s detail, which cashes out both as relevant social *information*, as Miller shows, and as critical political *knowledge*. McCarthy herself took the novel to be about "the mirage of political and social progress which misled the young in the 1930s."[71] But what emerges in the margins of this mildly disenchanted political epistemology are distinct glimmers of liberal activism. To be sure, as Schaub importantly elucidates, McCarthy joined Trilling and other New York intellectuals in displacing their sense of the defeat of socialism and political radicalism onto a cultural and psychological critique of mass society.[72] In *The Group*, however, McCarthy supplements this sense of defeat with detailed observations of the incrementalist project of welfare-state building, particularly in the realms of medicine and health-care politics. Evinced in the episodes of Blue Cross and clinic care discussed earlier, this commitment also becomes visible in the romantic fates McCarthy delivers to certain characters. The most sympathetic and unscathed characters in the novel are Jim Ridgeley and Polly Andrews, who discover each other and get married near its end. He is a progressive medical doctor with "a bit of the do-gooder in" him (*G* 298); she is a lowly medical technician who respects but does not join the Trotskyites due to their belief in "permanent revolution" (294). One of the Vassar graduates, Polly surmises on the heels of her marriage "that she must be the only girl in the Class of '33 who was happy" (307). Here, we might say, the novel's metonymic realism aspires to the condition of Galbraith's symbolism while maintaining an arm's length from Trilling's aesthetic existentialism. Polly and Jim are a modest pair, but they aren't for all that without their novelistic and political significance.

World Health Tyranny

Metonymy and symbol were distinctions surely too fine for nonfictional midcentury liberal activists who were busy with medical and health-care affairs of both local and global proportions. On the one hand, they had to contend with an entrenched, vigorous, and effective conservative lobby, the AMA, which more or less backed the idea that medical care be treated like a commodity, albeit one that its providers couldn't advertise and that deserved subsidization for the poor. One could hear progressive liberals' collective groan when Senator Robert Taft put forth his National Health Program in 1949, which insisted on a traditional fee-for-service system: "It has always been assumed in this country that those able to pay for medical care would buy their own medical service, just as . . . they buy their own food, their own housing, their own clothing, and their own automobiles."[73] Federal assistance was to be offered to the poor, notwithstanding the manner in which a two-tier system stigmatized the disadvantaged with its means test and subjected medical care to the discretionary logic of charity (*STAM* 284).

On the other hand, the ambitious goals of liberals' ostensible ally—the ultraliberal offshoot of the UN, the World Health Organization (WHO)—threatened to render indistinguishable totalitarian and liberal world systems. This postwar institution helped to shape the discursive conditions in which health care could indeed look like another noxiously happy object, one that decided in advance and for everyone the material components of happiness and thus reinforced the dominant "tautology," as Ahmed calls it, whereby "what is good is happy and what is happy is good."[74] To be sure, in Western intellectual and political history good health has long been closely tied to happiness, whether as an external aid to the Aristotelian soul's effort to act in accordance with virtue (arguably a necessary but insufficient condition) or as a Cartesian rival for the status of summum bonum (arguably a cause as well as an effect). But in the immediate postwar era no institution did more to make health and happiness synonymous than the WHO. Whereas Article 25 of the UN's Universal Declaration of Human Rights merely envisioned everyone's "right to a standard of living adequate for the health and well-being of himself and of his family, including food, clothing, housing and medical care and necessary social services," the WHO Constitution promoted a comprehensive definition of health, one that implied causal relays between health, happiness, and world peace. It rejected the conventional definition of health as "the absence of disease or infirmity," redescribing it as "a state of complete physical, mental and social well-being." This all-encompassing first principle directly followed the WHO Constitution's opening declaration, which held that health was "basic to the happiness, harmonious relations and security of all peoples."[75] No one less than President Truman reiterated this specific relay between health and happiness. In a 1948 cable to Geneva upon the

US Congress's approval of US membership in the WHO, after saluting the WHO's prioritization of combating "controllable diseases" such as tuberculosis and malaria, Truman concludes, "Through WHO we once again testify to our faith in [the] UN as [a] great instrument for reaching those goals of common understanding and mutual happiness among nations which alone can lead to peace and security for all peoples."[76]

This early positive reinforcement notwithstanding, there was no shortage of objections to the WHO's world picture and design. The AMA was deeply suspicious of its tilt toward "socialized" medicine and played a significant lobbying role in the Eightieth Congress's temporary block on US membership.[77] In the ensuing decades not only conservatives but American liberals, who were largely sympathetic to the WHO mission, reflexively cringed before its grandiose vision. As bioethicist Daniel Callahan observed around the same time that Foucault formulated his biopower thesis, "The worst wars of the 20th century have been waged by countries with very high standards of health," thus calling into question the WHO's presumed alignment of health and peace. Although this claim stopped well short of Foucault's biopolitical totality, Callahan further noted that the WHO's wall-to-wall definition of health "turns the enduring problem of human happiness into one more medical problem, to be dealt with by scientific means."[78] Whereas the UN's phrasing hinged on the idea of *adequacy*, the WHO's keyword was *completeness*. This ambition, Callahan cautioned, "makes the medical profession the gatekeeper for happiness and social well-being," or even "the final magic-healer of human misery."[79] To make matters yet more alarming, the WHO's first general-director and author of the WHO Constitution's preamble, the Canadian military psychiatrist Brock Chisholm, was a proponent of a centralized world government—as well as of compulsory sterilization and eugenics. He disdained the global situation of conflicting nation-states and envisioned the WHO as guided by an apolitical creed of functional internationalism.[80] One didn't have to be a member of the AMA or a red-baiting member of Congress to see that the subsumption of happiness under the WHO apparatus could eventuate in a "tyranny of health." Such strenuous functionalism would be anathema as well to left-leaning modernists such as Adorno and Horkheimer who discerned fascist undercurrents in instrumental rationality. The WHO vision of blanketing the planet with its version of health, in other words, threatened to render health "synonymous with virtue, social tranquility, and ultimate happiness."[81]

Possibly the most expansive depiction of a world guided by a WHO-like regime was authored by the midcentury American science fiction writer James Gunn. Published in segments in the mid-1950s, his novel *The Joy Makers* (1961) portrays the manifestations of happiness, health, virtue, and tranquility as deeply intertwined, both in the near future and in more distant stages of a happiness revolution. By the end, though, the tranquility achieved is so deep that it might as well be slaughter. In the initial stage, a medical doctor affiliated with the nonprofit company Hedonics, Inc. deploys a high-tech chair to diagnose as well as treat a client. An introductory offer (a limited-service contract) quickly but only temporarily cures the client Josh's viral infection and ulcer as well as his habitual anger. Those who have agreed to an unlimited service contract, which requires signing over all of one's assets, have gained a new lease on physical, mental, and ethical life. Josh's dowdy middle-aged wife, Ethel, for instance, positively glows with cheer: "Her face became radiant, haloed somehow with joy so that she became ageless, eternally youthful, filled like a lamp so full of peace and happiness that it overflowed incandescently."[82] Similarly, the labor union agent who usually causes Josh so much trouble no longer wants to argue or pound the table (*JM* 30). Already happiness, health, and benevolence have become inseparable. The second stage takes place about a century later, in the "golden age" of applied hedonics, when happiness is now a right and a duty (49). Here the master Hedonist is in his midfifties but has the strength, health, and looks of a thirty-year-old athlete (48). He is highly trained and disciplined, and his happiness derives from practicing techniques of self-control: the devaluation, suppression, substitution, and sublimation of unreasonable desires. But as medical doctor, teacher, and therapist of a populous "ward," he labors happily to find less demanding solutions to his patients' happiness problems. He thus advises one homely, enervated young woman suffering from unrequited love to have weekly diagnostic sessions that will raise her blood pressure, improve her thyroid, and tone up her body; he also certifies her for "minor plastic surgery" in hopes that someone will fall in love with her (56). With medical practice and affect therapy joined at the hip, Gunn thus suggests that in this golden age, practicing the "art" of happiness depends on maintaining a "careful balance between objective reality and subjective attitude" (81, 146). This is how the master Hedonist's ward achieves a remarkable 97 percent on the Hedonic Index (79).

Equally important, achieving 97 percent happiness depends on the commitment and competence of an expert in medicine and psychology to ascertain each individual's unique means of achieving maximum personal happiness. The fact that the master Hedonist has almost forgotten his own name, Morgan, on account of its long disuse in his "position" as "manipulator of people's happiness," is but one indication of his functionalist dedication to his vocation (100). "You can't standardize happiness," the master Hedonist insists (81), expressing as vehement a commitment to the doctor-patient relationship as any midcentury member of the AMA. Indeed, in many respects *The Joy Makers* resembles an allegorical brief in support of the AMA's professional ideology precisely when American medical practice had reached its own "golden age," enjoying as it did in the early postwar decades "a historically unprecedented peak of prestige, prosperity, and political and cultural influence—perhaps as autonomous as a profession could be."[83]

In its version of a medical and hedonic golden age, *The Joy Makers* underscores the crucial nature of the master Hedonist's autonomy by portraying the disastrous consequences of eliminating him from the scene and putting humanoid "mechs" in his place. Morgan's benevolent, conscientious, artisanal paternalism is doomed once the WHO-like governing body, the Hedonic Council, determines that happiness belongs not to "art" but to "true science" and that nothing short of "one hundred per cent happiness" will suffice (*JM* 81). This decision ushers in a standardization of happiness controlled by various machines that the council installs to manage the efficient and reliable delivery of delusion-inducing narcotics. Morgan is rendered superfluous; his resistance to the new system incurs the council's life-threatening wrath, and he escapes with a group of malcontented colonists to Venus, where he serves primarily as a medical doctor and only gradually persuades the colonists to adopt the principles of applied hedonics. By the time the offspring of one of these colonists returns to Earth from Venus a century later, the council's administration of happiness has been entirely supplanted by the alien population of "mechs." Apart from one rebellious girl, all five billion living humans now dwell "submerged" in amniotic fluid with nutrients delivered through an umbilical cord (154). Here is a picture of world happiness as health: these human beings are perfectly secure and tranquil, they suffer no disease or infirmity, and they have the potential to live thousands of years in "embryonic bliss" (155). As they're all "dreaming long, slow, happy, fetal dreams" (154), Gunn also implies that all five billion are dreaming the same dream—until, that is, the colonist hero from Venus starts to wreck the machines. It isn't clear whether it's the narcotized state or the mechanical standardization that revolts him more. In any case he has already killed one such aged fetus and is prepared to let die "five billion totally happy people" and to do so without a shred of "guilt" (164). Mass slaughter or euthanasia indeed appears preferable to the universal distribution of comatose happiness and social tranquility.

If *The Joy Makers* thus resembles a dystopian inversion of the WHO's conception of health as a happy "state of complete physical, mental, and social well-being," it also takes on the hues of a horror story in league with the AMA to scare Americans into believing that progressive attempts to reform the health-care system amounted to a full-blown government take-over. In the same mid-1940s years that UN affiliates were drafting the WHO Constitution, the AMA was busy lobbying Congress, which conservatives temporarily reclaimed in 1946, and carrying out a public relations campaign to stigmatize President Truman's agenda as socialism.[84] When Gunn portrays the Hedonic Council as achieving through stealthy gradualism the power of a totalitarian state, granting itself immunity from legal suits that could block its machine dreams of 100 percent sentient happiness, he redescribes, in effect, the WHO as a rogue world government detached from any electoral process. Quintessentially utilitarian, such a state need no longer justify or defend its actions; it need only make its people happy.

Translating the Ominous into the Medical

At first glance the stealth gradualism structuring *The Joy Makers* may appear to resemble the incrementalist narrative that I suggest in the earlier chapter on Gwendolyn Brooks does much to bind the trope of happiness, properly construed, to welfare-state activism in a relation of mutual justification. But encoded in the numerically slight difference between Morgan's pursuit of 97 percent happiness in his patients and the Hedonic Council's mandate of 100 percent happiness is what the medical historian Carl F. Ameringer would call a "nonincremental" change: one born from a dramatic shift in ideology rather than from the expanded application of established principles and practices. In the real world of health-care policy, it wasn't Gunn's dystopia of government takeover but its opposite that threatened to undo liberal activism's incremental efforts to distribute health care and insurance more equitably. Ameringer points to the ideological triumph in the 1970s of the law and economics movement, led by such figures as Robert Bork, Richard Posner, and Clark Havighurst, whose free-market commitments and so-called consumer welfare (or public choice) theory ushered in a "health care revolution." As he sums up the situation, "If economists, such as Milton Friedman, provided the kindling for the health care revolution, then [these three legal scholars] supplied the kerosene."[85] Their work was crucial to the Supreme Court's decision in the 1975 case *Goldfarb v. Virginia State Bar*, which ruled that "the learned professions," including law, engineering, and medicine, were no longer exempt from the antitrust Sherman Act; this decision laid the foundation for the deregulation of the health-care industry over the ensuing decades, which enabled the rise of for-profit enterprises.[86]

These nightmarish and reactionary scenes—one fictional, one historical—of nonincremental development in the politics of health care help to throw into relief the alternative value and procedural system that sustained liberal-activist praxis and eventuated in the passage of landmark legislation, the Social Security Amendments of 1965. Notwithstanding the momentousness of this legislation—with Title XVIII providing for Medicare and Title XIX for Medicaid—its incrementalist structure is unmistakable. Medicare had the appearance of a universal health-insurance scheme for a so-called deserving population, the elderly; it thus merely extended the pension plan already in place and in many cases involved nongovernmental organizations such as Blue Cross to serve as fiscal intermediaries.[87] Medicaid was for all intents and purposes an extension of the Kerr-Mills Act of 1960, that is, "an extension of medical payments under state welfare provisions rather than a new health service program" that targeted the medically indigent.[88]

Critics of this legislation tend to dwell on its aggravation—like so many of President Johnson's War on Poverty initiatives—of a two-tier system in which poor people were stigmatized as recipients of the state's charitable largesse and the middle class were beneficiaries of what they're entitled to by right of their contributory past. However incontrovertible this critique, it also serves to detract attention from the challenges liberal activists faced in even framing socioeconomic disparities in terms of rights-based justice. In the realm of health-care politics, the utilitarian grip held fast. For instance, one of the most influential macroanalyses of the medical system came from welfare economist Kenneth Arrow. His 1963 essay, "Uncertainty and the Welfare Economics of Medical Care," laid out the problems of treating health care the same as any other marketable commodity. As though seeking to head off the free-market ideologues at the pass, he takes direct aim at the "lack of realism" in flamethrower Milton Friedman's approach to competition models.[89] He explains that actually existing "nonmarketable" elements, such as the communicable nature of some diseases, prevent the free-market pricing structure from operating efficiently in the medical industry. He draws on Talcott Parsons's sociology to outline other sources of nonmarketability such as the "expected behavior of the physician," which unlike the typical businessman is not "governed" by sheer self-interest but by "concern for the customer's welfare."[90] Whereas Paul Starr critiques Arrow (alongside Parsons) for bolstering the medical profession's authority and thus hampering the era's progressive agenda (*STAM* 225–27), Ameringer places more weight on Arrow's positive contribution to the discursive relay conjoining the "public-interest theory of regulation" that was dominant in the Progressive and New Deal eras and the midcentury "professional regime" that maintained physicians' near monopoly on their profession's pricing and delivery schemes.[91] But whether they characterize Arrow as a drag on the progressive movement or an agent in it, neither sees him as operating within the discourse of rights-based justice.

That is, neither mistakes Arrow for midcentury political philosophy's beacon of socioeconomic justice, John Rawls. To repeat briefly my earlier account of this pair, as early as 1958 Rawls took the idea of justice as fairness to be a repudiation of the utilitarian idea of justice as "a kind of efficiency" backed (at best) by benevolence.[92] This utilitarian idea informed dominant midcentury theories of welfare economics, including Kenneth Arrow's—one of Rawls's direct targets[93]—and played out as an ideology of rational choice supplemented (again, at best) by regulatory oversight. In the hands of competent administrators, utilitarian tools may well improve the general welfare, Rawls argued, but according to its own macroprinciples, utilitarian justice *cannot exclude* a cost-benefit analysis. Hence its potential endorsement not only of an inequitable distribution of resources but also of *slavery*. The utilitarian idea of justice thus negated Rawls's guiding liberal principle of respect for human dignity and autonomy.[94] Arrow effectively concedes as much in his essay on medical care, notwithstanding his ultimate advocacy for government intervention in the health-care industry. In an explanatory discussion of Pareto optimality—"the allocation of resources to services which will make all participants in the market better off"—he acknowledges the potential betrayal of the disadvantaged. If there is to be change from within an achieved state of optimality, he says, "we cannot indeed make a change that does not hurt someone; but we can still desire to change to another allocation if the change makes enough participants better off and by so much that we feel that the injury to others is not enough to offset the benefits."[95] He thereby accepts in principle that the least advantaged could receive an even worse allocation of resources—a proposition that Rawls's theory of justice precludes due to its unreasonableness from the standpoint of the original position, from which emanates the maximin principle. To be sure, Arrow goes on to explain that slavery per se is not really a threat, since the sources of nonmarketability alluded to earlier include "social or historical controls, such as those prohibiting an individual from selling himself into slavery."[96] In other words, slavery isn't an option in Arrow's welfare economics, not because of any moral principle of fairness or autonomy but because of history and custom.

In what follows I argue that Paula Fox's early novels make visible the incremental yet enormously consequential effects of a Rawlsian approach to justice on 1960s health-care politics. In her 2001 memoir, Fox describes how as a child she "learned" from black household servants "what justice was."[97] One particular incident drove home this lesson. It was when Fox's father was in the middle of spanking her for a trivial offense and the black maid protested, "Mr. Fox! That isn't right! That isn't fair!" Fox goes on to describe how, years later, she often thought about this woman's brave action, in which "a sense of justice in her had outweighed the risk" of reprisal.[98] Fox carries forward this sense of justice into her fictional renditions of contemporary New York life, which involve significant trips to the hospital. In a 2004 interview with the *Paris Review*, Fox mentioned that her very first publication was a series of articles she wrote for the *People's World* (a labor paper based in San Francisco) in the mid-1940s on the Kaiser medical care program.[99] By the time she published her first novel, *Poor George*, in 1967, she had been married for about five years to Martin Greenberg (who, along with his brother Clement, was an editor of *Commentary* for some years) and had circulated on the margins of the New York intellectual scene. She became acquainted with Alfred Kazin and the Trillings, among others, and developed a lasting friendship with Irving Howe. This novel, as though taking the thematic baton from another New York intellectual, Mary McCarthy, culminates in an emergency hospital visit in which an employer-based Blue Cross plan serves the protagonist very well. By the time Fox published her second novel, *Desperate Characters*, in 1970, the Medicaid program had been operative for a few years. This program serves a fleeting character less than well, but it leaves, in conjunction with an earlier episode in a Brooklyn hospital's emergency room, an indelible, justice-affirming mark on the novel.[100]

In many ways, Fox's second novel appears to rewrite her first. In mapping out their interconnections, we'll begin to see how the medical care theme enables Fox not only to keep the novelistic enterprise in touch with politically inflected sociology in the manner of McCarthy but also to engage existential issues in the manner of Trilling. This latter engagement, however, entails crucial qualifications that amount to a rewriting of Trilling's investment in the medical situation. Recall that for him, near-fatal illness becomes in *The Middle of the Journey* an occasion for John Laskell to hover on the brink of abyss, to nurse a tragic, disenchanted sense of the world, and thus to insist on a politics of modulation in which, to repeat Amanda Anderson's claim, an "appreciation of complexity over action" is the "precondition for any renewed or appropriate political engagement."[101] Trilling's posture, then, is essentially retrospective; it is born (understandably enough, given its 1947 publication) out of a post-Holocaust regard for catastrophe. Akin to Walter Benjamin's abused angel of history, Laskell's backward fixation on his brush with death thus assumes the status of a moral necessity as well as an existential one—as though it would be a colossal betrayal for him to turn around and commit to a future of actual decision-making.

By contrast, Fox's summoning of the contemporaneous medical situation, some twenty years later, figures a stay *against* the abyssal, indeed, a stay against complexity. Her protagonist George Mecklin's propensity for "complex . . . reflection" is connected to his "enervating" way of moving through life in a "permanent blur."[102] Treatment in the hospital following his near-fatal medical emergency restores not only his physical well-being but also his existential outlook. In *Desperate Characters* one of the main characters, Sophie Bentwood, who is a professional translator, complains to herself about the English rendition of a sentence from the book she's reading on the New

York subway, *Renée Mauperin* by the Goncourt brothers: "'Illnesses do their work secretly, their ravages are often hidden.' It would sound, she thought, less medical and more ominous in French, more universal."[103] In Sophie's lexicon, the adjective *medical* appears synonymous with *clinical* or *bureaucratic*, indicating the translation's failure to capture an essentially tragic and universal human condition evoked in the original French. Trilling's existentialism lingers on. But from the novel's broader perspective, *medical* signals a salutary move away from tragic consciousness. More precisely, it binds tragic consciousness to the contingencies of everyday life; it defines the tragic downward. The novel argues in effect that the better (that is, more equitable) medical care a society has, the less tragic it is. Fox discloses the political and existential merits of siding with the "medical" over and against the "ominous," implying that the choice is a matter not merely of personal health but also of social justice, one that is predicated on a commitment to the future. However angst-ridden its patients, a postwar medical system can accommodate only so much existential complexity.

The intertextual connections between Fox's two novels revolve around three general components of her fictional style and substance: construal of character and interpersonal relations, scenes of physical crisis and subsequent medical treatment, and movements of plot toward difficult resolutions. These components operate with relative consistency in the realist idiom, but a fourth component—namely, Fox's numerous references to avant-garde art and theory—gains over the arc of the two novels a kind of allegorical valence.[104] Although these references are realist in origin, drawn as they are from midcentury aesthetic practice and theory, I want to suggest that in the second novel they coalesce into metacommentary on aesthetic form and genre. This metacommentary ultimately serves to hammer home, by way of allegorical accumulation and action, a broad endorsement of welfare-state justice, obtained through incrementalist means. The intensification of this motif between the first novel and the second mirrors another incremental shift, namely, that between the first novel's acknowledgment of the virtues of Blue Cross and the second novel's acknowledgment of the virtues of Medicaid: welfare-state justice and aesthetic thought, as it were, soldier on.

As far as their characters are concerned, both novels could have been titled *Desperate Characters*. Both are populated with liberal bourgeois professionals—teachers, lawyers, psychoanalysts, radio personalities, and so forth—along with urban artist-hipsters who make the parties these professionals attend in Brooklyn and Greenwich Village edgier but also more dispiriting. Both focus on domestic couples in or approaching middle age who are exhausted by their marriages (Emma, George's wife, appears to suffer from chronic fatigue syndrome). The troublesome state of these marriages loosely corresponds to the spouses' perception of inhabiting dissolute and inauthentic worlds. Whether it's the ascendance of youth culture's indulgent dissipation—exemplified by their preoccupation with long hair, their use of "jelly" words like "wow," and their belief in the "great oneness of everything" (*DC* 63, 81)—or their own generation's enervated passivity, in contrast to the Trotskyite activism in the 1930s of their older New York intellectual friends (81–82), these couples have seemingly acquiesced to the syndrome of quiet desperation that Thoreau diagnosed as the affliction of mass society. Indeed, despite their educated capacity to name and analyze this syndrome (120), their sense of purposeless, monotonous floundering rivals Prufrock's malaise, while their view of the contemporary social and environmental landscape—with its campaign posters of "an Alabama presidential candidate star[ing] with sooty dead eyes" over "crawling, suppurating urban decay" (119)—echoes Doctor Eckleburg's valley of ashes. It is against this backdrop of inner and outer dystopia that Fox puts into motion two dramas of medical-institutional restitution.[105]

With George Mecklin in the first novel and Sophie Bentwood in the second serving as the primary agents of drama, Fox's realism imbues her focal characters with interiority but importantly withholds from them the capacity to develop. Their static quality is not primarily a matter of debased self-deception, as is the case, say, in Richard Yates's 1961 novel about suburban malaise, *Revolutionary Road*. The main character of that novel, Frank Wheeler, after the death of his wife April following a botched home abortion, reveals his hollowness to anybody who'll listen to him, now a "walking, talking, smiling, lifeless man."[106] Rather than condescending satire, Fox's realism invites characterological scrutiny. What kinds of difficult (or desperate) characters, she seems to ask, is the liberal bourgeois class of the 1960s liable to produce? Conversely, how will these flawed characters cope with the sociopolitical order they inhabit and perpetuate? More to the point, will the sociopolitical order, exemplified by the medical system, be able to treat these flawed characters in a manner that affirms its underlying principles of social justice?

To address this last question, the critic Jennifer Schuessler's insight that Fox is "interested less in psychology than in the deforming straitjacket of character" serves as a good departure point for examining how Fox's characters shed light on systemic conditions.[107] Schuessler's claim dovetails with Fox's invocation, in the *Paris Review* interview, of the dictum attributed to Novalis that "character is fate."[108] But Fox is hardly the Bellovian novelist pursuing moral and existential questions of how a good man should live or how an adventurous man such as Augie March might achieve a good enough fate.[109] Rather, by mobilizing flawed characters, Fox is able to contrive a faintly static and abstracted mode of literary realism that foregrounds the systemic features of the contemporary world. More specifically, this form of realism throws into relief the features of the midcentury welfare state's value system. We'll see that Fox's novels reveal this system's modes of justifying its values, even when specific policy decisions fail to do these values full justice.

To put this novelistic problematic somewhat differently, later in the same 2004 interview, Fox finds herself mostly agreeing with the interviewer's suggestion that her construal of character conforms to Joyce Cary's take on fiction's problem with realistic characters. According to Cary, the interviewer says, quoting, "Real people are too disorganized for books. They aren't simple enough.... [Thus realism's heroes and heroines] are essentially characters from fable, *and so they must be to take their place in a formal construction which is to have a meaning*." Fox replies that "Cary was right."[110] Decades earlier Fox described a near-epiphanic experience of discovering the operations of "analogy," that is, how a "literal representation" of something became "something else," or how "concrete stories" held "transcendental meanings."[111] But at the same time that she warms to the proposition of fiction's creation of meaning through formal construction and simplification, she holds onto the proposition that fiction remains concrete, that it can "suggest things" about "the complexity of human life."[112] It is by means of this axis of empirical plausibility (or suggestiveness) and formally constructed "fable" that Fox steers her novels away not only from Yates's satirical condescension but also from the dialectic of character presiding over Trilling's novel. Whereas *The Middle of the Journey* dramatizes existential complexity by modulating between political disenchantment and dubious hope for a post-Holocaust world—a novelistic frame that is fundamentally committed to character as a function of psychology (in Trilling's case, specifically

Freudian psychology)—Fox delineates a dialectic between flawed or compromised persons and postwar liberal activism's value system, a system that she shows must indeed struggle to sustain and justify itself. By gesturing toward the ongoing pressure on liberal activism to expand welfare-state justice, specifically in the realm of health care, her novels deploy characters to embody perspectival and experiential increments of what Joyce Cary—while reaching for the fable—would call meaning.

In the case of *Poor George,* Fox portrays the virtues of a Blue Cross system by escalating the insured protagonist's conditions of personal crisis to a point of near fatality, when he is shot by the neighbor in the Hudson Valley whom he befriended (more precisely, befrenemied). This situation precipitates a rush to the Peekskill hospital. Among all the deformed characters inhabiting these two novels, George Mecklin may be the most sympathetic. An English teacher at a private high school on the Upper West Side, George has an eye, ear, and nose for the city's "air of decay and desolation" (*PG* 6). He is disturbed by the grotesque yet ordinary pathologies he observes around him, such as the near collision of a "blind Negro" pedestrian and a seemingly obtuse boy, afflicted by junk toys, "whose head was encased in a transparent bubblelike helmet" called a "Space Scout" and who is first shaken and then "smacked" by a "massive" woman, likely his mother (4). This is not a world that is easy to love. George also dislikes *Moby Dick* because he has "no passion for revenge" (14), which furthermore makes him "especially careful" when marking the exam on this novel of a ninth grader because "one had to be fair to people one hated" (21). George is someone who, although feeling "vaguely oppressed as far back as he can remember," nonetheless harbors "an undefined but powerful sense of possibilities" (14).[113] In addition to his pained sensitivity and vague optimism, George is put off by his smug neighbor, Charlie Devlin, whose "nose for culture and happiness" sniffs out all the available "in" people to host on his vapid radio program called "Happy People" (26, 65, 66). Charlie and his wife Minnie's cynical superiority and fraudulent hipsterism are what prompt George's consternation about midcentury Americans' pursuit of happiness: "Was the nearest you could come to happiness a feeling of unqualified self-justification? If that were true, probably the Devlins had attained bliss" (169). Some ten years after Humbert Humbert's confirmation of this happiness logic (discussed briefly in chapter 3), Fox will answer George's question by ultimately displacing a happiness conditioned by cynical self-justification with a happiness conditioned by competent hospital care justified by the welfare state.

By ratcheting up the tension in the novel's plot, Fox draws attention to the difficulty of achieving this displacement. Here I summarize its blunter points; most gripping perhaps is that Charlie shoots George outside the Devlin home. Long before that, George fails at his attempt, in effect, to homeschool a juvenile delinquent—the neighborhood peeping tom and ugly racist named Ernest—who earlier had broken into the Mecklin home (and later steals a radio) and who will eventually betray George by having quick daytime sex with Emma, his despondent, increasingly estranged wife. This cuckolding incident precipitates a violent quarrel between the spouses, followed by Emma's abrupt and conclusive departure. Marital crisis then escalates into George's drawn-out crisis of existential purpose, culminating in an alcohol-drenched tour through Greenwich Village with a colleague from the school who spends his summers impersonating a bohemian "inaction painter" (*PG* 176) and who practically deafens George with his nonstop talk. This Walpurgisnacht winds down and then winds up again when George finally decides to head home but out of desperate confusion finds himself instead prowling around the Devlin home, as though channeling the sluggard Ernest. When Charlie suspects a burglar and comes out of the house with barrels firing, the jig seems up for poor George.

In a grimmer novel—say, Horace McCoy's 1935 *They Shoot Horses, Don't They?*—George would have been put out of his misery by dying from the gunshot wound. But in *Poor George* the protagonist not only lives to see another day but finally enters a realm of the 1960s system that does not reek of "decay and desolation": the Peekskill hospital. A notable aspect of this late episode in the novel is the layered intricacy of its social and health-care politics. The snidely racist Charlie Devlin is put in his place by a black paramedic who is conspicuously less than deferential. The critical nature of the emergency—a gunshot wound to the chest that threatens lung collapse and "tension pneumothorax" (*PG* 201)—is entwined with the authoritative impatience and general irritability yet total competence of the medical team. So too, the lead doctor's sarcastic response to George's timorous report of his Blue Cross coverage—"Congratulations" (202)—stands cheek by jowl with George's "awful" contemplation of "the democracy of [his] body" (203), suggesting that medical crisis may generate the very idea of the political.

As for this specific idea of the political, it is worth remarking that for a brief period in the late 1940s Fox lived in Peekskill (with her second husband Richard Sigerson, who, according to her biographer, started a PR agency devoted to medical and pharmaceutical products during this time).[114] Fox also fondly tells of meeting Paul Robeson in the 1940s, once sharing a cab with him.[115] Earlier she had become well versed in leftist politics, primarily through tutorial sessions with her supercilious first husband, rendered into fiction in *The Western Coast*. Yet in *Poor George* there is no mention of the infamous Peekskill riots of 1949—featured prominently in E. L. Doctorow's *The Book of Daniel*—when anticommunist, antiblack, and anti-Semitic forces combined to stir up violence against attendees of a benefit concert featuring Robeson and organized by the radical left. This voluminous silence, I suggest, doesn't so much signal a betrayal of the left as a yielding to its moderate wing, whose progressive but decidedly incremental measures are on extended display in the hospital episode.

What first stands out in the episode is the way George comes to terms with his situation. Whereas Trilling's John Laskell convalesces in the privacy of his New York apartment and McCarthy's Kay Petersen pays extra for a private room in the Payne Whitney, Fox's George declines the luxury of solitude, despite guilt-ridden Charlie's readiness to cover extra expenses (*PG* 210). He opts instead to be treated in a room with four beds (201). This spatial arrangement frames the novel's dialectic between flawed person and functional welfare-state system. Not unlike Laskell, George is at first awash in fearful "knowledge of his own death" (202), which the sounds of three sleeping patients do nothing to alleviate (203). Their presence seems even to exacerbate George's estranged sense of losing existential ground to the clamoring democratic demands of his bodily material:

> His body seemed to be appallingly spread out, lost to him, the *he* that had been its everything. Had he imagined that he was the sole support of all his cells? And that *he* was really more significant than the cells of his lungs, his sweating fingertips? The democracy of the body was an awful thing to contemplate; he had believed he *was* what he thought; what he really was was an unstrung weight adrift. (203)

Afflicted by this "awful" experience of a pure, mindless version of "democracy," George is "adrift" in the direction of Sophie Bentwood's "ominous" territory. As morning arrives, however, George begins to recover from his dark night of the soul. Mindless democracy is reined in by the goodwill country of medicine, which is demarcated by the constructed space of the hospital room and the purposeful activity of other beings in it. The patients in the room include "an elderly Negro" who is too ill to interact—and soon dies—as well as a "young man" with whom George exchanges stares and who extends a morning greeting (205). Evenly distributing their attention around the room, nurses in "starched" white also alternate between "star[ing] impassively" at him and "friendly" yet "forbidding" interaction (204, 205). When George learns that the black patient's death "is not to be mentioned here" (206), we come to see that this suppression does not signal existential, racial, or moral evasiveness, as in *The Middle of the Journey*, but rather the hospital system's commitment to the present and future time of the living. "People did not die in time but out of it" (206), George thinks, indicating his growing ease with his specific life and time in his specific body amid the specific contingencies of the 1960s system. This is a system that clearly has familiarity with death but does not for all that accommodate its abyssal awfulness, as Laskell's existentialism demands. The ominous, here, is methodically translated into the medical.

It is also telling that George's relation to the nursing staff develops in a completely different manner from Laskell's. Like him, George grows emotionally attached to his private nurse. But unlike him, he's capable of treating her as a social and sexual equal, one he can imagine "out of the hospital, walking down the street emitting faint sexual cries" (*PG* 207). Whereas Laskell, to recall, imagines Nurse Paine as a maternal figure—"the nanny or the governess" (*MJ* 47)—and disdains the sexy Nurse Debry, George thinks his nurse "is a little like Emma," his wife (*PG* 207). Yet he harbors no delusions of a long-term acquaintance; he may feel "awful" when she announces her imminent departure, due to his recovery (207), but just as she predicts, "he . . . forget[s] about her" soon after she leaves (209). In this hospital room Fox presents system and persons as more or less calibrated to one another.

Perhaps no moment better captures the novel's insistence on the system's attempt at equitable beneficence toward its living citizens than when George the beneficiary finds himself deeply "interested" in all the "procedures" being done to him:

> His pulse, his blood pressure, his respiration, the antibiotics, the sedatives, all grew intensely significant. He waited greedily for examinations and questions and hypodermics. Even the mysterious thoughtfulness of Miss Hyslop, his nurse,

as she looked at the connections where the tubes entered his body, filled him with a kind of joy. (*PG* 205)

No longer swamped by pure democracy, George experiences happiness as induced by his collaboration with the medical system in giving impersonal yet purposeful attention to his body's welfare. Here the novel turns an affective and symbolic corner. Rather than permitting the Devlins to monopolize the symbolic meaning of Americans' pursuit of happiness, Fox offers a decisive alternative. On view at the end of *Poor George* is a system-justifying "kind" of "joy" that midcentury liberal activists can believe in.

Drawing on Happiness

By the mid-1960s, however, the picture of a medical system financed by the middle-class's prepaid insurance plans such as Blue Cross would not be cause for sustained celebration. It was certainly an improvement, when it came to hospital access and distributive equity, over the discretionary sliding-scale model preferred by the medical profession. And as *Poor George* lightly suggests, the quality of medical care that the middle class came to expect tended also to improve the care that the underprivileged received.[116] But the "drive and enthusiasm" of Blue Cross's early advocates (*STAM* 296) would give way to suspicion that its mission of nonprofit public welfare had been overtaken by its concerns as a business operation. Having phased out of its status as an experiment of "pragmatic humanitarianism" and then as a movement of "dogmatic privatism"—albeit one subsidized by tax exemptions—it entered a new phase of managerial "stabilization."[117] By the 1960s its public-interest ideology was deeply compromised by such decisions as replacing "community rating" with "experience rating" so as to compete with commercial insurance companies for accounts with employer groups and unions.[118]

It was also becoming clear that the aged and indigent were increasingly neglected by the current insurance-based system. For one thing, they could not afford the premiums; for another, it had "an inflationary effect . . . on the cost of medical care," thus leaving them worse off (*STAM* 333). Although Blue Cross may have once seemed a promising "test case for democracy," as historian David J. Rothman has put it, by the 1960s its many deficiencies were glaringly visible.[119] The Democrats' landslide victory in 1964 offered a legislative opportunity for launching incremental yet dramatic correctives in the form of Medicare and Medicaid.

If these new programs, especially the latter, became the test case for social justice in the late 1960s, then *Desperate Characters* may be understood as a kind of gloomy amicus brief in social justice's favor. As mentioned earlier, explicit references to Medicaid are minimal in the novel, but the presence of this program—alongside that fabled site of medical trouble, the city hospital's emergency room—is key to its narrative force. On the one hand, these references register the stark socioeconomic disparities afflicting the country, which the setting of a gentrifying Brooklyn does much to underscore. On the other hand, they figure a form of redistributive inclusiveness that, no matter how desperate its middle-class characters, the novel labors to endorse. Plath's clean and efficient hospital plainly won't do as a Galbraithian symbol of happiness, but Fox's dingy and crowded city hospital proves more promising.

The novel's central characters are gentrifying "pioneer[s]" Sophie and Otto Bentwood, who dwell amid the blight of 1960s Brooklyn (*DC* 5). Everywhere around their beautifully maintained brownstone they perceive the physical and moral decrepitude of "the slum people" (13). With the disparity between public squalor and private opulence fully in view, the novel's realism corroborates Galbraith's claims. Its action revolves around a medical emergency: Sophie is bitten while feeding a stray cat and fear sets in that the cat might be rabid. Sophie has access to doctors in private practice, but she neither demands one nor wants to go to the nearby hospital. Meanwhile her dread worsens. Sophie's reluctance to seek treatment is eventually overcome, but she persists in indulging in a morbid syllogism: "*If I am rabid, I am equal to what is outside*" (151). This phantasmatic desire amounts to a yearning to embody the public hospital—more precisely, to embody her dim view of it—whose "odor of despair," "special claustrophobic warmth," and general dilapidation "combined the transient quality, the disheveled atmosphere of a public terminal with the immediately apprehended terror of a way station to disaster" (101, 102, 103). As Fox tracks Sophie's literal and psychic steps toward, into, and away from the hospital, she exposes her character's susceptibility to the Plath syndrome while also indicating alternatives to it.

To begin with, Fox represents Sophie's overdetermined reaction to her need for emergency medical care as a function of her fortressed privacy, thus indicating how the public squalor/private opulence problem preys even on the wealthy. When a psychiatrist friend to whom Sophie shows her bite worries as much about her mental health as about the bite (*DC* 23–24), we see how readily Sophie might inhabit a Plath poem. For all her identificatory yearning to merge with the denizens of squalor, she exhibits an obsessive will to privatize, suggestive of a kind of overproduction of personal capital. As Otto's estranged law partner, Charlie, tells her, she is "enslaved by introspection" (39), which she herself at one point calls her "secret hoarding" (58). Guilt-laced inwardness is her specialty stock, and cultivating the conditions of panic—and then yielding to panic—allows Sophie to retreat even further from the public realm and thus to increase the hoard of her personal self. In other words, the panic precipitated by the cat bite manifests itself in her very imagination of the "outside" as rabid: she projects her inner affliction onto a world totality. As this psychopersonal wealth of dread and guilt takes the form of projective yearning, it also funds Sophie's nimble flipping of spatial metaphors. This is visible when she mulls over the "rules" she violated while involved in an extramarital affair; she concludes that "ticking away inside the carapace of ordinary life and its sketchy agreements was anarchy" (62). That is, her "inside" is already "equal" to her "outside": in experiencing the social world as rabid and the domestic world as anarchic while exhibiting contempt for the bracing antidote to both worlds' afflictions—namely, consensual "agreement"—Sophie has, like Plath's speaker in "Tulips," all the makings of an affect alien a la Ahmed's social phenomenology. Ahmed's suspicion of the welfare state extends to consensus liberalism's structural formation, which entails, in her argument, an "immanence of coercion, the demand for agreement," both affective and political. "After all," she argues, "agreement can mean not only 'the action of pleasing or contenting'" but also "'the act of consenting.'"[120] According to Sophie's and Ahmed's lights, then, there's little chance in the postwar era for the *ominous*—the anarchic, the rabid, the coercive—to translate into the *medical*.

Fox, however, is rather chary of this psychopolitical logic. Her close but severe narrative perspective conveys both psychological intimacy and sociological distance. The scenes in the hospital, although grim in their portrayal of the facility's inadequate resources, cultivate this distance by demonstrating (as in *Poor George*) the competence of medical practitioners and their interactions with other patients. Among them is an unnamed ER patient who, after a long and painful wait for the treatment he receives, returns to his wife and children in the waiting room, energetically "waving a piece of paper, [with] a bullying look of cheerfulness on his face" (*DC* 104). With hard-won, difficult cheer emerging in the novel's space of critical distance, Fox fashions something like a Galbraithian symbol, a validation of the public health-care sector.

This validation, however qualified, is all the more remarkable because by the late 1960s New York City's medical care had severely deteriorated—despite, according to public-policy historian James Colgrove, the city's "long tradition of innovative public health activities" and Mayor John Lindsay's earlier commitment to "public authority" as an instrument of change.[121] Colgrove stresses the "realistic" nature of its public-health professionals' "vision of change," by which he means their "incremental rather than radical" strategies and expectations.[122] But efforts to prioritize prevention and population analysis over cures and individual patient care were routinely outstripped by daily crises demanding immediate hospital attention.[123] The emergency room, as historian Beatrix Hoffman explains, often became the destination "of first resort" for "all types of patients, from the poor and uninsured to the middle class."[124] Ever since the 1946 Hill-Burton Act facilitated a boom in hospital construction and expansion, these institutions were largely expected to have well-functioning emergency rooms. By the 1960s, although "transformed into overcrowded purgatories [and] staffed by gruff administrators and harried nurses and physicians, where patients waited for hours," these ERs served as a "community resource" both for emergency and nonurgent care.[125] Meanwhile, Medicaid funds were often diverted to private hospitals at the expense of neighborhood clinics, and white flight patterns left a third of the city's remaining population medically indigent.[126] Adding to these difficulties, community activists who reasonably regarded poor health as a form of injustice and charity care as an affront to the "self-esteem" of the disadvantaged carried their protests so far as to interfere with the delivery of some public-health services.[127] Once again, this world is not easy to love. Whatever the practical setbacks, however, the deliberately incremental efforts of the Great Society era were generally keyed to ideas of social justice: "Clinicians, community activists, politicians, and policy-makers sought to create new models of medical care that were more equitable and efficient than those of the past."[128]

Formally mirroring this incremental process, Fox's novel constructs a set of interlocking scenes that capture, even as one punningly involutes, these deeply compromised but not ominous conditions. These scenes appear in sequential order, essentially spanning the novel's weekend time frame. The first is the scene mentioned earlier in which the Bentwoods' friend, fellow gentrifier, and party host, the psychiatrist Dr. Holstein, discovers, right after unsuccessfully phoning various physician friends on Sophie's behalf, that someone has thrown a stone through his window (*DC* 21–23). Here Fox plays Sophie's access to private-practice medicine against the hostile, anonymous protest of the underprivileged. The second takes place the next evening in their home when an agitated black man in a "leopard pillbox hat" and "brilliant red shawl" knocks at their door and pleads with them to let him use their telephone, referring to the other neighbors who have shut the door on him as "inhospitable cats" (98). Here Fox's rabies-resonating pun infuses the scene with ambiguity: Who exactly is the poisonous cat? Whose lack of hospitality is under review? Fox also plays the Bentwoods' simultaneous suspiciousness and submission—they let the man in but wonder if they've been swindled of the cash he persuades Otto to loan him—against a possibly cannier version of protest than that of the window-breaking stone thrower. A third interlocking scene takes place later the same evening at the ER wing of the nearby hospital, where Sophie feels "helplessly . . . reduced in size" by the high desk of the ER clerk, while Otto, in search of his health-insurance card, "attack[s] his pockets brutally as if he were mugging himself" (102). Here Fox plays the couple's financial health against their psychosocial deficiency and anxiety, now turned completely in on themselves.

The interlocking quality of these scenes constitutes an important dimension of Fox's narrative purpose. She is less interested in tightening the screws on her flawed characters (in the manner, say, of Yates) than in conveying, in the small episodic units of a weekend, the mutually damaging disparity between the economically privileged and their disadvantaged neighbors. Yet by lacing these scenes with vague allusions to the rabies threat, she also keeps in play the socially binding structure of the welfare state. We begin to see why the specific affliction of rabies is crucial in this novel: the disease may be life threatening to Sophie, but its infectiousness also renders her a potential danger to the public. In this sense rabies functions as a realist metonym, a medical trope that cashes out as both personal crisis and public concern, as a matter of both curative and preventive care. This is why animal bites must be reported to the police, as the ER nurse informs her, and why the city's board of health handles rabies cases. "All you have to do is go there and they'll take care of it," she explains (*DC* 107). Would that all maladies were rabies cases, the novel implies. But Sophie's attachment to the ominous reveals as well the ready availability of rabies as lurid metaphor. That is, rabies evokes its own disparity. It allows Fox to pit Sophie's hyperbolic and self-privatizing fantasies about sick society against the novel's critical consciousness. Through a prioritization of realist metonym over lurid metaphor, Fox brings to light the public-health system's commitment to carrying out its curative and preventive tasks despite inadequate resources. In this dystopian yet realistic drama of health care, there is drama enough.

The novel's drama of disparity coalesces around a singular figure: Sophie's hand. After being bitten but before going to the hospital Sophie regards her wounded hand as an "alien object, . . . something that had clamped itself to her" (*DC* 29). The hand thus functions for her as an objective correlative of sick society, a deeply unhappy object. At the hospital, however, this hand is treated gently and with respect. Once Sophie is transferred from the "desolation" of the waiting room to the treatment room's "atmosphere of welcome," she finds herself amid practical problem solvers: "Here was conversation, work, solutions" (105). Specifically, here is a black male attendant who, with professional competence, controverts Sophie's fantasy of her hand's alienability. "I'm not gonna take that hand away from you," he reassures her, as he "coaxingly" gets her to show it to him (106). True to form, Sophie copes with this standard-issue pleasantry by accessing a regressive, antiquated form of personalization. She imagines the black attendant as personal property—of the antebellum variety. "She felt that old-time reassurance that she had once thought the natural property of dark people—as though they were superior caretakers of frail white flesh" (106). Sophie's psychic economy is more retrograde than that of even Plath's affect alien.

But Fox's broader scope insists on the ER's atmosphere of public welcome by suggesting that respect for Sophie's hand entails respect for the publicness of public health. At first her hand is "arrested midway between" herself and the attendant; soon, as she waits for a nurse to prepare a tetanus shot, her hand is "resting . . . on the counter like an exhibit" (*DC* 107). And at first only the nurse, "sloppy-mouthed, looked" on, but as others in the room overhear the conversation about the portent of rabies shots, "everyone was watching her openly" (107). All the while the attendant continues to call her "honey" and "dear" but also attends to someone else, "an old woman" whose "face softened in hopefulness at his approach" (107). In this slight but revealing moment, the black attendant uses the very same language on the old woman (who also suffers a hand injury) that he used earlier with Sophie. "Across from [the Bentwoods], the Negro attendant was bending over the old woman. 'Let's see your hand, dear. Let's just see it. I won't take it away from you. Ah, that's a good girl'" (109). Other details fill out the public-health picture: the nurse who informs Sophie about the Board of Health "smile[s]" at her in sympathy, and hospital orderlies go about their tasks "indifferently" (108, 105). A nurse even jokes about a Persian kitten available for adoption, if Sophie desires one (107). This scene's wide distribution of impersonal respect, professional solicitude, and casual, transferrable geniality stands as the happy face of the public hospital.

Importantly, however, the Bentwoods aren't the only ones chastened by public health care's idea of happiness. Fox's scope widens to include an unnamed Medicaid beneficiary. At the pharmacy after leaving the hospital, the Bentwoods encounter a man whom the druggist treats "brusquely" because the man wants to fill a prescription but doesn't have the proper Medicaid ID (*DC* 110). The man meets the druggist's "opposition," the embodiment of the "vagaries of official procedure," with muted frustration: "'Shit, shit, shit . . .' he said without emphasis, even, it seemed, without anger" (111). Then he walks out the door and drops the prescription on the floor. This is not exactly a scene of satisfactory interaction between person and system, but in Fox's grim way it suggests the plausibility of calibrating one's affective economy to the bureaucratic imperatives of public health. Although negatively inflected, this man's absence of anger reveals the upside of having welfare-state institutions in the vicinity to absorb the emotional sting. What you lose in personal happiness you might gain in examples of your own anger management.

Still, this little scene of frustration registers the challenge that a realist novelist committed to portraying welfare-state justice faces. Institutional embodiment inevitably fails to capture the political-liberal idea. The element of universal fairness gets lost in the dynamics of pictured interaction and the distribution of attention. In *Desperate Characters* a web of references to artistic practice and art objects evolves into a metacommentary on this problem of representation. To borrow Irving Howe's phrase, cited earlier, it casts "a semi-allegorical shadow of meaning" over the novel's metonymic realism and thereby draws attention to its underlying ideas, both moral and political. In addition to its many references to the visual arts, including the technique of contour drawing, a Munch engraving, and the "sketchy" agreements mentioned earlier, the novel exploits—indeed, arguably depends on—the punning potential of the line.[129] When Sophie's fantasies of a rabies infection and the medical treatment for it turn morbid, her husband admonishes her "to draw a line. This is just a medical procedure.... You don't draw enough lines" (*DC* 110). The novel ends with Otto throwing a bottle of ink "violently at the wall," toward which they both turn to "see the ink running down to the floor in black lines" (156). Here Otto exemplifies the opposite of Harvey Walling, the inaction painter in *Poor George*, whose "paintings had a dreary similarity: muddy paint had been laid on canvas with a palette knife, swollen circles bulging on one side like diseased tires" (*PG* 177). Rather than evoking bulging three-dimensionality, the signs of linearity in Otto's wall art enable Fox to highlight flatness and borders and thus to suggest parallels between the function of the formal outside in aesthetic theory and its (more freighted) ethical function in social justice. These parallels become crucial to the novel's portrayal of the difficult interplay between welfare-state health and happiness.

I return now to the medical prescription that the thwarted Medicaid beneficiary lets drop: its flat, papery status suggests its relevance to the novel's shadow of allegorical meaning. The scene follows in fact closely in episodic sequence on the heels of Otto's statement to Sophie about drawing lines, about accepting a standard (if rare) medical procedure for what it purports to affect, namely, a person's well-being. That discussion appears a couple of paragraphs earlier, as the pair leaves the hospital. Now inside the drugstore, the "line" marking an emotional limit worth observing resurfaces in the form of a "glass partition" behind which two pharmacists work (*DC* 110). This glassy barrier to access on demand itself stands as a kind of medical procedure—as does the prescription, as does the prescription without the proper ID documents. The Medicaid beneficiary's nonviolent paper drop thus figures on the one hand another controverted will (akin to Sophie's surrender of her alienated hand) but on the other hand an acknowledgment of the virtue of procedural rules—rules devised in the interest of public health and social justice. As Rawls pointed out in 1958, public institutions "may be antiquated, inefficient, [and] degrading... without being unjust."[130]

In the context of the novel's broader allegorical picture, these lines and this paper drop—signaling acquiescence to the welfare state's depersonalizing authority—contribute to a visual grammar that contests the art form associated with Sophie, namely, the contour drawing. This art form gains a foothold when Sophie gazes out the back door and likens the residential scene to a contour drawing: "At the back of the house, dogs imprisoned in small yards ran in circles. Telephone cables, electric wires, and clothes lines crossed and recrossed, giving the houses, light poles, and leafless trees the quality of a contour drawing, one continuous line" (*DC* 72). Although she accepts the technology of the line, she seems to crave the contour drawing's illusion of voluminous, three-dimensional personalization. She tries to bring her underprivileged neighbors who aren't physically present into focus so as to feel the claims that their lives, unbeknownst to them, make on her. It's a charitable gesture. What Fox goes on to suggest, however, is that imagining the palpability of other people's private lives is inadequate to the claims the external world—the welfare state as a system—makes on the citizen subject. By the end of the next paragraph we see Sophie drifting from window to window, as though trying but failing to sustain her connection, "wishing herself dressed and out, yet staring passively at the street as though she were waiting for a sign" (73). It's as if she were George Mecklin in the early, abyssal throes of his hospital ordeal, overcome by the cells of democracy's intimate body. The contour form does not suffice.

Indeed, Sophie's alignment with the contour form implicates both her earlier embrace of inner anarchy and her later insistence on the outer world's rabid illness. Both phantasmatic scenarios require the contour drawing's illusion of three-dimensional space. The first is particularly revealing, as Sophie's anarchic infidelity is predicated on her desire for privacy, that is, for secrecy. When Charlie alerts her to her enslavement to introspection, to her being overly "tangled in personal life" (*DC* 39), what he doesn't quite see (despite her vague confession of infidelity) is how much she prizes secrecy as the doubly interiorized structure of private feeling. It is in this sequestered space that she experiences personal happiness. More precisely, it is here that she introjects someone else's personal happiness. Her affair with Francis Early—the habitually "smiling" man whom Otto befriends and introduces to her, who "makes [Otto] feel cheerful," and to whom Sophie "happily" gives domestic gifts—maintains its value insofar as she can keep it secret (51, 54, 59). Francis may be the genial and cynical hedonist (not unlike Charlie Devlin but suaver) who takes advantage of both spouses' emotional vulnerabilities (before returning to his Long Island wife with Munch engraving in tow). Sophie, however, is the one who engages in "secret hoarding" (58). She is the one who requires a special inner place to store her happiness memories, to which she habitually returns despite the waning intensity of their pleasure. Next to Otto in bed, for instance, after the cat bite, "she began to tell herself about Francis. She often told herself that story, easing herself to sleep" (49).

The volume and mass of this specific contour drawing may be shrinking, but later she still mobilizes the contour form to imagine herself merging with the rabid outside while simultaneously preserving a purchase on happiness. Anarchy and privatized happiness, by this domestic calculus, become interchangeable variables, whereas consensual agreement remains "sketchy"—dubiously flat—and hence unable to meet the allure of three-dimensional experience. Agreement, from this perspective, looks too much like a Medicaid prescription. Sophie thus resembles the kind of spectator of illusionistic art who Clement Greenberg suspects still seeks to "escape into it from the space in which he himself stands."[131] Her privatized life, not just her relation to contour art, takes this form. Her mode of dedifferentiating inside and outside is essentially the antithesis of Greenberg's account of how, in abstract art, "pictorial space has lost its 'inside' and become all 'outside.'"[132] Her version of dedifferentiation amounts to a self-envelopment in mass and volume, replete with a tiny loophole of retreat for storing secrets.

But with the novel ending as it does—with Otto flinging Sophie's ink bottle at the wall in a fit of distress—Fox mobilizes the midcentury discourse of visual art to attempt a kind of final rapprochement between a person's private attachment to three-dimensionality and the welfare state's conceptual requirement of systemic flatness. That Otto is the agent of this reconciliation may at first glance seem grotesquely ironic. Cranky, disdainful of 1960s counterculture, impervious to his estranged law partner's entreaties, and compromised by racial prejudice, Otto is neither as open to possibility as George Mecklin nor as wounded. But he does emerge over the course of the novel as the one who provides antidotes to Sophie's hoarding impulse and ominous anarchy. Sophie describes him to an old friend she visits on Saturday as "not much given to introspection" (*DC* 89), but we readers see that he exhibits a different kind of introspection from hers, one that involves an assessment of his flawed character from the standpoint of liberal morality. When Sophie asks him why he suspects that the black home invader in the pillbox hat is lying, his discomfiting response, "My prejudices, I suppose," indicates a recognition of his moral failings (100). When he earlier explained to Sophie that his refusal to reconcile with Charlie is based not on personal spite or obstinacy but on evidence of Charlie's malicious betrayal, he turns the same evaluative eye to his professional life (96–97).

Not surprisingly, then, Otto is the one who deems consensual agreement a valuable thing.[133] This position, too, is informed by introspection, as is evinced in his assessment of the fallout with Charlie:

> "We agreed," he said. "We agreed it would be best to dissolve the partnership. We were reasonable. Even Charlie was that . . . we had a meeting . . . discussed procedures. The next day, the very next morning, this rancor appeared, these recriminations against me began. It was like retribution, as though he were punishing me. It hadn't been my idea to end the thing. Charlie was the one who was *radical* about it. I knew there were difficulties. You *know* I knew that! There always are. And I know it's a failure of something in me, that I can't feel more about what preoccupies Charlie. But I think about it. I care about justice . . . I care. (DC 95, ellipses and emphasis in original)

Although framed by a sense of failure and frustration, Otto's references to agreement, procedure, and justice go far to ventilate the suffocating atmosphere of Sophie's contoured privacy.

Otto's name is a dead giveaway of this character's ethical and aesthetic fate in the novel. It connects a commitment (overly rigid, perhaps) to obligation—"ought to"—to abstract art. Its palindrome structure and its constitution entirely of circles (aughts) and crosses, like a ticktacktoe game, point to a lively two-dimensionality, a symmetrical but decentered flatness that runs this way and that. When he throws the bottle at the wall, causing ink to run "down to the floor in black lines," he makes something like a draft of a draft of a Jackson Pollock allover sketch or a Cy Twombly scribble. Both artists have been associated by some critics with primal-action expressiveness—what, in the present discussion, would count as a contour concept—and Otto's emotional gesture clearly squares with this aesthetic tradition. But contemporaneous critics bring attention to these artists' exploration of the relation of painted (or scratched) lines to flatness.

Greenberg will understand abstract art's ambition to be one of provoking a "more physical and less imaginative kind of experience than the illusionist picture."[134] It aspires to reduce itself to its essence of "flatness and the delimitation of flatness."[135] By contrast, Michael Fried will see abstract art's ambition as engaging the "continuing problem of *how* to acknowledge the literal character of the support." The difference between merely staging the minimal conditions of art (which is Fried's alternative description of Greenberg's sense of art's timeless, irreducible essences) and the livelier (because it is ever-changing) acknowledgment of these minimal conditions is visible, I think, in Fox's depiction of the ink lines' course from wall to floor. Here the repetition with a difference—redundancy of support, perpendicular shift—calls attention to "the generic conditions of their inescapable framedness."[136] Otto may be no more talented an abstract artist than Sophie is a contour illusionist, but his art form, as it reflects his political form, goes a long way toward extricating this married couple from their merely absorptive private life together and visualizing their place in the welfare-state system, a system framed by the idea of justice as fairness.

Writing Mute Liberalism
Peter Taylor, the South, and Journeyman Happiness

Peter Taylor had an anecdote about his sister who, once having met William Faulkner at a party, asked for advice to pass on to an aspiring writer, her brother: "And one of the things he said was to 'Read *Anna Karenina* and *Anna Karenina* and *Anna Karenina*.'"[1] Left untold is whether Taylor then plowed through the novel three times over. But he did pay tribute to its famous opening sentence, using verbatim the most common translation of its initial clause, "Happy families are all alike," for the title of his third collection of short stories in 1959. Inside the book, an epigraph reattached the amputated line: "Happy families are all alike; every unhappy family is unhappy in its own way." Critics have tended to look to the second half of Tolstoy's epigram for corroboration of their interpretive approach to Taylor's work, assuming reasonably enough that Taylor, like Tolstoy, inclined toward realist fiction of tumultuous domestic life. As David M. Robinson puts it, Taylor creates "chronicles of the myriad ways that families devise to make themselves unhappy."[2] With unhappy families supplying "the clearest indices of the social unease in the modernizing South," Taylor bucks "postwar public cultural assumptions . . . [by] insisting on the complexity and tension lying beneath the presumably placid surface of the American middle class."[3] Viewed this way, in which Taylor exposes discomfiting truths beneath the false front of placidity, his impulse to demystify would dovetail with the midcentury social critics, discussed in earlier chapters, who routinely disparaged happiness as a symptom of middle-class complacency and self-deception.

But while it's important to recognize Taylor as a chronicler of the South undergoing difficult transition, the conversion of him into a lightly historicizing writer of family psychology and interpersonal relationships—no matter how complex or tension-filled those relationships are—invites the kind of complaint that John Updike lodged in his *New Yorker* review, namely, that Taylor "retains an unslaked appetite for the local nuance," for "tracing teacup tempests among genteel Tennesseans."[4] Without a wider range of turmoil, this argument goes, without life-wrenching betrayals, infidelities, and mental breakdowns, without abortions, suicides, and imprisonment, Taylor's families simply aren't miserable or dysfunctional enough to reflect the modernizing South, let alone the American middle class. With a Howellsian fondness for anodyne narrative, Taylor enervates his own obsession with the South's "omnipresent past"; instead of Faulkner's "violent modernist gestures," Updike grumbles, Taylor "stirs" the dark waters of the past "with a Jamesian sort of spoon." His "leisurely, laggard prose" makes him a writer not only of yesterday but "for yesterday."[5]

Taylor certainly was engrossed by the upper-middle-class southern family and its insipid travails, but this social world also provides the platform, this chapter argues, for Taylor's exploration of the status and fate of liberalism in the South. Taylor is indeed better understood as a follower of Henry James (whom he revered) than as a bloodless Faulkner. A midcentury observer of southern manners, Taylor brings sufficient attention to "local nuance" to detect the barely legible strain of liberalism embedded in southern culture. He treads the path cleared by James, whose "ethnography of manners," Nancy Bentley explains, entailed not simply "reporting" on but also "creating" a sense of available cultural forms; for "writing fiction is one of the ways in which manners become intelligible as the stuff of a larger totality," that is, of a culture.[6] To a certain degree Bentley's argument extends from Lionel Trilling's, who famously identified "a culture's hum and buzz of implication," its "half-uttered or unuttered or unutterable expressions of value," as the aspect of modern life to which James's novels of manners give voice.[7] Manners are thus "the things that for good or for bad draw the people of a culture together and that separate them from the people of another culture."[8] But whereas Trilling promotes the superiority of this mode of fiction over books that devolve into "moral righteousness," Bentley stresses the way novelists of manners—with their awareness of both "table manners" and "tribal manners"— tap into imperialism's "language of colonial discovery" to develop a literary "authority, whose office it is to communicate between a civilization and the forms of otherness that the civilization's own powers have 'discovered' and aspired to master."[9] If Trilling's James stands as a paragon of literary virtue for high-mindedly resisting the moralistic enterprise, Bentley's James manages to reclaim moral virtue from the immoral colonialist enterprise only by way of making self-abjection a literary virtue. That is, he intertwines his ethnographic expertise in observing, defining, and subordinating otherness with narrative dramas of a self-consciously *over*civilized observer's "panic of agency" and "agonies of uncertainty."[10]

Taylor's ethnography of southern manners may be loosely understood to split the difference between Trilling's and Bentley's insights on James. Born and raised in America's internal colony, the South, Taylor emerges as a kind of indigenous ethnographer who neither overcompensates for his privileged position by staging agency panic nor disavows midcentury liberalism's moral component.[11] He is an empathic but sufficiently aloof expert who renders intelligible what the culture of the South "is like." This is a phrase Taylor invokes repeatedly in both his nonfiction and fiction; it indexes an analogical sensibility inflected and constrained by ethnographic purpose. It betokens the small but crucial gap of writerly awareness and activity that separates him from other southerners. The gap overtly structures, for example, Taylor's widely admired story from 1977, "In the Miro District." Its first-person narrator, now in "late middle age," opens his account of his vexed boyhood relationship with his Confederate hero grandfather by distinguishing himself from his parents. They had insisted on adhering to the southern tradition of pairing off old and young members of the family, but "living their busy, genteel, contented life together in the 1920s they didn't have the slightest conception of what that old man [his] grandfather was like. Or of what that boy, their son, was like either.... *They weren't people to speculate about what other people and other times were 'like.'*"[12] By contrast, the narrator clearly is one such person. Even though the narrator goes on to offer few conjectures or even figurative analogies, his attention to a surfeit of nuance constitutes speculation in the etymological sense of observation from the vantage point of a *watchtower* (*specula*). In this case the watchtower takes the form of the narrator's many intervening decades of life experience and self-awareness. This positioning distinguishes him—but, importantly, not by much—from life-immersed nonwriters such as his parents.

He thus models what amounts to Taylor's guiding literary theory, namely, that the very act of writing down stories amounts to analogical praxis and to an inductive mode of interpreting, understanding, and generalizing what something "is like" from the particular circumstance or specific incident. Taylor liked to say that even writing down "word for word" the stories that his mother frequently told led to his "discovery" of what the South was like.[13] Therein lies the incrementalist dividend of Taylor's literary project. Like the other incremental realists examined in this book, moreover, Taylor's ethnographic style does not neglect the distinction—as Trilling implies James's does—between the "good" and the "bad." "It may be," Taylor once said, "that a writer's most important possession, after his talent, is his sense of belonging to a time and place, *whatever the disadvantages or injustices or cruelties* of that time and place may be."[14] Evincing here as much commitment to a liberal ethos as to authorial competency, Taylor fashions his ethnographic incrementalism into a "sense" capable of noticing the midcentury South's peculiar institutions of disadvantage, injustice, and cruelty.

By contrast, the southerners he lives among see only tradition and a way of life. Taylor hailed from one of Tennessee's most prominent families. His maternal side included a Jackson-era general, state governors, a congressman, and a US senator, whereas his paternal side included a Confederate colonel and a speaker of the Tennessee House of Representatives; both sides contained lawyers and businessmen galore. This intimate acquaintance with the professional-managerial class helps to explain why Taylor's ethnographic fiction often revolves around businessmen, lawyers, politicians, university professors, administrators, and the like. Only rarely do these characters or their family members exude happiness. But their unhappiness points beyond domestic unease. By reframing the conceptual and rhetorical function of the happiness trope in relation to these characters, this chapter brings into focus Taylor's representation of liberalism's beleaguered situation, in terms both of political efficacy and cultural sensibility. Viewed this way, Taylor's stylistic moderation—the subdued tone, the first-person narrator's digressive manner of reminiscence, the mildness of dramatic situations—looks less like a deficiency in realist grit and more like the cultivation of a circuitous and recessive form, one that mirrors the plight of the liberal white southerner. To borrow Trilling's language, Taylor undertakes quietly to "half-utter" the faint but not insignificant signs of liberal culture in the South.[15]

Whereas the first half of this chapter traces out Taylor's project of observing southern manners from the minority perspective of the nearly silenced midcentury southern liberal, the second half turns to Taylor's more successful liberal figures. For Taylor's "sense of belonging to a time and place" also draws attention to actually existing alternatives to these peculiar institutions, that is, to modern institutional practices that embody the liberal creed. A handful of stories whose protagonists enact liberalism's flickering traction turn out also to be stories in which happiness thrives and is effectively pitted against southern grief. Through portrayals of more or less happy southern professionals who validate their lives spent in the modern university, Taylor "creates" a kind of ethnographic reality. The manners of these institution men—what Taylor in one story figures as a "journeyman"—constitute a cultural form too, Taylor implies.[16] These stories narrate justifications for this southern liberal manner as a viable alternative to—or an intelligence lurking within—the South's dominant culture of reactionary conservatism.

Taylor's aesthetic education made him particularly alive to Agrarian and neo-Agrarian varieties of conservatism. He often noted that it was Allen Tate who helped him see that "literature and ideas [were] more important than anything else in the world."[17] Tate was only the first among his many Agrarian modernist tutors; also influential were John Crowe Ransom, Andrew Lytle (a close friend of Taylor's father), Robert Penn Warren, and Cleanth Brooks. This pedagogical, aesthetic, and social movement was essentially grounded in hostility to liberalism. As Eric Aronoff explains, the Agrarians were deeply committed to modern anthropology's idea of cultural pluralism, which shored up their vision of the South's fundamental difference from American modernity. He zeroes in on the ways New Critics participated, "alongside other literary critics, linguists, anthropologists, and artists," in constructing the idea of culture as a "count noun" (rather than a mass noun), which gave rise to claims "both progressive and reactionary, liberal and conservative" about regional unity and difference.[18] Ransom and Tate were particularly keen to envision connections between the way the South becomes meaningful through its concrete, "infinitely particular" cultural homogeneity and the way the "meaning" of an aesthetic object such as a poem "arises from the internal dynamic of parts forming an integral whole."[19] Ideologies of regional totality and aesthetic totality thus mutually reinforced Agrarian antipathy toward the abstracting, utilitarian forces of the nation-state—which was, at best, a "spurious" culture.[20] Politicizing this ideology in the terms of governmental policy, Cleanth Brooks stressed in a 1965 essay how "the artist and the writer are traditionally 'agin' the government," because the southerner's "sense of community" cannot abide "something so rigidly dead as an Establishment."[21] These high-minded reactionaries exemplify the tendency of elite groups, according to the anthropologist Mary Douglas, ritualistically to "exaggerat[e] the difference" between those "within and without" their charmed circle such that "a semblance of order is created."[22]

Taylor inhabited this ordered milieu as a genial but self-distancing interlocutor. Not one to embrace what he once called "flaming liberal" progressivism, he resisted his mentors' Agrarianism less openly and "rude[ly]" than his good friend Randall Jarrell.[23] But he did describe himself as "very liberal" and as one who "had friends who were very much in the left wing in New York." He also acknowledged being "very conservative" in that he was "very protective of the South" and "resented" northern criticism.[24] We'll see that in his fictional writing, Taylor takes advantage of this entangled background to float, almost surreptitiously, liberal ideas and values while softly smothering the Agrarian aesthetic and cultural ideology. He absorbs his mentors' extremism into an aesthetics of moderation partly by devoting himself to the short story—considered a minor form, generally unloved by Agrarians—and partly by nodding toward but deflecting the Agrarian and neo-Agrarian preoccupation with the tragic, the violent, and the grotesque. He thus deprives southern identitarianism—its insistence on cultural difference—of its literary oxygen.

Disquieted Silence

Peter Taylor's resentment of the North's criticism possesses a long genealogy, ironically a liberal one that goes back to the nineteenth century and the politics of Reconstruction. The historian Morton Sosna explains that not just "diehard Dixiecrats" but "white Southern liberals of all persuasions exhibited [sectional, unprogressive] attitudes, such as sensitivity over 'outside interference' with the South's racial problems."[25] His book *In Search of the Silent South* (1977) helps to illuminate Gunnar Myrdal's remark in *The American Dilemma* (1944) that "Southern liberalism is not liberalism as it is found elsewhere in America or in the world."[26] The book's title takes its key words from George Washington Cable, the postbellum South's exemplary liberal dissident in Sosna's account, who deemed a statue of Robert E. Lee in New Orleans an emblem of the South's liberal potential, one that remained, "in the din of boisterous error round about it, all too mute."[27] "In other words," as

Sosna glosses Cable's rhetorical figures, "the social conscience of the South remained as silent as Lee's statue."[28] Cable's 1885 invocation of the "Silent South" and his efforts to induce its speech constitute the first expression in a chronological series of largely frustrated efforts to liberalize racial, economic, and electoral conditions in the South. By the time of Peter Taylor's young adulthood, New Deal iterations such as the Southern Conference on Human Welfare (founded in 1938); its offshoot, the Southern Conference Educational Fund (founded in 1942); and the Southern Regional Council (founded in 1944) had launched their forays. In addition to criticism from civil rights advocates for concentrating on improving black people's material conditions while accommodating Jim Crow segregation, these New Deal liberals suffered devastating attacks from the South's conservative bloc, whether by way of red-baiting and race-baiting or electoral defeats, such as the "crushing" ones of 1950, recounted by Sosna, in which senatorial primaries occasioned the ouster both of the "political hero of Southern liberals, [Senator] Claude Pepper" by segregationist George Smathers in Florida and of the former university president Senator Frank Graham by Dixiecrat Willis Smith in North Carolina.[29] Not even liberals' retreat into cautious moderation induced much support. In 1958 one of its most vocal and progressive members, Aubrey Williams, would write that "the rank of the 'liberal white Southerners' has been considerably thinned."[30] Here was another lost cause in the making.

These self-conscious southern liberals, however, did have one important resource at their disposal: the tradition of storytelling. One prominent white southern liberal, the newspaperman Ralph McGill, made this point in his 1963 book, *The South and the Southerner*, and indeed did so in language so strikingly similar to Taylor's as to raise curiosity about the authors' mutual familiarity:

> It is *the fate of the Southerner to be involved in his region*, always to feel himself held by it. He may never have believed the myths. The often *cruel injustices* of the rigid formula of race may have offended him and aroused him to open opposition. The cost of parochialism and injustice, not merely to the Negro but to the material and spiritual welfare of his own people, may long have been on his conscience. *But nonetheless, he is part of what he has met, and been. And the past, in tales of his grandparents, his great-aunts and uncles, has been in his ears from birth.*[31]

When Sosna reproduces this passage in his preface he aptly notes that McGill represents the views "not just of any Southerner but of a particular kind of Southerner," that is, of a "white racial liberal."[32] Whether as journalist or literary ethnographer, then, it is specifically the southern liberal whose awareness and attention renders visible the region's "disadvantages or cruelties or injustices," to recall Taylor's slightly different phrasing. In his fiction, Taylor applies this awareness not only to the racial situation but also to gender and economic inequities.[33] He is the storyteller who is poised, "belonging to a time and place" and steeped in family tales, to write about the Silent South in a manner that captures its predicament of muteness.

In two short stories, "In the Miro District," referred to earlier, and "The Elect" (1968), Taylor makes prominent use of the trope of silence to foreground southern liberalism's problem of expanding or even locating its base. To begin with the slighter story, "The Elect," Taylor suggests that the problem lies very deep, at the level of self-recognition. The narrative takes place on the day after a gubernatorial election in the large home of the winning candidate, a judge, whose troubled wife is the story's focal character. References to campaign stops in Lawrenceburg and Cedar Point place it in southern Middle Tennessee. In its broad strokes the story's theme certainly conforms to Robinson's account of "social unease in the modernizing South." At the start, the wife reflects on her reluctant though effective participation in her husband's campaign, compelling her as it did "to begin climbing on platforms and making a spectacle of herself" in the new, vulgar era of television politics and to lose touch with her wifely duties and the pleasures of running a household, which she had done for "many happy years."[34] While her husband still sleeps, her old-fashioned genteel self yearns for "some small measure of privacy" to be restored (CS 390). But by the end of this story of a few hours, after her thoroughly modernized husband has gotten up and about, she is provoked into conceding through tears of pent-up humiliation that "this should be the happiest day of our life," and she finally comes to terms with the unseemly world of contemporary politics by resolving "never [to] shed another tear as long as she lived" (406). Between these opening and closing moments, Taylor briefly shifts his focus to the governor-elect, who upon awakening recoils from the morbid silence of the house: "Pulling on his robe, he went into the hall and listened for some sound of life. Hearing none, he moved on to the head of the stairs. Still only the silence, the unspeakable, intolerable silence of this private house" (393). Genteel privacy and silence are thus conjoined and embodied both by house and wife.

Before the story concludes with the wife's tearful outburst and tearless resolve, Taylor subtly modulates this figure of obsolete gentility into a figure of undeclared but attentive liberalism. Specific ideological positions are conspicuously absent from Taylor's portrayal of the governor-elect and his aides. As though to insist on depoliticizing a story about politicians, the wife will identify Bess Truman and Mamie Eisenhower, the wives of presidents from both major parties, as "the two most sympathetic figures in American public life" (CS 391). They serve as models of dignity that help her cope with the difficulty of modernizing her personality. But over the course of her silent reflections on her public activity during the campaign, her private self (the one belonging to the silent house) turns out to be her greatest political—specifically, liberal—asset. At brunch, her son-in-law and husband gratefully recall both her effective manner of breaking an awkward "silence" following one of many hecklers' attacks in a mill town and the "sight" soon thereafter of her shaking hands down the line of mill workers—"those old codgers and those young roughnecks," as her husband calls them (404). At the time, she had responded to the heckler's mockery of "the genteel judge" by defending "the decent good manners she had always encouraged in him" (404). Now, at the table, the wife's own memory returns silently to this scene, exhibiting more intuitive awareness than her husband of the harsh labor conditions that give rise to heckling codgers and roughnecks:

> While she had stood there in the rain, it had come over her that there were no middle-aged men among the mill hands. There were only smooth-faced young boys, mixed with young boys who had at some point turned into rough-faced old men. Her heart had gone out unreservedly to those young boys and those old boys. (CS 405)

Recalling the way she mulled yet again, "at home that night" (CS 405), over the absence of middle-aged men, the campaign wife registers in private silence the abuses of a labor system that prematurely deforms men into aged weaklings ("old boys"), depriving them of what is supposed to be the prime of life. Notoriously antiunion, the South's mill industries (textile and timber being the main sorts) were central to the region's expanding economy, while their "labor-intensive operations" paid egregiously low wages.[35] Indeed, they contributed to a new social order replete with new manners. As the historian Numan V. Bartley notes, "From the midforties to the midfifties, industry expanded impressively while the value added per employee declined relative to the national average." This gave rise to the typical southern industrial town's Milltown section, which was as "easily recognizable" as Uptown and Colored Town and which resembled a northern "tenement district" in its poverty.[36] He cites a 1942 study of a mill region in North Carolina that reported that it was "as unthinkable" for an uptown person to bring home a millhand to dinner as it was "to invite a Negro."[37] In this context the ladylike silence of Taylor's campaign wife, as a manner of reflection on the millhands, figures this new social chasm. It also figures more generally the difficulty a southern liberal, particularly a female, would have in converting private judgment into politically active speech. She appears more empathic for shaking labor's hands at all and yet more muted for not sharing her liberal judgments even with her husband. Her two invocations of happiness similarly remain private, depoliticized expressions of a muted self. They are a far cry from Galbraith's vision of "symbols" of welfare-state, public-sector progress.

Still, in her limited way, the governor-elect's wife becomes Taylor's ethnographic proxy, attending to the cruelties and injustices of the midcentury southern economy. His short story may thus be understood to extend by a half century the social and narrative logic that Richard Godden has persuasively argued marks James's fiction of manners. Focusing primarily on *The Bostonians*, with its upper-class southern hero, Basil Ransom, in search of northern capital, Godden suggests that James's novelistic form gives expression to an "economy of manners."[38] James may dwell on leisure-class interests in both proprietary wealth and discriminating social knowledge, but he also can't help but testify to this class's exploitative relation to the underclasses. In the world constructed by the discriminating novelist, those exemplifying a "poverty of manner"—not unlike Taylor's codgers and roughnecks—tend to circulate in what, Godden notes, James calls democracy's "social dusk."[39] That Taylor's protagonist is "troubled ... most" by the sense "that she had shaken their hands with a genuine cordiality" rather than in the transactional spirit of a "professional" (*CS* 405) underscores Taylor's portrayal of a midcentury southern liberal ethos that may be honored only—or most earnestly—in the breach of privacy and introspective reflection. He sheds light on a class conflict, in the lingering image of heckling millhands, while also suggesting how the reaction to such conflict dissolves into the South's dusky silence.

The liberal voice becomes slightly more audible within the densely entangled plotline of "In the Miro District." Here, the late-middle-aged protagonist-narrator considers himself more or less liberated from Tennessee traditions—one who "managed to get away" ("Miro"159)—and is now capable of applying a liberal filter to his reminiscences. The object of his reminiscence is his grandfather and how he, in late adolescence, brashly confronted this Confederate hero's resolve to remain silent on the Civil War. An extended examination of this story should demonstrate the import of Taylor's "appetite for the local nuance," for he exposes deeply troubling aspects of the southern manner—not least, the contemptible self-serving politics behind the stoic dignity of the silent grandfather—as well as the difficulty of owning up to such moral deficiency.

From one standpoint, "In the Miro District" belongs to a cluster of stories (including two other *New Yorker* stories, "What Do You Hear from 'Em?" [1950] and "Miss Leonora When Last Seen" [1960]) in which family or town difficulties with an eccentric elderly Old South personage—a relic of bygone interpersonal, social, and economic mores—reveal the depredations of the modernizing impulse once the personage abandons his or her Old South manner and, by taking on a role that befits the New South, becomes a mildly grotesque caricature. In "In the Miro District," this transformation is the direct although unintended consequence of a conflict between grandfather and grandson. The conflict, as told by the grandson, arose from the grandfather's unexpected discovery of his grandson, then a recent graduate of Wallace, Nashville's prestigious prep school, in sexual dalliance with a young woman—not just any young woman, which the grandfather had previously shown himself willing to tolerate, but a "Ward Belmont girl" from a Nashville family as exclusive as his own. The narrator believes that this transgression of the Old South code was the last straw, as evidenced soon thereafter by the grandfather's turnabout behavior. He shed his country farmer eccentricities and at long last did what his daughter and son-in-law had pined for: he moved into their large home in Nashville's tony Acklen Park neighborhood, he donned a black suit and shoestring tie, he resumed attendance of Confederate Reunions, and he became willing to speak in appropriate ways about his experience in the Civil War. As the narrator explains, "In those days in Nashville, having a Confederate veteran around the place was comparable to having a peacock on the lawn or . . . to having one's children in the right schools" ("Miro" 201). The grandfather, in other words, refashioned himself: once a nuisance-obstacle *from* the Old South, he became a consumer-friendly icon *of* the Old South.

But if this pitiful transformation represents one ethnographic report Taylor wants to deliver, a more problematic one emerges from the circumstantial details surrounding the grandfather's silence on the Civil War and what these, pieced together, reveal about the South's unwillingness to acknowledge the war's single most glorious result, the emancipation of black people, let alone to envision emancipation as only a first step in the betterment of an oppressed race. This absence of acknowledgment, the narrative tacitly implies, dovetails with the way so-called Old South relics such as the grandfather managed in fact to modernize sufficiently in the postbellum era to maintain their wealth and power and to keep emancipated blacks socioeconomically subordinated. In other words, they remained active participants in a culture that perpetuated "disadvantages or cruelties or injustices." Taylor himself, in an interview, once acknowledged quite candidly the *longue duree* of preserving wealth and power that a family such as his own enjoyed. Rejecting conventional southern wisdom that "a whole new class of people had come in and got rich," he cites W. J. Cash's esteemed classic, *The Mind of the South* (1941), as the work that convinced him that "the same families held power in the South after the Civil War as before."[40] The fictional family of "In the Miro District" serves to confirm Cash's point, with Taylor, as the liberal ethnographic shadow behind the narrator, disclosing the negative psychological and socioeconomic consequences of this multigenerational success—as both historical reality and a family's untold story. These details emerge bit by bit over the course of the narrator's many explanatory digressions. The most important revolve around the grandfather's traumatic kidnapping by night riders. With the narrator fixated on the grandfather's Old South farmer persona, it is only through the unfolding account of this incident that the grandfather's New South career in law and business emerges.

The ethnographic force of Taylor's long short story stems in part from the fact that substantial details comprising the kidnapping event derive from true stories that Taylor's paternal grandfather Colonel Robert Zachary Taylor told about his run-in with night riders at Reelfoot Lake.[41] Although the incident gained national attention, it is not well known today. Some background information here should thus help to clarify the stakes of Taylor's fictional version. First, Taylor did alter a few minor facts. The kidnapping took place in

1908, for instance, not 1912, and Taylor's grandfather spent about 36 hours in hiding, not ten days. These alterations aside, it is worth noting that some forty years after his Agrarian mentor Robert Penn Warren looked to the history of his hometown, Guthrie, Kentucky, for his first novel, *Night Rider* (1939), in order to explore the mystique of southern vigilantism, Taylor looked to family lore to demystify the mystique.[42] Warren's novel drew on the years-long discord early in the twentieth century between monopoly capital and local tobacco growers that provoked the original formation of the Night Riders group. Also known as the Silent Brigade, they were the militant branch of the Dark Tobacco District Planters Protective Association, which farmers in Kentucky and Tennessee organized in their ostensibly populist struggle against the American Tobacco Company, also known as the Trust. With monopolistic impunity (until 1911), "the Trust allegedly assigned price quotas and purchased only at that level," Thomas H. Winn explains, thus preventing planters from receiving what they considered a fair price for their crops."[43] The association struck back by controlling the supply and refusing to sell unless the price rose. The association's big farms had sufficient resources to ride out the boycotts, but "smaller growers, sharecroppers and tenant farmers could not as easily absorb a sustained yearly loss of income."[44] If the association couldn't persuade or cajole these small farmers to stick to the boycott, its leaders stigmatized them as hillbilly accomplices and then sent its secret band of night riders to destroy their crops and property and physically intimidate them.[45] At first glance, this resistance movement appeared to be the virtuous work of local, traditional agrarians who were only attempting to fend off the modernization of their livelihood and way of community life. The association itself, however, was led by modernized urban elites—not the small-time local growers—who profited considerably from the traditional socioeconomic system. It is also known that the conflict perpetuated the subordination of black farmers and that some members of the association "resented the large number of black sharecroppers or tenant farmers and . . . used Night Rider tactics and reputation to coerce or intimidate" them.[46]

The vigilantism in the Reelfoot Lake area was much smaller in scale and looser in structure, but it grew out of a similar conflict between capital and locals. During the nineteenth century a series of entrepreneurial land developers sought to consolidate private ownership of the lake and thus force out (or force fees on) the settlers—mostly poor farmers, who had been fishing and hunting there ever since the 1811–1812 earthquakes created the lake (and the Native Americans were removed). By the early twentieth century the legal situation had become very complicated; suffice it to say that Robert Zachary Taylor and Quentin Rankin, "two of the state's most prominent attorneys," facilitated the incorporation of the West Tennessee Land Company so that the major landowner could develop the area for sportsmen and force locals "to sell their fish through [third party] leasees or face fines and prison."[47] They also became major shareholders. These company leaders thus became the target of vigilantes who modeled themselves on the Black Patch tobacco growers' secret band, with its clannish "fealty oath, password, notions concerning regalia," and so forth. For seven months "the Reelfoot region writhed in an atmosphere of terror and violence."[48] Similar to the Black Patch organization, the leaders of the Reelfoot group included the community's wealthy and respected farmers. And, seemingly even more than the Black Patch vigilantes, the Reelfoot band "wandered from its primary objective" of destroying the West Tennessee Land Company's control of the lake to meting out punishment to others in the area as personal and social retribution.[49] Tennessee state officials largely ignored these so-called backwoods crimes until the murder and near murder of the company men, Taylor and Rankin.

Instead of focusing on a perpetrator of vigilante terrorism, as Warren's novel does, Taylor dwells on the perspective of a surviving victim. Thickly mediated by layers of temporal and narratorial distance, that perspective, however, is none too sympathetic. According to the grandson in the present day of the 1970s, the grandfather liked well enough to tell about the abduction of himself and his law partner by "a band of hooded nightriders" ("Miro" 162), the subsequent murder by lynching of his partner, his own narrow escape, and the ten-day ordeal of hiding in the swamps and bayous before reaching safety. We also learn that after the near-death experience he switched from a pipe to cigarettes because the latter calmed his nerves, that he shaved off his beard and moustache because they reminded him of the swamp's stench, and that he stopped attending the annual reunions for Confederate veterans. More important than these indices of trauma is the oblique manner in which the narrator relates specific details of the event to his contemporary readers: first, by way of the narrator's description of *his* fraught, gushing delivery of the tale *to* his grandfather and, second, by way of the narrator's recollections of one night when he was a young child and overheard the grandfather tell the tale to fellow sportsmen on a hunting trip at Reelfoot Lake. In addition, the narrator explains that he includes the tale only because it helps to clarify the significance of the later confrontation that precipitated the grandfather's transformation, which appears to be his main concern. With these elements of circuitous indirection and redirection, the narrator produces a form of evasiveness that suggests the gravitational pull of his grandfather. If in the grandfather's case evasion amounts to silence on the Civil War and its historical import, in the narrator's case it is symptomatic, Taylor implies, of a southern liberal struggling to find his voice amid the silence both of his grandfather and of southern liberalism.

The narrator's fraught delivery of his grandfather's tale to his grandfather (as told to us readers decades after the episode) occurred after the grandfather discovered him at home binging on his parents' liquor with friends and even after these friends had left. Somewhat inebriated, he effectively taunted the grandfather with his own story, revealing how often he'd heard it as well as his contempt for its Faulknerian grandiosity. Indeed, toward the end of this scene, his delivery had escalated in style and tone to the point of Faulknerian parody. Worth quoting at length, the cumulative sentences, the repeated references to "rage," the watery setting, and the tale-telling reflexivity all create the sense that we've stepped into, say, the "Old Man" section of Faulkner's novel *The Wild Palms*:

> I went on and on. "Tell me again how you, alone, escaped! How the nightriders made a bonfire on the banks of the bayou and put a rope around Captain Tyree's neck, torturing him, pulling him up and letting him down until he finally said, 'Gentlemen, you're killing me.' And then one of the men said, 'That's what we aim to do, Captain.' And they yanked him up for the last time. How a moment later, when all eyes were on the strung-up body of your friend, your law partner, your old comrade-in-arms from the War days and with whom you had come there only as 'two friends of the court,' to settle old land disputes made not by any man on earth but by an earthquake a hundred years before almost to the day, how at that moment, really in one of your wicked explosions of temper—afterward it was your rage you remembered most clearly—you vowed to survive (vowed it in your rage) and yourself bring to justice those squatters-turned-outlaws. And seeing your one chance to escape, you, in your saving rage, dived into the brackish water of the Bayou du Chien—you a man of sixty and more even then. ("Miro" 176–77)

To all this and more, the grandfather listened, blinking his eyes and laughing his "sardonic courtroom laugh" but no longer really listening. "Finally," the narrator reports, "I was silenced by his silence" ("Miro" 177). He does go on to fill in yet more details related to the incident and speculates that, if he had "encouraged him," his grandfather would have likely picked up where he left off (177), because for him, the grandfather, telling the tale yet again held deep personal significance. "It meant how many times he had successfully avoided reminiscing about the War" (178). Here the more disturbing implication of his "silence" comes into focus. Not only was the grandfather silent about the war and thus his participation in prolonging slavery and wrecking the Union, but he also managed to co-opt and burnish with Faulknerian intensity the scene of ultimate torment for blacks and slaves. He positioned himself as slave-*like* or black-*like*, transferring to himself the heroic glamour of escaping a slave's or black man's worst nightmare, the terroristic actions of a lynch mob.

Taylor deepens the sense of harm done by the grandfather's silence in his portrayal of the narrator's recollection of the hunting trip he went on as a young child. The narrator notes that during the day, when the men were out hunting, he was "left in the hunting lodge on the lake's edge in the care of the Negro man who had been brought along to do the cooking" ("Miro" 181). In fact, what he remembers most "clearly" about the trip was being "all alone in the lodge with Thomas" and "listen[ing] to [his] doleful singing in the kitchen" while gazing at the lake (182). The narrator adds no more commentary about Thomas, but he has provided sufficient information for us to see that Thomas's situation around 1916 was more or less what it would have been around 1816, in terms of his lowly occupation and doleful spirit. In an interview Taylor once noted that there had been college-educated servants in his family's employ who couldn't find stable work in any professional field and thus were compelled to return to domestic service.[50]

This racialized economic order, the story implies, was much to the grandfather's liking. It squared with the narrator's later observation that the one hotel in the resort town Beersheba that "had its attraction" for the grandfather was graced with an "ancient and unreconstructed atmosphere" created in part by the "old slave quarters [that] were still standing" nearby ("Miro" 190). Back at the lodge, Thomas's domestic service had created the cozy yet rustic conditions for the men's late-night storytelling, overheard by the child, who they had supposed was asleep. What particularly struck him then, according to his recollection, was the grandfather's tale about another horrific aspect of his Reelfoot ordeal: the hallucinations he suffered while on the run from the night riders. Here we learn much more precisely why the grandfather was not interested in speaking about the Civil War. These hallucinations magnified his sense of persecution such that his flight from the night riders took on the aura of fleeing "hooded men mounted on strange animals charging toward him like the horsemen of the apocalypse" (183); equally important, the hallucinations merged this crisis of 1912 with the earthquake crisis of 1811–1812. Shaped by "the accounts he had heard or read" about the geological cataclysm (183), his visions became biblical and cosmic, effectively erasing the historical significance of the years occupying the exact middle of this hundred-year period—the time of the Civil War:

> [T]he whole earth seemed to be convulsed and its surface appeared as it must have in primordial times. And he imagined that he was there on that frontier . . . [with all the newly arrived American settlers who were] in flight, like so many Adams and Eves, before the wrath of their Maker. . . . [I] heard him speak of [these events] as though they were real events he had experienced and heard him say that his visions of the earthquake were like a glimpse into the eternal chaos we live in, a glimpse no man should be permitted, and that after that, *all of his war experiences seemed small and insignificant matters—as nothing*. And it was after that, of course, that he could never bring himself to go back to those [Confederate] reunions. ("Miro" 184–85, emphasis added)

The grandfather's mythographic and Christological end run around the Civil War's significance in American political and socioeconomic history brought self-vindication and self-authentication to his silence on the Civil War. It would resonate not only with Faulknerian naturalism but also with what Richard Godden has shown to be an Agrarian infatuation with the primordial. John Crowe Ransom, for instance, was deeply interested in Eastern Christianity because it was indifferent to Christ the Son, who rendered the Godhead a mere father and thereby aligned the Western church with a "definitive historical polity."[51] This is a theology that resists the market economy; it is one of the means, Godden suggests, by which the Agrarians built an *iconographic* frame for the Old South, wherein sacred, infinitely particular, unparaphrasable, and embodied mythography transcended realist historiography.[52] A realist mode of historiography, however, is what their student Peter Taylor would later rely on.

Taylor's multiple invocations of the word *like* in "In the Miro District" serve to dramatize this historiographical bifurcation. To recall, the story opens with the narrator distinguishing himself from his parents on the grounds that he's more reflective than they were, more apt "to speculate about what other people and other times were 'like'" ("Miro" 159). It turns out that he also possessed this ethnographic sensibility as a boy, evinced by his recounted face-off with his grandfather: "'Tell me what it was like,' I suddenly began now in a too loud voice. 'Tell me what it was like to be kidnapped by those nightriders'" (172). In this very same paragraph, the narrator notes that he had been "thinking about all the times we had been left together like this when I was a little boy" (172), indicating that *like* is keyed to realistic resemblance, to an epistemology of the typical or the generalizable. But when the grandfather likens his escape from night riders and his hallucinated experience of the earthquake to an apocalyptic "glimpse into the eternal chaos," mythic iconography has steamrolled over realist ethnography. It is no wonder, then, that the breaking of his spirit by his grandson's transgression of the Old South code and the resumption of his talk about the war rendered him a kind of performance artist. He became an artificial Confederate, issuing platitudes that conformed to what his son-in-law (the armchair historian of southern military strategies and tactics and what-if scenarios) wanted to hear. In this manner the grandfather allegorized the Agrarian sensibility, which liked to melodramatize the displacement of its cherished traditionalism. Its predominant alternative to visionary iconography of the Old South was to imagine the New South as a debased confection of costume and chitchat.

Indeed, Cleanth Brooks looks to one of Peter Taylor's most admired stories to expound on this Agrarian worldview. As mentioned earlier, "Miss Leonora When Last Seen," first published in the *New Yorker* in 1960, resembles "In the Miro District," among other stories, in its treatment of an Old South figure who suffers the indignity of being rendered obsolete by New South modernization. A brief examination of Brooks's treatment of "Miss Leonora When Last Seen,"—or more precisely, of what he overlooks in his treatment of it—reveals how the Agrarian sensibility actively participates in the silencing of southern liberalism. First, he delineates and affirms other South-identified critics' accounts of the southern way: "a genuine folk culture"; family life; community affection; a tragic sense of history tinged with guilt, failure, and pessimism; and a distrust of modern abstraction and of the modern belief in progress.[53] Then Brooks turns to a "very concrete" southern figure in contemporary literature, "the middle-aged spinster who has cultural aspirations," who in his view embodies "a positive instance of Southern attitudes and values."[54] He considers Taylor's Miss Leonora a particularly illuminating example.

Not without reason does Brooks dwell on Miss Leonora's Old South eccentricities: "It is natural that an author writing about what is happening to the older culture of the South should choose a woman to typify the anticommercial, traditional spirit, with its indifference to, if not actual antipathy toward, progressive measures, and its fixation on the concrete and the personal."[55] He also summarizes well enough the story's plot and situation: Miss Leonora Logan has left the small hometown of Thomasville in a futile attempt "to avoid being served with papers authorizing the condemnation of her house and land for public use." The townspeople have long resented the powerful Logan family's prevention of the town's modernization and economic development, and Miss Leonora, although "enmeshed in a past way of life, doomed to extinction," nevertheless "stand[s] in judgement over the 'citified place' that Thomasville now aspires to be."[56] Similar to the grandfather in "In the Miro District," Miss Leonora registers this disapproval by "surrender[ing]" to the town's "shallow modernity," trading in what Brooks calls her "genuine eccentric[ity]" for "the disguise of creatures whom she evidently regards as fakes and therefore as truly grotesque."[57] She has literally transformed her looks so as to resemble the South's middle-class internal tourist-consumer who goes about "seeking out antiques and country hams."[58] Brooks also draws attention to the ambivalence and mild anguish that the first-person narrator, a former pupil of Miss Leonora's and now a middle-aged hotelkeeper, exhibits as he slowly peels back the circumstantial layers that account for Miss Leonora's sad transformation.

But what Brooks tellingly scants is the Logan family's modus operandi, which might be called New South absenteeism. He references a few of their specific successes in keeping the town old-fashioned—the thwarting of plans to bring a railroad line, a cotton mill, and a snuff factory into the area.[59] But the narrator tells us a good deal more. To begin with, he takes note of the profusion of development projects that generations of the Logan family have prevented from materializing in the (fictional) West Tennessee town, from the time they founded it in 1816 up to the present. First there were the nineteenth-century industrial interests—the aforementioned railroad, cotton mill, and snuff factory. Then there was the charity institution—the insane asylum—around the turn of the century. Finally, there was a string of government projects designed to modernize the region's economy: "Just after the First World War, there was talk of our getting the new veterans' hospital. During the Depression, we heard about a CCC camp. At the beginning of the Second World War, people came down from Washington and took option on big tracts of land for 'Camp Logan.' Very mysteriously all of those projects failed to materialize."[60] As recent as 1952 "some Logan" "arranged to have the Memphis-Chattanooga bypass built . . . instead of bringing the new highway through town" (*CS* 517). Taylor's diffident narrator is uneasy about the town's decision finally to stick it to the latest Logan generation (it condemns Miss Leonora's property in order to build a modern public high school there). But he is also aware that the Logans' "one idea . . . always to keep the town unspoiled" has nearly snuffed it out (507). The town's population of 1,800, "counting white and colored," is 500 fewer than in 1880 (517). More to the point, the Logans aren't among them. In fact, the narrator observes, over the last century and a half, few Logans have ever lived there. In the early years Logan "men came and went only as their interest in the cotton crops required" (515). In the nineteenth century it had been from their positions as the state's chief justice or governor, or as the sons of men in those positions, that they shaped the town's destiny. In more recent decades the absenteeism has only worsened:

> By [the turn of the century] none of the Logan men was coming back here very much except to hunt birds in the fall. They had already scattered out and were living in the big cities where there was plenty of industry and railroads for them to invest their money in; and they had already sold off their land to get the money to invest. But they didn't forget Thomasville. No matter how far up in the world a Logan may advance, he seems to go on having sweet dreams about Thomasville. Even though he has never actually lived here himself, Thomasville is the one place he doesn't want spoiled. (*CS* 516)

What Taylor's ethnographic realism insists we see in this story, more so even than in "In the Miro District," is the South's deep-seated and generations-long manner of constructing a picture of Old South authenticity. Long before there was a New South there were self-serving political and economic machinations at work to create the fantasy of an Old South. In the post-*Brown* era of the narrator's adulthood, Taylor's wide-angle lens does not omit the effects of these machinations on race relations. The mild irony is that the aristocratic Miss Leonora is far kinder and more generous to the town's black population than are its ordinary white citizens. The ugly irony is that "there are people here who dislike the memory of the Logans even more than they do the prospect of integration. They are willing to risk integration in order to see that last Logan dispossessed of his last piece of real estate in Thomasville" (CS 515). This town, Taylor suggests, has been not only economically damaged but also morally stunted by the southern manner.

In Brooks's discussion of Miss Leonora's compelling southern eccentricity he turns to a decidedly nonsouthern sociologist to support his claims. He doubts that Taylor's narrator "has ever read David Riesman's *The Lonely Crowd*, but he knows an 'inner-directed person' when he sees one," which leaves the narrator torn between his "belie[f] in progress" and his admiration for "Miss Leonora's non-conformity."[61] By the end of the essay Brooks has converted the character trait of inner-directedness into an index of "the numinous" in "human nature," praising the story—as though it were written by, say, Flannery O'Connor—for "respond[ing]" to this nature "with a kind of religious awe."[62] Brooks implies by his overdrawn opposition that the liberal narrator is a mere other-directed conformist who finds himself diminished before the authenticity of an eccentric who "attempt[s] to find grace and meaning in life and to live her own life with a certain style."[63] Brooks thus commits the same fallacy perpetrated by numerous other critics who adopt Riesman's character typology and claim Riesman's nineteenth-century type—the inner-directed individualist—to be the genuine American article. In so doing Brooks erases the condition of personhood that matters most to Riesman: autonomy. Elsewhere I have discussed at length critics' tendency to overlook this third term or to assume that it is synonymous with inner-directed nonconformity.[64] Suffice it here to note briefly that Riesman was not insensible to the critical predicament his sociology created. He was quick to joke in his 1961 preface to the reissue of *The Lonely Crowd* how "everybody from the free enterpriser to the socialist has come out against conformity."[65] In an essay that predates the book's original 1950 publication by a few years, he also took pains to distinguish between nonconformity and autonomy, referring to "Bohemians and rebels" who "are not usually autonomous; on the contrary, they are zealously tuned in to the signals of a defiant group that finds the meaning of life in a compulsive non-conformity to the majority group."[66] He would go on to concede, in the 1961 preface to *The Lonely Crowd*, that "the confusion between autonomy and inner-direction that many readers fell into reflects our own inability to make the idea of autonomy a more vivid and less formal one," but he also attributed the confusion to Americans' "strand of nostalgic thinking."[67] In Brooks's nostalgia-tinged, numina-seeking hands, one effect of lauding Miss Leonora's eccentricity at the expense of the narrator's more conventional observations about small-town realities in West Tennessee is that he thickens the cone of silence around the already muted voice of the liberal South.

Institution Men and Their Happier Family Members

Whereas Brooks exhibits ideological deafness to the conceptual proposition of autonomy that informs the midcentury liberal disposition, Taylor exemplifies the necessity of validating it. A cluster of short stories and a short play that take place outside the South but are populated by southerners register the value of cultivating this disposition. The affective results of this cultivation, as embodied by his characters, are not always or completely pretty. But we'll see that the trope of happiness emerges in most of these works as the measure of liberalism's success, however modest or compromised, in gaining some traction in the value system of southerners. In these works, Taylor comes as close as we might imagine a midcentury southerner may come—and still be described by Agrarians as a southern writer—to a liberal justification of happiness. Three such stories, "Dean of Men" (1968), "1939" (1955), and *"Je Suis Perdu"* (1958), all center on the lives of university men—an administrator, a creative writer, and a historian, respectively. Operating in what Mark McGurl has dubbed "the program era," in reference to the rise after World War II of creative writing programs in institutions of higher education, the men in Taylor's stories significantly find their autonomous voices and qualified happiness within these institutions. The modern university, in other words, becomes as important to each man's affective life and self-definition as the more traditional institution of the family. They embrace, to borrow McGurl's schema, the institution as "a social *technology*, a way of mobilizing human and other resources to achieve external ends," rather than as "an embodiment of *tradition*, a place where the authority of past practices is contained and conserved."⁶⁸

The force of these stories' validation of modern institutional life becomes more visible when set against the backdrop of Taylor's short play, *The Death of a Kinsman* (1949). It dramatizes the crippling effects of insisting on the family unit—indeed, on happy-family unity—as the institution of choice precisely because it authorizes long-held conservative traditions. The play's explicit invocations of the happy family take us back to where this chapter began: to the title of Taylor's third collection of stories, *Happy Families Are All Alike*, and the accompanying epigraph. Since Taylor's literary forte was the short story, it makes sense that he cited Chekhov more often than Tolstoy as an important influence. It thus also makes sense that his best use of Tolstoy was not only titular and epigraphic but epigrammatic. What makes less sense is the content of Tolstoy's epigram. First, why should happiness homogenize and unhappiness differentiate? Second, in terms of literary realism, whether Tolstoy's or Taylor's, it's hard to imagine what a happy family would even look like (or, for that matter, an unhappy family). To be sure, a *family*, unqualified by affect, makes perfect empirical sense—as, say, a biological, legal, anthropological, or ethnographic unit—but a *happy* family seems phantasmally transpersonal. The attribution of emotional unity to a plurality of persons, whether in reference to a lasting disposition or a passing sensation, quashes the separate affective lives of each of its members. This is why Nabokov, in his 1957 novel *Pnin*, finds it easy to satirize the "progressive, idealistic" character named Dr. Wind, a devotee of group psychotherapy who "dreamed of a happy world consisting of Siamese centuplets, anatomically conjoined communities, whole nations built around a communicating liver."⁶⁹ Emblematic of Taylor's sense of the happy family's status as an empty category is the fact that the volume *Happy Families Are All Alike* contains no story with that title. As objects of realist representation, happy families aren't all alike; they're nonexistent.

But in Taylor's work they're nonexistent in an important way: through the conspicuous emptiness of the category, he calls attention to the transpersonal family as a figure of dubious totality, prompting questions about the discursive work such figurations perform. In the South at midcentury, the question of totality was anything but idle. The era witnessed the resurgence of a strident southern agrarianism, exemplified by the publication in 1953 of the now-classic collection of essays, *Southern Renascence*, edited by Louis D. Rubin Jr. and Robert D. Jacobs. Both reinforcing and reinforced by the era's Cold War conservatism, the volume aspired to articulate a totalizing cultural identity for the South, distinct at its core from a so-called northern identity. As Richard M. Weaver put it in his contribution to the volume, a "lack of common denominators" is what ultimately separates the South from the North.[70] In other words, culture, as a kind of branding device, becomes for neo-Agrarians what Walter Benn Michaels has more recently called "a primary technology for disarticulating difference from disagreement."[71] Once disarticulated from a deliberative politics organized around consensus-building and policy-making, the South's difference could be figured as identitarian totality.

In the volume's lead-off essay, titled "The Southern Temper," the author Robert B. Heilman enumerates some half-dozen "sense[s]" that constitute this regional temper or state of mind, among them a "sense of totality" (others include the elemental, the ornamental, the concrete, and the representative).[72] It is worth quoting Heilman's elaboration of totality's entailments, which is as sweeping as it is compressed:

> [I]t is a sense of time, of the extent of human need and possibility, of world and of spirit. It appears in Faulkner's style; in the critical focussing on the organic whole; in the anti-nominalism which has been most explicitly formulated by Richard Weaver; in [Allen] Tate's emphasis on mythic or non-scientific values; in the conjunction, in numerous pieces of fiction, of violence and spiritual awareness—a conjunction disturbing to readers who are used to taking one part of the whole at a time; in the penumbra of mystery—a mystery to be accepted, not solved—always bordering the clean light of [Eudora] Welty's characters and scenes; in the nostalgia, so frequent in [Katherine] Porter, for the reality felt behind the stage of action; in the questioning of nostrum and panaceas which can exist only by treating a part of human truth as if it were the whole; in suspecting our inclination to separate the present from all the rest of time, to exhaust all devotion in the religion of humanity, and to consider scientific inquiry as the only avenue to truth.[73]

As the references to Faulkner and other writers indicate, Heilman's commitment to such totality ideals as organic wholeness, myth, spirit, and the penumbra of mystery is largely aesthetic. He leaves it to Weaver to delineate the economic stakes. In the volume's subsequent essay, titled "Aspects of the Southern Philosophy," Weaver puts some of these same ideologemes to work to formulate an absolutist position against midcentury liberal ideas of wealth redistribution—absolutist in that its premises nullify the possibility of ethical, rational disagreement. Declaring the desire for redistribution (what Weaver and other midcentury conservatives called "leveling") to be motivated by the "modern spirit of envy," Weaver insists that "Southern people today" lack this "distemper."[74] He goes on to cite the "poor success of trade unionism" in the South, along with southerners' "hesitancy about tampering with a prevailing dispensation," as evidence of this absent envy.[75] Moreover, according to Weaver, "the typical Southern farmer or millhand tends to regard fortune, like nature, as providential." In other words, the unequal distribution of wealth, income, and, consequently, opportunity is simply "part of the inscrutable provision" of an organic social totality to which southerners don't so much consent as, by descriptive definition, belong. This southern "piety" contrasts with the northern mode, which "could be most generally described as a respect for ideas. Essentially the Northerner is a child of the Enlightenment; and his theology is very much like Tom Paine's, . . . [whose] own mind is his church."[76] Identitarian southernness is thus at once producer and product of a compensatory transpersonal totality. However pervasive the region's poverty or severe its income disparities, the South's actually existing economy, now imbued with the penumbra of theological mystery, is both a function and a sign of a far weightier providential dispensation that is distributed evenly throughout the totality.

Taylor's *Death of a Kinsman* works to deflect these neo-Agrarian pretensions. This one-act (two-scene) play dramatizes one northern woman's self-imperiling challenge to the southern temper and totality, tracking her futile attempt to achieve a redistribution of sorts within a southern household's affective economy. By the same token, the play stages the self-inflicted injuries incurred by the southerner who insists on maintaining the totality phantasm—the happy family. The play's more obvious plotline has to do with a live-in spinster aunt's sense of place and purpose within a traditional southern family, currently dwelling in Detroit. Besides this Aunt Lida, the Wade household comprises the parents, their several young children, black servants, and the northern white spinster housekeeper, Miss Bluemeyer. On the part of both Aunt Lida and the pregnant Mrs. Wade there is growing recognition of the way southern familial customs severely circumscribe their lives. As the pregnant Mrs. Wade explains to her husband, the reason she and her aunt never quarrel is that "[we] have played our roles so perfectly, as we've always seen them played in Tennessee. She, the maiden aunt, responsible and capable! I, the beautiful young wife, the bearer of children, the reigning queen!"[77] If it is clear from this spousal exchange (which ends with Mrs. Wade in tears) that a life of adhering to prescribed gender roles has its ups and downs, it is also clear that Mrs. Wade's affliction—the mother-woman syndrome made familiar to us by Kate Chopin—is not serious enough to unravel the family unit. She will not embark on a final fatal swim a la Edna Pontellier.

Far more problematic are the unscripted prickly encounters that the blood relatives have with the housekeeper. Miss Bluemeyer emerges as Aunt Lida's principal rival; she is her demographic peer but one who bears simultaneously enviable and suspicious distinctions. She is enviable on account of being independent and skilled enough to obtain gainful employment, as opposed to being more or less tolerated according to the southern family custom of taking in elderly widowed or maiden aunts. Yet Miss Bluemeyer is suspicious because, as hired employee, she embodies the menacing distemper of Weaver's nonsouthern leveler. While she harbors no grievance regarding her financial remuneration, she seems to begrudge her exclusion from the family's distribution of affective wealth. At least that's how Aunt Lida views her.

Tensions escalate, erupting into Aunt Lida's voiced disdain when Miss Bluemeyer expresses more sorrow than anyone in the Wade family over the recent death of their blood relative, an elderly cousin who was distant from the close-knit Wade family but resided nearby and with whom the housekeeper turns out to have had an indirect yet sympathetic acquaintance because of her friendship with the cousin's neighbor.[78] Insulted by the housekeeper's silent reproaches and angling to recruit Mrs. Wade as an ally in her suspicion, Aunt Lida plays the happy-family card: "And it's our happiness that is her hell, mind you, Margie. She can't abide the sight of our family happiness. . . . She cannot endure the presence of our happiness. Particularly not mine" (*DK* 129). She goes on to describe Miss Bluemeyer as "mean and jealous" and full of "resentment and hatred." Needless to say, Aunt Lida's "tirade," her "fit of temper," as Mr. Wade subsequently calls her speech, betrays her own deep-seated resentment toward the household rival (129). My point here, however, is not so much that this exhibition of rivalry—envy's cousin—shows neo-Agrarians to be in denial of the psychological disposition of actually existing southerners. Rather, it is that Taylor mobilizes psychological realism to stage the fallacy of the neo-Agrarian identitarian logic of totality. Fixated as Aunt Lida is on maintaining full possession of the family's happiness wealth, she is blind to the housekeeper's deeper concerns.

Aunt Lida doesn't see that it isn't so much a share of the family's wealth of happiness that Miss Bluemeyer wants as it is a liberalization of the family's means of emotional distribution. She wants the family to engage in emotional commerce with her. This commerce would entail reciprocity, that is, an acknowledgment of her independent (or nonorganic) but effectual participation in the household's affective economy. Specifically, she wants the Wades to respect her bereavement. She is offended by the fact that on this morning of the small funeral service, the Wades poke fun at one another, get preoccupied with changing a chandelier's lightbulb, and "laugh hysterically" at Aunt Lida's mimicry of each Wade child's "different way of pouting while being reprimanded" (*DK* 126, 127). She expresses moral indignation by glowering at them in the hall during their bulb-changing antics and staring intently at their mirthful play in Mrs. Wade's bedroom. She conveys her sense of entitlement to personal recognition by mentioning, when serving Mrs. Wade her coffee, that she made herself a cup at the same time, implying the two women's social equivalence. She also reminds Mr. Wade that she is "not one of the servants," marking her distinction from the black members of the household (119). Mr. Wade accepts this distinction at face value, but even on learning of Miss Bluemeyer's acquaintance with his relative, he doesn't think to invite her to the service any more than he thinks her sorrow ought to make him feel bad or to constrain the family's fun. Similarly unyielding, Aunt Lida exhibits no gratitude when she sees the flowers that Miss Bluemeyer and her friend Madge sent to the funeral chapel; to the contrary, she churns with indignation, sitting "through the whole service as stiff as a broom," according to Mr. Wade's report, and plotting the housekeeper's dismissal (133). For all her pains, then, Miss Bluemeyer fails to persuade the Wades to feel bad about the death of their kinsman or indeed to feel any altering effect of her presence within the household.

If her failure to achieve the affective redistribution she desires testifies to the southern temper's immunity to nonsouthern persuasion or argument, it nonetheless makes visible the southern family's reliance on racial difference to codify and absorb expressions of affective discord. Through such means, the family perpetuates the phantasm of the happy organic totality replete with internal hierarchy. That is, while Miss Bluemeyer's self-differentiation from the household's black servants registers her own racial anxiety, it also reveals the depth and fixity of socioeconomic subordination that structures black servitude and props up familial totality. In the Wade household this structure becomes visible through talk about uppitiness. The black servants do get "uppity" now and again, as Aunt Lida accuses the "girl" Lennie of nearly sounding (*DK* 141), but uppitiness itself gets coded as the heightened temper that black servants are permitted to express now and again. As Lennie retorts to Aunt Lida, "Wull, there's uppitier niggers than I be in this house" (141). Sounding uppity is part and parcel of black servants' knowing their place. This is why Lennie's back talk doesn't enrage Aunt Lida the way Miss Bluemeyer's wreath of flowers does. Reinforcing the sense of totality as it ritualizes the household's internal hierarchy, black uppitiness sustains the happy family's happiness. The legitimacy of this transpersonal phantasm would appear effectively reaffirmed.

And yet the play suggests that, even for southern believers, the days of this phantasmatic totality may be numbered. If we return to Aunt Lida's "fit of temper," we see how Taylor's stage directions indicate that Aunt Lida's vision of family happiness—and her ambition to manipulate this solidarity into a strategy for firing Miss Bluemeyer—is partly undone by the rivalry that fuels her hostility. After Mr. Wade objects to her "tirade," Taylor writes, "*Aunt Lida stares blankly at Mr. Wade for a moment[.] . . . She is not smiling and she makes no answer. She doesn't seem to have heard what he said*" (*DK* 129). She thus betrays the effect the household killjoy has had on her equanimity. Aunt Lida will eventually get her way with Miss Bluemeyer; she even stirs Mrs. Wade to wonder pitifully at Miss Bluemeyer's criticism of their "happy family life" (*DK* 149). But Miss Bluemeyer first finds an opportunity for her own withering tirade: "I understand a good deal of how this family business works," she blurts out to Mrs. Wade. "It makes a woman safe and sure being related this way and that way to everybody around her. And it keeps you from having to bother about anybody else, since they are not 'kinfolks'" (*DK* 147). In having Miss Bluemeyer speak modern truth to southern power and leaving Aunt Lida at the end of the play "*sit[ting] with her hands over her face*" (150), Taylor hints at the self-sabotaging price paid for the insistence on the happy family as the South's gold standard while simultaneously implying its unreality. Aunt Lida's self-withdrawal in shame suggests that, as the southern temper rises, the idea of southern totality threatens to collapse under its own shrill insistence.

It happens that in the same year that *The Death of a Kinsman* was republished in *The Widows of Thornton*, the leftist sociologist C. Wright Mills published a review in *Dissent* of Russell Kirk's book *The Conservative Mind*, which had appeared in 1953, the same year as Rubin and Jacobs's *Southern Renascence*. Mills uses the occasion less to bash conservative ideology than to suggest that the problem with midcentury conservatives is that they haven't been able to find the political ideology they seek; instead, "what they have managed to create is a mood," which entails an "absence of mind," by which Mills means an absence of reason.[79] This deficit of ideology, Mills observes, derives primarily from the conservative commitment to providential intent, to the "mystery of traditional life," and to a natural social hierarchy—all of which leave them bereft of any practical political leg to stand on. As Mills puts it, "When we examine [the conservative mood] carefully we find that it is largely assertion, without arguable support, and that it seems rather irrelevant to modern realities, and not very useful as a guideline of political conduct and policy."[80]

If the resemblance between the conservative *mood* and the southern *temper* is obvious enough, it's worth underlining the difference in attitude between Mills and a neo-Agrarian such as Weaver. Whereas Mills disparages the absence of "arguable support"—and later worries that the United States, "a conservative country without any conservative ideology," stands to lose all of its geopolitical credibility—Weaver would see this absence as exactly the point of imagining southern conservatism *as* a mood or temper or spirit.[81] Mood is generally considered not an absence of mind but an affective state of mind, an emotional color that pervades the mind, which is to say, a kind of totality that is insensible to argument. Taylor's short story, "*Je Suis Perdu*," which his editor at the *New Yorker*, William Maxwell, considered a "mood piece," at once extends the author's exploration of the happy family trope and illustrates the way institutional affiliation and professional practice contribute to the demotion of the totalizing form that mood embodies.[82] This demotion is shown to constitute a kind of existential disorientation or loss for the protagonist—hence the story's title—but it also registers an acknowledgment of mood's all-pervasive presence and even influence without accepting the mood totality as determinative. In contrast to the critic Jonathan Flatley's recent insistence on privileging mood in "critical practice," Taylor's story suggests why we might not want to do so.[83] Flatley's authoritative starting point isn't a neo-Agrarian but instead continental philosophy's near equivalent, Martin Heidegger. His theory of mood underwrites Flatley's conjoining slide between claims about critical reading and claims about a "collective affective atmosphere."[84] Heidegger's idea of *Stimmung* as "primordial" matters to Flatley because it putatively "establish[es] the conditions for our encounter with the world, before cognition and volition" and therefore "exert[s] a broad but foundational form of judgment."[85] For Taylor, mood is too moody to earn such high regard or to cohere into a transpersonal unit. Mood does alter the protagonist's sensibility, but it doesn't in fact change his mind about much. He can thank his institutional affiliation and professional occupation for that.

The story revolves around an unnamed professor of history who is wrapping up a year-long research project in Paris for a book "about certain Confederate statesmen and agents who, with their families, were in Paris at the end of the Civil War, and who had to decide whether to go home."[86] Echoing Milton's pair of poems, the narrative is divided into two sections, "L'Allegro" and "Il Penseroso." It starts out with the protagonist cheerfully reflecting on the smooth and pleasant way things have worked out for him, his wife, and their two young children. Having experienced "phenomenal" luck over the course of the year, he now finds it "hard to think of anything that had not worked out in their favor" ("*Je*" 252), from finding an apartment and a doctor who would come at midnight to attend his daughter's medical emergency to hiring a maid and, not least, completing his research. As he wanders about the Luxembourg Gardens one last time by himself, however, he can't help being struck by a mood of melancholy, at first seemingly causeless:

> He simply could not imagine what it was that had been able to depress his spirits so devastatingly on a day that had begun so well.... He was so eager to dispel this sudden gloom and return to his earlier mood, however, that he turned to walk back to the spot and see what else might have struck his eye. Above all, it was important for it to be something outside himself that had crushed his fine spirits this way, and that was thus threatening to spoil his day. ("*Je*" 260)

Continuing his search, he "hope[s] to discover ... something tragic or pathetic which he might hold responsible for the change" or at least to discover some "unhappy or unpleasant-looking person." But all around him are people who look "relatively happy ... as happy, almost, as he must have appeared not five minutes earlier" ("*Je*" 261). As this slight mystery unfolds, with the protagonist finally turning inward, he discovers that his mood affliction "sprang from the same thing his earlier cheerful mood had come from—his own consciousness of how well everything had gone for him this year" and "always" 262). He's bothered both by how predictable his life and career have become and that "his matter of *being*" what he is means he won't be something else. If the mood helps reveal this problem to himself, he has sufficient resources of memory and judgment to deem it not much of an insight: "This, too, was a tiresome, recurrent thought of his—very literary, he considered it, and a platitude" (263).

The protagonist may well be wrong about the source of his gloomy mood, since it is finally dispelled by the arrival of something external, his daughter. But Taylor here is less interested in the accuracy of the protagonist's self-diagnosis than in staging the subtle interactions and crucial distinctions between mood, feeling, memory, cognitive thought, judgment, and volition. First, it is notable that even when his gloomy mood is in full swing, the protagonist's cognitive capacities are not impaired. They function well enough for him to search actively for his mood's source. Conversely, even after identifying the gloomy mood's cause, the mood remains. Furthermore, despite the sudden appearance of his daughter in the park and change of mood, the protagonist is able to "gather his wits" and turn his thoughts to what his wife must be doing back in the apartment ("*Je*" 265). Yet he isn't quite able to witness the dissipation of the gloomy mood. Rather, he finds himself "wondering where his dark mood had gone. It was not just gone. He felt it had never been" (267). Further still, he now "feel[s] resentful" toward his daughter because "he wanted the mood of despondency to return, and he knew it wouldn't for a long while. . . . He felt he had been cheated. But this was not a mood, it was only a thought. He felt a great loss—except he didn't really feel it, he only thought of it" (267).

Whatever these passages' semantic slippages and the protagonist's self-corrections imply about the specific imbrications of mood, feeling, thought, and judgment, the important point is that Taylor portrays mood as one among many elements constituting a person's interiority—and, in terms of cognitive judgment and practical agency, far from the most important one. This portrayal accords with Charlie Altieri's account of the way mood is both intensely personal and yet independent of the subject's "practical orientations."[87] The affective intensity of mood, Altieri goes on to explain, is in relay with "the abstracting mind," such that "the experience of wholeness ceases to be merely abstract and takes on an almost material form as a presence."[88] Taylor implicitly stresses the "almost" in that phrasing so as to ward off more forcefully than Altieri does the seduction of a neo-Agrarian world-spirit totality.[89] In his story a mood is what comes and goes, apart from intention, will, or even commensurate feeling. It is an affective condition that suddenly "come[s] upon" the protagonist in an "unreasonable way" ("Je" 262). Mood, then, becomes emblematic of the perpetual haphazardness of being a subject in the world.

For Taylor, I suggest, mood parallels what a person more broadly experiences as a subject in history, due to being born into a particular time and place. An appreciation of historical contingency is what enables Taylor to think of "the cultural and social aspects of the South [as] just the tables and chairs and furnishings of [his] life."[90] In contrast to the neo-Agrarian sacralization of region, this Jamesian attitude cashes out as little more than the broadest and plainest of maxims, if not outright truisms: "And one does have to live in the world that he actually inhabits."[91] In Taylor's story the turn from personal situation to pragmatist historicity is mediated on the one hand by the protagonist's dejected sense of belatedness and on the other hand by his professional engagement with the history of other people. While in the throes of his "melancholy and gloom" ("Je" 262), he wishes he'd come to Paris earlier, feeling that in his approaching middle age, "he had come to Paris too late ... and that he ... might as well not have come" at all (265). But what emerges alongside his recovery of cheer is an affirmation of his own time and place. By story's end, Taylor's modern historian has come around to be about as unlost as he was at the start: he "acknowledged claims that others had on" his life in the present, accepting "ideas and truths and work and people that he loved better even than himself" (267). The inclusion of "work" here is key: the very logic of his academic research—both its external purpose of advancing modern knowledge (to recall McGurl's framework) and the specific topic he studies—practically insists on this recovered value system. To be sure, the Confederate men he has researched needed to decide whether to return home, but just as surely, they didn't get to decide to be born in the time and place of the Civil War.

With the support of a university institution that invests resources to produce this kind of knowledge, the protagonist is poised to write a book about other persons' situational contingencies in which autonomous decision-making matters. His own condition of autonomy becomes vivid over the course of the story's slow-motion portrayal of his drama of reflection and self-assessment. Neither an eccentric nor an other-directed conformist, his wide and abstracting distribution of attention—to ideas, truths, work, and people—registers the minimal relevance of mood, however pervasive, to his commitment to his life projects. The totality of a temper, southern or otherwise, will have little hold on him. Significantly, Taylor's protagonist finishes his walk in the park without incident. Indeed, unlike Aunt Lida's final gesture of shame, with her hands over her face, when this man's daughter appears in the park near the end of the story, "[h]e [gives] her a big squeeze with his arms and [holds] her a moment longer on his knee" ("*Je*" 267). That's what we might call empirical evidence of two happy family members who have no use for transpersonal totality.

The other two stories in this cluster bring the institutional workplace into firmer focus. In two ways—one trivial, the other not—"Dean of Men" picks up where "*Je Suis Perdu*" leaves off. With another academic at its center, the story's main events take place soon after this professor returns from a Fulbright-funded research year abroad (in Italy rather than Paris) to the small liberal arts college that employs him. Less trivial, when things at the college don't go well for him, they go undeservedly and unforgettably poorly—testament to which is the fact that some decades after the events the unnamed man is compelled to write them down for his adult son. This ruminating letter constitutes the story. Based loosely on events Taylor experienced at Kenyon College in the 1950s, the protagonist's workplace may appear to have become an institution of cruel optimism rather than an auspicious alternative to conservative institutionalism. It should thus prove instructive once again to juxtapose a critical account predicated on the fundamental suspicion of liberal institutions with one that is not. What Lauren Berlant's psychosocial theory would foreground in a "situation tragedy" such as this short story is how a liberal arts college, embodying liberalism's most high-minded "promises," manages to suck the life out of a man without his knowing it, because he, as a member of the professional-managerial class, depends on its structure of value to imagine himself as flourishing, as leading a purposeful, good life.[92]

When an "injustice done" to him precipitates a "professional crisis," and even his young daughter declares the college president's actions "unfair," it looks as though the protagonist's value system, to which he has been conscientiously true throughout a delicate professional negotiation, has failed him. [93] And yet he cannot abandon either the value system or the institution that ostensibly dignifies it. By the time he writes the letter to his son, he has outlived those early injustices by decades and has become a dean and then president at a different college. But the subdued tone with which he relates this crisis, along with evidence of a painful aftermath—the job resignation, the physical relocations for other jobs, the divorce, and the second marriage—may appear symptomatic of "the affective attachment to what we call 'the good life,' which is for so many a bad life that wears out the subjects who nonetheless, and at the same time, find their conditions of possibility within it."[94] Despite the narrator's self-description as having led "a happy, active life" (*CS* 38), it may be hard to resist the diagnosis that he has succumbed to one of modernity's life-damaging cruelties—its relentless optimism.

Such a diagnosis, however, would miss, I think, the larger point of Taylor's story. Just as in "*Je Suis Perdu*," the location of the protagonist's time and place is central to the way the story works out the significance of the narrator-protagonist's self-assessment. The narrator dwells extensively on other times and places—indeed, almost to the extent of obscuring the reality and import of his own time and place. But this near effacement is pivotal to Taylor's insights into what we might call the distinction between organization man and institution man at midcentury. No longer a proprietary entrepreneur, the white-collar man made renowned by such social critics as William Whyte and C. Wright Mills is a figure of downward mobility and diminished agency. As Andrew Hoberek notes, even academics suffered under the evolving conditions of labor and class identity: "In the postwar period, intellectual work was definitively reconfigured as something that took place within institutions . . . , most importantly, [within] the expanding system of higher education. . . . [As] organization men par excellence, their employment symboliz[ed] the ultimate degradation of creative mental labor within the white-collar workplace."[95]

By contrast, Taylor's southern man in a northern institution is a figure of salutary displacement and belatedness. His institution man is one who, like the organization man, follows on the heels of proprietary giants, but unlike him, he discovers untapped resources and puts them to institutional use. He exemplifies the midcentury social liberal whom historian Howard Brick describes as relatively unconcerned about traditional relations of capital on account of postwar society's evolution toward noneconomic motivations, cooperative values, and an intricately connected mixed economy. The social liberal adopted a revisionist "postcapitalist perspective" that discerned in "the institutions of contemporary society" a wide variety of "private and public, economic and political, 'autonomous' and 'prescribed' ... activities."[96] This perspective enabled him to apply a "flexible, pragmatist style" of engagement to institutional problem solving.[97] In Taylor's story the narrator-protagonist exhibits sufficient knowledge of longitudinal history, at least in the hindsight of narration, to appreciate rather than bemoan his diminished portion, describing without much fanfare how he parlayed it, when faced with personal crisis, into opportunity. He registers this historical awareness first and comparatively briefly by addressing his adult son's situation in the late 1960s, describing himself as "not unsympathetic" to his son's antiwar position and, more broadly, his bohemian ethos (CS 3). Still, the narrator predicts that this "wonderful generation," the game-changing baby boomers, will not "succeed in going very far along the road [it is] on" (3). Without sarcasm or hostility, he implies that his son might do well to lower his expectations. As the narrative unfolds, we see why. With much less reticence he turns to the worlds of recent proprietary giants—his father and grandfather. From these sections of the narrative we learn what happens when presumptuous men, one in the world of high finance and law and the other in the world of high politics and government, are shocked by the recognition of failure resulting from the same sort of unexpected betrayal and unjust subterfuge that the narrator experienced. What happens is that they take it out on others. In each case, the proprietary man's reaction was to retreat into the world of family. Each had a traditional family to retreat to, and each indulged his bitterness at the expense of his wife and children—the father by becoming "lonely and bored" at home (23) and the grandfather by becoming a "coarse-tongued old tyrant" (15). Such destinies are what the protagonist has avoided, he implies, by sticking with the institution, despite its flaws. "But at least I am not tyrannizing over old women and small children," he explains to his son. "At least I don't sit gazing into space while my wife . . . waits patiently to see whether or not I will risk a two-heart bid" (38). Indeed, the "happy, active life" he claims for himself seems to be his first wife's as well (38). The dissolution of their marriage enabled her return to work, allowing her to enjoy a long academic career.

If a cruel and unjust crisis within the modern institution turns out to be an opportunity for more equally redistributing pursuits of happiness and for creating institution women alongside institution men, the point of Taylor's 1968 story is not to recommend cruelty and injustice or even utilitarian consequentialism. The narrator's subdued tone remains a check on any enthusiasm the outcomes, isolated from their causes, might elicit. Further, he isn't oblivious to the costs of his decisions: "The books one might have written after that first one. More important, one may sacrifice the love, even the acquaintance of one's children. One loses something of one's self even" (*CS* 38). This is what it means to muddle through with incrementalism's hope of doing less harm than good. Having become what Mills disparages as the "administrator, idea-man, and good-will technician," the narrator-protagonist affirms that lowered expectations about but ongoing commitments to the robust if flawed midcentury system of liberal institutions has its ethical and epistemological advantages.[98]

Belatedness Revalued

The critic John Burt has described Taylor's Pulitzer-winning novel, *A Summons to Memphis* (1986)—for which "Dean of Men" is a kind of trial run (insofar as the novel also thematizes the effects of a proprietary father's reaction to betrayal)—as emblematic of Taylor's literary-historical situation: it "provides a metaphorical way of describing the literary predicament of a belated generation of Southern novelists, a generation that must sever its consuming ties with the Renascence generation but must also risk its vitality as novelists if it succeeds in breaking the tie."[99] This insight into a generation's belatedness is important, but I would suggest here that it is slightly misplaced. Taylor doesn't so much risk as gain vitality from loosening the tie. It is, to be sure, a more modest sort of vitality, but it is also less reckless and less aggrandizing at others' expense. When he thematizes belatedness, as we have seen, the character feeling belated manages nonetheless to convert the "predicament" into opportunity not by shrinking but by widening the gap between himself and previous generations of proprietary giants, be they Confederate statesmen for the historian, a Confederate hero-grandfather for the prep student, or a ruling-class father and grandfather for the college administrator. In "In the Miro District" the late-middle-aged narrator recalls how he, as a youth in search of an identity distinct from his forebear, knowing that he "wasn't and couldn't be like him," wondered what he himself "*was* like. Or if, merely as a result of being born when I was and where I was, at the very tail end of something, I was like nothing else at all, only incomparably without a character of my own" ("Miro" 190). Once again, the ethnographic technology of likeness performs its office. Here it functions as a distancing mechanism that provides cognitive access to the experience of belatedness without asserting that the narrator-protagonist, much less the author, still inhabits that subject position decades later.

Indeed, we might question whether the condition of belatedness applies at all to Taylor. The author who invents a narrator-protagonist who experiences belatedness as being empty of character need not himself feel empty of character, either personal or authorial. Although Taylor's wife, children, other relatives, friends, students, colleagues, and interviewers would be in the position to vouch for his lively personality, his story "1939"—originally published in the *New Yorker* under the title "A Sentimental Journey"—may be understood to model and affirm the kind of authorial vitality he imagined himself to exemplify. A brief portrait of an artist as a young man, the story seizes on its time and place with alacrity. It presents intimations of what might be called postsouthern timeliness. Based on a Thanksgiving weekend road trip to the East Coast that Taylor made with his Kenyon roommate, Robert Lowell—both of whom, to recall, followed John Crowe Ransom there—its ties to the South could hardly be looser or more tactfully yet emphatically loosened. The reminiscing narrator, now a college professor and creative writer, describes an altercation they had and its aftermath. On the train back to Gambier, after botched reunions with girlfriends, their mutual sense of betrayal reaches its tipping point; they're prepared for the feud to turn physical. But rather than an all-out thrashing that might purge but also escalate their anger and abjection to Faulknerian heights, they find themselves in nothing more than a shoulder-shoving match. The narrator doesn't pretend to know quite how or why:

> Apparently neither of us felt any impulse to strike the other with his fist or to take hold and wrestle. . . . We shoved each other about the little room for nearly half an hour, with ever increasing violence, our purpose always seeming to be to get the other through the narrow doorway and into the passage. ("1939" 243)

However much the "violence" here increases, the narrator explains that the shoving match "was all over" even before the arrival of the conductor, "an old man with an inquiring and rather friendly look on his face." If the conductor has "waited," as the narrator surmises, "in the hope of seeing something of [a] spectacle," he's also "satisfied" that they've called it quits ("1939" 243). As though to decrease any possible suspense, the narrator also explains in advance that he "know[s] from a later examination of [his] arms and chest and back that [he] was covered in bruises" (243) but otherwise uninjured. Objects in the train car are likewise undamaged: "We had not even upset the spittoon. Even Jim's glasses were safe on the leather seat" (243–44). And after the Taylor stand-in returned to his seat, he "fell asleep at once. It was a blissful kind of sleep, . . . a fine sort of sleep" (244). Some bruises, blissful sleep, and eyeglasses intact: it's difficult to imagine an outcome more underwhelming and more unlike, say, the predicament that O'Connor's Hulga, in "Good Country People," finds herself in after the Bible salesman runs off with her prosthetic leg.

What's conspicuously missing from Taylor's scene of conflict is the sense of exalted violation that the neo-Agrarian Marion Montgomery locates in Flannery O'Connor. Montgomery promotes her fiction of "grotesqueness" as indicative of "a fascinating healthiness in southern writing, whose power comes finally not from its local materials but from the writer's sense that, good or bad, we are members one of another and violate each other and must pay for the violation (usually through violence) because of the wrathful love of whatever gods we believe in."[100] This process, of course, mirrors the South's broader sense of violation. As Michael Kreyling puts it, "The defeat of the South summed up the history of the cumulative tragedy of the Western, Christian ideal, and conferred instant longevity and authority on the South."[101] Whereas O'Connor heightens this sense of wrathful and righteous violation in "Good Country People" by leaving Hulga "sitting on the straw in the dusty sunlight" with a "churning face," Taylor unwinds his story in the opposite direction.[102] On the final bus ride from Cleveland, his two college boys, after the shoving match, end up "sitting side by side" and keeping "up a continuous flow of uninhibited and even confidential talk about [them]selves" ("1939" 244). He does, however, invite momentary suspicion that a homosocial urge to violate has been repressed and then displaced onto a later interaction. Upon returning to Douglass House and discovering their seven housemates "sprawled about [their] big room in various stages of undress," the Taylor stand-in's reaction comes close to divine wrath: "I remember my first feeling of outrage. The sacred privacy of that room under the eaves of Douglass House had been violated; this on top of what had happened in New York seemed for a moment more than flesh and blood could bear" (245). But even this displacement is something of a ruse, for what follows is distinctly conciliatory and deflationary: "Then, all of a sudden, Jim Prewitt and I began to laugh," with Jim demanding something to eat. Jokes follow. Finally, "everyone laughed—a little nervously, perhaps, but with a certain heartiness, too" (245). With this socioemotional cliché of laughter, the narrator signals a departure from Southern Renascence aesthetics and an embrace of a liberal aesthetics of civility.

According to Montgomery, the genuine southern writer should herself enjoy a longevity engendered by violence: "Ultimately a writer with this sense of violation and its consequences will leave the longest scar on the world. (For art itself is a species of violence.)"[103] In distinct contrast to this glorification of scar-searing art, the narrator of "1939" describes himself as a "journeyman writer" whose bruises have long healed. He is "a type of whom Trollope might have approved, but one who has known neither the financial success of the facile Harvard boy [who passes through Kenyon and goes on to make it big in Hollywood] nor the reputation of Carol Crawford [the stand-in for Jean Stafford]. Yet this man behind the lectern is a man who seems happy in the knowledge that he knows—or thinks he knows—what he is about" ("1939" 222). It is from this double-gesturing position of simultaneously confident and diffident self-assertion, of both knowing oneself and acknowledging the limits of one's (self-) knowledge that Taylor's "happy" narrators typically speak. The trope of the "journeyman" doesn't just chime with the story's account of youthful artists on their literal and figurative journeys of life; it is also the means by which Taylor carved out a vocational space between the two writerly identities he wished to dissociate himself from. On the one hand, he cringed at the idea of being an "amateur," a term he associated with regional writers who couldn't rise above their local color quaintness. On the other hand, he was averse to the identity of the "professional" writer, one who wrote for financial profit. One thus discovers yet another virtue of the institution: Taylor understood his college or university employment as valuable precisely because it meant that he didn't have to publish to support his family; he could therefore envision writing time as not in conflict with family time.[104]

For this chapter the journeyman figure has significance that far surpasses

Taylor's autobiographical evocations. Indeed, it surpasses his important redirection of southern aesthetic value away from Agrarian pretensions and toward more secular, less extremist fictional practice. This figure stands, I suggest, as southern liberalism's most vital response to Galbraith's call for new symbols of happiness. To come full circle, the journeyman writer embodies not only a postsouthern loosening of ties to Agrarian ideology but also a tightening of ties to midcentury America's most formidable liberal critic, Lionel Trilling. Some four years before the original *New Yorker* publication of "1939," the figure of the journeyman writer appeared in Trilling's renowned essay "William Dean Howells and the Roots of Modern Taste," first published in the *Partisan Review*—where, as it happens, Taylor's Stafford stand-in will soon publish sections of her novel ("1939" 236). In this essay Trilling routes his revaluation of Howells through a discussion of Trollope, including Henry James on Trollope. In "1939" the Lowell stand-in accuses the Taylor stand-in of imitating Henry James (241). As the critic Albert J. Griffith observes, when the narrator aligns himself with Trollope, Taylor probably had Henry James's version of Trollope in mind. James is the one who, after all, "attributes to Trollope . . . [a] 'complete appreciation of the usual,'" which Griffith rightly sees in Taylor's work as well.[105] As though channeling Trilling, Griffith goes on to say that "Taylor takes the commonplace subject matter of a William Dean Howells and runs it through the rarified mind of a Henry James."[106] Taylor liked to think that a story's meaning "should seem mere happy coincidence" rather than the effect of conspicuous symbolism.[107] To employ the terms of this chapter, this happiness corresponds roughly to the achievement of ethnographic analogy. But it also seems a fitting conclusion to this chapter to apply the phrase "happy coincidence" to the near concurrence of Trilling's and Taylor's invocation of the journeyman figure. Without overloading this phrase with cultural-historical meaning, I do want to argue for the importance of Trilling's essay, as it promotes this figure's key relevance to midcentury literature, culture, and politics.

The passage in which he invokes the journeyman figure has the Jamesian quality of a self-implicating, part-laudatory, part-reproving judgment that stakes its intelligibility on the reader's receptivity to an enlarged context:

> Howells' ambitiousness reached its peak in youth and then compromised itself, or democratized itself, so that in much of his work he is only the journeyman,

a craftsman quite without the artist's expectably aristocratic notions, and in his life, although he was a child of light and a son of the covenant, he also kept up his connections with the Philistines—he was, we remember, the original of James's Strether; and when such a man complains about America, we do not say that his case is special, we do not discount and resist what he says, we listen and are convinced.[108]

Here Trilling simultaneously compares the journeyman writer unfavorably to the artist and esteems his social views; he arrays Howells's democratic sensibility against aristocratic elitism but aligns it with compromise and the uncultured middlebrow. Appearing early in this serpentine essay, the passage sets the stage for Trilling's case for listening more closely to the Howellsian frequency. But its ambivalence, I suggest, registers both the strength of the case and the difficulty, indeed the likely futility, of making it persuasive.

The broad concern of Trilling's essay is the worrisome "charisma" of modernist art and thought. Self-consciously turning the tables on his own inclinations, Trilling is troubled by the "power we respond to when we find [charisma] in our literature in the form of alliances with the dark gods of sexuality, or the huge inscrutability of nature, or the church, or history."[109] It accounts for "our preference for the hidden and ambiguous, for our demand for 'tension' and 'tragedy.'"[110] Trilling urges readers to see that their taste for charismatic literature corresponds to "our growing disenchantment with the whole idea of the political life, the feeling that . . . we do not willingly consent to live in a particular society of the present, marked as it is bound to be by a particular economic system, by disorderly struggles for influence, by mere approximations and downright failures."[111] A fixation on the "failures and injustices" of "capitalistic society" has led to a total repudiation of "bourgeois reality" such that only when a writer like Faulkner in *As I Lay Dying* portrays the "family's extremity of suffering" do we care to include the family theme in the "American literature of any pretensions."[112] This excess of aesthetic and political alienation demands reconsideration of the kind of conscientious, genial literature that Howells and Trollope offered. As James observed about Trollope, there "is something remarkably tender and friendly in his feeling about all human perplexities; he takes the good-natured, temperate, conciliatory view."[113] As for Howells, Trilling notes that he "was committed totally and without question to civil life."[114] These two writers' democratic "appreciation of the usual" may have left them with little to say about "heroic moral intensity" or the "irresistible temptation of disintegration," but they saw with acute insight ordinary virtues and social integration on the not impossibly distant horizon of modern life.[115]

The critic Mark Krupnick notes that this "attempt to recover the lost imagination of happiness was a serious project," one to which he justifiably deems Trilling, with his constitutive ambivalence and inclination toward modernist malaise, not up to the task. Consolation for Krupnick seems to arrive in the form of an entire generation's inadequacy: "If Trilling was not adequate to it, neither was any other writer of the fifties."[116] Howells becomes for Trilling a kind of ego ideal who offers only temporary respite from the modern intellectual's compulsive turn to the plight of tragic consciousness.[117] For confirmation of Trilling's inadequacy, one need only look to the note of futility with which he closes out the Howells essay: "The extreme has become the commonplace of our day," he bemoans. "This is not a situation which can be legislated or criticized out of existence, but while it endures we are not in a position to make a proper judgment of Howells, a man of moderate sentiments"; we may thus be "disqualified from making any literary judgments at all."[118]

But however halfheartedly Trilling undertook the project of imagining happiness, this book has urged a revision of Krupnick's judgment of the midcentury American scene. Along with Taylor, the other writers featured here prove quite adequate to the task not only of imagining happiness but also of justifying its symbolic value within the regime of welfare-state liberalism.

CODA
The Politics of Contemporary Happiness

This book's account of postwar American fiction's validation of welfare-state liberalism chimes with claims recently advanced by Jonathan Bell and Timothy Stanley. In their introduction to *Making Sense of Liberalism*, they insist that, despite liberalism's "shortcomings" as a proposition and practice, "it remains a vibrant movement full of potential."[1] Some of the essays in their volume importantly trace out this vibrancy all the way up to present-day politics. Would that one could do the same with respect to the specific discourse of happiness and welfare-state symbology. But the last few decades have witnessed the ballooning of two prohibitive trends: the pursuit of happiness science and the postmodern critique of the value of happiness. The preceding chapters have touched on this critique here and there while saying very little about the long, dubious history of happiness science.[2] By way of conclusion, then, I offer here a highly compressed summary analysis of how the contemporary confluence of happiness science and postmodern happiness critique has resulted in the nearly total eclipse of the political potential of happiness as a welfare-state proposition.

Once again, it helps my argument to proceed by literary example. Anybody seeking a window onto the contemporary discourse of happiness could do worse than to start with Richard Powers's 2009 novel *Generosity*. As we've come to expect from a Powers novel, it exhibits the author's command of the relevant scientific idiom—in this case, positive psychology and neuroscience. He mobilizes their conceptual staples (hedonic set points, allelic correlations, peak experiences, negativity biases, contentment graphs, illusory self-reports, and so forth) to portray Americans' obsession with happiness. Like other dark yet playful satires (for instance, DeLillo's *White Noise*), the novel waxes hyperbolic as it depicts a biotech-consumer-media complex committed less to the well-being of society or the flourishing of individuals than to the acquisition of the sheer experience of happiness. For this world's movers and shakers, the sooner the happiness gene can be isolated and marketed by biotech futurists the better.

Satiric exaggeration, however, does not obscure the novel's credible picture of the ideological and institutional conditions enabling happiness science to elevate the techne of happiness above—and largely to segregate it from—other matters of social and political import. In this world the status of happiness is settled: as contemporary America's uppermost value, it is a utility that affirms itself. This premium on happiness has a long, venerable history, dating back (in Western thought) to Greek antiquity, but in the contemporary era the happiness cult has generated a good deal of opposition. Among postmodern critics, specifically, objections range from the epistemological to the political: for Slavoj Žižek happiness permits the evasion of difficult knowledge and desire; for Claire Colebrook happiness insists, in a bad way, on giving a life narrative meaning; for Heather Love and Sara Ahmed happiness perpetuates compulsory social norms; for Michael Hardt and Antonio Negri happiness is bound up with proprietary bourgeois hegemony.[3] Yet for all the pressure such critiques have put on the value of happiness, they turn out, in an important sense, to reinforce rather than to unsettle its privileged status. In what follows I argue that postmodern and poststructuralist criticism effectively collaborates with happiness science to segregate happiness from normative politics, specifically from considerations of human flourishing and welfare-state justice. I trace out the parallel ascendance first of happiness science's disavowal of everything political, owing largely to its behavioral and geneticist methodologies, and then of postmodernism's displacement of welfare-state liberalism by a politics of recognition and/or of radical deterritorialization coded as "joy." Both modes of disowning normative politics serve only to strengthen what Powers suggests is technofuturism's co-optation of happiness. This cooptation, moreover, strengthens technofuturism's hold on the very idea of the future.

Generosity's portrayal of contemporary technofuturism provides a seriocomic glimpse of the hazards of a national obsession such as happiness. Intercutting three parallel narratives, the novel revolves mainly around the well-intended but nearly disastrous efforts of Russell Stone, a part-time university instructor of creative nonfiction, to protect one of his students, the Kabyle-Algerian refugee Thassadit Amzwar, from the biotech-consumer-media complex that wants to profit from her DNA, her ova, and her genuinely glowing personality. She's a genetic freak whose "hyperthymia" makes her happy all the time. This condition affects not only her preponderant experience of positive affect over negative affect (her PA to NA ratio) but also her overall sense of life satisfaction, despite enduring all kinds of terrible misfortune. In addition, the novel tracks the comings and goings of Dr. Thomas Kurton, the neuroscientist and biotech entrepreneur who will eventually sequence parts of her genome, and of Tonia Schiff, the producer-host of a popular television science show who has made Kurton a household name. All three narrative arcs dramatically intersect when Thassa appears on an Oprah-like talk show. Russell is in the studio audience (along with Candace Weld, the psychotherapist he has recruited to help Thassa and who is his subsequent love interest); Kurton is a fellow guest on the show; and Schiff and her crew are filming the show for their own show. They all witness Thassa's near meltdown, an event that precipitates her devolution into little more than a spectacular object and subject of happiness.

The web formation of these storylines allegorizes the mutually reinforcing conditions, in the "consumer-genomics era," of the happiness cult and the commercialization of science.[4] Powers portrays this matrix as both dynamic and ominous: it enables biotech futurists, television hosts, bloggers, and YouTubers alike to propagate the fantasy of genetically enhanced well-being for all, or at least for those who can afford it; ironically, the main thing standing between *Brave New World*'s happiness dystopia and us, the novel suggests, is unregulated capitalism. The "British ethicist" Anne Harter, who spars with Kurton on television, may well criticize his expensive "breakthroughs" for widening the gulf "between the haves and have-nots" (*G* 61), but Powers makes the proposition of ubiquitous happiness resulting from socioeconomic equality seem even worse. In the novel, Kurton is the one who thinks ubiquitous happiness would be wonderful. He deems Huxley's book "one of the most dangerous, hope-impeding, ideological rants ever written"; the author must have been "stunted by some virtuous vision of embattled humanism" (192). Kurton thinks that "for most of human history" storytelling compensated for "short and bleak" lives and that "now that we're on the verge of living the long, pain-reduced lives that our brains deserve," we need a different kind of art (151). But "we" readers of *Generosity* are meant to have more trouble identifying with this biotech maverick than with Powers's "throwback characters" (236), the melancholic Russell and solicitous Candace. We are encouraged to be glad for once that we can't afford something. For if biotech's envisioned therapies were technically feasible and economically available, we might never be able to justify being cranky or sad, much less to enjoy reading about characters who are. While everyone who meets Thassa adores her, one of her classmate-groupies worries, "Is there something broken with her? Or something really . . . fixed?" (50). Is it, for instance, a good thing that after another classmate-groupie sexually assaults her, Thassa harbors no anger and refuses to press charges against him?

Generosity never fully answers whether Thassa's hyperthymia is a good thing or a bad thing *for her*; the genetic condition seems both to endanger and protect her. But the novel does imply that what's really "fixed," in a quite different sense, is the contemporary language game of happiness. It at once trivializes happiness by isolating it and monetizes happiness by promoting it. The novel, I've suggested, attributes this fix to the contemporary moment's fluid systemic forces. This moment, it goes without saying, has a history. In addition to the biotech-consumer-media complex that Powers depicts, the last three decades both of the social science of happiness and of postmodern cultural theory have done much to fix the language game of happiness. The social science of happiness got its kick start, according to many in the field, in 1984, when Ed Diener published his landmark article on subjective well-being in *Psychological Bulletin*—the same year, notably, that Fredric Jameson published his landmark article on postmodernism in *New Left Review*. As it happens, the two articles perform similar functions within their respective disciplines. They both take stock of an area of inquiry emerging from the postwar era. Whereas Jameson identifies postmodernism's general break with modernity as a late 1950s phenomenon, Diener identifies the roots of his discipline in the work of midcentury humanistic psychologists (such as Abraham Maslow and Carl Rogers) who broke with moderns' Freudian and behavioralist past.[5] Moreover, as they proceed to describe and evaluate these developments, each proposes methodological innovations meant to improve his discipline's strategies of inquiry, offering these proposals as instructional *maps*.

Diener opens his essay with a succinct declaration that clears the way for happiness science's segregation and promotion of its object of study: "Throughout history philosophers considered happiness to be the highest good and ultimate motivation for human action."[6] This theory of value and motivation becomes the discipline's operative premise. Rarely subject to intramural challenge, it presumes a social consensus, beyond the discipline, of happiness's supreme utility. Yet, as Diener observes, now that external criteria for defining and evaluating happiness (such as Aristotelian virtue and Christian holiness) have been superseded by subjective criteria (such as the frequency and intensity of positive affect and assessments of life satisfaction), of paramount interest to him is the development of better techniques for measuring and defining subjective well-being. Hence the need to sort out correlations from causes, to reduce distortions in self-reports, and to elaborate theoretical approaches (primarily theories of motivation and causes) that "can be tested empirically in relation to SWB."[7] This subjective turn certainly conforms to liberal modernity's respect for individual self-determination, but it also steers happiness science toward a "prudential psychology," which no longer considers happiness's relation to liberalism's other core values.[8] Diener's methodology thus enables researchers "to map more completely" but also more exclusively the terrain of subjective happiness.[9]

Jameson's widely influential theory offers postmodern criticism similar methodological leverage. Combining historicist description and historiographical assertion, his 1984 essay identifies "the constitutive features of the postmodern."[10] These features have become so familiar as hardly to need mentioning: simulacral depthlessness, the waning of historicity alongside the waxing appeal of a perpetual present, the waning of affect alongside the fragmentation of the subject, and the waning of political or critically active artistic expression alongside the allure of the commodity form. As these phenomena render postmodernism "the cultural dominant of the logic of late capitalism," they register what Jameson calls "a whole new economic world system."[11] If Jameson's description has encouraged critics to dwell on (and claim as emblematic) certain cultural patterns while ignoring others, equally significant is the way Jameson supplements his historicism with a critical methodology appropriate for inhabiting the "totalizing space of the new world system." His idea of "cognitive mapping" is meant in part to replace the purportedly obsolete dream of "critical distance."[12] Rather than being merely "mimetic"—that is, rather than restricting its epistemological reach to empirical phenomena and falsifiable theory, as Diener's map does—Jameson's cognitive map will "enable a situational representation on the part of the individual subject to [a] vaster and properly *unrepresentable* totality."[13] No one gets anywhere in the postmodern world without a guide to its immanent evanescence.

With cognitive map in hand, cultural critics may now (to borrow Jameson's idiom) transcode Louis Althusser's old duality of ideology and science into a new dialectic of material situation and unrepresentable totality and thereby find themselves in inventive relation to the world's immanence.[14] For Jameson's methodological instruction makes available a new kind of affective-critical orientation. Instead, for instance, of reading Bob Perelman's "schizophrenic" poem, "China," as evidence of morbid alienation and anxiety, the cognitive map reveals the poem's gesture toward "*absent* text[s]"; thus "the unity of the poem is no longer to be found within its language, but *outside* itself." Jameson's brief but exquisite reading of Perelman's poem reveals how the schizophrenic style "becomes available for more *joyous intensities*."[15] Yet aesthetic relief from late capitalism is not all Jameson seeks. The dialectic he proposes between the world and its unrepresentable, absent, radical otherness is also meant to enable utopian-minded political activists to "regain a capacity to act and struggle" in the "political form of postmodernism." From aesthetic intensification to political intervention, then, the cognitive map offers its users "radically new forms" of engagement.[16]

The influence of Jameson's critical paradigm is evident in postmodern critiques of happiness—for instance, in the work of Sara Ahmed, a prominent critic in affect, queer, and cultural studies, and of Michael Hardt and Antonio Negri, coauthors of best-selling academic books of political theory. This influence is registered in their respective projects of transcoding "joyous intensity" into affective and political alternatives to mainstream happiness. In 2008 Ahmed edited a special issue of *New Formations* on the politics of happiness, publishing a monograph on the subject in 2010. In 2009 Hardt and Negri concluded their massive trilogy—*Empire*, *Multitude*, and *Commonwealth*—with a brief chapter on happiness. I take both sets of criticism to be particularly robust examples of the postmodern assault on the function and value of happiness within welfare-state liberalism. They both take part, alongside happiness science, in undoing liberalism's dialectical tension between happiness and justice. Ahmed's and Hardt and Negri's specific modes of intervention reveal, in my view, troubling implications for the rubbing of normative happiness off the political-economic map.

For Ahmed, the brave new world portended by Huxley and Powers has already arrived. Long before the pharmaceutical industry's success in marketing ever-new variants of soma-like drugs, and long before any fictional or real biotech industry's dream of isolating the happiness gene, sociopolitical claims to the promise of happiness became the scourge of modernity. The trouble arose from "philosophy's foundational tautology: what is good is happy and what is happy is good."[17] In this moral economy, happiness is what conventional moderns desire; happiness is what they feel when they obtain or achieve that desire; and happiness is a sign of their moral desert. Ahmed thus accepts as social truth Diener's premise of happiness's cultural status as the highest good and ultimate motivation. Despite their incompatible approaches to the politics of happiness, this premise is what allows her to isolate happiness no less than Diener does as the great problem to focus on.

Ahmed is deeply suspicious of this dominant structure of feeling; she contends that happiness marginalizes negative emotions and the people who have them. But not just anybody who has them: the figures of significance are melancholy migrants wounded by racism, killjoy feminists angered by gender subordination, and unhappy queers estranged by familial hope. For unlike most people who have internalized the imperative to be happy, marginalized persons suffer delegitimation twice over: they are socioeconomically underprivileged, and nobody likes their attitude. It gets worse: the "powers-that-be . . . , in wanting our happiness," might also "forbid recognition of sadness as that which gets in the way" both of manifest happiness and of the desire for it.[18] Ahmed takes more interest in the recognition of psychosocial injury than in the potential redress of the political-economic conditions that underlie susceptibility to such injury. By her lights, negative affect performs the same function as other, more recognizably permanent markers of identity: it grants political authenticity and authority to fixedness.[19]

From the liberal-democratic standpoint, oppressed persons usually have good reason to be angry about and frustrated by unfair practices of discrimination and inequality. But Ahmed does not look at things from the liberal-democratic standpoint. She is as suspicious of consensus liberalism's structural formation as she is of modernity's cult of happiness. Indeed, the political structure and the psychosocial cult are functionally homologous. The promotion of happiness "involve[s] an immanence of coercion, a demand for agreement": if you find the right things agreeable, then "those around you 'agree' with your agreement." This is how institutions arising from democratic consensus menace the population. "After all, agreement can mean not only the action of pleasing or contenting" but also "the act of consenting."[20] Ahmed's style of rhyming here bespeaks her sense of an unbroken continuum between social psychology's capture of affective life and the social contract's capture of political will.

More precisely, this rhyming bespeaks the collapse of the political realm into the affective realm. The whole point of being an "affect alien" is to register "unhappiness with and rage about injustice."[21] But this focus on the negative affect of persons whom liberals are bound (both likely and obligated) to recognize as victims of injustice makes it difficult to see the ideological corner into which Ahmed has backed the politics of happiness. It is not just a corner organized around the preference of recognition over redress; it also construes an alignment between *un*happiness and righteousness—without, however, offering an account of justice. Ahmed relies on the immediate legibility of the very kinds of injustice that consensus liberalism, with its commitment to equal rights and fairness, make legible. She thus exhibits symptoms of cryptonormativism, resembling innumerable postmodern critics who, to borrow Ruth Leys's description, "implicitly espouse certain political beliefs and norms, such as the value of democracy, without providing reasons for these beliefs because their theoretical position precludes them from doing so."[22]

The preclusion of liberalism's mechanisms for promoting future justice and happiness helps to explain why Ahmed defends queer theorist Lee Edelman's notorious antifuturism as "still affirming something in the act of refusing affirmation."[23] Such ineluctable affirmation dovetails with her own sense that it's important as a political activist to affirm "something." It turns out by the end of the book that Ahmed can't entirely disaffirm happiness. She takes up the project of transcoding Jameson's sense of joyous intensity into the figure of the "silly" and "happy-go-lucky" person who puts the "hap" back into happiness by being open to contingent "possibility."[24] The utilitarian tautology of the good being happy and the happy being good is thus displaced by a postmodern tautology of the good being chancy and the chancy being good. In neither scenario is there room for liberalism's dialectical tension between the institutional promotion of objective fairness and the experiential value of subjective well-being.

From the standpoint of governmental policy it's difficult to imagine without drifting into cartoonish fantasy what a quirky, happy-go-lucky institution would even look like. And yet this is close to what Hardt and Negri have in mind when, at the end of their book *Commonwealth*, they return to Spinoza's concept of joy as the solution to the problem of bourgeois proprietary happiness. Writing joyous intensity jumbo large—institutionalizing it globally—they envision "altermodernity's" displacement of modern, postmodern, antimodern, and hypermodern regimes. In the era of modernity, Hardt and Negri argue, Enlightenment government's "faith in progress" was fine for its time.[25] But it's too teleological for today's globalized multitude; it's too predictably driven toward contemporary theories of social democracy (such as those advanced by Jürgen Habermas and John Rawls), which remain preoccupied with inequitable distribution of wealth and the scarcity of resources.[26] In altermodernity, there's no property and no scarcity; government thus embraces Spinoza's intuition that "we still don't know . . . what a body can do and a mind can think. And we will never know the limits of their powers" (379). In this new nonorder, government's key function is to promote the potentiality of "becoming," of "growing powers," and of "open[ing] new possibilities."[27] In other words, happiness, redescribed as joy, becomes the affective proxy for political agency. It infuses a charmed circle in which radical novelty is good and the good is radically novel. This is how, as Bruce Robbins notes in his review of *Commonwealth*, Hardt and Negri's fans are encouraged to "confuse politics with science fiction."[28] They adopt a weltanschauung that seems to relish technofuturism even more than Powers's Kurton does.

In Powers's near-futuristic novel, to recall, it is a message of radical, joyous difference that Thassa embodies, that her genetic freakishness delivers to the biotech-consumer-media complex in the form of hyperthymia. And the scientist-entrepreneur Kurton devises an ethos to fit the moment, one that any Spinozan could appreciate. He expresses it in the television debate, cited earlier, with the ethicist Anne Harter, whose surname indicates her big heart but whose presence recedes as the novel unfolds. Her ineffectualness signals the hegemonic triumph of Kurton's capitalizing technofuturism whereby "ethics" itself will have to "catch up" to the popular desire to "live longer *and* better" (G 63). Earlier in the novel we learn that in addition to his research work in isolating gene complexes, Kurton "writes ecstatic pieces about the coming transhuman age" (24). The only "duty" he recognizes "is to proceed as if limits to our ability did not exist. We are collaborators in creation" (25). Here Kurton's fantasy of the transhuman becomes indistinguishable from Hardt and Negri's prophecy of Spinozan possibility.

In sum, Powers's novel and Ahmed's and Hardt and Negri's theories of the politics of happiness suggest why subverting the nation-state's plans for the future well-being of its citizens—by remaining true to recognizable identitarian misery, by seizing the silly, unplanned day, or by inventing radical new powers—possesses so much allure. These actions are constitutively dramatic, at once rebellious and playful. But they also severely scant the potential for conceptualizing a dialectical relation between happiness and welfare-state liberalism's sense of possible justice. In the face of such exacting propositions for a normative politics that, as we've seen throughout this study, keeps happiness within its purview, contemporary happiness science and biotech markets have a lot to answer for. In contrast to postmodern styles of opposition, welfare-state activism actually challenges their operative logic. A Nietzschean postmodernist such as Žižek, of course, will hardly be moved by the endeavor made here to revalue happiness in relation to redistributive justice. For him the latter idea will have as much traction as the sham liberal values from which it emanates. But for historians and cultural critics who inhabit the contemporary era but haven't completely ceded to its postmodern visions of politics and affect, a consideration of postwar accounts of subjective happiness in relation to social welfare might help to relax the antihappiness reflex that critics of all stripes, bombarded almost daily with media reports on happiness, have understandably developed.

Notes

Introduction

1. Philip Roth, *Reading Myself and Others* (New York: Farrar, Straus and Giroux, 1975), 175–77. More recently, Eric Klinenberg has made similar points about the library's role in cultivating a young person's sense of trust and responsibility. See his *Palaces for the People: How Social Infrastructure Can Help Fight Inequality, Polarization, and the Decline of Civic Life* (New York: Crown, 2018), 38.

2. John Kenneth Galbraith, *The Affluent Society* (Boston: Houghton Mifflin, 1958), 283. Hereafter abbreviated as *AS*, with page references appearing in the text.

3. As the historian John Patrick Diggins puts it, "In the 1950s the classical notion of liberalism as the preservation of life and property simply became peace and prosperity *for the majority*." *The Proud Decades: America in War and Peace, 1941–1960* (New York and London: Norton, 1988), 131, emphasis added.

4. Friedrich A. Hayek, *The Road to Serfdom* (Chicago: University of Chicago Press, 1944), ix, xv.

5. J. Donald Moon, introduction to *Responsibility, Rights, and Welfare: The Theory of the Welfare State*, ed. J. Donald Moon (Boulder, CO: Westview, 1988), 7. For a more skeptical account of Galbraith's agenda, see Sean McCann, "'They Make Their Own Tragedies Too': Harvey Swados and Postwar Liberalism's Discourse of Dependency," in *Literary/Liberal Entanglements: Toward a Literary History for the Twenty-First Century*, ed. Corrinne Harol and Mark Simpson (Toronto: University of Toronto Press, 2017), 304–5.

6. Lionel Trilling, "William Dean Howells and the Roots of Modern Taste," in *The Opposing Self: Nine Essays in Criticism* (New York: Viking, 1955), 87, 92.

7. Herbert Marcuse, *Eros and Civilization: A Philosophical Inquiry into Freud* (1955; repr., New York: Vintage, 1962), 237.

8. Russell W. Davenport, "A *Life* Round Table on the Pursuit of Happiness," *Life* 25, no. 2 (July 12, 1948): 96. Hereafter cited as *Life*, with page references appearing in the text.

9. There was one racial exception: the views of one married black couple who participated in a preliminary discussion were cited (*Life* 104, 107).

10. Richard Godden, *Fictions of Capital: The American Novel from James to Mailer* (Cambridge, UK: Cambridge University Press, 1990), 172.

11. Wendy Wall, *Inventing the "American Way": The Politics of Consensus from the New Deal to the Civil Rights Movement* (Oxford, UK: Oxford University Press, 2008), 165.

12. Wall, *Inventing*, 172.

13. Wall, 201, 202.

14. John Higham, "The Cult of 'American Consensus': Homogenizing Our History," *Commentary* 27 (February 1959): 94.

15. Higham, "Cult," 96.

16. Diggins, *Proud Decades*, 113–14.

17. E. L. Doctorow, *The Book of Daniel* (1971; repr., London: Penguin Classics, 2006), 14. Hereafter abbreviated as *BD*, with page references appearing in the text.

18. Daniel more obliquely implies that his wife, Phyllis, is marked by a similar morbidity. When they go to Washington, DC, for the Pentagon protest, the charming room they've procured in an elderly woman's house allows Phyllis to feel "serenely happy suspended in this quiet room in the absolute stillness in this house" (*BD* 309). Rather than appreciate this capacity for serenity, Daniel likes to subvert it, evinced by his habit of subjecting her to psychosexual torment. For egregious instance (often cited by critics), on the day after Susan's suicide attempt, he demands, while driving down the highway, that Phyllis remove her pants—under threat of increasing the vehicle's speed—and then proceeds first to fondle her genitalia and next to brand her buttock with the cigarette lighter (74). There is no explanation for this action, and no remorse. Earlier he had described himself as a "betrayer"—as "the kind of betrayer who betrays for no reason" (20).

19. Giorgio Agamben, *Homo Sacer: Sovereign Power and Bare Life*, trans. Daniel Heller-Roazen (Stanford, CA: Stanford University Press, 1998), 7.

20. Agamben, *Homo Sacer*, 8, 9.

21. Agamben, 9–10.

22. Agamben, 134, 186.

23. Agamben, 188.

24. Agamben, 79.

25. Doctorow once described his novel's nonlinearity in terms of the influence the television show *Laugh-In* had on him while he was drafting it: "[Its] idea of discontinuity and black-outs and running changes on voice and character—it was that kind of nerve energy I was looking for." It was written "out of a spirit of transgression." *E. L. Doctorow: Essays and Conversations*, ed. Richard Trenner (Princeton, NJ: Ontario Review Press, 1983), 41, 47.

26. Daniel's acquiescence to this logic becomes particularly cruel when he passes on Susan's psychic affliction of trauma to the next generation, his infant son. In Riverside Park, as though reversing Freud's fort/da game of emotional loss and recovery, he

throws the boy higher and higher into the air while catching him closer and closer to the ground, so that the boy is ultimately "locked in absolute dumb dread" (*BD* 161). With the infant scared nearly to death—"concentrating on his fear" of "the breathtaking flight" and "even more terrifying fall"—while the father entertains a "murderous feeling" (161), the scene figures a multigenerational continuity of the psychically damned. Personal-political wreckage is chronic: from executed father to sadistic son to terrorized grandson. Daniel's history of the present maps the reduction of happiness to zero.

27. Doug Rossinow, "Partners for Progress? Liberals and Radicals in the Long Twentieth Century," in *Making Sense of Liberalism*, ed. Jonathan Bell and Timothy Stanley (Urbana: University of Illinois Press, 2012), 19–20.

28. See T. V. Reed, "Genealogy/Narrative/Power: Questions of Postmodernity in Doctorow's *The Book of Daniel*," *American Literary History* 4, no. 2 (Summer 1992): 295; and Michael Szalay, *Hip Figures: A Literary History of the Democratic Party* (Stanford, CA: Stanford University Press, 2012), 245.

29. Fredric Jameson, "Postmodernism, or the Cultural Logic of Late Capitalism," *New Left Review* 146 (1984): 70.

30. Fredric Jameson, "Periodizing the 60s," *Social Text* 9/10 (Spring/Summer 1984): 183.

31. The terms of anthropology seem the most appropriate way to account for a modern nation-state's assertion of certain basic values, such as being educated rather than ignorant and healthy rather than ill and seeking to flourish over a lifetime rather than to wither. As the Marxist critic Robin Blackburn puts it, "The requirements of human flourishing have certain material and ideal components and these furnish an anthropological basis for the notion of 'human rights' and popular recognition of this fact helps to give rights claims their traction." See "Reclaiming Human Rights," *New Left Review* 69 (May/June 2011): 137.

32. Wendy Wall notes how poorly the mainstream consensus model served movements such as Martin Luther King Jr.'s push for civil rights: "Powerful as it was, the language of national consensus also had profound limits. In adopting this rhetoric, King and others were forced to abandon other languages—international socialism, black nationalism, and perhaps most important, human rights—that had propelled movements for equality in earlier decades." See Wall, *Inventing*, 285–86.

33. Ian Balfour and Eduardo Cadava, "The Claims of Human Rights: An Introduction," *South Atlantic Quarterly* 103, nos. 2/3 (Spring/Summer 2004): 280–81.

34. Balfour and Cadava, "Claims," 281.

35. Balfour and Cadava, 293.

36. United Nations, preamble, Universal Declaration of Human Rights, last accessed October 10, 2012, http://www.un.org/en/universal-declaration-human-rights/.

37. Samuel Moyn, "The Universal Declaration of Human Rights of 1948 in the History of Cosmopolitanism," *Critical Inquiry* 40, no. 4 (Summer 2014): 369, 380.

For criticism of Moyn's dismissal of the significance of the UDHR (and other pre-1970s texts) in the history of nonwelfarist rights, see Blackburn, "Reclaiming Human Rights," 126–38.

38. Harry K. Girvetz, *The Evolution of Liberalism*, intro. Arthur Schlesinger Jr. (London: Collier, 1963), 233.

39. With regard to consensus, the General Assembly could announce unanimous approval of the UDHR in December 1948, but only in the shadow of abstention on the part of several communist and authoritarian countries and the absence of numerous others. Still, as Edmund Fawcett comments in his recent longitudinal study, *Liberalism: The Life of an Idea*, "The achievement was large nevertheless, and so recognized at the time. The moral climate was palpable. . . . December 1948 may properly be counted as a moment when liberal democracy was recognized as a global, not a narrowly Western, aspiration." See *Liberalism: The Life of an Idea* (Princeton, NJ: Princeton University Press, 2014), 293.

40. See, for instance, Wendy Brown's critique of Michael Ignatieff, whose human rights defense she characterizes as tantamount to a defense of neoliberal free-market individualism at the expense of collective governance in "'The Most We Can Hope For . . .': Human Rights and the Politics of Fatalism," *South Atlantic Quarterly* 103, nos. 2/3 (Spring/Summer 2004): 451–63; and Bruce Robbins and Elsa Stamatopoulou's discussion of the UDHR's neglect of indigenous collective rights and colonized states' rights to self-determination in "Reflections on Culture and Cultural Rights," *South Atlantic Quarterly* 103, nos. 2/3 (Spring/Summer 2004): 419–34.

41. Amartya Sen, *The Idea of Justice* (Cambridge, MA: Harvard University Press, 2009), 57, 92. It's worth noting that Sen, Arrow, and Rawls joint-taught a seminar on rationality and justice at Harvard in 1968. See S. M. Amadae, *Rationalizing Capitalist Democracy: The Cold War Origins of Rational Choice Liberalism* (Chicago: University of Chicago Press, 2003), 258. I discuss at greater length Rawls's engagement with Arrow's social choice theory in "The Idea of Happiness: Back to the Postwar Future," in *Postmodern/Postwar—and After*, ed. Jason Gladstone, Andrew Hoberek, and Daniel Worden (Iowa City: University of Iowa Press 2016): 127–40. Katrina Forrester, in her recent account of Rawls's massive influence on political philosophy, contends that "by the end of the 1950s, the architecture of his theory was in place," including his commitment to consensus as "a 'heuristic device' to yield justifiable principles for judgment that would allow room for change." She also notes that Rawls was a beneficiary of the GI Bill. See Katrina Forrester, *In the Shadow of Justice: Postwar Liberalism and the Remaking of Political Philosophy* (Princeton, NJ: Princeton University Press, 2019), 3, 5, 6.

42. John Rawls, "The Sense of Justice" (1963), in *John Rawls: Collected Papers*, ed. Samuel Freeman (Cambridge, MA: Harvard University Press, 1999), 115.

43. John Rawls, "Justice as Fairness" (1958), in *John Rawls: Collected Papers*, ed. Samuel Freeman (Cambridge, MA: Harvard University Press, 1999), 66, 70.

44. Rawls, "Justice as Fairness," 66.

45. Rawls, 50.

46. John Rawls, "Distributive Justice: Some Addenda" (1968), in *John Rawls: Collected Papers*, ed. Samuel Freeman (Cambridge, MA: Harvard University Press, 1999), 158.

47. John Rawls, *A Theory of Justice* (Cambridge, MA: Harvard University Press, 1971), 549, 550. Hereafter abbreviated as *TJ*, with page references appearing in the text.

48. Perhaps even more relevant to this study than Rawls's odd figure of the flourishing grass counter is Rawls's invocation of aesthetic objects as analogical "exemplars of human flourishing" (*TJ* 550). He likens the fulfillment of an aspirational life plan to "compositions, paintings, and poems," for they exemplify "a certain completeness which though marred by circumstance and human failing is evident from the whole" (550).

49. Ursula K. Le Guin, "The Ones Who Walk Away from Omelas" (1973), in *30/30: Thirty American Stories from the Last Thirty Years*, ed. Porter Shreve and B. Minh Nguyen (New York: Penguin, 2006), 211.

50. Le Guin, "Omelas," 213. This abject child occupies the position of the slave that, Rawls argues, utilitarianism logically permits. See "Justice as Fairness," 67. By contrast, his contract doctrine is premised on equal liberty. In later essays, "Constitutional Liberty and the Concept of Justice" (1963) and "Distributive Justice" (1967), he strengthens the argument by introducing the idea of an original position in which contracting members "do not know their own talents and abilities. That is, they have no knowledge of how they will fare in the competition for positions in an open society." See "Constitutional Liberty and the Concept of Justice," in *John Rawls: Collected Papers*, ed. Samuel Freeman (Cambridge, MA: Harvard University Press, 1999), 81. He deduces that this "veil of ignorance" would compel the social contract to eliminate caste hierarchies because no rational person would take the risk of becoming a slave. See "Distributive Justice," in *John Rawls: Collected Papers*, ed. Samuel Freeman (Cambridge, MA: Harvard University Press, 1999), 132. In this point of the doctrine lies arguably the most consequential distinction between Rawls's theory of justice as fairness and utilitarian welfare economics.

51. Heather Love, "Small Change: Realism, Immanence, and the Politics of the Micro," *Modern Language Quarterly* 77, no. 3 (September 2016): 434, 436. For a full account of Love's theory of close but not deep reading, see Heather Love, "Close but Not Deep: Literary Ethics and the Descriptive Turn," *New Literary History* 41, no. 2 (Spring 2010): 371–91.

52. Love, "Small," 434, 435, 437.

53. Quoted in Love, 433.

54. Girvetz, *Evolution*, 18.

55. Quoted in Deak Nabers, "The Martial Imagination: World War II and American Culture," *American Literary History* 25, no. 1 (Spring 2013): 117, 118.

56. Robert Warshow, "The Gangster as Tragic Hero" (1948), in *The Immediate Experience: Movies, Comics, Theatre and Other Aspects of Popular Culture* (1962, enlarged ed., Cambridge, MA and London: Harvard University Press, 2001), 97–98, emphasis added.

57. Hence also the emergence of the gangster film, according to Warshow, the refreshing antidote to happy Americanism, thanks to the gangster's devotion to sadistic rationality that inevitably turns in on itself—thereby satisfying the moviegoer without eliciting happiness. See Warshow, "Gangster," 99–103.

58. Richard Yates, *Revolutionary Road* (1961; repr., New York: Vintage, 2008), 347.

59. C. Wright Mills, *White Collar: The American Middle Classes* (London: Oxford University Press, 1951), xiii.

60. Flannery O'Connor, *Wise Blood*, in *Three by Flannery O'Connor* (1952; repr., New York: Signet, 1983), 51.

61. O'Connor, *Wise*, 101, 102

62. Mills, *White*, xx, emphasis added.

63. Walter Benn Michaels, *The Shape of the Signifier* (Princeton, NJ: Princeton University Press, 2004), 30.

64. Girvetz, *Evolution*, 16.

65. Nabers, "Martial," 117.

66. Irving Howe, introduction to *Beyond the Welfare State*, ed. Irving Howe (New York: Schocken, 1982), 12.

Chapter 1

1. Philip Roth, *Letting Go* (1962; repr., New York: Ballantine, 1985), 340, 341. Hereafter cited as *LG*, with page references appearing in the text.

2. Seized by a sudden inspiration to write a poem, Libby manages only to write down and weirdly cobble together famous lines from poems learned in college.

3. Darrin McMahon, *Happiness: A History* (New York: Grove Press, 2006), 463.

4. Philip Roth, *Portnoy's Complaint* (1969), in *Novels 1967–72*, ed. Ross Miller (New York: Library of America, 2005), 435. A devotee of FDR's "Four Freedoms," which Rockwell illustrated to much popular acclaim, Portnoy seems to have in mind one illustration in particular, namely, the freedom from want (466). Rockwell had depicted this freedom as a privatized and thoroughly American affair: a cheery Thanksgiving feast, with family posed agreeably around the supper table while Grandma sets down the platter of roast turkey and Grandpa prepares to carve. Of course, Portnoy himself is another kind of middle-class monstrosity, and, as though not wanting him to have the last word on the Rockwell aesthetic, Roth revisits this scenario decades later in *American Pastoral* (1997). In voluptuous and ambivalently loving detail, Roth portrays the Swede, who reveres Thanksgiving, as yearning to inhabit a Rockwell picture forever.

5. Cf. Stanley Cavell: "The achievement of human happiness requires not the

perennial and fuller satisfaction of our needs as they stand but the examination and transformation of those needs." *Pursuits of Happiness: The Hollywood Comedy of Remarriage* (Cambridge, MA: Harvard University Press, 1981), 4–5. See also Robert Kaufman's account of a constructivist-idealist aesthetics in "What Is Construction, What's the Aesthetic, What Was Adorno Doing?," in *Aesthetic Subjects*, ed. Pamela R. Matthews and David McWhirter (Minneapolis: University of Minnesota Press, 2003), 366–96; and Christine Korsgaard's account of normativity as first-person reflective endorsement in *The Sources of Normativity* (Cambridge, UK: Cambridge University Press, 1996). For a very different view of Roth's early view of happiness, see Bernard Rodgers's book, *Philip Roth* (Boston: Twayne, 1978). He sees a parallel between Roth's orientation and Chekhov's suggestion that "behind the door of every contented, happy man there ought to be someone standing with a little hammer and continually reminding him with a knock that there are unhappy people, that however happy he may be, life will sooner or later show him its claws, and trouble will come to him" (171–72).

6. Jonathan Freedman, *Klezmer America: Jewishness, Ethnicity, Modernity* (New York: Columbia University Press, 2008), 164–65.

7. Ross Posnock, *Philip Roth's Rude Truth: The Art of Immaturity* (Princeton, NJ: Princeton University Press, 2006).

8. That Roth sought in *Letting Go* to explore the status of art in the context of this midcentury discourse of happiness was certainly not lost on one of his friends from his Chicago years, on which much of this novel was based. Thomas Rogers, in his own 1950s-era Chicago novel, *The Pursuit of Happiness* (New York: New American Library, 1968), has the minor character Jane Kauffman settle into Roth's novel while the central character, her boyfriend William Popper, selects Croce's *Aesthetics* for bedtime reading (11).

9. Howard Mumford Jones, *The Pursuit of Happiness* (Cambridge, MA: Harvard University Press, 1953), 131–32. Hereafter cited as *PH*, with page references in the text.

10. Immanuel Kant, *Groundwork of the Metaphysics of Morals*, in *Practical Philosophy*, trans. and ed. Mary J. Gregor (Cambridge, UK: Cambridge University Press, 1996), 70, 71.

11. Similarly viewing America as having traded its founding documents for a mess of happy pottage, Hannah Arendt, who quotes Jones's passage on phantoms and delusions in *On Revolution* (1963), longs for the eighteenth century, when "Americans knew that public freedom consisted in having a share in public business, and that the activities connected with this business by no means constituted a burden ... [but rather] a feeling of happiness." Arendt, *On Revolution* (London: Penguin, 1990), 119.

12. Melvin Tumin, "Popular Culture and the Open Society," in *Mass Culture: The Popular Arts in America*, ed. Bernard Rosenberg and David Manning White (New York: Free Press, 1957), 551, 554.

13. C. Wright Mills, *The Sociological Imagination* (New York: Oxford University

Press, 1959), 3; and Mills, *White Collar: The American Middle Classes* (London: Oxford University Press, 1951), 80.

14. Catherine Jurca, *White Diaspora: The Suburb and the Twentieth-Century American Novel* (Princeton, NJ: Princeton University Press, 2001), 19, 147.

15. Richard Pells, *The Liberal Mind in a Conservative Age: American Intellectuals in the 1940s and 1950s* (New York: Harper and Row, 1985), 146.

16. Lionel Trilling, "William Dean Howells and the Roots of Modern Taste," in *The Opposing Self* (New York: Viking, 1955), 103; Mark Krupnick, *Lionel Trilling and the Fate of Cultural Criticism* (Evanston, IL: Northwestern University Press, 1986), 98, 110.

17. David Riesman, "The Saving Remnant: An Examination of Character Structure," in *Individualism Reconsidered, and Other Essays* (Glencoe, IL: Free Press, 1954), 120.

18. Helen Howe, *We Happy Few* (New York: Simon and Schuster, 1946), 250, 342. No relation to Irving Howe, Helen Howe was the sister of the eminent Harvard law professor Mark Howe (to whom Howard Mumford Jones dedicated his book) and thus also the aunt of Susan Howe and Fanny Howe.

19. David Riesman, "The Ethics of *We Happy Few*," in *Selected Essays from Individualism Reconsidered* (New York: Doubleday, 1954), 41, 42, 43.

20. Riesman, "Ethics," 30, 45.

21. Charles Altieri, *The Particulars of Rapture: An Aesthetics of the Affects* (Ithaca, NY: Cornell University Press, 2003), 10. Building on Kant's ideas of art's expressive particularity and aesthetic judgment's purposiveness without a purpose, Altieri aims analogously to redeem reflexive, imaginatively productive, affective experience for its own existential sake (14–16). This is precisely what Libby, redounding as it were aesthetic purposiveness *with* affective purpose, cannot accomplish.

22. The argument I advance here contrasts with Joseph Landis's. He claims that "what grieves Roth most is the awareness that normalcy has, like a Procrustes' bed, truncated the range of life, excluding on the one hand the embrace of aspiration, the exhilaration of wonder, and on the other the acceptance of suffering." Landis, "The Sadness of Philip Roth: An Interim Report," in *Critical Essays on Philip Roth*, ed. Sanford Pinsker (Boston: Hall, 1982), 165.

23. Philip Roth, *Goodbye, Columbus and Five Short Stories* (1959; repr., New York: Vintage, 1993), 51. Hereafter cited as *GC*, with page references appearing in the text.

24. The fact that Neil seems not to know the name of the "boy" says less about a possible racist habit of mind that deindividuates male blacks (after all, Neil doesn't call the boy "boy" to his face) than it does about the limitations of institutional solicitude. On the one hand, there is only so much Neil as a librarian can do to improve the lot of a child from the housing projects; on the other hand, institutional surveillance is checked and the black boy's privacy is protected by his anonymity.

25. Pells, *Liberal Mind*, 222, 228.

26. David Riesman, "Some Observations on Changes in Leisure Attitudes," in *Selected Essays from Individualism Reconsidered*, 129–30.

27. Robert D. Leigh, *The Public Library in the United States* (New York: Columbia University Press, 1950), 139.

28. Leigh, *Public Library*, 7.

29. Douglas Raber, "Inquiry as Ideology: The Politics of the Public Library Inquiry," *Libraries and Culture* 29, no. 1 (1994): 50.

30. Douglas Raber and Mary Niles Maack, "Scope, Background, and Intellectual Context of the Public Library Inquiry," *Libraries and Culture* 29, no. 1 (1994): 27.

31. Redmond Kathleen Molz, "The Public Library Inquiry as Public Policy Research," *Libraries and Culture* 29, no. 1 (1994): 65. See also Redmond Kathleen Molz and Phyllis Dain, *Civic Space/Cyberspace: The American Public Library in the Information Age* (Cambridge, MA: MIT Press, 1999), 93–97.

32. J. Roland Pennock, "Political Development, Political Systems, and Political Goods," *World Politics* 18, no. 3 (1966): 433.

33. Pennock, "Political Development," 420.

34. Pennock, 6.

35. Pennock, 7–11.

36. Pennock, 17–18.

37. Leigh, *Public Library*, 7.

38. Howard Brick, *Transcending Capitalism: Visions of a New Society in Modern American Thought* (Ithaca, NY: Cornell University Press, 2006), 2.

39. For an account of how this phrase entered the PLI's broad-based forum as well as of the negative reactions of professional librarians to the PLI's acceptance of this seeming reality, see Alice I. Bryan, "The Public Library Inquiry: Purpose, Procedures, and Participants," *Libraries and Culture* 29, no. 1 (1994): 21–22.

40. Leigh, *Public Library*, 19, 48, 49.

41. Raber and Maack, "Scope," 45.

42. Robert L. Lineberry, *Equality and Urban Policy: The Distribution of Municipal Public Services* (Beverly Hills, CA: Sage Publications, 1977), 14.

43. Frank Levy, Arnold J. Meltsner, and Aaron Wildavsky, *Urban Outcomes: Schools, Streets, and Libraries* (Berkeley: University of California Press, 1974), 260.

44. Levy, Meltsner, and Wildavsky, *Urban Outcomes*, 1, 3.

45. Levy, Meltsner, and Wildavsky, v.

46. Levy, Meltsner, and Wildavsky, 251.

47. Levy, Meltsner, and Wildavsky, 224.

48. Levy, Meltsner, and Wildavsky, 182, 231.

49. Leigh, *Public Library*, 142.

50. Andrew Hoberek, *The Twilight of the Middle Class: Post–World War II American Fiction and White-Collar Work* (Princeton, NJ: Princeton University Press, 2005), 94.

51. Levy, Meltsner, and Wildavsky, *Urban Outcomes*, 174.

52. Diversity of activity and people is a central theme of Susan Orlean's recent tribute to public libraries and librarians in *The Library Book* (New York: Simon and Schuster, 2018). Focusing on the library system in Los Angeles, she presents a world of kaleidoscopic variety at opening time:

> People poured in—the hoverers, who bolted from their posts in the garden, and the wall-sitters, and the morning fumblers, and the school groups, and the business people, and the parents with strollers heading to story time, and the students, and the homeless, who rushed straight to the bathrooms and then made a beeline to the computer center, and the scholars, and the time-wasters, and the readers, and the curious, and the bored—all clamoring for [items and services]. (6)

53. Riesman, "Some Observations," 145.

54. Riesman, 147.

55. Philip Fisher, *The Vehement Passions* (Princeton, NJ: Princeton University Press, 2002), 46.

56. Philip Fisher, *Vehement Passions*, 45, 218.

57. Roth's alertness to Bellow is well-known and need not be elaborated here. Suffice it to note that, in his preface to the thirtieth anniversary edition of *Goodbye, Columbus*, Roth included Bellow among the two dozen writers high on his reading list at midcentury. He also identified the influence of *Commentary*, which is where "Looking for Mr. Green" first appeared, during this period. This preface also appeared in the *New York Times*. See "Goodbye Newark: Roth Remembers His Beginnings," *New York Times*, October 1, 1989, https://www.nytimes.com/1989/10/01/books/goodbye-newark-roth-remembers-his-beginnings.html.

58. Saul Bellow, "Looking for Mr. Green," *Commentary* (March 1951): 255. Hereafter cited as LFMG, with page references appearing in the text. By contrast, Roth's parlay is modest. A summer in the life of a public librarian occasions, at its most extreme, weak sociological generalizations about young suburban mothers (discussed earlier) and a hopeful daydream about the current generation of Newark's black population, which Neil envisions following in the migratory footsteps of upwardly mobile Jews (*GC* 90). His curbed perspective, I'm suggesting, permits the novella to keep the objectives of midcentury liberal activism in view.

59. Richard Wright, *Black Boy*, intro. Jerry W. Ward Jr. (1945; repr., New York: HarperPerennial, 1998), 244–53.

60. Gwendolyn Brooks, *Report from Part Two* (Chicago: Third World Press, 1996), 13; and James Atlas, *Bellow: A Biography* (New York: Random House, 2000), 25–26.

61. Brooks, *Report*, 14.

Chapter 2

1. Gwendolyn Brooks, *Maud Martha* (1953; repr., Chicago: Third World Press, 1993), 43. Hereafter cited as *MM*, with page references appearing in the text.

2. Robert Genter, *Late Modernism: Art, Culture, and Politics in Cold War America* (Philadelphia: University of Pennsylvania Press, 2010), 152.

3. Abram Kardiner and Lionel Ovesey, *The Mark of Oppression: Explorations in the Personality of the American Negro* (1951; repr., Cleveland: Meridian Books, 1962), 89, 109.

4. John P. Jackson Jr., *Social Scientists for Social Justice: Making the Case against Segregation* (New York: New York University Press, 2001), 10. See also Ellen Herman, *The Romance of American Psychology: Political Culture in the Age of Experts* (Berkeley: University of California Press, 1995), 174–207.

5. Kardiner and Ovesey, *Mark*, 387.

6. Alain Locke, "The High Price of Integration: A Review of the Literature of the Negro for 1951," *Phylon* 13, no. 1 (1952): 16.

7. Robert M. Hughes, "The End Products of Oppression," *Phylon* 12, no. 4 (1951): 393, 394.

8. Ralph Ellison, "*An American Dilemma*: A Review," in *The Collected Essays of Ralph Ellison*, ed. John F. Callahan (New York: Modern Library 1995), 339. Ellison's review was written in 1944 but first published in *Shadow and Act* (1964).

9. Marguerite Cartwright, "Descendants of Bigger Thomas," *Phylon* 14, no. 1 (1953): 117, 118.

10. Hubert Creekmore, "Daydreams in Flight," *New York Times Book Review*, October 4, 1953, 4.

11. For an explicit comparison of the two characters, see, for instance, Patricia H. Lattin and Vernon E. Lattin, "Dual Vision in Gwendolyn Brooks's *Maud Martha*," *Critique* 25 (Summer 1984): 180–88; and Valerie Frazier, "Domestic Epic Warfare in *Maud Martha*," *African American Review* 39 (Spring–Summer 2005): 133–41. It is also worth noting in this context that Ralph Ellison similarly recognized Richard Wright's very own—and autobiographical—protagonist of *Black Boy* as Bigger Thomas's opposite number. In "Richard Wright's Blues," his 1945 review of *Black Boy*, Ellison insists that we take note of the black man's positive potentiality:

> And just as Wright, the man, represents the blooming of the delinquent child of the autobiography, just so does *Black Boy* represent the flowering—cross-fertilized by pollen blown by the winds of strange cultures—of the humble blues lyric. There is, as in all acts of creation, a world of mystery in this, but there is also enough that is comprehensible for Americans to create the social atmosphere in which other black boys might freely bloom.

"Richard Wright's Blues," in *The Collected Essays of Ralph Ellison*, ed. John F. Callahan (New York: Modern Library 1995), 130–31. As we'll see later in this chapter, Brooks will similarly deploy tropes of blooming and flowering—indeed, putting them to dazzling and almost obsessive use—to convey the potentiality of black girls and boys.

12. See Mary Helen Washington, "'Taming All That Anger Down': Rage and

Silence in Gwendolyn Brooks's *Maud Martha*," in *Black Literature and Literary Theory*, ed. Henry Louis Gates Jr. (New York: Routledge, 1984), 249–62; Frazier, "Domestic Epic Warfare"; and Harry B. Shaw, "*Maud Martha*: The War with Beauty," in *A Life Distilled: Gwendolyn Brooks, Her Poetry and Fiction*, ed. Maria K. Mootry and Gary Smith (Urbana: University of Illinois Press, 1989), 254–70.

13. Alan Brinkley, in *The End of Reform: New Deal Liberalism in Recession and War* (New York: Alfred A. Knopf, 1995), shows that popular support for welfare-state expansion began to wane as early as 1937.

14. Thomas W. Pogge, "Human Flourishing and Universal Justice," in *Human Flourishing*, ed. Ellen Frankel Paul, Fred D. Miller Jr., and Jeffrey Paul (Cambridge, UK: Cambridge University Press), 337.

15. Those I designate *liberal activist* here the political studies historian Ira Katznelson designates *reconstructionist*. He identifies Dahl and Lindblom among a handful of important adherents to a postwar "political studies enlightenment." As he tells the story in *Desolation and Enlightenment: Political Knowledge after Total War, Totalitarianism, and the Holocaust* (New York: Columbia University Press, 2003), such public intellectuals "confronted the sources and character of their cheerless age" but "refused to abandon the liberal, secular, and pluralist values" that others—from T. S. Eliot to Adorno and Foucault—"renounced" (xiv). These reconstructionists sought "to rouse the liberal imagination and to situate it realistically to produce means with which to advance a decent politics" and to pursue usable "political knowledge and institutional creativity" (42). Inquiry into the legitimacy of the liberal nation-state and its institutions was a central preoccupation (108ff.).

16. Michael Omi and Howard Winant, *Racial Formation in the United States: From the 1960s to the 1990s*, 2nd ed. (New York: Routledge Press, 1994), 98.

17. Lauren Berlant, *Cruel Optimism* (Durham, NC: Duke University Press, 2011).

18. Thomas Hill Schaub, *American Fiction in the Cold War* (Madison: University of Wisconsin Press, 1991), 33.

19. Lionel Trilling, *The Liberal Imagination*, intro. Louis Menand (1950; repr., New York: New York Review of Books, 2008), xv–xvi.

20. Trilling, *Liberal*, xix, xx.

21. Trilling, xvi–xvii, xxi.

22. David L. Chappell, "The Triumph of Conservatives in a Liberal Age," in *A Companion to Post-1945 America*, ed. Jean-Christophe Agnew and Roy Rosenzweig (Malden, MA: Blackwell, 2006), 321.

23. In *The Other Blacklist: The African American Literary and Cultural Left of the 1950s* (New York: Columbia University Press, 2014), Mary Helen Washington also notes Brooks's connections to leftists in Chicago, who would likely have been familiar with Parrington's work (183–84).

24. Marc Moreland, "The Welfare State: Embattled Concept," *Phylon* 11.2 (1950): 164.

25. Moreland, "Welfare," 164.

26. Moreland, 164. For an informative account of Byrnes's career, see Robert L. Messer, *The End of an Alliance: James F. Byrnes, Roosevelt, Truman, and the Origins of the Cold War* (Chapel Hill: University of North Carolina Press, 1982).

27. Moreland, "Welfare," 166, 167.

28. Moreland, 167, 168, emphasis added.

29. Moreland, "Welfare," 169.

30. Dona Cooper Hamilton and Charles V. Hamilton, *The Dual Agenda: Race and Social Welfare Policies of Civil Rights Organizations* (New York: Columbia University Press, 1997), 2.

31. Hamilton and Hamilton, *Dual Agenda*, 4, 6–7.

32. See also Jeff Manza, "Race and the Underdevelopment of the Welfare State," *Theory and Society* 29 (2000), 828.

33. Maria K. Mootry, "'Down the Whirlwind of Good Rage': An Introduction to Gwendolyn Brooks," in *A Life Distilled: Gwendolyn Brooks, Her Poetry and Fiction*, ed. Maria K. Mootry and Gary Smith (Urbana: University of Illinois Press, 1989), 11.

34. It should be noted that yet another important work of African American fiction from the period, Paule Marshall's *Brown Girl, Brownstones* (1959), addresses the theme of real estate ownership and its role in securing African American upward mobility. The novel reveals the vexed ambivalence of an immigrant community of Barbadians in Brooklyn, whose formation of the Association of Barbadian Homeowners and Businessmen does much to advance some interests of the community while debilitating others. Later in this chapter I suggest that an earlier iteration of vexation (which Marshall stages in the mutual and destructive hostility of the protagonist Selina's parents) is significantly tempered in *Maud Martha* by the active presence of a government institution—specifically, the Home Owners' Loan Corporation (HOLC), established in the early stages of the New Deal.

35. George E. Kent, *A Life of Gwendolyn Brooks* (Lexington: University Press of Kentucky, 1990), 108.

36. For detailed accounts of the Clark experiments and their use in *Brown v. Board of Education*, see Jackson, *Social Scientists*, 135–45; and Gwen Bergner, "Black Children, White Preference: *Brown v. Board*, the Doll Tests, and the Politics of Self-Esteem," *American Quarterly* 61, no. 2 (2009): 299–332.

37. Harry K. Girvetz, *The Evolution of Liberalism*, intro. Arthur Schlesinger Jr. (1950; rev. ed., London: Collier, 1963), 177. First published under the title *From Wealth to Welfare: The Evolution of Liberalism* (Stanford, CA: Stanford University Press, 1950), Girvetz added new chapters and more recent statistics and references to the revised edition. Unless otherwise noted, the passages cited appear in both editions.

38. John Stopford, *The Skillful Self: Liberalism, Culture, and the Politics of Skill* (London: Lexington Books, 2009), 30.

39. Quoted in Brent Hayes Edwards, "Black Serial Poetics: An Introduction to Ed Roberson," *Callaloo* 33, no. 3 (2010): 626.

40. Edwards, "Black Serial Poetics," 627, 629.

41. Edwards, 636n17.

42. Betty Friedan, *The Feminine Mystique*, intro. Anna Quindlen (1963; repr., New York: Norton, 2001), 250.

43. Jane Elliott, "Stepford, U.S.A.: Second-Wave Feminism, Domestic Labor, and the Representation of National Time," *Cultural Critique* 70 (Fall 2008): 32–62.

44. Girvetz, *Evolution*, 171–72, 178.

45. Girvetz, 176, 177.

46. Girvetz, 177, 236. The second passage appears only in the revised edition.

47. Girvetz, 178, 233, 253.

48. Girvetz, 268, 331. The second and third passages appear only in the revised edition.

49. Girvetz, 134.

50. Girvetz, 154.

51. Girvetz, 133, 154.

52. Girvetz, 395n21.

53. Quoted in Herman, *Romance*, 197. David Riesman more playfully invoked the topology of the "frontier" to suggest the social awkwardness of middle-class "explorers" in the strange new suburb, a theme I take up in the next chapter. See David Riesman, "Some Observations on Changes in Leisure Attitudes," in *Selected Essays from Individualism Reconsidered* (Garden City, NY: Doubleday, 1954), 138.

54. Gwendolyn Brooks, *Report from Part One* (Detroit: Broadside Press, 1972), 68. Hereafter cited as *RPO*, with page references appearing in the text.

55. With respect to her attentiveness to the institutional environment and liberal activism, Maud Martha is indeed a kind of surrogate for Brooks herself. In 1951 Brooks published a piece of nonfiction, "They Call It Bronzeville," which contains material that reappears in *Maud Martha* almost verbatim. In this piece Brooks serves as tour guide of Bronzeville for the curious but uninitiated "white Stranger" (61). Early on she takes note of the "Bronzeville citizen" who "never stops fighting to improve conditions. He fights at the polls, he fights in the meetings of his leagues and associations, he fights in his petitions and in his letters to the press and the President" (61). Over the course of the article Brooks references with visible pride a dense network of public and private institutions, among them: Princeton Park, Coppin Chapel, African Methodist Episcopal church, the Regal Theatre, the offices of the Chicago *Defender*, the Johnson Publishing Company, the South Side Community Art Center, the Parkway Community House, Provident Hospital, the Parkway Ballroom, the Metropolitan Funeral System Association, and not least, the George Cleveland Hall Branch Library. Gwendolyn Brooks, "They Call It Bronzeville," *Holiday* (October 1951): 60–64ff. I'm grateful to Adrienne Brown for bringing this piece to my attention.

56. Quoted in Price Fishback, Jonathan Rose, and Kenneth Snowden, *Well Worth Saving: How the New Deal Safeguarded Home Ownership* (Chicago: University of Chicago Press, 2013), 37.

57. Ira Katznelson and Barry R. Weingast, "Intersections between Historical and Rational Choice Institutionalism," in *Preferences and Situations: Points of Intersection between Historical and Rational Choice Institutionalism*, ed. Ira Katznelson and Barry R. Weingast (New York: Russell Sage, 2005), 15–16.

58. Fishback, Rose, and Snowden, *Well Worth Saving*, 47, 117.

59. Fishback, Rose, and Snowden, 47, 50.

60. Fishback, Rose, and Snowden, 49.

61. For information on the HOLC's residential security maps, initiated in 1935 (that is, after most of its loans were issued), and its loan practices with regard to race, ethnicity, and neighborhood, see Amy E. Hillier, "Who Received Loans? Home Owners' Loan Corporation Lending and Discrimination in Philadelphia in the 1930s," *Journal of Planning History* 2, no. 1 (2003): 3–24; James Greer, "The Home Owners' Loan Corporation and the Development of the Residential Security Maps," *Journal of Urban History* 39, no. 2 (2012): 275–96; and James Greer, "Historic Home Mortgage Redlining in Chicago," *Journal of the Illinois State Historical Society* 107, no. 2 (2014): 204–33.

62. Girvetz, *Evolution*, 334–45. This discussion appears only in the revised edition.

63. See Roy José DeCarvalho, *The Founders of Humanistic Psychology* (New York: Praeger, 1991).

64. Abraham Maslow, *Motivation and Personality*, 3rd ed. (1954; New York: Harper and Row, 1987), 66.

65. Maslow, *Motivation*, 3rd ed., xx, xxv; Abraham Maslow, *Motivation and Personality* (New York: Harper and Row, 1954), 202. The contradictory combination of elitist and democratic liberal elements comprising Maslow's psychology has been widely discussed. See, for instance, Allan R. Buss, "Humanistic Psychology as Liberal Ideology: The Socio-Historical Roots of Maslow's Theory of Self-Actualization," *Journal of Humanistic Psychology* 19, no. 3 (1979): 43–55; and Bill Cooke, Albert J. Mills, and Elizabeth S. Kelley, "Situating Maslow in Cold War America: A Recontextualization of Management Theory," *Group & Organization Management* 30 (2005): 129–52. As Buss notes, Maslow's examples of self-actualizers "were democratic, autonomous, individualistic[;] and, true to the liberal penchant for piecemeal progress, they preferred to work from within rather than from without the system on matters relating to social injustice" (48). They also comprised only "the one percent of the general population" (52).

66. See also William Davies, *The Happiness Industry* (London: Verso, 2015), 146.

67. V. J. McGill, *The Idea of Happiness* (New York: Praeger, 1967), 322.

68. McGill, *Idea*, 334–35.

69. McGill, 346.

70. Stopford, *Skillful*, 22, 23, emphasis added. In this passage Stopford draws specifically on John Rawls's idea of the veil of ignorance to posit the ethical value of the "unknown" in framing arguments about an individual's conceptions of the good.

71. Lorraine Hansberry, *A Raisin in the Sun*, in *Norton Anthology of African American Literature*, 3rd ed., vol. 2, ed. Henry Louis Gates Jr. and Valerie Smith (New York: Norton: 2014), 482. Hereafter cited as *RS*, with page references appearing in the text.

72. For a concise account of the Hansberry family's activism and the series of Supreme Court cases that brought restrictive covenants to an end—as elements of a broader context for understanding Wright's *Native Son*—see Catherine Jurca, *White Diaspora: The Suburb and the Twentieth-Century American Novel* (Princeton, NJ: Princeton University Press, 2000), chap. 4.

73. Robert A. Dahl and Charles E. Lindblom, *Politics, Economics, and Welfare: Planning and Politico-Economic Systems Resolved into Basic Social Processes* (1953; repr., New York: Harper Torchbook, 1963); Charles. E. Lindblom, "The Science of 'Muddling Through,'" *Public Administration Review* 19, no. 2 (1959): 80.

74. Dahl and Lindblom, *Politics*, 4, 83–84.

75. Dahl and Lindblom, 82, 85.

76. Lindblom, "Science," 81.

77. Dahl and Lindblom, *Politics*, 28, 34.

78. Lindblom, "Science," 81; Dahl and Lindblom, *Politics*, 87.

79. Lindblom, "Science," 88n9; Dahl and Lindblom, *Politics*, 60.

80. Dahl and Lindblom, *Politics*, 61–62.

81. Dahl and Lindblom, 88.

82. Mark McGurl, "Being and Time Management" (lecture, Concordia University, Montreal, November 3, 2016).

83. Tyler T. Schmidt, *Desegregating Desire: Race and Sexuality in Cold War American Literature* (Jackson: University of Mississippi Press, 2013), 100.

84. Genter, *Late Modernism*, 98. See also Jackson, *Social Scientists*, 111–12.

85. Genter, *Late Modernism*, 156.

86. See Kent, *A Life*, 62.

87. Ralph Ellison, "The World and the Jug," in *The Collected Essays of Ralph Ellison*, ed. John F. Callahan (New York: Modern Library, 1995), 162.

88. Houston A. Baker Jr., *Blues, Ideology, and Afro-American Literature: A Vernacular Theory* (Chicago: University of Chicago Press, 1984), 69, 77.

89. Paul Engle, "Chicago Can Take Pride in New, Young Voice in Poetry," in *On Gwendolyn Brooks: Reliant Contemplation*, ed. Stephen Caldwell Wright (Ann Arbor: University of Michigan Press, 1996), 4. Engle had been instrumental in the preceding years in honoring Brooks with awards at the annual Midwestern Writers' Conference. See D. H. Melhem, *Gwendolyn Brooks: Poetry and the Heroic Voice* (Lexington: University Press of Kentucky, 1990), 18. On Engle's recruitment of Margaret Walker, see Mark McGurl, *The Program Era: Postwar Fiction and the Rise of Creative Writing* (Cambridge, MA: Harvard University Press, 2009), 150.

90. Dan Jaffe, "Gwendolyn Brooks: An Appreciation from the White Suburbs,"

in *On Gwendolyn Brooks: Reliant Contemplation*, ed. Stephen Caldwell Wright (Ann Arbor: University of Michigan Press, 1996), 55, 58.

91. Omi and Winant, *Racial Formation*, 16–17.

92. Kent, *A Life*, 156.

93. See, for instance, Lattin and Lattin, "Dual Vision"; Barbara Christian, "Nuance and Novella: A Study of Gwendolyn Brooks's *Maud Martha*," in *A Life Distilled: Gwendolyn Brooks, Her Poetry and Fiction*, ed. Maria K. Mootry and Gary Smith (Urbana: University of Illinois Press, 1989): 239–53; Dorothy Randall Tsuruta, "Regional and Regal: Chicago's *Extraordinary* Maud Martha," in *Gwendolyn Brooks's Maud Martha: A Critical Collection*, ed. Jacqueline Bryant (Chicago: Third World Press, 2002): 41–68; Larry R. Andrews, "The Aliveness of Things: Nature in *Maud Martha*," in *Gwendolyn Brooks's Maud Martha: A Critical Collection*, ed. Jacqueline Bryant (Chicago: Third World Press, 2002), 69–89; R. Baxter Miller, "'Does Man Love Art?': The Humanistic Aesthetic of Gwendolyn Brooks," in *A Life Distilled: Gwendolyn Brooks, Her Poetry and Fiction*, ed. Maria K. Mootry and Gary Smith (Urbana: University of Illinois Press, 1989): 100–115; and Mehlman, *Gwendolyn Brooks*.

94. Houston A. Baker Jr., "The Achievement of Gwendolyn Brooks," in *A Life Distilled: Gwendolyn Brooks, Her Poetry and Fiction*, ed. Maria K. Mootry and Gary Smith (Chicago: University of Illinois Press, 1989), 21–23.

95. Trilling, *Liberal*, xxi.

96. Baker, "Achievement," 28.

97. Baker, 23.

98. Kenneth W. Warren, *What Was African American Literature?* (Cambridge, MA: Harvard University Press, 2011), 80.

99. Warren, *What Was*, 53–54.

100. Gwendolyn Brooks, *Report from Part Two* (Chicago: Third World Press, 1996), 12. It is worth noting in this context that Brooks uses the language of flourishing in this autobiography's vehement endorsement of the black family as well as of government infrastructure. Too much attention is given to "Black failings," she insists; "there are also the *firm* families: the durable, effective and forward youngsters; the homes regularized and rich with intelligence, affection, communication and merriment. The necessary corrective programs *must flourish*—individual, state, national, world. But the already-successes must be announced, featured, credited" (134, emphasis added in the second instance).

101. Schmidt, *Desegregating Desire*, 92. See also Patricia Andrews-Keenan, "South Side Community Center Turns 75," *Chicago Gallery News*, December 22, 2014, http://www.chicagogallerynews.com/news/2014/12/south-side-community-art-center-turns-75.

102. Arthur P. Davis, "Integration and Race Literature," *Phylon* 17, no. 2 (1956): 142.

103. Brooks, *Report from Part Two*, 77.

104. For a detailed account of the pedagogy Brooks developed for the Blackstone Rangers workshop, see Stephen Schryer, *Maximum Feasible Participation: American Literature and the War on Poverty* (Stanford, CA: Stanford University Press, 2018), 64–65.

105. Omi and Winant, *Racial Formation*, 98.

106. Howard Brick, "Optimism of the Mind: Imagining Postindustrial Society in the 1960s and 1970s," *American Quarterly* 44, no. 3 (1992): 356. See also Irving Howe's introduction to the collection of essays, *Beyond the Welfare State*, where he describes the Marxist view, in which "the welfare state arises mainly from the political foresight and shrewd manipulations of the business classes." Irving Howe, introduction to *Beyond the Welfare State*, ed. Irving Howe (New York: Schocken, 1982), 5.

107. Brick, 356, 357.

108. Gwendolyn Brooks, *The World of Gwendolyn Brooks* (New York: Harper and Row, 1971), 315. Hereafter cited as *WGB*, with page references appearing in the text.

109. Brick, "Optimism," 372.

110. Berlant, *Cruel*, 25.

111. Berlant, 122.

112. Berlant, 24, 115.

113. For details regarding the Mecca's history (and Brooks's brief employment there as a young woman) as well as an extraordinarily trenchant account of Brooks's reportage aesthetics in this poem, see chapter 5 of C. K. Doreski, *Writing America Black: Race Rhetoric in the Public Sphere* (Cambridge, UK: Cambridge University Press, 1998).

114. Berlant, *Cruel*, 174.

115. Berlant, 176.

116. Berlant, 10.

117. Miller, "Does Man," 103.

118. Hortense J. Spillers, "Gwendolyn the Terrible: Propositions on Eleven Poems," in *A Life Distilled: Gwendolyn Brooks, Her Poetry and Fiction*, ed. Maria K. Mootry and Gary Smith (Urbana: University of Illinois Press, 1989), 225.

119. I am grateful to Liesl Olson at the Newberry Library for confirming the absence of this quasi-epigraph in earlier editions.

120. In a 1969 interview Brooks abjured the interviewer's assertion that "many" of her "characters . . . make a pitiful attempt to be what they cannot be," politely but firmly insisting that only a few of them do this: "Some of them are very much interested in just the general events of their own lives" (*RPO* 154). My point takes this defense a step further, suggesting that Brooks ultimately has trouble presuming that even those "some" have no saving remnant of inner awareness.

Chapter 3

1. Patricia Highsmith, *The Price of Salt* (1952; repr., New York: Norton, 2004), 261. Hereafter cited as *PS*, with page references appearing in the text.

2. Steven Knapp, *Literary Interest: The Limits of Anti-Formalism* (Cambridge, MA: Harvard University Press, 1993), 100, 101. Slightly later Knapp identifies this mode of literary interest specifically with "liberal agency" (103).

3. Jennifer Worley, "The Mid-Century Pulp Novel and the Imagining of Lesbian Community," in *Invisible Suburbs: Recovering Protest Fiction in the 1950s United States*, ed. Josh Lukin (Jackson: University Press of Mississippi, 2008), 108. For a broader account (and extensive bibliography) of midcentury lesbian pulp fiction's publishing and reception history, see Yvonne Keller, "'Was It Right to Love Her Brother's Wife So Passionately?': Lesbian Identity, 1950–1965," *American Quarterly* 57 (2005): 385–410. For an analysis of the historiographical significance of contemporary journalistic and academic reading practices of this fiction, see Christopher Nealon, "Invert-History: The Ambivalence of Lesbian Pulp Fiction," *New Literary History* 31 (2000): 745–64.

4. Michael Warner, *The Trouble with Normal: Sex, Politics, and the Ethics of Queer Life* (New York: Free Press, 1999), 8–9.

5. United Nations, Article 26 (and elsewhere in slightly different wording), Universal Declaration of Human Rights, last accessed October 10, 2012, http://www.un.org/en/documents/udhr/indix.shtml.

6. United Nations, preamble, Universal Declaration of Human Rights, last accessed October 10, 2012, http://www.un.org/en/universal-declaration-human-rights/.

7. See Johannes Morsink, *The Universal Declaration of Human Rights: Origins, Drafting, and Intent* (Philadelphia: University of Pennsylvania Press, 1999), for a painstakingly thorough account of the deliberations informing the UDHR, including delegates' efforts to preserve its "outright secularism" by avoiding talk of God and natural law (289).

8. Unlike Highsmith's letter-writing fans, literary critics tend to downplay all this happy positivity. Sara Ahmed, who critiques modernity's imperative to be happy, devotes two footnotes in *The Promise of Happiness* to the novel, observing in each that the "cost" of happiness is high, involving as it does Carol's loss of custody of her child. See Sara Ahmed, *The Promise of Happiness* (Durham, NC: Duke University Press, 2010), 247, 249. Critics who offer extended analyses of the novel's representation of liberal norms come to more illuminating although similarly qualified conclusions. Victoria Hesford locates the strength of *The Price of Salt* in its response to the Cold War containment strategy's reach into private life. She argues that the novel "turns" the "domestic ideology of the middle-class home as a source of national strength and normality inside out, revealing the undertow of violence and sexual unconventionality that both prop up the public function of the middle-class home and constantly threaten to tear it apart." See Victoria Hesford, "Patriotic Perversions: Patricia Highsmith's Queer Vision of Cold War America in *The Price of Salt*, *The Blunderer*, and *Deep Water*," *Women's Studies Quarterly* 33 (2005): 217. Even Joan Schenkar's account of the novel as a kind of personal fairy tale (for an author who never lived happily ever after with anybody), into which Highsmith "poured her most exalted

feelings," foregrounds its "close[ness] in spirit to the sadistic cruelties of the Brothers Grimm." See Joan Schenkar, *The Talented Miss Highsmith: The Secret Life and Serious Art of Patricia Highsmith* (New York: St. Martin's, 2009), 271, 281. The happy ending, these critics imply, is best appreciated under the sign of compromise, violence, and vulnerability. My point here is not to minimize the sense of precariousness that Highsmith infuses the novel with; it is, rather, to see this precariousness operate in the service of dramatizing the legitimacy of happiness.

9. Schenkar, *Talented*, 213.

10. Patricia Highsmith, *Strangers on a Train* (1948; repr., New York: Norton, 2001), 106, 265.

11. Patricia Highsmith, *The Talented Mr. Ripley*, in *The Talented Mr. Ripley, Ripley Under Ground, Ripley's Game*, intro. Grey Gowrie (1955; repr., New York: Knopf, 1999), 38.

12. Michael Trask, "Patricia Highsmith's Method," *American Literary History* 22 (2010): 588, 605.

13. Grey Gowrie, introduction to *The Talented Mr. Ripley, Ripley Under Ground, Ripley's Game*, by Patricia Highsmith (New York: Knopf, 1999), xvi.

14. Tom Perrin has argued persuasively that Highsmith's novel exemplifies this genre's tendency to narrate a protagonist's coming to adequate terms with the world through compromise and maturity. See Tom Perrin, "Rebuilding *Bildung*: The Middlebrow Novel of Aesthetic Education in the Mid-Twentieth-Century United States," *Novel: A Forum on Fiction* 44 (2011): 392–93. My focus here is on what Rita Felski has drawn attention to in one of the genre's subdivisions—the "novel of self-discovery." See chapter 4, "The Novel of Self-Discovery: Integration and Quest," of her book, *Beyond Feminist Aesthetics: Feminist Literature and Social Change* (Cambridge, MA: Harvard University Press, 1989), 122–153.

15. Sara Ahmed, "Multiculturalism and the Promise of Happiness," *New Formations* 63 (2006): 124.

16. In *A Game for the Living* the outwardly cheerful protagonist questions whether logic pertains to happiness: "Theodore thought he was as happy as anyone logically could be in an age when atomic bombs and annihilation hung over everybody's head, though the world 'logically' troubled him in this context. Could one be logically happy?" Patricia Highsmith, *A Game for the Living* (1958; repr., New York: Atlantic Monthly, 1988), 5. In *The Price of Salt* Highsmith implies that, yes, there is a logic to happiness but also that the specific logic in question considers the conditions internal to liberalism's value system, not to the world's given menaces.

17. Educated at Barnard, Highsmith subscribed to the *Partisan Review* in the 1940s and read the works of such prominent liberals as Daniel Bell and David Riesman. Schenkar notes Highsmith's *Partisan Review* subscription (*Talented*, 132). Andrew Wilson, in *Beautiful Shadow: A Life of Patricia Highsmith* (New York: Bloomsbury, 2003), notes her familiarity with Bell and Riesman, 187, 221.

18. Joseph Haroutunian, *Lust for Power* (New York: Scribner, 1949), 19.

19. Haroutunian, *Lust*, 10–11.

20. Howard Mumford Jones, *The Pursuit of Happiness* (Cambridge, MA: Harvard University Press, 1953), 17.

21. David Riesman, "Abundance for What?," in *Abundance for What? and Other Essays* (Garden City, NY: Doubleday, 1964), 304, 305; Eric Larrabee, *The Self-Conscious Society* (Garden City, NY: Doubleday, 1960), 156–57, 167. For fuller historical accounts of the rise of Americans' self-doubt, in "the very hour of achievement, of triumph over fascism and totalitarian government," see Warren Susman, "Did Success Spoil the United States? Dual Representations in Postwar America," in *Recasting America: Culture and Politics in the Age of Cold War*, ed. Lary May (Chicago: University of Chicago Press, 1989), 22. On the "plight of the privileged," see Richard Pells, *The Liberal Mind in a Conservative Age: American Intellectuals in the 1940s and 1950s* (New York: Harper and Row, 1985), 186. On Americans' "choking on our own abundance, trapped by our own technological detritus," see Jackson Lears, "A Matter of Taste: Corporate Cultural Hegemony in a Mass-Consumption Society," in *Recasting America: Culture and Politics in the Age of Cold War*, ed. Lary May (Chicago and London: University of Chicago Press, 1989), 43–44.

22. Since at least Émile Zola's *Au Bonheur des Dames* (1883), the department store has been a favored emblem of lively consumerism, prominent as well in such American classics as Kate Chopin's "A Pair of Silk Stockings" (1897) and Theodore Dreiser's *Sister Carrie* (1900).

23. Joyce Appleby, "Consumption in Early Modern Social Thought," in *Consumer Society in American History: A Reader*, ed. Lawrence B. Glickman (Ithaca: Cornell University Press, 1999), 143. Other critics argue yet more strongly for the ethical significance of commerce and consumerism. Lawrence B. Glickman, for instance, observes the close link between the commercial nexus and social justice in a modern democracy, in that one person's money becomes as good as another's and thus prohibits the restriction of consumption to particular groups. See Lawrence B. Glickman, "Introduction: Born to Shop? Consumer History and American History," in *Consumer Society in American History: A Reader*, ed. Lawrence B. Glickman (Ithaca: Cornell University Press, 1999), 13. Michael Schudson likewise considers consumption from the perspective of social welfare: "What particular consumer goods mean will vary from one society to another and one era to another. But what remains constant is the goal that people should have goods sufficient so that they will not be ashamed in society. Societies should be organized so that no one falls below a level that provides access to the consumer goods required for social credit and self-respect. The protection of human dignity or, more broadly, the ensuring of human 'capability to function' is not relative." Michael Schudson, "Delectable Materialism: Second Thoughts on Consumer Culture," in *Consumer Society in American History: A Reader*, ed. Lawrence B. Glickman (Ithaca: Cornell University Press, 1999), 354.

24. Michael W. Clune, *American Literature and the Free Market, 1945–2000* (Cambridge, UK: Cambridge University Press, 2010), 4.

25. Clune, *Free Market*, 12, 168.

26. Lionel Trilling, "The Kinsey Report," in *The Liberal Imagination*, intro. Louis Menand (1950; repr., New York: New York Review of Books, 2008), 234, 241.

27. Trilling, "Kinsey," 226, 236, 240.

28. Trilling, 232.

29. Schudson, "Delectable Materialism," 345, 348.

30. Terry Castle, "The Ick Factor," *The New Republic*, November 10, 2003, 32, 33.

31. Vladimir Nabokov, *Lolita* (1955; repr., New York: Berkley, 1977), 136.

32. Nabokov, *Lolita*, 57, 59.

33. Nabokov, 152.

34. Nabokov, 16, 125.

35. Christine Korsgaard with G. A. Cohen et al., *The Sources of Normativity* (Cambridge, UK: Cambridge University Press, 1996), 229.

36. Korsgaard, *Sources*, 227–28, 242.

37. Korsgaard, 161, 228.

38. Alfred Kinsey et al., *Sexual Behavior in the Human Female* (Philadelphia: W. B. Saunders, 1953), 9.

39. David Riesman, "Some Observations on Changes in Leisure Attitudes," in *Selected Essays from Individualism Reconsidered* (Garden City, NY: Doubleday, 1954), 138.

40. Riesman, "Some Observations," 126, 139, 140.

41. David Riesman, *Thorstein Veblen: A Critical Interpretation* (1953; repr., New York: Seabury Press, 1960), 174, 176.

42. Riesman, *Veblen*, 174.

43. Colin Campbell, "Consuming Goods and the Good of Consuming," in *Consumer Society in American History: A Reader*, ed. Lawrence B. Glickman (Ithaca: Cornell University Press, 1999), 21.

44. For a brilliant but very different psychoanalytic reading of the function of the fetish in lesbian love, see Teresa de Lauretis, *The Practice of Love: Lesbian Sexuality and Perverse Desire* (Bloomington: Indiana University Press, 1994).

45. Larrabee, *Self-Conscious*, 160.

46. "True lovers," as Korsgaard puts it, "learn how to be made for each other." *Sources*, 242.

47. Andrew Wilson, *Beautiful Shadow: A Life of Patricia Highsmith* (New York: Bloomsbury, 2003), 163.

48. Stanley Cavell, *Pursuits of Happiness: The Hollywood Comedy of Remarriage* (Cambridge, MA: Harvard University Press, 1981), 4–5.

49. Warner, *Trouble*, 24–25.

50. Warner, 69.

51. Korsgaard, *Sources*, 161.

52. Although there might be room in the Highsmith motel for Warner's affirmation of queer-positive riskiness in promiscuity, there's none for Lee Edelman's idea of radical queer negativity. Referring to modernity's "dream of eventual self-realization," he recognizes this ideology's force in modernity but implies that its status is a corrosive delusion born of the psychic Imaginary, not an imaginative ideal worthy of pursuit. Lee Edelman, *No Future: Queer Theory and the Death Drive* (Durham, NC: Duke University Press, 2004), 10. Polemically sick and tired of liberalism's commitment to futurity, particularly of the way it routinely expresses this commitment in its cult-like devotion to figures of "the Child," Edelman looks for figures of queerness that demolish "the social order and the Child in whose name we're collectively terrorized" (29). He favors a radical negativity whereby queerness figures a "death drive, [an] intransigent jouissance" of illegibility and antisocial senselessness (27). From his standpoint, Highsmith's road-tripping duo can appear only quaintly inadequate, although he might relish Carol's lost custody.

53. Patricia Highsmith, *Plotting and Writing Suspense Fiction*, revised and updated (New York: St. Martin's Griffin, 1983), 134.

54. Highsmith, *Plotting*, 26, 136.

55. Highsmith, xi, 17.

56. Highsmith, 3, 27, 137.

57. Highsmith, x, xiv, 143.

Chapter 4

1. Sylvia Plath, *Ariel* (New York: Harper and Row, 1965), 10–12, lines 1, 15–16. Hereafter line numbers of "Tulips" are cited parenthetically in the text.

2. Abigail Cheever, *Real Phonies: Cultures of Authenticity in Post–World War II America* (Athens: University of Georgia Press, 2010), 69.

3. Sara Ahmed, "Multiculturalism and the Promise of Happiness," *New Formations* 63 (2006): 126.

4. Ahmed, "Multiculturalism," 125, 126.

5. Ahmed, 126.

6. Sara Ahmed, *The Promise of Happiness* (Durham, NC: Duke University Press, 2010), 243n8.

7. Michel Foucault, *Technologies of the Self: A Seminar with Michel Foucault*, ed. Luther H. Martin, Huck Gutman, and Patrick H. Hutton (Amherst: University of Massachusetts Press, 1988), 147.

8. For President Roosevelt's 1944 State of the Union address, in which he identified these rights, see http://www.fdrlibrary.marist.edu/archives/address_text.html. For the United Nations Universal Declaration of Human Rights, see http://www.un.org/en/universal-declaration-human-rights/.

9. Norman Daniels, "Rights to Health Care and Distributive Justice," *The Journal*

of Medicine and Philosophy 4, no. 2 (1979): 177, 178, 181. See also the editors' introduction to a 1976 collection of essays on bioethics, medicine, and health-care politics: "There has been a fundamental change in American society. An interest in human rights and social justice, kindled first by the issues of race and war, has spread to other areas of social policy including health. The public concern for questions of justice and welfare has led us to challenge traditional assumptions and traditional ethical premises. The questions now being asked are more health policy questions, questions of distribution and priority." Robert M. Veatch and Roy Bronson, eds., *Ethics and Health Policy* (Cambridge, MA: Ballinger, 1976), xx.

10. Daniels, "Rights," 186.

11. Bruce A. Ackerman, *Social Justice in the Liberal State* (New Haven, CT: Yale University Press, 1980), 57.

12. Brian Barry, *Why Social Justice Matters* (Cambridge, UK: Polity, 2005), 70.

13. Barry, *Social Justice*, 72.

14. Barry, 71–72.

15. Rosemary Stevens, *The Public-Private Health Care State: Essays on the History of American Health Care Policy* (New Brunswick, NJ: Transaction, 2007), 158–59.

16. Deborah Nelson, "Plath, History, and Politics" in *The Cambridge Companion to Sylvia Plath*, ed. Jo Gill (Cambridge, UK: Cambridge University Press, 2006), 22.

17. Susan Sontag, *Illness as Metaphor* (New York: Farrar, Straus and Giroux, 1978), 26.

18. Sontag, *Illness*, 4.

19. Sontag, 3, 4.

20. Sontag, 69.

21. John Kenneth Galbraith, *The Affluent Society* (Boston: Houghton Mifflin, 1958), 283.

22. Galbraith, *Affluent*, 252.

23. Galbraith, 257.

24. Galbraith, 188–90, 288–89. Central to Galbraith's case for decreasing the disparity between public squalor and private opulence was recognizing the injustice of *relative* poverty. In an affluent society, he argued, poverty is relative but nonetheless socially corrosive; it must be measured not in terms of adequacy of income for sheer survival but in terms of "the minimum necessary for decency" (323–24). Otherwise poor people are "degraded" by the community in an objective or "literal sense": "They live outside the grades or categories which the community regards as acceptable" (324).

25. Paul Starr, *The Social Transformation of American Medicine* (New York: Basic Books, 1982), 21. Hereafter cited as *STAM*, with page references appearing in the text.

26. Talcott Parsons, *The Social System* (New York: Free Press, 1951), 428.

27. Parsons, *Social*, 435.

28. Parsons, 436.

29. Stephen Schryer, *Fantasies of the New Class: Ideologies of Professionalism in Post–World War II American Fiction* (New York: Columbia University Press, 2011), 40.

30. Sources for this information include Starr, *Social Transformation*; Robert Stevens and Rosemary Stevens, *Welfare Medicine in America: A Case Study of Medicaid* (New York: Free Press, 1974); Carl F. Ameringer, *The Health Care Revolution: From Medical Monopoly to Market Competition* (Berkeley: University of California Press, 2008); and Daniel M. Fox, David Rosner, and Rosemary A. Stevens, "Between Public and Private: A Half Century of Blue Cross and Blue Shield in New York," *Journal of Health Politics, Policy and Law* 16, no. 4 (1991): 643–50.

31. Lionel Trilling, *The Middle of the Journey*, intro. Lionel Trilling (1947; repr., New York: Avon, 1975), 12. Hereafter cited as *MJ*, with page references appearing in the text.

32. Lionel Trilling, *The Liberal Imagination*, intro. Louis Menand (1950; repr., New York: New York Review of Books, 2008), 57. Hereafter cited as *LI*, with page references appearing in the text.

33. For a fascinating account of the broader midcentury reception history of *Princess Casamassima* among politically minded writers such as Ralph Ellison and James Baldwin, see Michaela Bronstein, "*The Princess* among the Polemicists: Aesthetics and Protest at Midcentury," *American Literary History* 29, no. 1 (2017): 26–49.

34. Robert Warshow, *The Immediate Experience: Movies, Comics, Theatre and Other Aspects of Popular Culture*, enlarged ed. (Cambridge, MA: Harvard University Press, 2001), 17.

35. Anthony Hutchison, *Writing the Republic: Liberalism and Morality in American Political Fiction* (New York: Columbia University Press, 2007), 94.

36. Amanda Anderson, "Postwar Aesthetics: The Case of Trilling and Adorno," *Critical Inquiry* 40, no. 4 (Summer 2014), 434, 435.

37. Anderson, "Postwar," 437.

38. Anderson, 435.

39. Anderson, 435, emphasis added.

40. Parsons, *Social*, 437, 441, 464.

41. Parsons, 451, 457, 461.

42. Parsons, 470.

43. Michael Szalay, "Lionel Trilling's Existential State," *Occasion: Interdisciplinary Studies in the Humanities* 2 (December 20, 2010): 6, http://occasion.stanford.edu/node/55.

44. Szalay, "Existential," 6, 10.

45. Szalay, 6.

46. Starr notes that this system did not always provide financial security, especially in rough economic times, but it did provide doctors with their desired professional security (*STAM* 236).

47. Lawrence B. McCullough, "Rights, Health Care, and Public Policy," *The Journal of Medicine and Philosophy* 4, no. 2 (1979): 206.

48. McCullough, "Rights," 207.

49. Warshow, *Immediate*, 13.

50. From the 1920s onward, medical care in rural areas generally deteriorated. There was a "gradual depletion of physicians in rural areas as a result of migration to cities and the diminishing output of medical schools. As the importance of hospitals to medical care became more widely recognized, the inadequacy of rural facilities also drew increasing criticism" (*STAM* 261). Moreover, hospital-oriented medical care tended to focus on acute needs rather than chronic conditions. See Rosemary A. Stevens, "Health Care in the Early 1960s," *Health Care Financing Review* 18, no. 2 (Winter 1996): 21.

51. Herbert Marcuse, *Eros and Civilization: A Philosophical Inquiry into Freud* (1955; repr., New York: Vintage, 1962), 228, 240.

52. Marcuse, *Eros*, 237.

53. Quoted in Mark Krupnick, *Lionel Trilling and the Fate of Cultural Criticism* (Evanston, IL: Northwestern University Press, 1986), 96.

54. Anderson, "Postwar," 436–37.

55. Michael Lind, "Conservative Elites and the Counterrevolution against the New Deal," in *Ruling America: A History of Wealth and Power in a Democracy*, ed. Steve Fraser and Gary Gerstle (Cambridge, MA: Harvard University Press, 2005), 250.

56. Mary McCarthy, *The Group* (New York: Harcourt, Brace and World, 1963), 314. Hereafter cited as *G*, with page references appearing in the text.

57. Brenda Murphy, "The Thirties, Public and Private: A Reassessment of Mary McCarthy's *The Group*," *Lit: Literature Interpretation Theory* 15 (2004): 83.

58. Murphy, "Thirties," 89. Michael Trask aptly calls McCarthy's style "oppositional literary realism" and "critical verisimilitude." See Trask, "In the Bathroom with Mary McCarthy: Theatricality, Deviance, and the Postwar Commitment to Realism," *Criticism* 49, no. 1 (Winter 2007): 10, 11.

59. Thomas Hill Schaub, *American Fiction in the Cold War* (Madison: University of Wisconsin Press, 1991).

60. Nancy K. Miller, "Women's Secrets and the Novel: Remembering Mary McCarthy's *The Group*," *Social Research* 68, no. 1 (Spring 2001): 179.

61. Quoted in Miller, "Women's Secrets," 175, 179.

62. Miller, "Women's Secrets," 174.

63. Lind, "Conservative," 262.

64. According to Layne Parish Craig, historians note that Margaret Sanger's alliance with "mainline eugenics ideology" did not derive from a shared racial ideology (or other theories of inherited weakness) but from her evidence of family weakness caused by the "actual production of large families," which led to "bad health in the mother and in the later children." Layne Parish Craig, *When Sex Changed: Birth*

Control Politics and the Literature between the World Wars (New Brunswick, NJ: Rutgers University Press, 2013), 90. Sanger was also concerned about the mortal risks to poor women of illegal abortion. See Carole R. McCann, *Birth Control Politics in the United States, 1916–1945* (New York: Cornell University Press, 1994), 14–17.

65. Schryer, *Fantasies*, 93–109.

66. David Riesman, with Nathan Glazer, *Faces in the Crowd: Individual Studies in Character and Politics*, abridged ed. (New Haven, CT: Yale University Press, 1965), 28.

67. Riesman, *Faces*, xiii. Riesman's distinctions between illustration and demonstration and between abstraction and documentation may help to make sense of the controversy surrounding McCarthy's acknowledgment, regarding *The Group*, of drawing on specific persons she knew at Vassar while disavowing the novel's status as a roman à clef. For a detailed account of this controversy, see Frances Kiernan, *Seeing Mary Plain: A Life of Mary McCarthy* (New York: Norton, 2000).

68. Eric Larrabee, "David Riesman and His Readers," in *Culture and Social Character: The Work of David Riesman Reviewed*, ed. Seymour Martin Lipset and Leo Lowenthal (New York: Free Press, 1961), 411.

69. David Riesman, *Selected Essays from Individualism Reconsidered* (Garden City, NY: Doubleday, 1954), xiv.

70. See Murphy, "Thirties," 83; and Trask, "Bathroom," 15.

71. Quoted in Miller, "Women's Secrets," 183.

72. Schaub, *American Fiction*, 50–65.

73. Quoted in Stevens and Stevens, *Welfare Medicine*, 21.

74. Ahmed, *Promise*, 202.

75. For the United Nations Universal Declaration of Human Rights, see http://www.un.org/en/universal-declaration-human-rights/. For the World Health Organization's Constitution, see https://www.ncbi.nlm.nih.gov/pmc/articles/PMC1625885/.

76. Quoted in John Farley, *Brock Chisholm, the World Health Organization, and the Cold War* (Vancouver: University of British Columbia Press, 2008), 63.

77. Farley, *Brock Chisholm*, 48–50.

78. Daniel Callahan, "The WHO Definition of 'Health,'" *The Hastings Center Studies* 1, no. 3 (1973): 80.

79. Callahan, "WHO," 81.

80. See Farley, *Brock Chisholm*, 4–5, 20–21, 173–74.

81. Callahan, "WHO," 82, 84.

82. James Gunn, *The Joy Makers* (1961; repr., Blacksburg, VA: Fantastic Books, 2010), 40. Hereafter cited as *JM*, with page references appearing in the text.

83. Ameringer, *Health Care*, 39.

84. Ameringer, *Health Care*, 38; Farley, *Brock Chisholm*, 67.

85. Ameringer, *Health Care*, 59.

86. Ameringer, 6. And yet, as Ameringer and other historians show, the actual

effects were more limited. To extend the kerosene metaphor, the health-care market turned out to be as likely to burn out as to flare up. As a growth market, it was susceptible to what one historian calls "considerable volatility." See Bradford H. Gray, "The Rise and Decline of the HMO: A Chapter in U.S. Health-Policy History," in *History and Health Policy in the United States: Putting the Past Back In*, ed. Rosemary A. Stevens, Charles E. Rosenberg, and Lawton R. Burns (New Brunswick, NJ: Rutgers University Press, 2006), 311. On the heels of the *Goldfarb* decision, a period of booming entrepreneurialism arose (Stevens, *Private-Public*, 152), particularly after "the Reagan administration decided to halt the federal support of HMOs and promote them as an investment opportunity" (Gray, "Rise and Decline," 323). But this initial boom of for-profit HMOs was short-lived, peaking in 1987, after which "consolidations and failures ensued"; a similar boom/bust cycle marked the 1990s (Gray, "Rise and Decline, 311–12).

87. Stevens and Stevens, *Welfare Medicine*, 50; Lawrence D. Brown, "Capture and Culture: Organizational Identity in New York Blue Cross," *Journal of Health Politics, Policy and Law* 16, no. 4 (1991): 667.

88. Stevens and Stevens, *Welfare Medicine*, 51.

89. Kenneth Arrow, "Uncertainty and the Welfare Economics of Medical Care," *The American Economic Review* 53, no. 5 (December 1963): 944.

90. Arrow, "Uncertainty," 949.

91. Ameringer, *Health Care*, 5. See also the difference of view between S. M. Amadae and Howard Brick, generalist historians of the period, in their assessments of Arrow's work and influence: Amadae, *Rationalizing Capitalist Democracy: The Cold War Origins of Rational Choice Liberalism* (Chicago: University of Chicago Press, 2003); and Brick, *Transcending Capitalism: Visions of a New Society in Modern American Thought* (Ithaca, NY: Cornell University Press, 2006).

92. John Rawls, "Justice as Fairness" (1958), in *John Rawls: Collected Papers*, ed. Samuel Freeman (Cambridge, MA: Harvard University Press, 1999), 64.

93. Rawls, "Justice," 66.

94. Rawls, 67.

95. Arrow, "Uncertainty," 942.

96. Arrow, 945.

97. Paula Fox, *Borrowed Finery: A Memoir* (New York: Picador, 2001), 191.

98. Fox, *Borrowed*, 54.

99. Paula Fox, "The Art of Fiction CLXXXI," interview by Oliver Broudy, *Paris Review*, no. 170 (Summer 2004): 41.

100. Medical episodes and details crop up frequently in Fox's work. For instance, in her third novel, *The Western Coast* (1972), the protagonist Annie Gianfala contracts appendicitis and undergoes an emergency operation; later she becomes involved in a years-long extramarital affair with the doctor who performed the surgery. Fox, *The Western Coast*, intro. Frederick Busch (1972; repr., New York: Norton, 2001). Fox's

2004 short story, "The Broad Estates of Death" (collected in *News from the World*), is about an adult son's visit to his dying father in a remote part of New Mexico and the medical treatment administered there by a local doctor and nurse. In a brief 2005 essay, "Way Down Yonder" (collected in *News from the World*), Fox recounts attending a surgical operation in 1942 in New Orleans. See Paula Fox, *News from the World: Stories and Essays* (New York: Norton, 2011).

101. Anderson, "Postwar," 435, 434. See also Anderson's earlier essay, "Character and Ideology: The Case of Cold War Liberalism," *New Literary History* 42 (2011): 222.

102. Paula Fox, *Poor George*, intro. Jonathan Lethem (1967; repr., New York: Norton, 2001), 53. Hereafter cited as *PG*, with page references appearing in the text.

103. Paula Fox, *Desperate Characters*, intro. Jonathan Franzen (1970; repr., New York: Norton, 1999), 73–74. Hereafter cited as *DC*, with page references appearing in the text.

104. In a brilliant 1980 afterword to a reissue of *Desperate Characters*, Irving Howe describes the genre of the short novel, in which "it is the trajectory of the action that counts," as "sometimes" imbued with "a semi-allegorical shadow of meaning." Irving Howe, "On *Desperate Characters*," afterword to *Desperate Characters*, by Paula Fox (Boston: Nonpareil Books, 1980), 159.

105. In an instructive essay, Phillip Barrish examines contemporary works of American speculative fiction that "imagine future dystopias defined by issues of health care access, distribution, and funding: defined, that is, by questions of policy or what might also be thought of as the political economy of health care." He persuasively argues that they reveal much more about health care as a system than do contemporary personal memoirs focused on illness and that, in contrast to realist fiction, the way they foreground setting "encourages us to recognize the large systems that subtend society as produced, rather than fixed or natural." See Phillip Barrish, "Health Policy in Dystopia," *Literature and Medicine* 34, no. 1 (Spring 2016): 106, 108. What I aim to show in this section of the chapter, however, is that Fox's near-dystopian yet decidedly realist fiction offers deeply intimate pictures of the everyday effects of an actual, recognizable, and evolving system on persons, interpersonal relations, and socioeconomic groups.

106. Richard Yates, *Revolutionary Road* (1961; repr., New York: Delta, 1983), 330.

107. Jennifer Schuessler, "Jigsaw," *New York Review of Books*, April 25, 2002, 47.

108. Fox, "Art of Fiction," 56.

109. See L. H. Goldman, *Saul Bellow's Moral Vision: A Critical Study of the Jewish Experience* (New York: Irvington, 1983), 31ff.

110. Fox, "Art of Fiction," 62, emphasis added.

111. Fox, *News from the World*, 172, 174.

112. Fox, "Art of Fiction," 62, 63.

113. The phrase "sense of possibilities" is repeated, in connection to George, two more times in the novel (*PG* 25, 153–54).

114. Bernadette Conrad, *Die Vielen Leben der Paula Fox* (München: C. H. Beck, 2011), 172.

115. Paula Fox, "Civil Society: Moments of Vividness and Promise," *Dissent* (Fall 1987): 594.

116. The political scientist Bo Rothstein argues that, in general, when the middle class is included in a welfare program, the quality of the service tends to improve: "It will demand high-quality service that prevents the well-known fact that services for poor people will become poor services." See Bo Rothstein, "Happiness and the Welfare State," *Social Research* 77, no. 2 (Summer 2010): 448.

117. Brown, "Capture," 651, 654, 658, 662.

118. Theodore R. Marmor, "New York's Blue Cross and Blue Shield, 1934–1990: The Complicated Politics of Nonprofit Regulation," *Journal of Health Politics, Policy and Law* 16, no. 4 (1991): 772; *STAM* 329. Commercial insurance companies could offer employers lower rates if their workers were healthy and low-risk—called "experience rating"—whereas the community ethos of Blue Cross meant that subscribers paid the same rate, that is, until pressures of competition led it to change its policies (*STAM* 329).

119. David J. Rothman, "The Public Presentation of Blue Cross, 1935–1965," *Journal of Health Politics, Policy and Law* 16, no. 4 (1991): 683.

120. Ahmed, *Promise*, 212.

121. James Colgrove, "Reform and Its Discontents: Public Health in New York City during the Great Society," *Journal of Policy History* 19, no. 1 (2007): 4.

122. Colgrove, "Reform," 23.

123. Colgrove, 3, 10.

124. Beatrix Hoffman, "Emergency Rooms: The Reluctant Safety Net," in *History and Health Policy in the United States: Putting the Past Back In*, ed. Rosemary A. Stevens, Charles E. Rosenberg, and Lawton R. Burns (New Brunswick, NJ: Rutgers University Press, 2006), 250, 257.

125. Hoffman, "Emergency," 254.

126. Colgrove, "Reform," 9, 15–16.

127. Colgrove, "Reform," 19. Colgrove describes how community activists interfered with health professionals' efforts to run a pilot program to screen poor children in slum neighborhoods for lead poisoning, which involved a door-to-door urine test that activists wanted control over (20–22).

128. Colgrove, "Reform," 3.

129. Other arty references include a gimmicky artist who becomes wealthy by reassembling typewriter keyboards "so that they spelled out mystic nonsense words" and the rival performance art of the artist's wife, in which she serves Jell-O with "nickels and dimes" instead of fruit dropped in, possibly "celebrating their new affluence" or "making an ironic comment" (*DC* 123, 124).

130. Rawls, "Justice as Fairness," 48.

131. Clement Greenberg, *Art and Culture: Critical Essays* (Boston: Beacon Press, 1961), 137.

132. Greenberg, *Art*, 136.

133. As though pressing the limit of the idea of consensual agreement, however, Otto also engages in nearly nonconsensual sex with his semisleeping wife (*DC* 145).

134. Greenberg, *Art*, 137.

135. Quoted in Michael Fried, *Art and Objecthood: Essays and Reviews* (Chicago: University of Chicago Press, 1998), 35.

136. Fried, *Objecthood*, 32–33, 37.

Chapter 5

1. Hubert H. McAlexander, ed., *Conversations with Peter Taylor* (Jackson: University Press of Mississippi, 1987), 163.

2. David M. Robinson, *World of Relations: The Achievement of Peter Taylor* (Lexington: University of Kentucky Press, 1998), 1.

3. Robinson, *World*, 2, 99.

4. John Updike, "Summonses, Indictments, Extenuating Circumstances," *New Yorker*, November 3, 1986, 158.

5. Updike, "Summonses," 158, 162.

6. Nancy Bentley, *The Ethnography of Manners: Hawthorne, James, Wharton* (Cambridge, UK: Cambridge University Press, 1995), 8.

7. Lionel Trilling, "Manners, Morals, and the Novel," in *The Liberal Imagination*, intro. Louis Menand (1950; repr., New York: New York Review of Books, 2008), 206.

8. Trilling, "Manners," 207.

9. Trilling, 219; Bentley, *Ethnography*, 1, 2, 9.

10. Bentley, *Ethnography*, 17, 18.

11. The historian Numan V. Bartley discusses the postwar South's status as the United States's underdeveloped internal colony: "An economic colony of the Northeast," it was afflicted by "absentee ownership of southern transportation and industry," which "drained away profits from the region." See *The New South, 1945–1980* (Baton Rouge: Louisiana State University Press, 1995), 3. See also the summary by Richard H. King of C. Vann Woodward's study of the post-Reconstruction period in which "Redeemer" oligarchs with "railroad, lumber, iron, and commercial interests" in the South abetted this situation, "turning the South into an economic colony of Northern and European business interests." Richard H. King, *A Southern Renaissance: The Cultural Awakening of the American South, 1930–1955* (New York: Oxford University Press, 1980), 265.

12. Peter Taylor, "In the Miro District," in *In the Miro District, and Other Stories* (New York: Knopf, 1977), 159, emphasis added. Hereafter cited as "Miro," with page references appearing in the text.

13. McAlexander, *Conversations*, 11, 42. Taylor also liked to describe the (distinctly

liberal) moral effect of writing down family stories. It was, for him, a "cognitive instrument": "As I put them down on paper, I began to see that in all these fine Southern stories blacks were getting the short end from women, who were getting the short end from men. I didn't know what they meant until I wrote them" (McAlexander, *Conversations*, 63). See also pp. 50, 78. Moreover, although Taylor did not see himself as a writer who "was going to go out and improve the world" (78), his liberal standpoint allowed that the world *could* be improved. This arrays Taylor against the Agrarians whose tragic vision, as John M. Grammer notes, "sanctioned a political quietism"; it could make "social problems ... seem just sadly inevitable." "Reconstructing Southern Literature," *American Literary History* 13, no. 1 (March 2001): 131.

14. McAlexander, *Conversations*, 13, emphasis added.

15. In arguing that Taylor is attentive to liberal culture and its near absence or enforced muteness, I attempt here to redirect the significance of Trilling's invocation of "half-uttered or unuttered or unutterable expressions of value" within a culture. These expressions need not obscure political elements but indeed may point directly to those political elements. This argument differs from the one Richard Godden makes about Trilling in his seminal book, *Fictions of Capital: The American Novel from James to Mailer* (Cambridge, UK: Cambridge University Press, 1990), 17–18.

16. See "1939," in *Happy Families Are All Alike* (1959; repr., Philadelphia: Lippincott, 1962), 222. Hereafter cited by title, with page references appearing in the text. Taylor occasionally applied this term to himself. See McAlexander, *Conversations*, 43.

17. McAlexander, *Conversations*, 116. See also pp. 50, 114.

18. Eric Aronoff, *Composing Cultures: Modernism, American Literary Studies, and the Problem of Culture* (Charlottesville: University of Virginia Press, 2013), 7, 159, 166. See also Scott Romine, *The Real South: Southern Narrative in the Age of Cultural Reproduction* (Baton Rouge: Louisiana State University Press, 2008).

19. Aronoff, *Composing Cultures*, 140, 150.

20. Aronoff, 19.

21. Cleanth Brooks, "The Southern Temper," in *A Shaping Joy: Studies in the Writer's Craft* (London: Methuen, 1971), 213.

22. Quoted in Michael Kreyling, *Inventing Southern Literature* (Jackson: University of Mississippi Press, 1998), 5–6.

23. Quoted in James Curry Robison, *Peter Taylor: A Study of the Short Fiction* (Boston: Twayne, 1988), 138; McAlexander, *Conversations*, 118.

24. McAlexander, *Conversations*, 93. The complicatedly left-leaning Robert Lowell, along with Jarrell, with whom he migrated to Kenyon College to study with John Crowe Ransom, counted among his very closest friends. According to his biographer, he voted twice for Adlai Stevenson See Hubert H. McAlexander, *Peter Taylor: A Writer's Life* (Baton Rouge: Louisiana State University Press, 2001), 139.

25. Morton Sosna, *In Search of the Silent South: Southern Liberals and the Race Issue* (New York: Columbia University Press, 1977), ix.

26. Quoted in Sosna, *Silent South*, viii.

27. Quoted in Sosna, 2.

28. Sosna, 2.

29. Sosna, 165. For discussions of liberal activism in the South, in addition to Sosna, see Bartley, *New South*, 38ff.; and Linda Reed, *Simple Decency and Common Sense: The Southern Conference Movement, 1938-63* (Bloomington: Indiana University Press, 1991. For a discussion of southern anticommunist hostility to liberals, see Anthony P. Dunbar, *Against the Grain: Southern Radicals and Prophets, 1929-1959* (Charlottesville: University Press of Virginia, 1981), 225-58.

30. Quoted in Sosna, *Silent South*, 170.

31. Ralph McGill, *The South and the Southerner* (Boston: Little, Brown, 1963), 218, emphases added.

32. Sosna, *Silent South*, vii. For an account of the failure of southern liberal academics and intellectuals such as V. O. Key, C. Vann Woodward, and Robert Penn Warren to embrace political liberalism, see King, *Southern Renaissance*. "This new liberalism," he writes, "was less a political program or a coherent theoretical position than an attitude" (277). This attitude, moreover, resembled Trilling's liberalism in displacing questions of socioeconomic justice with questions of sensibility (King, *Southern Renaissance*, 332n75).

33. The liberal journalist W. J. Cash similarly invoked "cruelty and injustice" in the concluding remarks of his influential book *The Mind of the South* (Garden City, NY: Doubleday, 1941), 426.

34. Peter Taylor, "The Elect," in *The Collected Stories of Peter Taylor*, intro. Richard Bausch (New York: Farrar, Straus and Giroux, 1969), 391, 400. Hereafter cited as *CS*, with page references appearing in the text.

35. Bartley, *New South*, 107.

36. Bartley, 107, 108.

37. Bartley, 109.

38. Godden, *Fictions*, 12.

39. Godden, 14.

40. McAlexander, *Conversations*, 167.

41. McAlexander, 50.

42. Warren's mystification has to do with the way, in this novel, he uses an episode of southern political history—the formation of an association of tobacco growers and its subsequent involvement in murderous vigilantism—as an occasion for exploring existential and metaphysical ideas of self-fulfillment. The protagonist Percy Munn's obsessive search for the essence—the truth—of selfhood (his own and others') places him at odds with the political group he's joined: "The thing which they had created, which they were, at this moment, in the act of creating, had no meaning as yet, no form. You couldn't tell—you couldn't ever tell what a thing was until it was dead, until the time for action was past." *Night Rider* (1939; repr., Nashville:

J. S. Sanders, 1992), 16. His idea of happiness follows this metaphysical suit. Contemplating the significance of his wife for him, Munn thinks that she embodies "the promise of happiness, happiness as a thing in itself, an entity separate from the past activities of his life" while also being "something concealed, preciously, at the center of his life" (160).

43. Thomas H. Winn, "The *Night Rider* Revisited: A Historical Perspective," *Southern Quarterly* 31, no. 4 (1993): 68.

44. Winn, "Revisited," 68.

45. Winn, 72.

46. Winn, 73.

47. Paul Jay Vanderwood, "Night Riders of Reelfoot Lake," *Tennessee Historical Quarterly* 28, no. 2 (1969): 126, 129.

48. Vanderwood, "Night Riders," 130, 131.

49. Vanderwood, 131. These actions included whipping a woman who attempted to divorce her husband (a clan member); whipping a man who played too much pool; whipping an elderly county squire for asserting in public the superiority of Negroes over night riders; and, predictably enough, destroying the property of a black farmer before murdering him and several members of his family for being arrogant. See Vanderwood, "Night Riders," 131–33.

50. McAlexander, *Conversations*, 139.

51. Godden, *Fictions*, 152–53.

52. Godden, 143ff.

53. Brooks, "Southern Temper," 198.

54. Brooks, 199, 205.

55. Brooks, 201.

56. Brooks, 200, 212.

57. Brooks, 212, 213, 214.

58. Brooks, 212.

59. Brooks, 201.

60. Peter Taylor, "Miss Leonora When Last Seen," in *The Collected Stories of Peter Taylor*, intro. Richard Bausch (New York: Farrar, Straus and Giroux, 1969), 516. Hereafter cited as *CS*, with page references appearing in the text.

61. Brooks, "Southern Temper," 211.

62. Brooks, 214.

63. Brooks, 211.

64. See Mary Esteve, "Shipwreck and Autonomy: Rawls, Riesman, and Oppen in the 1960s," *Yale Journal of Criticism* 18 (Winter 2005): 323–49.

65. David Riesman, with Nathan Glazer and Reuel Denney, *The Lonely Crowd: A Study of Changing American Character*, abridged ed. (New Haven, CT: Yale University Press, 1969), xxx.

66. David Riesman, "The Saving Remnant," in *Individualism Reconsidered and Other Essays* (Glencoe, IL: Free Press, 1954), 117.

67. Riesman, *Lonely*, lvi.

68. Mark McGurl, *The Program Era: Postwar Fiction and the Rise of Creative Writing* (Cambridge, MA: Harvard University Press, 2009), 151.

69. Vladimir Nabokov, *Pnin* (1957; repr., New York: Vintage International, 1989), 52.

70. Richard Weaver, "Aspects of the Southern Philosophy," in *Southern Renascence: The Literature of the Modern South*, ed. Louis D. Rubin Jr. and Robert D. Jacobs (Baltimore: Johns Hopkins University Press, 1953), 23.

71. Walter Benn Michaels, *The Shape of the Signifier: 1967 to the End of History* (Princeton, NJ: Princeton University Press, 2004), 16.

72. Robert B. Heilman, "The Southern Temper," in *Southern Renascence: The Literature of the Modern South*, ed. Louis D. Rubin Jr. and Robert D. Jacobs (Baltimore: Johns Hopkins University Press, 1953), 3.

73. Heilman, "Southern Temper," 10.

74. Weaver, "Aspects," 21, 22.

75. Weaver, 22.

76. Weaver, 20–21, 22, 23.

77. Peter Taylor, *The Death of a Kinsman*, in *The Widows of Thornton* (1954; repr., Baton Rouge: Louisiana State University Press, 1994), 135–36. Hereafter abbreviated as *DK*, with page references appearing in the text.

78. The elderly cousin seems to be one of those "plain people" to whom Taylor refers in an interview and to whom a southern family will typically lay claim, despite being practical strangers, in order to hold onto social and economic power. See McAlexander, *Conversations*, 168.

79. C. Wright Mills, "The Conservative Mood," in *Power, Politics, and People: The Collected Essays of C. Wright Mills* (New York: Oxford University Press, 1963), 208.

80. Mills, "Conservative Mood," 209.

81. Mills, 220.

82. Quoted in McAlexander, *Peter Taylor*, 140.

83. Jonathan Flatley, "Reading for Mood," *Representations* 140 (Fall 2017): 139.

84. Flatley, "Reading," 144.

85. Flatley, 144, 145.

86. Peter Taylor, "Je Suis Perdu," in *Happy Families Are All Alike* (1959; repr., Philadelphia: Lippincott, 1962), 253. Hereafter abbreviated as "*Je*," with page references appearing in the text. It is worth noting that Taylor embarked on a similar venture in 1955, funded by a Fulbright grant (McAlexander, *Peter Taylor* 132). For a discussion of the important institutional role of philanthropic foundations for creative writers in the early postwar era, see chapter 5, "The Foundations of Criticism," of Evan Kindley's book, *Poet-Critics and the Administration of Culture* (Cambridge, MA: Harvard University Press, 2017).

87. Charles Altieri, *The Particulars of Rapture: An Aesthetics of the Affects* (Ithaca, NY: Cornell University Press, 2003), 56.

88. Altieri, *Particulars*, 60.

89. To put it another way, Taylor's story draws on but also deflates the paradox-inflected account of Milton's poems advanced by his mentor Cleanth Brooks in *The Well Wrought Urn*. Predictably enough, Brooks locates a "paradox" in the way Milton organizes tropes of light and optics, with the "inward eye" necessitating the "veil" of night's blackness "to conceal a brightness which is in reality too intense for human sight." Brooks, *The Well Wrought Urn* (New York: Harcourt, Brace, and World, 1947), 64. It is through this paradox that the "secular" figure—the pensive melancholic—glimpses "religious" truth (65). Taylor's short story also plays with these tropes and figures, most pointedly in the way the daughter's blue eyes "were literally dazzling in the sunlight ("*Je*" 266). Further, this pensive melancholic likens her blue eyes to "the park's own blue heaven," the sky (266). And while he admits the "mysterious power" the young girl has on him, nothing paradoxical or religious enters the scene. Taylor insists on the sufficiency of the empirical world and the secular experience of it.

90. McAlexander, *Conversations*, 86.

91. McAlexander, 117.

92. Lauren Berlant, *Cruel Optimism* (Durham, NC: Duke University Press, 2011), 176.

93. Peter Taylor, "Dean of Men," in *The Collected Stories of Peter Taylor*, intro. Richard Bausch (New York: Farrar, Straus and Giroux, 1969), 4. Hereafter cited as *CS*, with page references appearing in the text.

94. Berlant, *Cruel*, 27.

95. Andrew Hoberek, *The Twilight of the Middle Class: Post–World War II American Fiction and White-Collar Work* (Princeton, NJ, Princeton University Press, 2005), 21.

96. Howard Brick, *Transcending Capitalism: Visions of a New Society in Modern American Thought* (Ithaca, NY: Cornell University Press, 2006), 171, 172.

97. Brick, *Transcending Capitalism*, 171.

98. Quoted in Hoberek, *Twilight*, 21.

99. John Burt, "After the Southern Renaissance," in *The Cambridge History of American Literature*, gen. ed. Sacvan Bercovitch, vol. 7, *Prose Writing 1940–1990* (Cambridge, UK: Cambridge University Press, 1999), 421.

100. Marion Montgomery, "The Sense of Violation: Notes toward a Definition of 'Southern' Fiction," in *On Matters Southern: Essays about Literature and Culture, 1964–2000*, ed. Michael M. Jordan (Jefferson, NC: McFarland, 2005), 55–56.

101. Kreyling, *Inventing Southern Literature*, 27.

102. Flannery O'Connor, "Good Country People," in *The Norton Anthology of American Literature*, gen. ed. Nina Baym, vol. 2, 5th ed. (New York: Norton, 1998), 2033, 2034. For O'Connor, the violent or "extreme situation" is what "best reveals what we are essentially," which for her was the mission of the writer. *Mystery and Manners*, ed. Sally Fitzgerald and Robert Fitzgerald (New York: Farrar, Straus and Giroux, 1969),

113. O'Connor also liked to formulate this argument in terms of a fiction of manners: "It is the business of fiction to embody mystery through manners" (*Mystery*, 124). This claim aligns her with southern traditionalism and against modernity: for "mystery is a great embarrassment to the modern mind" (124).

103. Montgomery, "Violation," 56.

104. McAlexander, *Conversations*, 41–43, 169.

105. Albert J. Griffith, *Peter Taylor*, rev. ed. (Boston: Twayne, 1990), 146.

106. Griffith, *Peter Taylor*, 146–47.

107. Quoted in McAlexander, *Peter Taylor*, 70.

108. Lionel Trilling, "William Dean Howells and the Roots of Modern Taste," in *The Opposing Self: Nine Essays in Criticism* (New York: Viking, 1955), 81.

109. Trilling, "William Dean Howells," 99.

110. Trilling, 99.

111. Trilling, 91.

112. Trilling, 91, 92.

113. Henry James, "Anthony Trollope," in *The Future of the Novel*, ed. Leon Edel (New York: Vintage, 1956), 237.

114. Trilling, "William Dean Howells," 92.

115. Trilling, 77, 102.

116. Mark Krupnick, *Lionel Trilling and the Fate of Cultural Criticism* (Evanston, IL: Northwestern University Press, 1986), 98.

117. Over the many decades the appeal of this plight has hardly slackened. It arguably reaches new heights of unequivocal expression in Jonathan Flatley's 2008 book, *Affective Mapping: Melancholia and the Politics of Modernism* (Cambridge, MA: Harvard University Press, 2008). Drawing on Walter Benjamin's account of Charles Baudelaire and modernity's conditions of estrangement, he regards attunement to disintegration and loss not so much a temptation as a psychic and political necessity, one that engenders for all intents and purposes a critical obligation to "melancholize" (Flatley, *Affective*, 1). With "the place of modernism" marking the gap between modernization's utopian promises and the reality of unfulfillment and failure, "the modern subject [is] in a precariously depressive position" (31, 32). The modern artist must thus devise a "historical-aesthetic methodology" for mapping out the sources and agents of misery (3). Tough luck, it seems, if your disposition, critical or otherwise, tends toward the sunny side.

118. Trilling, "William Dean Howells," 103. Trilling's own campus short story, "Of This Time, of That Place" (1943), suggests the difficulty he had renouncing the immense appeal of the charismatic figure. See Lionel Trilling, *Of This Time, of That Place, and Other Stories* (New York: Harcourt Brace Jovanovich, 1979). The story's figure of charisma is an innocent, an intellectually ambitious eccentric—indeed, "mad" (90)—undergraduate whom the protagonist morally fails. A poet and professor at an esteemed liberal arts college, the protagonist essentially betrays the young man by

going along with institutional machinations engineered by the dean to have him expelled. This social violence, the story makes clear, indicates the institution's embrace of mediocrity and its concomitant intolerance of the (charismatic) struggle toward intellectual excellence. For valuable analyses of this short story, see William M. Chace, *Lionel Trilling: Criticism and Politics* (Stanford, CA: Stanford University Press, 1980); and Robert Henn, "Trilling's University and the Creation of Postmodernism," *Arizona Quarterly* 65, no. 1 (Spring 2009): 55–83.

Coda

1. Jonathan Bell and Timothy Stanley, introduction to *Making Sense of Liberalism*, ed. Jonathan Bell and Timothy Stanley (Urbana: University of Illinois Press, 2012), 2.

2. Probably the best account of the long history of happiness discourse, dubious and otherwise, is Darrin McMahon's monograph, *Happiness: A History* (New York: Grove Press, 2006). Also valuable is V. J. McGill's *The Idea of Happiness* (New York: Praeger, 1967).

3. See Slavoj Žižek, *Welcome to the Desert of the Real: Five Essays on September 11 and Related Dates* (London: Verso, 2012); Claire Colebrook, "Narrative Happiness and the Meaning of Life," *New Formations* 63 (2008): 82–102; Heather Love, "Compulsory Happiness and Queer Existence," *New Formations* 63 (2008): 52–64; Sara Ahmed, *The Promise of Happiness* (Durham, NC: Duke University Press, 2010); and Michael Hardt and Antonio Negri, *Commonwealth* (Cambridge, MA: Harvard University Press, 2009).

4. Richard Powers, *Generosity: An Enhancement* (New York: Picador, 2009), 271. Hereafter abbreviated as *G*, with page references appearing in the text.

5. Fredric Jameson, "Postmodernism, or the Cultural Logic of Late Capitalism," *New Left Review* 146 (1984): 53; Edward Diener, "Subjective Well-Being," *Psychological Bulletin* 95 (1984): 547.

6. Diener, "Subjective," 542.

7. Diener, 563.

8. Daniel M. Haybron, "Philosophy and the Science of Subjective Well-Being," in *The Science of Subjective Well-Being*, ed. Michael Eid and Randy J. Larsen (New York: Guildford Press, 2008), 21.

9. Diener, "Subjective," 563.

10. Jameson, "Postmodernism," 58.

11. Jameson, 58, 85.

12. Jameson, 87, 88.

13. Jameson, 89, 90, emphasis added.

14. Jameson, 91.

15. Jameson, 74, 75, emphasis added here and in the preceding sentence.

16. Jameson, 92.

17. Ahmed, *Promise*, 202.

18. Ahmed, 213.

19. For an example of necessary fixedness, Ahmed turns to the Indian-born father of a modern tomboy in the 2002 British romantic comedy *Bend It Like Beckham*. The middle-aged migrant injured in his youth by a racist incident will be diminished, indeed falsified, if he lets geniality take the place of melancholy. His "stubbornness" testifies to the racism that is "going on and ongoing"; further, it testifies to the necessity of defying the socially coercive terms by which "the very act of recognizing injustice in the present is read as a theft of [other people's] optimism." Ahmed, *Promise*, 162. Leaving aside the dubiousness of this zero-sum affective phenomenology, what's important to see here is that the personal quality of stubbornness figures the very impossibility of redress.

20. Ahmed, *Promise*, 212.

21. Ahmed, 222.

22. Ruth Leys, "The Turn to Affect: A Critique," *Critical Inquiry* 37, no. 3 (2011): 452.

23. Ahmed, *Promise*, 161.

24. Ahmed, 218. As it happens—a little too conveniently—the character who best embodies this ideal of immanent contingency is the quirky young woman Poppy in Mike Leigh's endearing 2008 film *Happy-Go-Lucky*. It's too convenient because Poppy also happens to be a deeply caring individual: she acts kindly and responsively "to the suffering around her"; she possesses the "ethical capacity" to be "affected by others." Ahmed, *Promise*, 220, 221. Rather mystifyingly, Ahmed implies a necessary connection between, on the one hand, embracing contingency, possibility, and chance and, on the other hand, caring about others. In doing so she creates a species of capricious utopianism in which (to tweak the commercial slogan of a Canadian telecom company) the future is—luckily—friendly.

25. Hardt and Negri, *Commonwealth*, 378.

26. Hardt and Negri, 18.

27. Hardt and Negri, 378, 379.

28. Bruce Robbins, "Multitude, Are You There?," *n+1* 10 (2010), http://nplusonemag.com/multitude-are-you-there.

Index

Ackerman, Bruce, 126
Addams, Jane, 75
Adorno, Theodor, 84–85, 135, 144, 152, 242n15
Agamben, Giorgio, 11–12, 16
Agrarian ideology, southern, 183–84, 195–96, 200, 218
Ahmed, Sara, 103, 124–25, 151, 169, 222, 226–28 249n8, 269n19; on "affect alien," 124, 228
Allport, Gordon, 75
Althusser, Louis, 39, 226
Altieri, Charles, 38, 209–10, 238n21
Amadae, S. M., 258n91
American Library Association (ALA), 43–44
American Medical Association (AMA), 126, 130, 132, 137–38, 150–52, 154–55
Ameringer, Carl F., 155–57, 257n86
analogy: in Bellow, 53; in Brooks, 77, 96; in Fox, 162; in Highsmith, 108, 113–14; and incremental realism, 4, 162; in Taylor, 181–82, 196, 215, 218
Anderson, Amanda, 135, 144, 159
Appleby, Joyce, 105
Arendt, Hannah, 16, 237n11
Aristotle, 8, 21, 34–35, 75–76, 151, 225
Aronoff, Eric, 183
Arrow, Kenneth: and health-care politics, 157–58; and social-welfare theory, 19, 21–22

Ashbery, John, 94
autonomy, 1, 15, 37, 75, 103, 108, 154, 157–58, 199–200, 211; in *Maud Martha* (Brooks), 57, 66, 71, 82, 85

Baker, Houston A., Jr., 85–86, 88–89
Baldwin, James, 85, 255n33
Balfour, Ian, 16
Barrish, Phillip, 259n105
Barry, Brian, 126–27
Bartley, Numan V., 188, 261n11, 262n29
Baudelaire, 267n117
Bell, Daniel, 250n17
Bell, Jonathan, 221
Bellow, Saul, 55; "Looking for Mr. Green," race in, 52–54
Benjamin, Walter, 159, 267n117
Bentham, Jeremy, 129
Bentley, Nancy, 180–81
Bergner, Gwen, 243n36
Berlant, Lauren, on cruel optimism, 60–61, 93–96, 211–12
Blackburn, Robin, 233n31, 234n37
Blackstone, William, 34
Blue Cross, 4, 132, 146–47, 156, 159–60, 164, 167
Boorstin, Daniel, 9
Bork, Robert, 156
Brick, Howard, 45, 92, 213, 258n91
Bronson, Roy, 254n9
Bronstein, Michaela, 255n33

Brooks, Cleanth, 183, 196–98, 199–200, 266n89
Brooks, Gwendolyn, 3, 55, 76–77, 247n100; and happiness, 87, 92; and integrationism, 84–92; and liberal activism, 70–71, 76–77, 83–84; as welfare-state liberal, 60–61. Works: *The Bean Eaters*, 94; "In the Mecca," 94–96; *Maud Martha*, 28, 56–61, 64–68, 71–74, 76–77, 81–85, 95, 98; *Maud Martha*, flourishing in, 71–72, 76–77; *Maud Martha* and incrementalism, 81–83, 155; *Maud Martha*, race and personality integration in, 57; *Maud Martha*, race and underprivilege in, 57; *Maud Martha*, realism in, 67; *Maud Martha*, welfare state and, 58, 64; *Report from Part One*, 86–92, 98, 248n120; *Report from Part Two*, 88–90, 247n100; "The Sermon on the Warpland," 99; "The Second Sermon on the Warpland," 99; *A Street in Bronzeville*, 86, 94; "The Sundays of Satin-Legs Smith," 95–98; "They Call It Bronzeville," 244n55; "We Real Cool," 93–94, 97–98
Brophy, Thomas D'Arcy, 7
Brown, Adrienne, 244n55
Brown, Wendy, 234n40
Bryan, Alice I., 239n39
Burt, John, 214
Buss, Allan R., 245n65
Byrnes, James F., 62

Cable, George Washington, 184–85
Cadava, Eduardo, 16
Callahan, Daniel, 152
Campbell, Colin, 113
Cartwright, Marguerite, 58
Cary, Joyce, 162–63
Cash, W. J., 190, 263n33

Castle, Terry, 108
Cavell, Stanley, 119, 236n5
Chace, William M., 267n118
Chambers, Whittaker, 133
Chappell, David L., 61
Chase, Stuart, 6
Cheever, Abigail, 123, 128
Chekhov, Anton, 201, 237n5
Chisholm, Brock, 152
Chopin, Kate, 204; "A Pair of Silk Stockings," 251n22
Clark, Kenneth, 58, 65
Clark, Mamie, 65
Clune, Michael W., 106
Colebrook, Claire, 222
Coleridge, Samuel Taylor, 61
Colgrove, James, 170, 260n127
Compte, Joseph, 66
consensus, cult of, 9
consensus liberalism, 6, 169, 177; American way and, 6–7; critique of, 227–28; happiness and, 7–9, 11; and incrementalism, 80; and race, 87
conservativism, midcentury, 58–59, 61, 70, 126, 207; and AMA, 150–52, 155; neo-Agrarian, 183–84, 202–3, 205–10
consumer agency, 101, 112, 117; and conspicuous consumption, 112–13; happiness and, 105–6; and overspiritualization or underspiritualization of goods, 107–8
consumerism, 102, 117; critique of, 104; and sexual preference, 106–10, 112–16
consumer society, 101–2, 104; and postwar suburbs, 111–12
Craig, Layne Parish, 256n64

Dahl, Robert A., 242n15; on incrementalism 59, 79–80, 82
Daniels, Norman, 126

Dardenne brothers, 94
Davenport, Russell W., 6–8
Davis, Arthur P., 85
De Lauretis, Teresa, 252n44
DeLillo, Don, *White Noise*, 221
Descartes, René, 126–27, 151
Diener, Ed, 224–25, 227
Diggins, John Patrick, 10, 231n3
Doctorow, E. L., 232n25; *The Book of Daniel*, 5, 10–15, 165, 232n18, 232n26; happiness in, 11
Doreski, C. K., 248n113
Douglas, Mary, 184
Dreiser, Theodore, *Sister Carrie*, 251n22
Du Bois, W. E. B., 88
Dunbar, Anthony P., 263n29
Duplessis, Maurice, 139
Dworkin, Richard, 126

Edelman, Lee, 228, 253n52
Edwards, Brent Hayes, 66
Einstein, Albert, 75
Eisenhower, Dwight, 44
Eisenhower, Mamie, 187
Eliot, T. S., 242n15
Elliott, Jane, 67
Ellison, Ralph, 58, 85, 241n11, 255n33
Emerson, Ralph Waldo, 34
Engle, Paul, 86, 88, 246n89

Faulkner, William, 67, 179–80, 194–95, 202, 215, 219; *Wild Palms*, 193
Fawcett, Edmund, 234n39
Felski, Rita, 250n14
Fiedler, Leslie, 103
Fisher, Philip, 49
Flatley, Jonathan, 208, 267n117
flourishing (individual), 4, 18, 20–22, 29, 59–60, 78–79, 83, 101–2, 221–22; and welfare state, 74, 99; *See also* Brooks: *Maud Martha*

Forrester, Katrina, 234n41
Foucault, Michel, 124–25, 135, 138, 144, 152, 242n15
Fox, Paula, 3, 23, 165; *Borrowed Finery: A Memoir*, sense of justice in, 158; *Desperate Characters*, 28, 129–30, 159–61, 168–78, 260n129; *Desperate Characters*, emergency medical care in, 168–69, 171–73; *Desperate Characters*, and incrementalism, 170–71; *Desperate Characters*, private happiness in, 175–76; *Desperate Characters*, race in, 166, 171–73, 176–77; *Desperate Characters*, visual art in, 164, 173–78; *News from the World: Stories and Essays*, 259n100; *Poor George*, 129–30, 158–59, 163–67, 169, 174; *Poor George*, emergency medical care in, 163–67; *Poor George*, happiness in, 163–64, 166–67; *Poor George*, race in, 166; *Poor George*, visual art in, 164, 174–75; *The Western Coast*, 165, 258n100
Freedman, Jonathan, 32
Freud, Sigmund, 34, 80, 133, 142, 163, 224. *See also* social science: neo-Freudian
Fried, Michael, 178
Friedan, Betty, 67
Friedman, Milton, 156–57
Fromm, Erich, 6, 36–37, 75, 142
Frost, Robert, 86

Gaddis, William, 106
Gaitskill, Mary, 94
Galbraith, John Kenneth, 29, 69, 254n24; and symbols of happiness, 1, 3, 19, 27, 130, 150, 168, 170, 188, 218; theory of social balance, 2
Gauguin, Paul, 32, 40, 48, 50–51
Genter, Robert, 85

Gerth, Hans, 85
Ginsberg, Allen, *Howl*, 10
Girvetz, Harry K., 18, 24, 27, 65–66, 68–70, 74
Glickman, Lawrence B., 251n23
Godden, Richard, 6, 188, 195, 262n15
Goldstein, Kurt, 75
Goldwater, Barry, 62
Goncourt brothers, 160
Gould, Beatrice, 8
Gowrie, Grey, 103
Graham, Frank, 185
Grammer, John M., 262n13
Gray, Bradford H., 258n86
Greenberg, Clement, 158, 176–78
Greenberg, Martin, 158
Greer, James, 245n61
Griffith, Albert J., 218
Gunn, James: *The Joy Makers*, 129–30, 156; *The Joy Makers*, happiness revolution in, 153–55

Habermas, Jürgen, 229
Hamilton, Charles V., 63
Hamilton, Dona Cooper, 63
Hansberry, Lorraine, 246n72; *A Raisin in the Sun*, 78–79
happiness: consensus liberalism and, 11; consumer agency and, 105–6; contemporary cult of, 222–23, 227; gene, 222, 226; health and, 151; imagination of, 220; incremental realism and, 4; jouissance as, 11; middle class and, 31–32, 34–35, 50; postmodern critique of, 221–22, 226–27; promise of, 124; pursuit of, 3, 5, 8–9, 19, 59, 68, 76, 101, 104, 163; redistributive justice and, 19; same-sex desire and, 118–19; science of, 127, 221–22, 224–25; sociological critique of, 32–35; in Spinoza, 63; symbols of, 1, 3–4, 27–28; as trope of flourishing, 60; welfare state and, 5, 21, 91–92; and WHO, 151–53. *See also* Galbraith; justification; utilitarianism; *and individual authors*
happy art, 31–32, 50; in *Letting Go* (Roth), 38
happy ending, in *The Price of Salt* (Highsmith), 29, 100, 103
happy family, 179, 201; in *The Death of a Kinsman* (Taylor), 203–4, 206–7
happy poems, in *Letting Go* (Roth), 31–32, 37
Hardt, Michael, 222, 226, 228–29
Haroutunian, Joseph, 104
Havighurst, Clark, 156
Hayek, Friedrich A., 2
Heidegger, Martin, 208
Heilman, Robert B., 202
Henn, Robert, 267n118
Hesford, Victoria, 249n8
Higham, John, 9–10, 12
Highsmith, Patricia, 3, 119; *A Game for the Living*, 103, 250n16; *Plotting and Writing Suspense Fiction*, 121–22; *The Price of Salt*, 28, 100, 102–8, 110–20, 249n8, 250n16; *The Price of Salt*, happiness in, 103, 113, 115; *Ripley Under Ground*, 103; *Strangers on a Train*, 102, 119; *The Talented Mr. Ripley*, 102–3
Hillier, Amy E., 245n61
Hitchcock, Alfred, 119
Hoberek, Andrew, 47, 212
Hoffman, Beatrix, 170
Home Owners' Loan Corporation (HOLC), 4, 73, 76–77, 243n34
Hook, Sidney, 6
Horkheimer, Max, 152
Howe, Helen, *We Happy Few*, 36, 238n18
Howe, Irving, 28, 85, 159, 173, 248n106, 259n104

Howells, William Dean, 4, 35, 47, 180, 218–20
Hughes, Langston, 78
Hughes, Robert M., 57
humanist psychology, 59, 75–76, 224
Humphrey, Hubert H., 18
Hutchison, Anthony, 134
Huxley, Aldous, *Brave New World*, 223, 226

Ignatieff, Michael, 234n40
incrementalism, 21, 44–45, 81–84, 135–36, 214; decision-making theory and, 4, 24, 59, 79–80, 83; and health care, 150, 156, 167; and medical care, 170; and nonincrementalism, 155–57; and Old Left activism, 165; and welfare state, 150
incremental realism, 22–28, 52, 160, 170–71, 182; and analogy, 4; and decision-making theory, 4; and symbols of happiness, 4. *See also* realism, literary
institutions: modern, 200; traditional, 200–201, 213. *See also* Taylor, Peter: institution men in; welfare state
integrationism. *See* race: and integrationist politics

Jackson, John P., 243n36
Jacobs, Robert D., 202, 207
Jaffe, Dan, 86, 88
James, Henry, 133, 144, 180, 182, 188, 210, 218–19, 255n33
James, William, 34, 75
Jameson, Fredric, 15, 23–25, 27, 224–26
Jarrell, Randall, 184, 262n24
Johnson, Charles, 94
Johnson, Lyndon, 156
Jones, Howard Mumford, 33–35, 41, 104
Jurca, Catherine, 35, 246n72

justice: distributive, 21, 141, 145–46; as fairness, 20, 22, 178; and health care, 125–27; and liberalism, 59; and medical care, 160–61, 168, 170, 174; redistributive, 4, 16, 19; socioeconomic, 3 59–60, 69, 77; utilitarian, 22; welfare-state, 5, 15, 28, 160, 173–74, 178, 222
justification: of flourishing 71–72; of government intervention, 126; of happiness, 59, 63, 68, 155, 164, 166–67, 200, 220; of incrementalism, 155; of welfare state, 155, 162–63

Kant, Immanuel, 38; on happiness, 33, 51
Kardiner, Abram, 57–58
Katznelson, Ira, 73, 242n15
Kaufman, Robert, 237n5
Kazin, Alfred, 158
Keller, Yvonne, 249n3
Kent, George E., 87
Kiernan, Frances, 257n67
Kindley, Evan, 265n86
King, Martin Luther, Jr., 233n32
King, Richard H., 261n11, 263n32
Kinsey, Alfred, 103, 107, 111
Kirk, Russell, 207
Klinenberg, Eric, 231n1
Knapp, Steven, 100, 120
Korsgaard, Christine, 237n5, 252n46; on liberal subjectivity and normativity, 110, 120
Kreyling, Michael, 216
Krupnick, Mark, 220

Landis, Joseph, 238n22
Larrabee, Eric, 104, 117, 149
Lasch, Christopher, 108
Lattin, Patricia H., 241n11
Lattin, Vernon E., 241n11
Lears, Jackson, 251n21

Lee, Don L. (Haki R. Madhubuti), 87, 91
Lee, Robert E., 184
Le Guin, Ursula K., "The Ones Who Walked Away," 21–22
Leigh, Mike, *Happy-Go-Lucky*, 269n24
Leigh, Robert D., 43–45
lesbian pulp fiction, 100–101, 120
Leys, Ruth, 228
liberal activism, midcentury, 1–5, 15, 25, 32, 45–47, 69–70, 81, 129, 155, 163; and African American activism, 63–64, 70, 76–77, 79; and distributive justice, 141; and health-care politics, 125, 127, 130, 156–57
liberal imagination, 29
liberalism: autonomy and, 15; critique of, 11–15, 61, 226–28; and ethics, 80; and integrationism, 60, 79, 85, 89–90; and universalism, 103. *See also* South, the
liberalism, welfare-state, 16, 28, 221; and happiness, 21; and health care, 137–39; and social contract, 24. *See also* consensus liberalism
liberal readers, 100–101; queer, 101, 120
liberal subjectivity (or personhood), 4, 64, 85, 109–10
libertarian ideology, 3
"*Life* Round Table on the Pursuit of Happiness, A," 5–9, 12
Lind, Michael, 145
Lindblom, Charles E., 242n15; on incrementalism 59, 79–80, 82
Lindsay, John, 170
Lineberry, Robert L., 45
Locke, Alain, 57
Locke, John, 34
Love, Heather, 23–24, 26, 222, 235n51
Lowell, Robert, 215, 262n24
Lytle, Andrew, 183

Mailer, Norman, 122, 147
manners: ethnography of, 180–81; fiction of, 188; novel of, 180; southern, 180–81, 182–83, 188–89, 199; underclasses' poverty of, 188
Mantovani, Paolo, 32, 52
Marcuse, Herbert, 4, 96, 141–42
Marshall, Paule, *Brown Girl, Brownstones*, 243n34
Maslow, Abraham, 224, 245n65; on self-actualization, 75–76
Maxwell, William, 207
McCann, Carole R., 257n64
McCann, Sean, 231n5
McCarthy, Joseph, 10
McCarthy, Mary, 3, 159; *The Group*, 129–30, 146–50, 165, 257n67; *The Group* and feminist sociology, 147–48; *The Group*, happiness in, 150; *The Group*, liberal activism in, 150
McCoy, Horace, *They Shoot Horses, Don't They?*, 164
McCullough, Laurence B., 138
McGill, Ralph, 185–86
McGill, V. J., 75–76, 268n2
McGurl, Mark, 83, 200, 210
McMahon, Darrin, 31, 268n2
Medicaid, 4, 28, 156, 159–60, 167–68, 170, 173–74, 176
medical patient: in Fox, *Desperate Characters*, 169–70; in Fox, *Poor George*, 166–67; in Parsons, 130–31, 136–37; in Plath, "Tulips," 123–25; in Trilling, *The Middle of the Journey*, 136–39
Medicare, 28, 156, 167
Messer, Robert L., 243n26
Michaels, Walter Benn, 27, 202
middle class, 29, 47, 65, 88, 168, 179–80, 197; exclusion from, 56; and happiness, 25–26, 31–32, 33–35, 40, 50,

179–80; and health care, 127, 132, 141, 147–48, 156, 167, 170; and public library, 49; and welfare state, 149
Miller, Arthur, 96
Miller, Nancy K., 147, 150
Miller, R. Baxter, 97
Mills, C. Wright, 26, 34, 41, 85, 96, 207, 212, 214
Milton, John, 266n89
mixed economy, 3–4, 28–29, 42, 213
Molz, Redmond Kathleen, 44–45
Montgomery, Marion, 216–17
mood, 207, 209–10; and idea of southern totality, 207–11
Moon, J. Donald, 3
Moreland, Marc, 74–75; and critique of conservativism, 62; on defense of welfare state, 61–64
Morsink, Johannes, 249n7
Moyn, Samuel, 18, 234n37
Murphy, Brenda, 146–47
Myrdal, Gunnar, 43, 58, 86, 184

Nabers, Deak, 24, 28
Nabokov, Vladimir: *Lolita*, 108–9; *Pnin*, 201
Nealon, Christopher, 248n3
Negri, Antonio, 222, 226, 228–29
Nelson, Deborah, 128
neo-Agrarian aesthetic ideology, 184, 202–3, 216–17
New Critics, 183
New Left, the, 10–15, 92–93
night riders, 190–93, 195–96
Nixon, Richard, 62

O'Connor, Flannery, 199, 266–67n102; "Good Country People," 216; *Mystery and Manners*, 266–67n102; *Wise Blood*, 26
O'Hara, Frank, 106

Old Left, the, 14–15, 161, 165
Olson, Liesl, 248n119
Omi, Michael, 60, 91
Orlean, Susan, 240n52
Ovesey, Lionel, 57–58

Parrington, V. L., 56, 61–62
Parsons, Talcott, 149, 157; on doctor-patient relationship, 130–31, 140
Pells, Richard, 251n21
Pennock, J. Roland, 44
Pepper, Claude, 185
Perrin, Tom, 250n14
Plath, Sylvia, 146, 172; *The Bell Jar*, 123; "Tulips," 123–25, 127–29, 132, 168–69
Plato, 76
Poe, Edgar Allan, 12–13
Pogge, Thomas W., on idea of flourishing, 59
Pollack, Jackson, 177
Porter, Katherine, 202
Posner, Richard, 156
Posnock, Ross, 32
poverty: health-care politics and, 157–58; medical care and, 141; rights and, 146, 156; rural, 141. *See also* underprivilege
Powers, Richard, *Generosity*, 221–24, 226, 229
public health, 126–27, 129, 170–72, 174
public library, 1, 4, 55; midcentury politics of, 42–48. *See also* happiness; Roth: *Goodbye, Columbus*
Public Library Inquiry (PLI), 43–45, 47–48

Raber, Douglas, 43
race (African American): and aesthetic judgment, 88–89; and Black Power movement, 60, 91; and home

race (African American) (*continued*)
 ownership, 64, 73–74, 78–79; and integrationist poetics, 85–86; and integrationist politics, 60, 64, 85–86; and liberal activism, 63–64, 70; and liberal consensus, 87; and liberal subjectivity, 64; and microaggression, 23; and midcentury social science, 57–58, 70; and Peekskill riots, 165; and prejudice, 57; and public library, 1, 28; and segregation, 57; and self-loathing, 57; and the South, 184–85; and underprivilege, 1, 28, 81; *See also* Bellow: "Looking for Mr. Green"; Fox: *Desperate Characters*; Fox: *Poor George*; Hansberry: *A Raisin in the Sun*; Roth: *Goodbye, Columbus*; Taylor: "In the Miro District"; Wright: *Black Boy*; Wright: *Native Son*
Rankin, Quentin, 192
Rankine, Claudia, 23–25, 27
Ransom, John Crowe, 183, 195, 215
Rawls, John, 5–6, 16, 157–58, 174, 229, 234n41, 235n48, 235n50, 245n70; on happiness, 19; idea of justice as fairness, 20; idea of primary goods, 20–21; and incrementalism, 21, 24; and social-contract theory, 6, 20
realism, literary, 3, 67, 83, 106, 130, 140, 144, 147, 162, 168, 173, 201; ethnographic, 196, 198; historiographic, 196; psychological, 205; and sociology, 149. *See also* incremental realism
Reed, Linda, 263n29
regional identitarianism, southern, 183–84, 210
Riesman, David, 35–37, 45–46, 49, 104, 111, 199, 244n53, 250n17, 257n67; and midcentury sociology, 149; on "Veblenism," 112–13

rights, civil, 185; and health care, 126, 130, 138, 156–57; and poverty, 146, 156–57; and Franklin Roosevelt, 125
rights, human, 16–19, 97; and welfare state, 17–18. *See also* Universal Declaration of Human Rights (UDHR)
Robbins, Bruce, 229, 234n40
Robbins, Lionel, 68
Robeson, Paul, 165
Robinson, David M., 179
Rockwell, Norman, 31, 38, 41, 236n4
Rodgers, Bernard, 237n5
Rogers, Carl, 224, 237n8
Rogers, Thomas, *The Pursuit of Happiness*, 237n8
Roosevelt, Eleanor, 75, 90, 102
Roosevelt, Franklin, 62, 73, 125, 132
Rossinow, Doug, 14
Roth, Philip, 1, 3, 10, 35, 54–55. Works: *American Pastoral*, 236n4; "Defender of the Faith," 52; "Eli, the Fanatic," 52; *Goodbye, Columbus*, 1, 32, 39–43, 240n57, 240n58; *Goodbye, Columbus*, public library in, 4, 28, 39–40, 92; *Goodbye, Columbus*, and race, 1, 4, 28, 39–40, 42–43, 47–52; *Letting Go*, 30–32, 37–39; *Letting Go*, expectation of happiness in, 30; *Portnoy's Complaint*, 31; "You Can't Tell a Man by the Song He Sings," 52
Rothman, David J., 167
Rothstein, Bo, 260n116
Rubin, Louis D., Jr., 202, 207

same-sex desire, 101–2; and consumer agency, 104–6, 112–15
Sanger, Margaret, 256n64
Schaub, Thomas Hill, 61, 147, 150
Schenkar, Joan, 249n8, 250n17
Schlesinger, Arthur, Jr., 19
Schmidt, Tyler T., 84
Schryer, Stephen, 149, 248n49

Schudson, Michael, 107–8, 112–13, 251n23
Schuessler, Jennifer, 162
Sedgwick, Eve, 93
Sen, Amartya, 19, 234n41
Shils, Edward, 149
Sigerson, Richard, 165
Smathers, George, 185
Smith, Willis, 185
social science, midcentury, 57, 59, 65, 70; instrumental, 149; neo-Freudian, 57, 75, 142; and personality integration theory, 59, 85
Sontag, Susan, on illness as metaphor, 128–29
Sosna, Morton, on the "Silent South," 184–86
South, the: and black farmers, 191; and emancipation of slaves, 190; and idea of southern totality, 201–3, 205–11; injustice in, 182, 185–86, 188, 190; as internal colony, 180; labor in, 187; liberalism in, 180, 182–86, 193, 218; modernization of, 179–80, 186, 189–91, 196–97; New South, 189–90, 196–97, 199; Old South, 189–90, 195–97, 199; and poverty, 191; race and, 184–85, 190, 199, 205
Southern Conference Educational Fund, 185
Southern Conference on Human Welfare, 185
Southern Regional Council, 185
Spillers, Hortense J., 97
Spinoza, Baruch, 62–63, 74–75, 228–29
Stafford, Jean, 217
Stamatopoulou, Elsa, 234n40
Stanley, Timothy, 221
Stark, Inez Cunningham, 89, 91
Starr, Paul, 130, 137, 157, 255n46
Stevens, Rosemary, 256n50; on national health care in United Kingdom, 127–28

Stevenson, Adlai, 262n24
Stopford, John, 76; on autonomy, 66
Stowe, Harriet Beecher, 140
suburbs, 111–12; sociological critique of, 41
Susman, Warren, 251n21
Szalay, Michael, 137–38

Taft, Robert, 151
Tate, Allen, 183, 202; *The Fathers*, 144
Taylor, Peter, 3, 86, 179, 261n13, 262n15, 265nn78, 266n89; and ethnographic style, 182–83, 190, 198; happiness in, 183, 213–14, 217; institution men in, 200, 207–8, 210–14, 217–18; trope of silence in, 186–87, 189–90, 193–95. Works: "Dean of Men," 29, 200, 211–14; *The Death of a Kinsman*, 201, 203–7; "The Elect," happiness in, 186; *Happy Families Are All Alike*, 201; "In the Miro District," 181, 186, 189–97, 214–15; "In the Miro District," race in, 194; *"Je Suis Perdu,"* 29, 200, 207–12, 266n89; "Miss Leonora When Last Seen," 196–200; "1939," 29, 200, 215–18; race in, 194; *A Summons to Memphis*, 214; "What Do You Hear from 'Em?," 189; *The Widows of Thornton*, 207
Taylor, Robert Zachary, 190, 192
Thompson, Clara, 142
Thompson, Morton, *Not as a Stranger*, 125
Thoreau, Henry David, 161
Tolstoy, Leo, 179, 201
Trask, Michael, 103, 256n58
Trilling, Diana, 159
Trilling, Lionel, 3, 35, 48, 61, 72, 88, 103, 149–50, 159, 262n15, 263n32; on "democratic pluralism of sexuality," 107; on Henry James, 133, 135, 180, 182, 218–19. Works: *The Middle of*

Trilling, Lionel (*continued*)
the Journey, 125, 129, 131–46, 159, 162, 165–66; *The Middle of the Journey*, happiness in, 135, 146; *The Middle of the Journey*, romantic sentimentalism in, 140, 142–43; "Of This Time, of That Place," 267n118
Trollope, Anthony, 217–19
Truman, Bess, 187
Truman, Harry, 7, 62, 151–52, 155
Tumin, Melvin, 34, 41
Twombly, Cy, 177

underprivilege, 19, 141–42; and health care, 167; and medical care, 170; and race, 57, 171; and women, 148. *See also* poverty
United Nations (UN), 4–5, 16–17, 19, 102, 125, 151–52, 155
Universal Declaration of Human Rights (UDHR), 4–5, 16–19, 29, 106, 110–11, 234n39; and personality development, 102
Updike, John, 180
Urban Outcomes: Schools, Streets, and Libraries (Levy, Meltsner, and Wildavsky), liberal activism and, 45–47
utilitarianism: critique of, 20, 68–69; and happiness, 3, 20, 22, 25, 129–30, 155; and health care, 138, 157; and social-welfare theory, 19; and welfare state, 144–46
Utrillo, Maurice, 38, 52

Vanderwood, Paul Jay, 264n49
Veatch, Robert M., 254n9

Walker, Margaret, 86
Wall, Wendy, 6–7, 233n32
Warner, Michael, 101, 253n52; on normality and sexual politics, 119–20
Warren, Kenneth W., 89

Warren, Robert Penn, 183; *Night Rider*, 191–92, 263–64n42
Warshow, Robert, 25, 134, 140, 236n57
Washington, Mary Helen, 242n23
Weaver, Richard M., 202–4, 207
Weingast, Barry R., 73
welfare state: and biopolitics, 124–25; and flourishing, 74, 99; and happiness, 5, 91–92, 164; and hospital emergency room, 159, 164–65, 168, 170; institutions of, 59–60, 64, 68, 85, 89–92, 148, 150, 171, 173; and middle class, 149; and paternalism, 2; and poverty, 2; and public library, 1, 4, 32, 92; and redistribution, 63; and socialism, 2; and socioeconomic justice, 3; and universalism, 63–64. *See also* justice: welfare-state
Welty, Eudora, 202
Whyte, William, 35, 212
Wilkie, Wendell, 6
Williams, Aubrey, 185
Williams, Raymond, 107
Williams, Roger, 62
Williams, William Carlos, 86, 123
Wilson, Andrew, 119, 250n17
Winant, Howard, 60, 91
Winn, Thomas H., 191
World Health Organization (WHO), 19, 130; and happiness, 151–55
Worley, Jennifer, 101, 120
Wright, Richard, *Black Boy*, 241n11; *Black Boy*, race in, 54–55; *Native Son*, 58, 85, 246n72; *Native Son*, race in, 55

Yates, Richard, *Revolutionary Road*, 26, 161, 171

Žižek, Slavoj, 222, 230
Zola, Émile, *Au Bonheur des Dames*, 251n22

Dorothy J. Hale, *The Novel and the New Ethics*

Christine Hong, *A Violent Peace: Race, U.S. Militarism, and Cultures of Democratization in Cold War Asia and the Pacific*

Sarah Brouillette, *UNESCO and the Fate of the Literary*

Sophie Seita, *Provisional Avant-Gardes: Little Magazine Communities from Dada to Digital*

Guy Davidson, *Categorically Famous: Literary Celebrity and Sexual Liberation in 1960s America*

Joseph Jonghyun Jeon, *Vicious Circuits: Korea's IMF Cinema and the End of the American Century*

Lytle Shaw, *Narrowcast: Poetry and Audio Research*

Stephen Schryer, *Maximum Feasible Participation: American Literature and the War on Poverty*

Margaret Ronda, *Remainders: American Poetry at Nature's End*

Jasper Bernes, *The Work of Art in the Age of Deindustrialization*

Annie McClanahan, *Dead Pledges: Debt, Crisis, and Twenty-First-Century Culture*

Amy Hungerford, *Making Literature Now*

J. D. Connor, *The Studios after the Studios: Neoclassical Hollywood (1970–2010)*

Michael Trask, *Camp Sites: Sex, Politics, and Academic Style in Postwar America*

Loren Glass, *Counterculture Colophon: Grove Press, the* Evergreen Review, *and the Incorporation of the Avant-Garde*

Michael Szalay, *Hip Figures: A Literary History of the Democratic Party*

Jared Gardner, *Projections: Comics and the History of Twenty-First-Century Storytelling*

Jerome Christensen, *America's Corporate Art: The Studio Authorship of Hollywood Motion Pictures*

The authorized representative in the EU for product safety and compliance is:
Mare Nostrum Group
B.V Doelen 72
4831 GR Breda
The Netherlands

www.ingramcontent.com/pod-product-compliance
Lightning Source LLC
Chambersburg PA
CBHW030610230426
43661CB00053B/1921